< >

THE ORIGINS OF MODERN
FREEDOM IN THE WEST

THE MAKING OF MODERN FREEDOM

General Editor: R. W. Davis

THE ORIGINS OF MODERN
FREEDOM IN THE WEST

≺ ≻

Edited by R. W. Davis

STANFORD UNIVERSITY PRESS
STANFORD, CALIFORNIA
1995

Stanford University Press
Stanford, California
© 1995 by the Board of Trustees of the
Leland Stanford Junior University
Printed in the United States of America

CIP data appear at the end of the book

Stanford University Press publications
are distributed exclusively by
Stanford University Press within
the United States, Canada, and Mexico;
they are distributed exclusively by
Cambridge University Press throughout
the rest of the world.

1000745214
0804724741

To the memory of Michael Steiner,
a fine young historian

Series Foreword

THE STARTLING AND MOVING events that swept from China to Eastern Europe to Latin America and South Africa at the end of the 1980s, followed closely by similar events and the subsequent dissolution of what used to be the Soviet Union, formed one of those great historic occasions when calls for freedom, rights, and democracy echoed through political upheaval. A clear-eyed look at any of those conjunctions—in 1776 and 1789, in 1848 and 1918, as well as in 1989—reminds us that freedom, liberty, rights, and democracy are words into which many different and conflicting hopes have been read. The language of freedom—or liberty, which is interchangeable with freedom most of the time—is inherently difficult. It carried vastly different meanings in the classical world and in medieval Europe from those of modern understanding, though thinkers in later ages sometimes eagerly assimilated the older meanings to their own circumstances and purposes.

A new kind of freedom, which we have here called modern, gradually disentangles itself from old contexts in Europe, beginning first in England in the early seventeenth century and then, with many confusions, denials, reversals, and cross-purposes, elsewhere in Europe and the world. A large-scale history of this modern, conceptually distinct, idea of freedom is now beyond the ambition of any one scholar, however learned. This collaborative enterprise, tentative though it must be, is an effort to fill the gap.

We could not take into account all the varied meanings that freedom and liberty have carried in the modern world. We have, for example, ruled out extended attention to what some political philosophers have called "positive freedom," in the sense of self-realization of the individual; nor could we, even in a series as large as this, cope with the enormous implications of the four freedoms invoked by

Franklin D. Roosevelt in 1941. Freedom of speech and freedom of the press will have their place in the narrative that follows, certainly, but not the boundless calls for freedom from want and freedom from fear.

We use freedom in the traditional and restricted sense of civil and political liberty—freedom of religion, freedom of speech and assembly, freedom of the individual from arbitrary and capricious authority over persons or property, freedom to produce and to exchange goods and services, and the freedom to take part in the political process that shapes people's destiny. In no major part of the world over the past few years have aspirations for those freedoms not been at least powerfully expressed; and in most places where they did not exist, strong measures have been taken—not always successfully—to attain them.

The history we trace was not a steady march toward the present or the fulfillment of some cosmic necessity. Modern freedom had its roots in specific circumstances in early modern Europe, despite the unpromising and even hostile characteristics of the larger society and culture. From these narrow and often selfishly motivated beginnings, modern freedom came to be realized in later times, constrained by old traditions and institutions hard to move, and driven by ambition as well as idealism: everywhere the growth of freedom has been *sui generis*. But to understand these unique developments fully, we must first try to see them against the making of modern freedom as a whole.

The Making of Modern Freedom grows out of a continuing series of conferences and institutes held at the Center for the History of Freedom at Washington University in St. Louis. Professor J. H. Hexter was the founder and, for three years, the resident gadfly of the Center. His contribution is gratefully recalled by all his colleagues.

R.W.D.

Contents

≺ ≻

Acknowledgments

Several foundations have generously supported The Making of Modern Freedom series. The National Endowment for the Humanities provided funding for planning meetings and also sponsored the autumn 1991 conference where this volume was first discussed. The Lynde and Harry Bradley Foundation contributed towards meeting administrative and support expenses at the Center for the History of Freedom. We are grateful for all the support we have received, including the strong backing we have always enjoyed from Washington University.

The Center wishes to thank Rosemary Kennedy who helped us to attain clarity and consistency in the early volumes of this series.

R.W.D.

CONTRIBUTORS

J. H. Baker
St. Catharine's College, Cambridge

William J. Bouwsma
*University of California, Berkeley
(Emeritus)*

R. W. Davis
Washington University

Donald R. Kelley
Rutgers University

H. G. Koenigsberger
University of London (Emeritus)

John Hine Mundy
Columbia University (Emeritus)

Douglass C. North
Washington University

Martin Ostwald
*Swarthmore College & University of
Pennsylvania (Emeritus)*

Brian Tierney
Cornell University (Emeritus)

≺ ≻

THE ORIGINS OF MODERN
FREEDOM IN THE WEST

<≻

Introduction

R. W. DAVIS

T HERE WAS NOTHING INEVITABLE about the growth of modern
freedom in the West. Around 1000 A.D., at the beginning of
the medieval period, there were no signs that would foreshadow
it. Poor, politically fragmented, and culturally backward, the West
was simply not in the same class as the great empires to the east,
the Moslem and the Chinese. If anything important were to be expected, it would have been only reasonable to expect it from them.

Yet 500 years later, the West was transformed. It was rich, powerful, and culturally alive. It was not politically united, but the monarchical states into which it was divided were formidable in their
own rights. And within them, too, there had been a blossoming of
political forms. The towns, built by their own trading activities,
were to a large degree governed by their own citizens. Representative institutions, parliaments and estates, had grown later than the
towns, and in part to draw them into the system of feudal government. True, save in England and what would become the independent Netherlands, representative bodies were beginning to face adversity by the end of the fifteenth century; but in those two countries
they were flourishing. The protection of the law had long been extended to property; now courts of law, especially in England, became increasingly concerned with the protection of people. How
does one account for the transformation? Douglass C. North answers this question in "The Paradox of the West," the first chapter
of this volume.

The Greeks are usually seen as the original progenitors of freedom. As the first to devise civil and political liberty, they obviously
have a strong claim to the title. Beyond that, they were also the
first to have a word, *eleutheria*, for the concept. Often, however,
those who borrow concepts see things through the spectacles of

their own times, which distort the original meaning or purpose; this certainly has been true of borrowing from the Greeks. What is the history of the word *eleutheria* in its own time? When did it assume a meaning similar to freedom, and why? Martin Ostwald in chapter 2 examines this question.

When one thinks of the medieval Church, one is likely to think first of a great spiritual institution. That it unquestionably was, but it was much else besides. The Church's spiritual power endowed it as well with great political power, making it an important and effective check on the assumption of despotic power by the state. The Church also provided a model of government for secular bodies, which imitated its choosing of its functionaries by election, and adopted representative institutions as suggested by the Church councils. By perpetuating Roman traditions of popular election and inspiring representative government, the Church was vital to the development of modern freedom, as Brian Tierney demonstrates in chapter 3.

The earliest secular institutions to follow the example of the Church in shaping their own governments were the towns of Italy. Public officials were elected. The number of those eligible for election tended to be large. The franchise was usually broad, and was often democratic. As might be expected, the resulting town governments provided effective protection to private property and other institutions essential for the carrying on of business. But they protected life as well as property. Though more dependent on outside authority than in Italy, towns elsewhere showed similar characteristics. They were the initial training grounds for laymen in the practice of free government, as John Hine Mundy shows in chapter 4.

As the towns were waxing wealthy, monarchs in the thirteenth and fourteenth centuries began to feel distinctly needy. The reason was costly and almost continuous warfare, which put impossible strains on traditional and not easily expandable revenues. The obvious solution was to tap the resources of the towns and of better-off rural residents. But these elements in society were made up of people who had long enjoyed considerable independence of thought and action. They could not easily be bullied. It made much more sense to gather their representatives together for negotiation over taxation and grievances. Such was the background of parliaments and estates all over Europe, as H. G. Koenigsberger demonstrates in chapter 5, the first of two on the subject that he has written in this volume.

In England in the seventeenth century parliamentary legislation would become the major vehicle for protecting the liberties of the subject. Before that, however, the common law courts were the main arena for such advances in freedom as took place. Two developments of outstanding importance for the making of modern freedom were the gradual whittling away of villeinage, and the growth of due process by such devices as habeas corpus. Most basic perhaps, psychologically as well as legally, was the disappearance of villeinage, which by 1600 left all Englishmen "free men." Habeas corpus protected the individual against arbitrary imprisonment by forcing state authorities to show just cause in a timely fashion. Both developments represented significant strides toward the modern conception of freedom dedicated to providing equal protection for all individuals. Unlike the common law in England, other systems of law seem not to have had much in the way of procedures for securing liberty: certainly nothing resembling habeas corpus. Nor did they have the flexibility to end servile status, which was thoroughly entrenched in Roman law, except by legislation. J. H. Baker in chapter 6 examines the key developments in the common law.

The Renaissance and the Reformation likewise promoted ideas of individual worth by exalting human potential. Briefly put, the Renaissance encouraged people to have faith in their ability to look after themselves in this world; while Reformation theology encouraged the belief that their passage to the next was a matter between them and God alone. Beyond putting a greater emphasis on the individual and what he or she could accomplish, the Reformation also encouraged the growth of ideas of freedom in more specific ways. John Calvin particularly, with his doctrine that lesser magistrates had both a right and a duty to lead in restraining and even overthrowing rulers who defied God's will, put a significant check on temporal authority and its power to command its subjects. William Bouwsma examines these kinds of questions in chapter 7.

In the main, resistance theories such as Calvin's were brought into play against the several monarchies that had emerged from the chaos and confusion of the fourteenth and early fifteenth centuries, physically strengthened by enhanced revenues and military might and psychologically more secure through the veneration of their subjects. Donald Kelley in chapter 8 first discusses the position of monarchs. He then turns his attention to the resistance theories with which they would have to contend in the later sixteenth and seventeenth centuries. In the course of that century and a half a queen of Scotland was forced to abdicate; a king was deposed and a new state established in the Netherlands; two kings of France were assassinated; one king of England was beheaded by the public executioner, and his second son forced into exile and supplanted by heirs more congenial to Parliament. All of these actions were taken in the name of liberty exercised under God's sanction, and seen as just retribution for unregenerate monarchs. Resistance theories obviously provided powerful arguments. Nor was their day done; they would continue to be important, most notably as furnishing the fundamental theoretical underpinning for the French Revolution.

Parliamentary institutions were to be of central importance in the two countries in which one can discern clear, albeit incomplete, outlines of the existence of modern freedom at the beginning of the seventeenth century. Nor was the connection between freedom and parliamentary institutions merely coincidental. The Dutch States General was carefully designed, mainly through the necessity of referral back to the provincial estates, in such a way as to make it no threat to Dutch liberties. The English Parliament, as has been suggested, made itself the champion of liberty during the seventeenth century, for reasons which are explored in detail in the volume after this one. H. G. Koenigsberger, in his second chapter, examines Dutch and English parliamentary institutions and their importance for freedom in the early modern period. At the same time, by comparing them with similar institutions elsewhere in Europe and carrying his investigation up to 1700, he is able to put them in a broad context and suggest the reasons for their survival and success. Professor Koenigsberger argues that the explanation is more a question of contingencies than of a special Dutch or British genius for parliamentary government.

It will not have escaped the reader's notice that the chapters in this volume touch on all the freedoms enumerated in our definition. Though it would have been anathema to Luther and Calvin, in the doctrine of every believer's direct relationship with God (Luther's "priesthood of all believers") lay the seed of the doctrine of religious liberty. Among its political liberties, ancient Athens allowed every citizen freedom of speech in the Assembly; as the English Parliament did every member in the sixteenth century. The early modern English courts were developing safeguards against capricious authority, as in habeas corpus. Medieval towns were very much concerned with freedom to produce and exchange goods and services. And institutions of church, state, and municipal government were developing mechanisms which would allow popular participation in the political process.

While all the parts were there, the sum in 1600 was still not modern freedom. Though freedom of speech of a sort existed in Athens, Socrates still had to drink the hemlock; and members of Parliament who, in the opinion of the monarch, carried their own freedom of speech too far were still forcibly reminded that it had limits. Yet though modern freedom was still unformed, it was from the earlier materials touched on that it was to be fashioned. This volume discusses the major building blocks appropriated from the ancient and medieval periods.

The Paradox of the West

DOUGLASS C. NORTH

THE SEARCH FOR THE ORIGINS of modern freedom entails both an inquiry into the conditions that gave rise to the demand for freedom and an inquiry into the origins of an ideology that promoted freedom as the basic ideal of a society—an ideology of such intellectual power that it is a driving force today in shaping the modern world. It is paradoxical that modern freedom is a product of a part of the world that was relatively backward a millennium ago. From our present day perspective there would appear to have been many more likely candidates for its birthplace—societies with more advanced economies, with more sophisticated scientific and technological knowledge, with more attention paid to the arts, literature, and the pursuit of knowledge in general. And, indeed, along with the progress of freedom in the West did come the relative advance of all those indicators of more advanced civilizations. Therefore a search for the origins of freedom must do more than focus on the polity; it must provide an explanation for the overall rise of the Western world.

A central thesis of this chapter is that economic growth and the development of freedom are complementary processes of societal development. Economic growth provides the resources (and leisure) to support more complex societies; and it is unlikely to persist in the *long run* without the development of political and civil liberties. A world of specialization and division of labor—the roots of economic growth—is going to nurture democratic polities and individual freedoms.

Why might there be such a relationship? The short answer is that well-specified and enforced property rights, a necessary condition for economic growth, are only secure when political and civil rights are secure; otherwise arbitrary confiscation is always a threat. Also credible commitment—an essential condition for the creation of capital markets—is not possible without an effective legal system, one that will impartially and systematically enforce agreements across time and space. A longer but more satisfactory answer entails an analysis of the interplay among the more complex, interdependent economies that arise from division of labor; of the consequent evolution of diverse interests and their gradual increase in bargaining power; of the ideas and ideologies that would be congenial to such growing diversity; and of the influence of these belief structures on incremental institutional change. Such an approach can then account for the gradual widening over time of the spectrum of individuals and groups to whom freedom and liberties would be extended.

In what follows I hope to spell out not only the interrelationships that characterized this evolution but also the limitations of and qualifications to the overall thesis. That there is an historical relationship between economic growth and the development of freedoms is evident: the pioneers of modern economic growth, the Netherlands and England, were also the pioneers in the development of representative government and civil freedoms (and the countries that were left behind in western European expansion, Spain and Portugal for example, failed to develop those freedoms). That the relationship is not perfect is equally evident: there were economies such as China that had periods of economic growth without producing either representative polities or individual freedoms, and in the modern world we may look at the Soviet Union after World War II or the experience of some Asian countries. Economic growth may be a necessary but is not a sufficient condition for the development of *modern* freedom. So the puzzle we must unravel is what set of unique conditions—ones not present in more advanced societies during the past millennium—set off economic growth and the development of freedoms in the West? But there is an even more fundamental underlying puzzle: why has economic growth itself been so exceptional?

By economic growth I mean sustained growth in output per head of population. Throughout the long era of human history total output has grown and population has increased; but improvement in overall human well-being associated with output growing faster than population has not been the automatic result. While the statistical data do not exist to give us unequivocal answers, per capita economic growth does appear to have occurred, for example, in the classical era in fifth century B.C. Athens before the internecine war with Sparta, in the era of Rhodian domination of the eastern Mediterranean, and during the first two centuries of the Roman Empire.[1] Economic growth, then, is not unique to the Industrial Revolution, despite a long scholarly tradition identifying the two. But sustained economic growth was the exception before the Industrial Revolution and, for that matter, after that revolution in eighteenth-century England. Indeed, it is only in the very modern era since World War II that economic growth has been widespread. And it is only in the modern era that modern freedoms have become widespread.

The sources of economic growth have variously been ascribed by economists to technology, human capital (education and skills of human beings), and economies of scale (falling costs associated with the growth of large-scale markets). While these are clearly proximate sources of productivity increase and hence growth, they are not the ultimate sources. If they were, growth long since would have become universal, because the desire for improvement in well-being appears to be a universal human trait and all societies would have to do would be to invest in the technologies or skills and knowledge that would produce such desirable results. But throughout history (and even in much of the modern world) societies have failed to make the necessary investments.

Societies do not make the necessary investments because the institutional and organizational structure does not provide the incentives to do so. The failures of human organization underlie not only economic backwardness but social, intellectual, and political backwardness as well. Indeed the search for efficient economic organization leads us to political organization, since it is the polity that defines and enforces the economic rules of the game. It is to the complex (and still not completely understood) interplay between the economy and the polity that we must turn to search for the clues that account for the rise of the West. In going back a millennium to search for the roots of modern freedom, we must look both to the institutional framework and to the intellectual context from which sprang the perceptions that guided human actions. Most important of all, we must explore the dynamics of change that propelled the West into world hegemony.

≺ I ≻

Initial Conditions

Since history is about how yesterday's choices affect today's decisions, any starting point is not just arbitrary but does violence to the essential continuity of history. If we take an initial snapshot of northwest Europe of a millennium ago we do so, therefore, with a self-conscious glance over our shoulder at the background sources of that landscape.

The western Roman Empire disappeared in the chaotic conditions of the fifth century A.D; a more or less arbitrary historical chronology dates the end of feudalism about a millennium later, in 1500. In between these dates western Europe gradually emerged from the anarchy that followed the collapse of Roman order and the overrunning of western Europe by Germanic tribes, to develop the political and economic structure which set the scene for subsequent developments. This evolution was basically conditioned by the heritage of Greco-Roman civilization which persisted (particularly in southern Europe), modifying and ultimately shaping many of the institutional arrangements that emerged in the sixth to the tenth centuries. The manor appears to be a lineal descendent of the Roman villa and the serf of the feudal world appears to be a descendant of the dependent *coloni*. Slavery, too, existed in the Middle Ages. Roman law continued and where order evolved served as the basis for the development of property rights.

The Church carried over the cultural heritage of the classical world to the Middle Ages. It was the lonely repository of learning (and indeed monasteries were frequently the most efficient farming centers of medieval Europe). A major possessor of material wealth, selling salvation in return for treasure and land, it was also characterized by asceticism, hermit life, and devout missionary activity. Most important, it provided a unified belief structure, an ideological frame of reference, that shaped perceptions in the medieval world. This common frame of reference served as the basis for the ongoing evolution of perceptions that would guide choices shaping the future of polities and economies.

Northwest Europe was a geographic contrast to the Mediterranean rim, the seat of Greco-Roman civilization. The latter was characterized by light and/or seasonal rainfall, light soils, and a varied agriculture ranging from viticulture and olive trees to cereals; the former by abundant rainfall, thick forests, and heavy soils that suited it to livestock and, with appropriate modifications of ploughs, cereal production. These climatic and geographic features determined the agrarian structure of the economies of northwest Europe.

These institutional, intellectual, and geographic background conditions of tenth-century life in northwest Europe must be set in the context of the most fundamental initial organizational condition—the lack of large scale economic and political order. The disintegration of the Roman Empire was followed by more than half a millennium of small scale political units. Whatever advantages had existed in large scale political-economic organization were absent or severely diluted in the era that followed. The Roman Empire did persist in the East until Constantinople was taken by the Turks in 1453; the Moslem world built on the charismatic faith of the new religion did create an empire spreading over North Africa and into Europe. But neither these exceptions nor the short-lived Carolingian Empire denies the critical point that the conditions that made possible a single empire governing the Mediterranean world had disappeared.

Assault from three directions, by Vikings, Moslems, and Magyars, imposed its stamp on the region. Vikings appeared off the coast of England in 786, of Ireland in 795, and of Gaul in 799. London was sacked in 841; Viking longboats moved up navigable rivers to attack such diverse towns as Rouen in the north and Toulouse in the south. Moslem corsairs roamed the Mediterranean and raided the coast from southern Italy to Provence. Hungarian horsemen raided Bremen in 915 and reached as far west as Orléans in 937.

The viable response was the fixed fortification, the heavily armored knight, and the hierarchical, decentralized structure of feudalism. The military result was something of a stalemate. The fortified town and (later) the stone castle were impregnable to all but the most persistent—and well financed—opposition that could undertake the siege necessary to starve out the inhabitants; warfare was typically small scale between heavily armored knights. The Vikings were repulsed at the siege of Paris in 885, Moslem raiders were defeated on the River Garigliano in 915, and the Magyars were defeated near Augsburg in 955. In consequence there was a revival of local order, an expansion of manors—ones being carved out of the wilderness, and a growth of towns. And it is in the context of these initial conditions that the complex interplay between political, economic, and military changes initiated the unique conditions that led to sustained economic growth.

Economic activity took place within the manor (with some exceptions) and in towns. Manorial organization was typified by a threefold division of land into the lord's demesne, the peasant holdings, and the commons. The majority of peasants were bound to the manor as serfs owing labor services and dues to the lord of the manor. They were subject to the lord's jurisdiction, had to seek justice in the lord's court, and were restricted in their movements and in their economic transactions.[2]

Traditional manorial organization provided scant encouragement for economic growth. The isolation of the manor inhibited specialization and division of labor and slowed the diffusion of technology when it did develop. The incentives imbedded in the customs of the manor provided little impetus for the rapid growth of skills and knowledge or technological change. The heavy plough with wheels, moldboard, and colter; the horsecollar; and the horseshoe did make their appearance although the shift from oxen to horses came mostly after the ninth century and then only slowly.[3] Likewise the shift from the two-field to the three-field system of crop rotation was a very gradual change. But population was growing at least from the tenth century on, most likely as a result of the relative improvements in order that followed the end of the incursions of Vikings, Moslems, and Magyars. And this population growth (and subsequent decline) would play a major role in altering the manorial organization.

The evolving towns were the centers of rapid economic—and political—change in response to the improved establishment of order over larger areas. Whether the numerous city republics of north and central Italy or the urban centers that grew up in the Low Countries in the tenth century, they were sources of dynamic changes resulting from the opportunities of expanding trade in the Mediterranean or the basins of the Scheldt and the Meuse and from ties both to south Europe and to the Baltic and North Sea coastal areas.

Prior to 1300 trade was carried on primarily by traveling merchants. Such traders often formed societies for mutual protection;

some of these even required their members to be suitably armed when traveling in caravans—an indication that problems of peace and order had not been settled completely. But after 1300 the importance of traveling merchants—and of fairs—began to decline.[4] The growth of trade fueled the growth of towns and the settlement of merchants further accelerated their development. The constraints imposed by geography and the high costs of land transport dictated their locations: at the head of a gulf (Bruges), where a road crossed a river (Maestricht), near the confluence of two rivers (Ghent), or at a breakpoint in transportation (Brussels).

< II >

The Sources of Institutional Change

The tenth to the sixteenth centuries in northwest Europe appear to have been a kaleidoscope of endless warfare at every level, from the local ubiquitous internecine conflicts of barons to the relatively large scale battles of the Hundred Years' War in which the English routed the French at Crécy, Poitiers, and Agincourt and the French turned the tables at Formigny and Castillion. They were also an era of radical demographic change, with population growth from the tenth to the fourteenth centuries and then a decline beginning in the early fourteenth century that probably persisted for 150 years before being reversed.

A changing military technology, from the longbow in the English victories to the artillery effective in the French victories to the pike phalanx that undid heavily armored French knights at Courtrai in 1302, led to profound changes not only in the nature of warfare but in the viable size of political units.[5] Warfare became more costly both because of the costs of training disciplined units and because of the increased capital costs of the offensive and defensive equipment. Whether the result was the dangerous employment of skilled mercenaries or the initiation of a professional standing army by Charles VII of France, political units needed more revenue to survive than could be obtained from a sovereign "living of his own" from traditional feudal sources. Yet if the fiscal needs of the sovereign had increased, the potential resources to generate additional revenue in the economies had also increased. Among these were growing trade, expanding markets, and widespread development of many economies.

The demographic decline of the fourteenth century was precipitous in urban populations, a result of the bubonic and pneumonic plagues. The immediate consequence was an absolute decline in the volume of trade and commerce and in the revenue available to be taxed or appropriated by princes. But the decline in commerce was not equal to that in population. The basic institutional structure of rules and laws persisted and provided the essential framework that would serve as the basis of growth when population revived. The impact of population decline on agrarian organization was more fundamental. A change in the land/man ratio made labor scarce and forced an increased competition among landlords, which ultimately altered the organization of the manor and of agriculture.

The revenue necessary to fiscally strapped rulers could be confiscated, could be borrowed (particularly from Florentine bankers), or could be traded by constituent economic groups in return for services provided by the sovereign. All these methods were tried. Confiscation killed the goose that laid the golden egg. Eventually Florentine (and other) bankers were burned by repudiation—but not before monarchs had been supported in expensive wars and some bankers had realized handsome profits from Crown monopolies and other favors from rulers. The third method, the exchange of services—particularly the granting and enforcing of property rights—for revenue, produced a wide variety of structural changes, from the protection of alien merchants, to the incorporation of guild and merchant law into legal codes and enforcement by the state, to the establishment of Parliament, Estates General, and Cortes.

≺ III ≻

Institutional Changes

The military and demographic/economic changes had profound implications for institutional and organizational change. The self-sufficient manor with dependent labor (serf, slave, or free) gradually gave way to a market-oriented agriculture, particularly pronounced adjacent to town and cities, with landlords and peasants bound together less by customary rights and obligations and more by an evolving structure of property rights. And institutional and organizational innovations further contributed to the growth of towns and cities and an expanding national and international commerce. The evolution of the bill of exchange and the development of techniques for negotiability and discounting required the development of centers where such events could occur—the Champagne and other fairs, banks, and eventually financial houses that would specialize in discounting. Marine insurance evolved from sporadic individual contracts covering partial payment for losses to standard printed contracts offered by specialized firms. Marine insurance was one way to spread risks; another was business organization that permitted either portfolio diversification or the aggregation of a number of investors in the commenda (an arrangement used in long-distance trade in which a sedentary merchant would despatch a "junior partner," usually a relative, to sell the cargo and obtain a return cargo), the regulated company, and finally the joint stock company.[6]

The mechanisms for contract enforcement appear to have had their beginnings in internal codes of conduct of fraternal orders of guild merchants, which were enforced by the threat of ostracism. These codes evolved into merchant law and spread throughout the European trading area; gradually they became integrated with common and Roman law and enforcement was eventually taken over by the state.[7]

It is important to recognize that the economic institutional structure was made possible by the evolution of polities that eventually provided a framework of law and its enforcement. Such a framework is an essential requirement for the impersonal exchange that is necessary for economic growth. The framework developed as polities gradually shifted from Mafia-like extortion to trading "protection and justice" for revenue. The initial impetus for this development was the desperate search for additional revenue; but as noted above that search could take several forms—confiscation or debt repudiation on the one hand or the trading (and enforcing) of property rights for revenue on the other.

Radically different results ensued from the divergent policies of rulers in the face of fiscal crises; but the one constant was the gradual emergence of the nation-state, whether in the context of the economic growth that characterized the Netherlands or of the stagnation that ensued from Spanish policies.

To understand the success of the Netherlands we must look back to the evolution of prosperous towns of the Low Countries such as Bruges, Ghent, and Liège; their internal conflicts; and their relationship to Burgundian and Habsburg rule. The prosperity of the towns, whether based on the wool cloth trade or metals trade, early on made for an urban-centered, market-oriented area unique at a time of overwhelmingly rural societies. Their internal conflicts reflected ongoing tensions between patrician and crafts and persistent conflict over ongoing efforts to create local monopolies which, when successful, led to a drying up of the very sources of productivity which had been the mainspring of their growth. The overall impact of the advent of Burgundian control was to discourage restrictive practices. In 1463 Philip the Good created a representative body, the States General, which enacted laws and had the authority to vote taxes for the ruler (although each province kept its own estate and the delegates to the States General were given limited powers). This assembly encouraged the growth of trade and commerce. The Burgundian (and later Habsburg) rulers themselves, in spite of vigorous opposition, actively discouraged monopoly privileges embodied in guild and trade restrictions such as those in the cloth towns of Bruges and Ghent. The rulers were supported by new centers of industry that sprang up in response to the favorable incentives embodied in the rules and property rights. The Burgundians and Habsburgs were rewarded by a level of prosperity that generated tax revenues that made the Low Countries the jewel in the Habsburg Empire. Eventually the ever more exacting revenue demands of Philip II led to revolt, the sacking of Antwerp, the successful separation of the seven northern provinces, and the rise to commercial supremacy of Amsterdam. And it was in the Netherlands and Amsterdam specifically that modern economic growth had its genesis.

Contrast this brief story of economic growth with the story of Spain. After centuries of strife with the Moors and ceaseless internal wars among feudal barons Castile and Aragon united, under Ferdinand and Isabella, to form a nation-state. When Charles V ascended the throne in 1516 the great era of Spanish hegemony over Europe was initiated. It was characterized by prosperity, with growing fiscal revenues from Aragon, Naples, Milan, and particularly the Low Countries. Increased revenues were matched by increased expenditures as Charles V maintained the largest and best equipped army in Europe. Maintaining and expanding the empire, however, was ever more costly; and when the Low Countries revolted against Charles V's successor, Philip II, the result was not only to lose a major source of revenue but to incur the additional expenses of war with the seven provinces. The fiscal crisis deepened as treasure from the New World declined. The desperate search for revenue led to granting local monopolies for revenue, to confiscations, and to ever higher rates of domestic taxation. The predictable results were a decline of trade and commerce and bankruptcies of the state in 1557, 1575, 1596, 1607, 1627, and 1647.

These contrasting stories of economic growth and decline have been, with appropriate but usually minor modification, repeated endlessly in history and in the modern world. Growth has been generated when the economy has provided institutional incentives to undertake productivity-raising activities such as the Dutch undertook. Decline has resulted from disincentives to engage in productive activity as a consequence of centralized political control of the economy and monopoly privileges. The failures vastly exceed the successes. Economic growth has been the exception; stagnation and decline have been the rule, reflecting a persistent tendency toward failure in human organization. But both the successes and the failures reflect more than institutional/organizational characteristics of societies. They also reflect perceptions, ideas, ideologies—the beliefs that guide human choices and actions.

≺ IV ≻

Cultural Beliefs and Societal Organization

Just what is the relationship between beliefs and the human condition? In his *The Protestant Ethic and the Spirit of Capitalism*,[8] Max Weber emphasizes beliefs. In contrast, the dedicated neoclassical economist assumes that ideas, ideologies—indeed beliefs in general—don't matter because people go about pursuing what is in their self-interest. But the economist assumes not only that self-interest always guides choices but that individuals know what is in their self-interest; that they have correct theories and hence make choices that will lead to the desired outcomes. In fact, however, humans face a world of uncertainty and the mental models that they construct to interpret the world around them and that determine their choices are models derived from their subjective—and typically very limited—experiences. In consequence diverse dogmas, myths, ideologies, and ideas have shaped and continue to shape human action.

But if ideas matter, just how do they matter? Weber is concerned to show that the religious ethic embodied in Protestantism—and specifically Calvinism—contained values that promoted the growth of capitalism. But which way does the causation run; and how do we know that both the values and the growth of capitalism did not stem from some other source?[9] Weber makes a connection between religious views and values, and between values and economic behavior; but he does not demonstrate how the consequent behavior would generate the growth of the specific institutions and organizations that produced a growing economic system.[10] Moreover Counter-Reformation Catholicism may have encouraged the same individualism and sense of discipline that Weber uniquely ascribes to Protestantism.

It will be useful to consider the relationship between behavioral beliefs and the evolution of specific institutional and organizational structures. A long-standing view of many scholars has been that individualist behavioral beliefs are congenial to economic growth. Alan Macfarlane's controversial *The Origins of English Individualism*[11] traces the sources of English individualism back to the thirteenth century or earlier. It paints a picture of a fluid, individualistically oriented set of attitudes towards the family, the organization of work, and the social structure of the village community. These attitudes were manifested in a set of formal rules dealing with property inheritance and the legal status of women.

More recently Avner Greif[12] compares Genoese traders with traders who had adopted the cultural and social attributes of Islamic society in the Mediterranean trade of the eleventh and twelfth centuries. He detects systematic differences in their organizational structures traceable to contrasting individualist versus collectivist behavioral beliefs. The traders from the Islamic world developed in-group social communications networks to enforce collective action which, while effective in relatively small homogeneous ethnic groups, do not lend themselves to the impersonal exchange that arises from the growing size of markets and diverse ethnic traders.

In contrast the Genoese developed bilateral enforcement mechanisms which entailed the creation of formal legal and political organizations for monitoring and enforcing agreements—an institutional/organizational path that permitted and led to more complex trade and exchange. Greif suggests the generality of these different belief structures for the Latin and Muslim worlds and then makes the connection between such belief structures in the European scene and the development of the economic institutions and organizations described briefly in the preceding section.

But if we accept that there were different behavioral beliefs in different societies and that they induced different forms of institutions and organizations, what produced the beliefs? The major candidate is religions since they were the dominant organized belief structures of the pre-modern world. The vast literature dealing with the effect of religious dogma on economic activity is, however, inconclusive since it is possible to pick out specific aspects of almost any religion that are antithetical to economic growth. Some of these are the Islamic opposition to insurance markets[13] and the Christian opposition to interest payments.

The proper focus, however, should not be on specific norms but on the learning process by which a particular belief structure—in this case religion—evolves. The learning process is a function of the way in which a given belief structure filters the information derived from experiences and the different experiences that confront individuals in different societies at different times. Thus one can argue that the Christian religious framework of the Middle Ages provided an hospitable filter for learning that led to adaptations congenial to economic growth; or alternatively that the specific geographic/economic/institutional context of the medieval Western world provided the unique experiences responsible for the resultant adaptations. In fact it was a combination of the two that produced the adaptations in the belief structure that were conducive to economic growth and political/civil freedoms. The belief structure embodied in Christian dogma was, despite some notorious contrary illustrations, amenable to evolving in directions that made it hospitable to economic growth. Both Ernst Benz[14] and Lynn White[15] maintain that Christian belief gradually evolved the view that nature should serve mankind and that therefore the universe could and should be

controlled for economic purposes. Such a view is an essential precondition for technological progress. But the unique institutional
conditions of parts of medieval/early modern Europe provided the
sort of experiences that served as the catalyst for such perceptions.
From this perspective Weber's Protestant ethic is part of the story of
this adaptation but is "downstream" from the originating sources.

≺ V ≻

What Happened Elsewhere

The foregoing analysis suggests that the western European experience was unique in both its institutional configurations and its belief structure. But it does not answer the fundamental question of
just what conditions are necessary and sufficient to induce economic growth and the evolution of freedoms. If economic growth is
a necessary condition, what additional attributes will assure the evolution of freedoms? We don't know—as is evident from the fumbling
efforts being made in the modern world to revive failed economies
and produce democratic polities. Therefore we have a less than satisfactory explanation for why in earlier times the more advanced economies and societies outside western Europe did not provide the setting for economic growth and the development of modern freedom.

A major failing of the literature of both economic history and
economic development is that the emphasis is upon technology as
the impetus for economic development. Hence we have many studies of technological failure or stagnation when in fact, the key to
growth is the institutional/organizational structure and its effect
upon incentives—incentives to invent and innovate, but also incentives to organize the production process more efficiently, to reduce
transaction costs in factor and product markets, to organize a judicial system to enforce contracts, to create a polity that will specify
and enforce property rights. Most importantly those incentives must
be maintained. In this context we may not know how to realize such
desirable objectives, but we do have some understanding of what
doesn't work. The following very brief analysis of two earlier advanced societies that failed to develop concentrates on those negative features.

China is the leading candidate to have produced sustained

growth and freedoms. The technological bias of historical scholarship has made a major puzzle out of the failure of that society to continue the development that made it a world leader in technology. Joseph Needham's massive scholarship[16] has provided us with detailed knowledge of China's early scientific and technological achievements. Over much of the more than two millennia since that country was unified it appeared to be more advanced than any other civilization and certainly during the Sung dynasty—tenth to the thirteenth centuries—gave indications of real economic growth. R. M. Hartwell asserts that the level of Chinese iron output in 1078 was equal to that of all of Europe in 1700.[17] As late as the Ming dynasty (beginning in the fourteenth century) China was preeminent in technology.

The search for an explanation of both periods of apparent real growth and technological creativity and other periods of slow growth or stagnation must explore changes either in the external environment or in the internal incentive structure that altered opportunities. Eric Jones argues that the non-Western world was more prone to disasters (floods, earthquakes, plagues) than was the West[18] and that the Jurchen and then Mongol invasions were a negative influence on growth.[19] He leaves open, however, whether such forces rather than the structural aspects of Chinese society were the critical deterrents.

Certainly changes in the external environment can account for a part of the uneven pattern of change; but a more abiding long run source of uneven evolution was the persistent character of the Chinese polity. It was not always or even usually a strong state, but it was a centralized state in which the decisions over property rights emanated from the center and could be and were changed by the whims of an emperor. Centralized decision making can produce periods of growth when a ruler perceives his or her interests are furthered by a set of rules that generate growth; but equally it can, and inevitably will, produce the reverse when a ruler, either because of fiscal crises or because of ideological beliefs, perceives his/her interests to be furthered by policies and hence incentive structures that induce stagnation. Chinese history is replete with arbitrary alterations in policies that fundamentally influence opportunities. In his *Oriental Despotism*[20] Karl Wittfogel had the wrong explanation for the centralization (a consequence of an irrigation system) but the right intuition that centralized controls are antithetical to development in the long run. Left unanswered is why the periods of growth did not lead to a breakdown of centralized controls and the evolution of freedoms.

Like China, Islam possessed technological, architectural, literary, and scientific credentials that made it appear a likely candidate for economic growth. The period from 700 to 1100 has been described as an Arab agricultural revolution[21] with the widespread diffusion of new crops and the promotion of new or the rehabilitation of old irrigation systems. Islamic law provided clearly specified individual rights to water and a tax system that encouraged agricultural investment. In commerce, merchants of the Islamic Empire pioneered in the fields of business organization and finance. Capital was usually pooled through either partnerships or the use of the commenda. Letters of credit and promissory notes were widely used in long distance trade.[22] In technology, the Arabs developed the lateen sail, were pioneers in paper production, and were pre-eminent in a number of areas of chemistry and metallurgy.

At its peak the Islamic Empire exceeded the Roman Empire, and as late as the seventeenth century it was a military threat to Europe. And even the assertion that the Islamic faith was not conducive to economic growth, an assertion that superficially appears attractive in the light of modern Islamic economics, has been challenged: Maxine Rodinson asserts that there is nothing in Islamic precepts that was contrary to fostering growth either in the past or in the present.[23]

But just what did prevent economic growth in the past, and for that matter in the present (aside from countries possessing oil)? It is certainly correct that individuals of Islamic faith have frequently exhibited all the individual acquisitive characteristics associated with achievement motivation and in *other settings* have been effective entrepreneurs. And that is precisely the point. It is the interplay between the belief structure and the external environment that shapes the evolution of a belief structure. Throughout most of history (with rare exceptions such as the Abbasid Caliphate of Baghdad in the ninth century) the external environment was not one that was conducive to intellectual evolution; to quote William McNeill, "by a curious and fateful coincidence, Moslem thought froze into a fixed mold just at the time when intellectual curiosity was awakening in western Europe—the twelfth and thirteenth centuries A.D."[24] Just as the environment of western Europe was influencing the evolution of the belief structure towards flexibility, the Moslem environment and specifically polity were enforcing conformity and stifling creativity. As in the case of China there were specific historical periods when a Moslem ruler fostered trade and commerce but others when the state exercised arbitrary control over property rights and practiced confiscation. The Ottoman Empire, for example, enjoyed heady success in the fifteenth century but evolved into a warrior, plundering state.

≺ VI ≻

Economic Growth and the Evolution of Freedom

None of the likely candidates to have originated modern freedom possessed the unique attributes of a belief structure and an institutional framework that were conducive to long-run economic growth and the evolution of freedoms. Just what setting might provide such a belief structure and institutional framework? Or to state the issue a little differently, why wouldn't any wealth-maximizing ruler encourage economic growth and grant more freedoms to his/her subjects? A ruler stands to get richer via more tax revenue by encouraging economic growth. This objective can be accomplished by providing incentives to promote productivity and by allowing constituents to retain a part of the increased income that results. However the ruler faces a tradeoff between the increased income he can obtain and the increased threat to his security as constituents have both more freedom of action and resources to overthrow him. The constituents too face the dilemma that the ruler may at some point renege on his promises and confiscate their accumulated wealth. The solution to the dilemma facing the parties is for the ruler and constituents to make bargains such that it is in both of their interests to live up to the bargains or for the ruler to bind himself/herself irreversibly to a course of action that will promote economic growth—for instance giving over rights and coercive power to constituents or their representatives. The latter policy will lead not only to the evolution of representative government but also to the rule of law.

Time is a crucial element in such a scenario. That is, such credible commitment can be realized only over a long period of time; the ruler can realize such gains only with long term agreements and constituents have no way of trusting an absolute ruler except by observing his/her conduct over time.

If we take a long enough time perspective something like this evolution appears to have occurred, and indeed it bears a superficial resemblance to English history. But when we examine the historical record carefully, much of it is at variance with this account. What is the matter with such a scenario? Why don't we observe such evolution in history? Is it because rulers weren't motivated by self-interest, rulers didn't know their own self-interest, they or the constituents didn't have the time to reach such agreements? Probably all of the above were factors, although given the historical record rulers do frequently appear to have been self-interested to the extent that they attempted to extract a maximum amount of (short term) wealth from constituents. But underlying motivation and the realizing of objectives is the belief structure that individuals possess. And the external environment determines the time horizons that ruler and constituents use in making decisions.

Not only are individuals not solely motivated by self-interest; achieving their objectives, whatever the motivation, entails their having theories about how to do so. How does a ruler know what will be the outcome of granting constituents more freedom? Even today we have wildly conflicting views about how to achieve economic, political, or social objectives. The belief structure that guided such decisions—and still does—is a hodge-podge of theories, dogmas, and ideological preconceptions sometimes leavened by informed evaluation.

And as for the external environment, the time horizon of rulers was—and still is—the short run, not just because in Keynes's memorable phrase "in the long run we are all dead" but because the very nature of the political process militates against long time horizons. Fiscal crises as a consequence of wars or internal conflict historically have been a major reason for the short time horizon of rulers; so has their mortality (although sometimes their time horizon has been leavened by the utility derived from hereditary succession).

But in addition to the cognitive belief structure and the external

environment there is still one other factor that we must tak
account in an understanding of the way societies evolve—and uua
is path dependence. Once on a particular path it is very difficult for
societies to alter directions radically. An economy with a tradition
of economic stagnation or growth is not easily changed to the other
direction. The explanation goes to the heart of the way institutions
affect societal performance. Institutions are the structure that humans devise to reduce uncertainty in their dealings with each other;
they are composed of formal rules such as laws and informal constraints such as norms of behavior and conventions. Institutions are
the key to the incentive structures which guide the way societies
evolve and therefore determine the kinds of organizations that will
arise to take advantage of the opportunities that the institutional
framework has created. Thus if we have laws and rules that reward
productive economic activity we can expect that organizations such
as partnerships and firms will emerge to take advantage of those
opportunities. And most important of all, the individuals in those
organizations will have a stake in perpetuating such laws and rules.
Thus the organizations that arise as a result of a particular institutional configuration result in turn in a powerful interest group
whose survival depends on maintaining that set of institutions.

But there is perhaps an even stronger force making for path dependence: the informal constraints of norms of behavior are derivative from the cognitive belief structure and therefore reinforce support for a given institutional framework. For that reason change
tends to be incremental and revolutions when they do occur are
never as revolutionary as the term implies. While the formal rules
can be changed overnight, the informal constraints are much more
impervious to change and impose a powerful drag on abrupt change.
Thus a tradition of economic growth and freedom has built-in support for its maintenance, just as a tradition of economic stagnation and totalitarian rule with centralized bureaucratic controls has
equally powerful organizational support (from the favored bureaucracy) for its perpetuation. Therefore even if a ruler did want to alter
the path of an economy away from stagnation to economic growth
he/she would face formidable opposition from the entrenched existing interests—as many rulers both in the past and in the present
have discovered.

≺ VII ≻

The Paradox of the West

We are now ready to unravel the paradox of the West. There are still gaps in our understanding and puzzles to be resolved. Moreover a more complete story would devote more attention to the costs associated with both economic growth and the development of freedoms. There were losers—lots of them along the way—whose conditions deteriorated in the course of the changes described. But overall the material conditions of human beings and the security of persons and property over a range of civil, political, religious, and economic activities improved.

Putting at the center of inquiry the institutional/organizational structure of the society, we can explore the interplay between economic and political organization in the context of changes wrought by changing perceptions of the participants or by forces external to them. The failures of the most likely candidates, China and Islam, point the direction of our inquiry. Centralized political control limits the options—limits the alternatives that will be pursued in a context of uncertainty about the long-run consequences of political and economic decisions. It was precisely the lack of large scale political and economic order that created the environment essential to economic growth and ultimately human freedoms. In that competitive decentralized environment lots of alternatives were pursued; some worked, as in the Netherlands and England; some failed, as in the cases of Spain and Portugal; and some, such as France, fell in between these two extremes. But the key to the story is the variety of the options pursued and the increased likelihood (as compared to a single unified policy) that some would turn out to produce economic growth. Even the relative failures in western Europe played an essential role in European development and were more successful than China or Islam because of competitive pressures.

The last point deserves special emphasis. The dynamic consequences of the competition among fragmented political bodies resulted in an especially creative environment. Europe was politically fragmented; but it was integrated in having both a common belief structure derived from Christendom, and information and transportation connections that resulted in scientific, technological, and artistic developments in one part spreading rapidly throughout Europe. To treat the Netherlands and England as success stories in isolation from the stimulus received from the rest of Europe (and to a lesser degree Islam and China) is to miss a vital part of the explanation. Italian city-states, Portugal, and Germanic states all fell behind the Netherlands and England; but banking, artistic development, improvements in navigation, and printing were just a few of the obvious contributions that the former states made to European advancement.

With the advantage of hindsight can we be more specific? The lack of large scale order in Europe in the early medieval period meant that the source of decision making was in the town or in the manorial/feudal hierarchy. This decision making was conditioned by the cultural heritage that shaped the initial perceptions of the participants. Let us begin with the role of the town on the continent of Europe.

The towns in medieval western Europe varied—from the Italian city-state, to fortress towns built in response to the threat of external aggression, to local administrative towns; but in all cases a key factor in their evolution was the degree of autonomy from external authority they enjoyed. It was the relative freedom of European towns from such authority that was an initial distinguishing factor as compared to towns elsewhere. As economic opportunities emerged with the relative increase in order and therefore a decline in the transaction costs of trade, the towns were in a position to take advantage of the new opportunities—whether it was the Mediterranean trade of the Venetians and Genoese or the woolen and metal trade of the Low Country towns with northwest Europe. The expansion of commerce led to the growth of a new interest group, commercial interests, alongside the traditional nobility, Crown, and clergy. Towns were able to gain liberties often over the opposition of nobles and clergy. This liberty to come and go, to buy and sell as they saw fit was as essential to economic growth as some security of property. The Protestant Reformation, evolving in the context of repression, introduced a concern for another liberty—liberty of conscience, the freedom to worship as one chose; and economic liberty, religious freedom, and representative government became intertwined issues.

The commercial expansion of the eleventh to the fourteenth centuries produced not only an increase in urban places but also the development of commercial networks linking together the trade of northwest Europe with that of the Mediterranean. The organizational framework of fairs, guilds, law merchant, and the organizations that facilitated the use of the bill of exchange required an institutional framework of political and economic order. Order necessitated both the creation of a framework of rules of the game inside the town and equally the establishment of rules and their enforcement that permitted exchange across political boundaries.

The political/economic order within Low Country towns was eloquently described by Henri Pirenne in his *Early Democracies in the Low Countries*.[25] Pirenne's story is one of the creation of the institutional infrastructure of democratic order within thriving town economies, which was gradually undermined by guild restrictions and conflict between patrician and lesser citizenry over control of the polity. But for Pirenne "the municipal democracies of the Middle Ages consisted, and could only have consisted, of privileged members. They did not, and could not, know the ideal of a liberty and an equality open to all."[26] For Pirenne this democracy was pragmatic and unleavened by intellectual pretensions of democracy and egalitarianism and therefore not like modern democracy.

That may be correct; but what Pirenne was describing was an integral part of a process of fundamental change. Political re-ordering and inevitable internal conflicts are everywhere in history a part of the process of economic expansion—a conflict internal to the town and its evolving interest groups but also external in its relationship with princes and rulers. To reiterate an ongoing theme of this chapter, change was overwhelmingly an incremental process, building onto and modifying the pre-existing institutional framework and constrained by the belief structure that prevailed. It is precisely that process of instutitional/organizational incremental evolution that Pirenne describes in his story of the way the various political and economic organizations evolved and interacted with each other. It is not an inevitable triumph of democracy that is taking place, but a struggle for control of the polity. And as for a belief structure that embodied modern sentiments of democracy and egalitarianism: that was surely not a part of the perceptions of that time, either in the town or in the countryside.

England evolved along a route to economic growth and freedom different from that of the Continent. Being an island made it less vulnerable to conquest and eliminated the need for a standing army. The belief structure, as Macfarlane makes clear, was different. The Norman conquest, the exception to British invulnerability to external conquest, produced a more centralized feudal structure than any on the Continent; but as the Magna Carta attests, the Crown could not overstep the traditional liberties of the barons who had dictated the charter's terms or of towns, foreign merchants, and villeins. England's political institutions also differed in several important ways from those of its neighbors on the Continent. The most important was the unity of its Parliament. There was a single Parliament for the entire country; no regional estates as in France, Spain, and the Netherlands. There was also no division into towns, clergy, and nobility. Maitland pointed out: "It is a noticeable fact that at a very early time, perhaps from the beginning, the citizens and burgesses sit together with the knights."[27]

Both on the Continent and in England the changing status of serf and free labor on the manor certainly was not guided by any change in the perception of their inferior status. Rather, the gradual evolution of longer leases, reduced obligations, and a shift to copyhold (in the West) reflected a change in the relative scarcity of labor as a consequence of population decline in the fourteenth century, the alternative opportunities that the towns provided, and the competition for labor that resulted.

In combination with the development of markets, towns, and trade as a consequence of the relative improvement of order and the demographic changes, we must consider the fiscal crises of princes. Such crises arose as a consequence of the ubiquitous warfare among competing political units and the growing costs of warfare. They played a key role in the political/economic changes that occurred. Between 1200 and 1500 the many political units in western Europe went through endless conflicts, alliances, and warfare and gradually evolved into nation-states. It was not so much the size of the political unit that was critical for survival as it was the ability to increase tax revenues. It had been customary for the ruler to receive revenue in kind and indeed in some cases to move the court from one part of the country to another to consume the goods and services in kind. With the growth of a money economy as a consequence of the economic expansion of the eleventh to fourteenth centuries, revenues became monetized; then in the fourteenth and fifteenth centuries they declined as a result of the fall in land rents, stemming from declining population.

A year of warfare resulted in as much as a four-fold increase in the costs of government—and warfare was endemic. Declining revenues and increasing fiscal costs posed an ever-worsening dilemma for European princes. Custom and tradition set limits on the exactions they could obtain from lesser lords and, as the Magna Carta attests, a king who stepped across the boundary of accepted custom faced the possibility of revolt. The king's vassals were sometimes as powerful as he and in concert were more powerful. Moreover vassals could and sometimes did combine with foreign princes to overthrow the king; therefore increased taxation of vassals could place a Crown in jeopardy.

While the degrees of freedom of princes varied, one option available to them, as we have seen, was to grant privileges—property rights—in return for revenue. As trade and commerce grew beyond the bounds of the town or manor, merchants found that the private costs of protection could be reduced by a larger coercive authority and were willing to pay princes to provide protection.

In order to prevent loss of revenue from evasions, rulers granted rights to alienate land or to allow inheritance, thereby establishing more secure and efficient property rights. Towns were granted trading privileges in return for annual payments; alien merchants were granted legal rights and exemptions from guild restrictions in return for revenue. Guilds received exclusive rights of monopoly in return for payments to the Crown.

The ubiquitous competition among the evolving nation-states was a deep underlying source of change and equally a constraint on the options available to rulers within states. Competition forced the Crown to trade rights and privileges for revenue, including, most fundamentally, the granting to representative bodies—variously Parliament, Estates General, Cortes—control over tax rates and/or certain privileges in return for revenue. Equally, competition among states offered constituents alternatives—states to which they might flee or send their moveable wealth, thus constraining the ruler's options.

But at this point there are divergent stories. Some bodies retained and expanded their status and provided the basis for the growth of representative government; others declined or withered away. It was the evolving bargaining strength of rulers vis-a-vis constituents that was decisive. Three considerations were at stake: the size of the potential gains the constituents could realize by the state taking over protection of property; the closeness of substitutes for the existing ruler—that is the ability of rivals (both within and outside the political unit) to the existing ruler to take over and provide the same (or more) services; and the structure of the economy which determined the benefits and costs to the state of various kinds of taxation.

In the Low Countries, for example, the productive town economies stood to gain substantially by the political order and protection of property rights provided first by the Burgundians and then by Charles V. The structure of the economy built around export trades provided the means for easy-to-collect taxes on trade but not at a level to affect adversely the comparative advantage of the trades. But the demands of Philip II led to the conviction that the economy would continue to prosper only with independence. The resistance was initiated on the authority of the States General which in 1581 issued the Act of Abjuration of allegiance to Philip II and claimed sovereignty for the provinces themselves.

Eventually the seven northern provinces succeeded in achieving independence. The resulting economic/political structure of Amsterdam and the Netherlands was one not only of efficient economic organization but with many of the basic attributes of political and civil freedoms. The powers of the newly independent country—the United Provinces—resided with each province and a unanimity rule meant that the States General must receive the unanimous votes of the deputations from each province (which voted as a unit). Cumbersome as that process was, this political structure survived. The polity not only evolved the elements of political representation and democratic decision rules but supported religious freedom (an important source of friction with the Spanish Crown). The de facto policy of the United Provinces was one of toleration in the sphere of religion; it was a policy that encouraged immigration of dissenters from various parts of Europe, many of whom contributed to the growth of the Dutch economy.

In England as on the Continent, traditional feudal revenues were a declining portion of total state revenues. England's external trade provided an increasing share of the revenue, including taxes on wine, general merchandise, and wool cloth; but it was the wool export trade in the thirteenth century that was the backbone of augmented Crown revenue. Eileen Power's classic story of the wool trade[28] describes the exchange among the three groups involved in that trade: the wool growers as represented in Parliament, the merchants of the staple, and the Crown. In an agreement the merchants achieved a monopoly of the export trade and a depot in Calais, Parliament received the right to set the tax, and the Crown received the revenue. William Stubbs summarized the exchange: "The admission of the right of Parliament to legislate, to inquire into abuses, and to share in the guidance of national policy, was practically purchased by the money granted to Edward I and Edward III."[29]

With the Tudors the English Crown was at the zenith of its powers, but it never sought the unilateral control over taxing power that the Crown of either France or Spain achieved. The confiscation of monastery lands and possessions by Henry VIII alienated many peers and much of the clergy and as a consequence "Henry had need of the House of Commons and he cultivated it with sedulous care."[30] The Stuarts inherited what the Tudors had sown and the evolving controversy between the Crown and Parliament is a well-known tale. Two aspects of this controversy are noteworthy for this analysis. One was the evolving perception of the common law as the supreme law of the land—a position notably championed by Sir Edward Coke—and the other was the connection made between monopoly and a denial of liberty as embodied in the Crown grants of monopoly privileges. To quote David Harris Sacks, "The concept of liberty grew in antithesis to the growth of a theory of state power which had its concrete expression in the creation of economic monopolies. The focus on the grievance of monopolies helped sustain a powerful intellectual connection between the protection of individual rights and the preservation of the commonweal."[31]

The Spanish Crown, in contrast, evolved into an absolutist monarchy. Aragon and Castile, the two regions making up the nation-state that emerged under Ferdinand and Isabella, were very different. The former (comprising Valencia, Aragon, and Catalonia) had been reconquered from the Arabs in the last half of the thirteenth century and had become a major commercial center. The Cortes reflected the interest of merchants and played a significant role in public affairs. Indeed, had Aragon determined the future of Spain its history would have been very different. But Castile, which had been continually engaged in warfare against Moors and in internal strife, had no such heritage of strong merchant groups. The Cortes was relatively less effective and Isabella succeeded in gaining control of unruly barons and of church policy as well. A centralized monarchy and resultant bureaucracy ensued and it was Castile that determined the institutional evolution of Spain (and ultimately of Latin America, as well).

The era of Spanish hegemony was made possible by the income from the Habsburg empire and the New World treasure, but as revenue from those sources declined the Crown of necessity turned to the desperate expedients of taxation and confiscation—with disastrous results. Economic monopolies and centralized political controls went hand in hand. The path that Spain was traveling proved durable and led to three centuries of economic stagnation and political instability which ended only with the demise of Franco in the mid-twentieth century. Moreover the Spanish heritage carried over into the new world of Latin America a set of institutions and organizations that produced neither sustained economic growth nor sustained political and civil freedoms.

The divergent evolution of the Netherlands and England, on the one hand, and Spain—and France—on the other, then, can be attributed immediately to the different bargaining strength of constituents and rulers and the three underlying sources of that bargaining strength: the gains to constituent groups of the state taking over protection of property; the closeness of substitutes for the existing ruler; and the economic structure which determined the yields to various taxes. And in turn we can trace the particular geographic/economic/institutional pattern that produced the divergent conditions. Bargaining strength may be the immediate source of change but it is not the complete source, and it would be misleading to ignore the complementary role played by the belief structure. Western Europe had the initial common belief structure of Latin Christendom. But that initial belief structure evolved differently in parts of Europe as a consequence of diverse experiences. In the Netherlands and England the experiences fostered the evolution of the belief structure in directions that led to modern perceptions of freedom. In contrast, Spanish experiences perpetuated not only the traditional hidalgo aversion to economic activity but also the beliefs underlying the medieval hierarchical order.

The evolution of the belief structure in England is most succinctly captured in J. H. Hexter's introduction to another volume of this series in which he contrasts the medieval liberties of England in 1500—"a changing body of particular claims under the protection of law for those who had them"—with the Petition of Right enacted by Parliament in 1628—a petition which concerns "itself with freedom at the level of its foundations. Its enactment is the decisive first step in the direction of modern freedom, of liberty as we know it in our world."[32]

Access to medieval liberties was determined by the hierarchical structure of the society; bondsmen—slaves, villeins, serfs, and other dependent individuals—were excluded from access. The Petition of Right, in contrast, established for all Englishmen a set of rights protected by law—a law enacted by Parliament. The changing perceptions about the rights of individuals, from the medieval views of status to the seventeenth century view of Englishmen as freeborn, reflected the evolution of the belief structure between 1500 and 1628. The positive combination of the belief structure with the particular conditions that existed in the Netherlands and England led to the institutional evolution of the economy and polity. It also fostered the intellectual changes that produced not just the Protestant Reformation but an evolving belief structure, and resultant behavior, conducive both to economic growth and to the evolution of freedoms. Contrasting circumstances in Spain, and to a lesser degree France, shaped the evolution of the belief structure in ways that reinforced their existing institutional structure and stifled both economic growth and political/civil freedoms.

The interplay between the belief structure and the external environment shaped immediate policies and choices and provided a rationale to support them: this story takes us half way there in the evolution of modern freedom. Ultimately, ideas of freedom took on an independent role. From such individuals as Hobbes, Locke, participants in the Scottish Enlightenment, and on the Continent Montesquieu, a powerful ideology would gradually evolve—one that would reshape the world. That is another story.

Freedom and the Greeks

MARTIN OSTWALD

THAT THE CONCEPT OF "FREEDOM" can properly be formulated only as the antithesis of "unfreedom" is a truth that can now be taken for granted.[1] However, this does not imply that every form of "unfreedom" has a corresponding "freedom" as its antithesis: "unfreedom" takes on a greater variety of guises than "freedom." To determine whether the former generated the latter or the latter the former is impossible. If we take "unfreedom" as denoting the dependency of one human being on another, be it in a social, economic, or political way, we may assume that it existed among mankind from time immemorial. Accordingly, we can expect to find an explicit or implicit distinction between the two from the time of which the earliest written documents have been preserved. In all societies on record, including the Greek, the earliest evidence indicates that a distinction between "unfree" and "free" is made only to indicate the difference in status of individual persons. The Greek contribution to notions of freedom is unique in that it is the first to extend this notion from individuals to the community that is the state. The Greeks developed political freedom in two senses: internally, they regarded a state as free if it was not ruled by a despot; and externally, if it was free from foreign domination.

To trace this development is the purpose of this chapter. Its parameters run from the first appearance of Greek in the so-called Linear B Texts (usually dated from c. 1450–1200 B.C.) of the Mycenaean period to the end of the classical period, whose last major exponent was Aristotle, who died in 322 B.C. After the Mycenaean texts, we encounter it in the Homeric epics which, though they had taken the form in which they have come down to us by the middle of the seventh century B.C., are believed to reflect conditions of the late Mycenaean. From there we shall proceed to the period begin-

ning with the great social and constitutional reformer Solon early in
the sixth century and ending at the eve of the Persian Wars, c. 490
B.C. The period following the Persian Wars down to the end of the
fifth century, which we examine next, is the most crucial for our
purposes, since it includes the flowering of the Athenian democracy
as well as the development of an Athenian empire. A final section
will be devoted to the fourth century, culminating in the work of
Aristotle, the tutor of Alexander the Great.

Before we begin our discussion, a few verbal ambiguities must be
cleared up. In a brilliant and influential recent discussion of freedom, Orlando Patterson has tried to show that slavery generated the
idea of freedom, and specifically that "women played a decisive role
in the Western social invention of *personal* freedom."[2] The point is
harder to prove than Patterson seems to realize. In the first place,
Finley has shown that "slave" is not a unitary concept in ancient
Greek,[3] which begs the question which form of "unfreedom" generated "freedom." A second problem is that we speak almost indif-
ferently of "freedom" or "liberty," while Greek uses only one term,
eleutheria, or its adjectival or verbal form (*eleutheros, eleutheroun*).
"Freedom" will be used in the following as the English equivalent
of *eleutheria*, and "slavery" as its opposite, equivalent to Greek
douleia.

≺ I ≻

Mycenae and Homer

In our earliest texts, there is no explicit contrast beween "free" and
"slave." In fact, when the Linear B tablets speak of male or female
"slaves" (*do-e-ro/a* or *do-e-los/a*) only the kind of work they do and
the fact that the term is usually followed by a genitive indicates
their dependent status.[4] Nowhere do we encounter an explicit contrast between them and a free person. In fact, no term corresponding
to what we call "free" is found in the tablets at all. In the rare instances in which the term *e-re-u-te-ro/a* (= *eleutheros/a*) is found
in Pylos, it seems to refer to "a free allowance deducted from an
official assessment [of linen]," an "authorized concession."[5] It is evidently an economic term, devoid of social or political meaning. As
in the case of "slave" the context provides no antonym that would

enable us to extrapolate from it an early meaning of "freedom."[6]

Although the Homeric poems, which are generally thought to reflect the conditions of the late ninth and early eighth centuries B.C., amply attest the use of slaves, *doulos/ē* is rarely used to describe them; various other terms, which differentiate them by the functions they perform, are more common. Equally rare are forms of *eleutheros*.[7] The few occurrences of both terms, however, leave no doubt that they describe the social status of an individual, especially the statuses from which and into which an individual passes as a result of war. Women lose their "day of freedom" (*eleutheron ēmar*) or embark on the "day of slavery" (*doulion ēmar*) (*Iliad* 6.463) when their husbands have fallen in battle, their city has been captured, and they have themselves become the booty of an enemy.[8] When this happens, the captive woman becomes a slave (*doulē*), sometimes the concubine of her captor (*Iliad* 3.409)—by whom she may have children (*Odyssey* 4.12). But males, too, can experience the "day of slavery" in the form of a reduction in their status.[9] When invaders have been successfully repelled, the "mixing bowl of freedom" is served to celebrate the event (*Iliad* 6.528), presumably less to celebrate the preservation of the status in which the full member of society found himself than to express gratitude that the loss of that status had been avoided. "Slavery" (*doulosynē*) is the lot of the fifty carding women whom Eurycleia supervises (*Odyssey* 22.423), and Odysseus comments that Laërtes's "slavelike looks" (*douleion eidos*) belie his royal bearing (*Odyssey* 24.252).

Just as the kind of work assigned to slaves shows no noticeable difference from that done by non-slave labor, "freedom" is not as significant a feature in differentiating members of the upper from those of the lower class as is membership in an aristocratic family (*oikos*).[10] Neither term is found in the Hesiodic poems, which are rough contemporaries of *Iliad* and *Odyssey*, even though we have contemporary archaeological evidence that slavery was common enough to have burial sites set aside for slaves. A fragment of Heraclitus shows that notions of freedom-slavery similar to those in Homer lasted into the early fifth century in some parts of the Greek world: it is war that has made some men slaves and others free, just as it has shown some to be gods and others human beings.[11] But by his time the identity of a free person was distinct and important enough to be made explicit.

≺ II ≻

From Solon to the Eve of the Persian Wars

We learn from the poems of Solon that far-reaching economic developments had adversely affected the social and political status of many Athenians, primarily those engaged in agriculture, which he sought to ameliorate through his reforms in 594 B.C. In doing so, he took a major step in extending the boundaries of "freedom" (*eleutheria*). It is likely, but not demonstrable, that Solon's ideas were ahead of the rest of the Greek world. Roughly contemporary evidence from places as far apart as Lesbos, Amorgos, and Megara shows that "freedom" had assumed dimensions that are not attested for Homeric times.

From Lesbos we have a substantial fragment of a poem by Alcaeus (born c. 620 B.C.) in which he attacks his political enemy Pittacus for projecting the image of "free men born of noble parents," even though his father was a Thracian drunkard.[12] We can infer from this that in his contemporary Lesbos a "free" man enjoyed an elevated social position among others who do not necessarily seem to have been unfree. Sure enough, there is in this context no unfree person with whom he is contrasted, but he does have the social distinction of belonging to an aristocratic family, superior to savage drunkards: he is a cultivated person. While Homer had not made much of the fact that Menelaus had a son by a slave woman (*Odyssey* 4.12), free and slave are distinct social classes here.

The negative side of this is seen in a line of Semonides of Amorgos (c. 600 B.C.), whose animal typology of women includes a lady born of a delicate mare who shuns "works of slaves" and anguish:[13] born into the upper social class, she does not want to demean herself by servile labor. The sentiment persists with a touch of Homeric language in Theognis of Megara a generation or two after Solon. In exile in Thebes, he maintains his aristocratic bearing: he still has his city; exile has not entailed "slavery" for him, and he will not let a girl, who had met her "day of slavery," tease him about his parentage (1210–15). But there is also a new dimension in that moral traits come to be associated with "free" and "slave." He boasts that, since he has never abandoned a friend, there is nothing "slavish" in his soul (529–30); and that he can now behave like a "free man," since his relationship with a boy, whom bad company had corrupted, has come to an end (1377–80). In warning Democles that a spendthrift might end his days in "slavery," he comes close to giving the term not only the moral but also the economic overtones it has in Solon (921–28). An opposite character is the skinflint who has never given his stomach a "free man's meal" (*eleutherion siton*) (915–16), a term that has the moral thrust of "liberal," "generous," rather than the social sense of "free."[14] It is in Theognis that we encounter the adjective *eleutherios* for the first time in Greek literature. In fact he goes so far as to make slavery its genetic opposite: "never has a slave's head grown straight; it always stands crooked on a slanting neck. No rose or hyacinth grows from a squill, no slave woman gives birth to a free and generous child (*teknon eleutherion*)" (535–38).

We can only assume that "freedom" already had these or similar connotations in Solon's time. Although his poems contain more social terminology than the remains of any other archaic poet, they are too fragmentary to serve as indicators of what was original with him and what he shared with his contemporaries. He differs from his predecessors in that he is the first author we know who explicitly opposes "freedom" and "slavery" and uses both in a metaphorical sense. Whether this is due to the accident of survival or presents radically new thinking we cannot tell.

The antinomy "freedom-slavery" is preserved in only one poem, in which he celebrates the achievements of his economic measures, the *seisachtheia*, through which, he claims, he "made free" the Earth, which had formerly been "enslaved," by removing the mortgage stones that had impaled her. In the same poem, moreover, he takes credit for "having brought back to Athens . . . many who had been sold abroad, some lawfully, some not, and others who had fled abroad, exiled by the constraint of debt; roaming around in many places, they no longer uttered Attic speech. Others again, whom degrading slavery held in bonds here at home and who trembled at their masters' whims, I made free."[15]

What strikes the reader at once is that "slave" and "free" here are not only used of individuals. They are also applied in a bold metaphor to a personified earth that has been "freed" from its "slavery," an image that gains power through its juxtaposition with men "freed" at home from the "slavery" to which they had been reduced.

Secondly, "freedom" and "slavery" are here for the first time in the surviving evidence predicated of a group, identified by a common fate. The effect of these two dramatic juxtapositions is that "slavery" becomes a corruption of the natural state of both the earth and of a group of men inhabiting it; "freedom" restores both to the status meant for them. Freedom is thus infused with a political value for which we have no evidence in earlier thought.

This poem is, unfortunately, our main source for understanding the nature of the emergency that Solon remedied. It is supplemented by some information to be gleaned from the second chapter of Aristotle's *Constitution of Athens* and Plutarch's *Solon* 13.3–4. From these sources it is evident that agrarian distress lay at the root of the trouble, and that Solon remedied it by removing encumbrances (*horoi*) from the land and restored their freedom to people who had lost it through some kind of indebtedness. The precise nature of their indebtedness and the reasons for their loss of freedom remain obscure.[16] Certain is that the gulf between rich and poor had widened, presumably because free men, called *hektēmoroi* in our sources, had incurred obligations to rich landowners, partly as sharecroppers, partly as ordinary borrowers, and had as a result lost their land and their personal freedom. Some had been enslaved at home, others were sold as slaves abroad, and others again had fled into exile. The reasons for defaulting on their obligations is attributed by Solon to the greed of the rich:

the mentality of the leaders of the people is immoral; much painful suffering is in store for them as a result of their great arrogance. They do not know how to curb their greed and how to enjoy in quiet order the cheer a banquet gives them . . . they get rich from the lure of immoral deeds. Sparing neither sacred nor public property they steal like robbers from any source they can, and do not even watch out for the solemn foundations of Justice. She is aware in silence of what is going on and what has gone on, but is sure to come in good time to exact the price. This comes at that point to the entire city as a wound none can escape, and quickly leads it into degrading slavery, which arouses from their sleep civil strife and war.[17]

While this is the only fragment of Solon's poetry that illustrates his view of the state of affairs before his reforms, there are two fragments, likely to have been written some decades after the reforms, in which he seems to warn the people of the "slavery" into which they can fall by turning the management of their affairs over to one man, presumably the tyrant Peisistratus:[18] "The city perishes at the hands of great men: through its ignorance the people has fallen into slavery to a sole ruler" (fr. 9.3–4); and "If you have suffered grievously through your own incompetence, do not attribute your subsequent lot to the gods. It is you who have exalted these men by giving them a guard, and it is for that reason that you have sunk into the state of degrading slavery." It is difficult to take "slavery" literally in these two passages. After all, the individual members of society enjoyed the status of free men even under the tyrant. It is rather the status of the people as a whole, deprived of effective power, and subject to the whims of one man, that has been reduced to "slavery." Although the meaning may be taken to be a metaphorical extension of the master-slave relationship, "slavery" has evidently become fully a political term. On the positive side, we can infer that a "free" man is a person who is politically the master of his own destiny in that he is not subject to the whims of a sole ruler: he is a citizen, an integral part of a community (*polis*) competent to decide its own aims.[19]

We have no evidence for over another century that the "slavery" of a people under a tyrant or monarch—and the concomitant concept of the "freedom" experienced by a community liberated from tyranny—was conceptualized in post-Solonian Greece. That no such evidence should have come down to us from the time of the Peisistratid tyranny—under which Athens fell some three decades after Solon's reforms and, as we saw, at a time when Solon may still have been alive—is not surprising. The freedom of speech required to dub the condition of the tyrant's subjects "slavery" will not have existed; it will have required the luxury of retrospect, enjoyed by later generations, to apply a description of this kind. Even after the first serious attempt at putting an end to the tyranny in 514 B.C., the "tyrannicides" Harmodius and Aristogeiton were praised for bringing "political equality" (*isonomia*), not "freedom," to Athens.[20] It is not until Herodotus's account of Athenian history, written more than half a century after the event, that the overthrow of the Athenian tyranny is said to have led to "freedom," hyphenated in one passage with "free speech" (*isēgoriē*).[21]

There is, however, one indication that the end of tyranny may have been regarded as tantamount to the establishment of "free-

dom" on the island of Samos. Herodotus informs us that after suc-
ceeding the tyrant Polycrates of Samos in 522 B.C., his lieutenant
Maeandrius "first of all, erected an altar and established around it a
sacred precinct to Zeus Eleutherios (= Zeus guarantor of freedom),"
and then declared to the assembled people that Polycrates's style of
"lording it (*despozōn*) over men like himself was not to his liking";
he declared political equality (*isonomiē*) and access to power for
all, reserving for himself and his descendants only six talents from
Polycrates's possessions and the priesthood of Zeus Eleutherios,
"whose sanctuary I have myself founded; to you I give freedom"
(Herodotus 3.142). To question the historicity of the foundation of
the cult, as some modern scholars have done, on the grounds that
we know of no other similar cults until some fifty years later will
not do.[22] Our only source, Herodotus, may have heard of the cult
from contemporaries of Maeandrius or their children, when he traveled in Samos some five or six decades after the event. His statement
that the altar "is now in a suburb" of Samos (3.142.2) suggests that
he had seen it and had learned its identity from native Samians.
Moreover, Maeandrius's action may be capable of more than one interpretation: inasmuch as he frowned on the "lordship" (*despozōn*)
exercised by Polycrates, he may have regarded as "freedom" the
status to which he aspired for the people of Samos, very much as
Solon looked upon those he had liberated from their indebtedness.
However, we have no way of discounting the possibility that the
concept of the "freedom" gained by a people after the fall of a tyrant
existed in Samos before it took root in other parts of the Greek
world. If so, the Maeandrius story as told by Herodotus is our earliest evidence of "freedom" as the condition attained by a people after
the demise of a tyrant.

<   III   >

The Persian Wars and their Aftermath

The most signal contribution of the Greeks to the idea of "freedom,"
its political dimension, is lacking—or at least stunted in its development—in the documents that have come down to us from the
ancient Near East. Since slavery was a universal phenomenon in all
ancient Mediterranean civilizations, there can be little doubt that

distinctions not only between master and slave but also between free man and slave were universally perceived. But being perceived does not automatically mean that they were made explicit.

The ancient Mesopotamian law codes abound with provisions for the treatment of slaves, especially of female slaves and those of their children who had been fathered by their masters.[23] But apart from the special attention given to *awēlum* in the Code of Hammurabi[24]—usually translated "seignior"—there seems to be no special designation for a "free" man. There is no notion of a person "free" in a political sense; on the contrary, there is some evidence that the absolute monarchs of Persia would regard their subjects as slaves.[25] Here the Hebrews, about whom we have more coherent information than about any other Near Eastern people, form an exception. In the first place, the institutions of the sabbatical year (*Exodus* 21:2) and the Jubilee year (*Leviticus* 25:10), which restored land to its original owner and emancipated the slave, caused slavery not to be envisaged as a permanent status; accordingly, the difference between "slave" and "free" remained more blurred than in other cultures, particularly since the Hebrew language does not differentiate, either, between a free servant and a slave.[26]

Moreover, the story of the exodus from Egypt is not couched in political terms. The Israelites were in Egypt a minority subjected to a slavery to which other subjects of the Pharaoh were not, and which is described in some detail in *Exodus* 1:10–14: they were deprived of personal rather than of a political freedom by the Egyptians, who "did set over them taskmasters to afflict them with their burdens. And they built for Pharaoh treasure cities, Pithom and Raamses" (11). Their "redemption" is not a progression from domination by a tyrant or occupation by an alien power to independence and freedom, but rather an escape from slavery to Pharaoh to service (= slavery) to God. This is stated explicitly at *Leviticus* 25:55: "for unto me the children of Israel are servants; they are my servants whom I brought forth out of the land of Egypt: I am the Lord your God."[27] The goal of their deliverance is the divine legislation at Sinai rather than the establishment of political autonomy. There is no notion of political freedom expressed in Near Eastern literature.

Herodotus is our main source for the decisive step which gave "freedom" the political dimension which the Greeks bequeathed to Western civilization. In his work there are three different kinds of "unfreedom" as antinomies to "freedom." The first contrasts with a financial kind of "freedom" not unlike the one we encountered on the Pylos tablet in the sense of "a free allowance deducted from an official assessment [of linen]."[28] It occurs only once and that in a comparison of Spartan and Persian customs in successions to the royal throne: in both cases the incoming king "frees" any Spartan from paying debts owed the king or the public treasury (6.59). In six passages "freedom" refers to the status of a person, as it did from Alcaeus on; but in Herodotus the term is usually contrasted with the "unfreedom" of a slave.[29] One passage contains the adjectival form *eleutherios* in a sense similar to its use in Theognis (535–38) to describe the free and open manner of Cyrus's answer to Astyages (1.116.1), and the adverb *eleutherōs*, used three times, invariably refers to uninhibited free speech (5.93.2; 7.46.1; 8.73.3).[30]

While the "freedom" expressed in these passages does not go beyond views we encountered before the beginning of the fifth century, by far the greatest number of "freedom" passages in Herodotus have a political thrust of which we do not hear before the Persian Wars. Solon had already called "slavery" the condition into which the city as a whole might fall, if it were to fall under a single ruler (*monarchos*), presumably referring to Peisistratus.[31] In Herodotus we regularly find the positive counterpart to this expressed as "freedom": a people is said to be "free," when it is not ruled by—or has overthrown the rule of—a single potentate. It is used of the condition of the Athenians both before (1.62.1) and after the tyranny of Peisistratus and his sons (5.55.1, 62.1–2, 63.1, 64.2, 65.5, 78, 91.1–2, 6.123.2 [*ter*]); it is used of the offer made by Maeandrius to the Samians after the death of Polycrates (3.142.2, 4; 143.3); of the help given by Euryleon to the Selinuntians to overthrow the rule of Peithagoras (5.46.2); and again of the Milesians after they got rid of their tyrant Aristagoras (6.5.1). Its most remarkable use, its application to the Spartans, who had never experienced an autocratic form of government, will be more profitably discussed later.

With two exceptions, this freedom in internal affairs is predicated only of Greeks. One of these is the condition of the Egyptians after the kingship of the priest of Hephaestus (2.147.2); the other, more apparent than real because it refers to the privilege of a noble family within a society, describes the position of the family of Otanes after Darius's accession to the throne, as the only "free" family in Persia in that "it is ruled to the extent that it is willing, so long as it does not transgress the laws of the Persians" (3.83.3).

A second political use of "freedom" in Herodotus describes the freedom of a state from domination by an alien power. "Freedom" from "slavery" is the condition of the Medes after their overthrow of Assyrian rule (1.95.2). It is also the political aim of the peoples who defended themselves against the encroachments of Sesostris in Egypt (2.102.4).

In most instances, however, it refers to the independence and freedom of particular tribes or cities, predominantly Greek, from Persian domination: Scythians (4.110.2), Thracians (7.111.1), but above all the Ionians of Asia Minor (1.6.3, 170.2; 4.133.2, 136.4, 137.1, 139.2; 5.49.2; 6.11.2; 8.132.1; 9.98.3), including Cyprians (5.109.2, 116) and Perinthians (5.2.1). Not surprisingly, Athens figures most prominently in this list, because in defending her freedom against Persian intrusion, she also defended her freedom at Marathon against a renewed tyranny of Hippias (6.109.3 and 6, [122.1]; 7.51.2; 8.140a.4, 143.1).[32]

What strikes us as remarkable is that Persia, too, is described as enjoying a "freedom" given by Cyrus when he freed the country from domination by the Medes (1.126.6, 127.1, 210.2; 3.65.7). His achievement is invoked by Darius in the "Constitutional Debate," held to determine the future constitution of Persia after the overthrow of a usurper, to argue for the restoration of monarchy on the grounds that it was one man (Cyrus) to whom Persia owed its freedom (3.82.5). It is invoked again successfully by Xerxes in staking his claim to succeed Darius: "he was the son of Atossa, daughter of Cyrus, and it was Cyrus who won freedom for the Persians." Xerxes is presented as urging this argument at the same time as the Spartan king Demaratus arrived as an exile at the Persian court (7.2.3).

That Herodotus is not cynical in predicating "freedom" of the Persians is shown by the fact that he uses the next memorable encounter between Demaratus and Xerxes as an occasion to lend substance to an extension of "freedom," which transcends the boundaries of particular cities and tribes and encompasses the whole of the Greek world. Two passages credit the Athenians with the liberation not just of their own city but of Greece from the threat of Persian domination (7.139.5; 8.142.3), and many more see the defeat of Persia as averting slavery from the Greeks as a whole and as establish-

ing their freedom (7.147.1, 157.2, 178.2; 8.77.2; 9.41.3, 45.2–3, 60.1).
Thus "freedom" becomes more than a social or political fact; it is a
value that characterizes the Greeks and distinguishes them from
their adversaries. Free individuals exist in all parts of the world as
masters of slaves; barbarians as well as Greek states can metaphori-
cally become "slaves" to a single ruler and can become "free" once
they terminate his control over them; Greek as well as non-Greek
states can live as slaves under foreign domination or be free and
their own masters.

But once "freedom" is predicated of the Greeks as a whole, it
becomes something different, something that is worth fighting for.
Herodotus defines it in the context of the discussion between Xerxes and Demaratus. Its scene is laid at Abydos on the Hellespont at
the moment when Xerxes has just proudly reviewed the troops he is
unleashing against Greece (7.101–4). Baffled that the Greeks intend
to offer resistance, he asks the Spartan exile:

How can a thousand, or ten thousand, or even fifty thousand men, all
equally free and not ruled by one man, offer resistance to an army as numerous as mine? . . . When ruled by one man, in the way we have it, fear is
likely to make them perform better than their own nature enables them to
do; forced by the whip, they would attack an army larger than their own.
But if left free and without control they would not do either of these things.

Demaratus, scrupulously claiming competence only to speak for the
Spartans, replies:

For myself I should not be able to undertake a fight against two men, and, if
it were up to me, not even with one. But if forced to do so, or if some important cause would spur me on, I would fight with the greatest pleasure
against any one of those men who claim to be a match for three Greeks. In
the same way, the Lacedaemonians are inferior to no man in single combat,
but fighting as a group are the best of all men. For although they are free,
they are not free in all respects: law lords it over them, and they fear this
master even more than your men fear you. They do whatever it bids, and
what it bids is always the same: it does not let them flee from battle no
matter how numerous their enemies are, it bids them stay in formation to
conquer or to die (7.103–4).

Demaratus claims to speak only of the Spartans, and the fact that
he is actually articulating a Spartan ideal is driven home by the story
of Sperthias and Boulis, who volunteered to go to Persia as hostages
for Sparta to expiate the treatment given earlier by the Spartans to

Persian ambassadors. When invited by the officer before whom they presented themselves to submit themselves to the Persian king and be rewarded, they replied: "The advice you give us, Hydarnes, is one-sided. Part of it is based on experience, but of the rest you have no experience: you know very well how to be a slave, but since you have never tasted freedom, you don't know whether it is sweet or not. If you were to experience it, you would advise us to fight for it not only with the spear but even with the battle-axe" (7.135.3).

Several factors suggest that Herodotus means to identify Demaratus's statement on the Spartan idea of freedom with the ideal which prompted the Greeks as a whole to resist conquest by the Persians. Demaratus is a Spartan, a representative of the dominant power in the Hellenic League, which had been formed to unify the Greeks against the Persians in 480 B.C. As such, he also represents a people which was unique in that it had never experienced tyrannical rule, but, possessing itself "freedom" in running its own affairs internally, prided itself for having assisted other states in liberating themselves from tyranny. Thus Sparta was more Greek than the rest of the Greek states, and in fostering "freedom" in other Greek states became instrumental in spreading to Greece as a whole her own highest political value. Spartan "freedom" explains Greek freedom.

Furthermore, as an exile Demaratus stood to gain nothing from exalting the political values of his country; on the contrary, as Herodotus makes clear, he had much to lose, if anything he said would displease Xerxes (7.101.3, 104.1–2). His statement has, therefore, the air of objectivity; his disclaimer to speak only for the Spartans is taken by the reader as a sign of modesty, and makes him all the more acceptable as an authoritative spokesman for the Greeks as a whole.

Finally, Herodotus had associated Demaratus's name with that of Xerxes at the moment when Xerxes succeeded Darius to the throne on the strength of his argument that he was also the grandson of Cyrus, to whom the Persians owed their "freedom" (7.2.3). By juxtaposing in the debate at Abydos Xerxes's view of "freedom" with that of Demaratus, Herodotus obviously wants his readers to take the colloquy as contrasting Greek with Persian political values.[33] Persian political "freedom" means no more than independence and absence of foreign domination; the unity it manages to create in military (and presumably also political) affairs is created by fear, force, and the use of the whip. Only in this way can individual performance exceed natural ability; it grants personal freedom only to the monarch: if the people were free from constraints there would be no unity and no extraordinary performance (7.103.4).

The Spartans, and with them the Greeks, fuse personal and political "freedom" into one. Their personal freedom is not the unrestrained (*aneimenōs*) variety, which seems to be the only one that Xerxes knows; but it is circumscribed by an objective social norm (*nomos*), which the Greeks fear more than a slave fears his master (*despotēs*). But, unlike the human master whom the Persians fear, this master has no whims, but is constant and consistent in his demands. And it is in response to its demands that the Greeks will prefer to stand their ground in battle and either to conquer or to die (7.104.4–5). In other words, the superiority of Greek over Persian political and social values is that while Persian ideas of "freedom" do not go beyond absence of foreign domination, the Greeks realize that even political freedom has parameters, but parameters set by a social norm rather than by an autocrat. In their eyes Persian "freedom" is nothing but "slavery."

Since Herodotus was born about 484 B.C., he is not likely to have written his account before the middle of the fifth century, that is, at least three or four decades after the end of the Persian Wars. There is no reason to doubt that he faithfully presents ideas held by his contemporaries about the Persian Wars. But since his writings contain political notions of "freedom" that we had not encountered before the beginning of the fifth century, we must now raise the question whether there is any independent evidence in documents from the first half of the fifth century to indicate that "freedom" already had taken on political dimensions about the time of the Persian Wars.

Here we encounter a difficulty in dating. Our most reliable evidence consists of a series of epigrams, preserved partly in stone but largely in literary texts, which celebrate exploits of the Persian Wars. Such epigrams are notoriously hard to date, especially since the ancients had the habit of republishing them, usually in an embellished inscriptional or literary form, when a suitable occasion arose.[34] In this way many of the epigrams attributed to Simonides— the most famous writer of epigrams at the time of the Persian Wars—

have come down to us in a form that is more likely to be fourth-century imitation than contemporary with the Persian Wars, so that we are left guessing whether a given occurrence of *eleutheria* or *douleia* is original or part of later rewriting.

These considerations make it possible but uncertain that two lines from a drinking song attributed to Anacreon, addressed by a certain Alcimon to the memory of his friend Aristocleides, who "had lost his young life fighting to avert slavery from his country,"[35] are the earliest surviving example of the idea that a country is "enslaved" when it is occupied by an alien power; it does not yet express the idea that a country not so occupied is "free." Anacreon, believed to have been born in Teos c. 570 B.C. and to have lived to a ripe old age, had too many imitators in antiquity to make us confident that this fragment belongs in the sixth century;[36] if it does, it still remains uncertain what the country is for which Aristocleides gave his life.[37]

A great number of epigrams and other poems have been preserved to commemorate Greek exploits in the Persian Wars; to celebrate victories in the battles of Marathon (490), Salamis (480), and Plataea (479); as well as to lament setbacks at Artemisium and Thermopylae (480). In trying to discover whether any of these see the Greek victories as the triumph of "freedom" and/or the prevention of "slavery," we are again hampered by the difficulty of dating. Many relevant documents became so popular that they were republished, decades and centuries later, usually in some contaminated form, and there are no infallible criteria to determine which were composed soon after the events they honor and which are later.[38]

There is fairly general agreement, however, that an epigram celebrating a sea battle as having prevented "all of Greece from seeing the day of slavery"—note the Homeric language—belongs to the period immediately following the battle of Salamis.[39] If this permits the inference that the possibility of all Greece being "enslaved" to a foreign power existed as early as Herodotus suggests it did, the positive side of this notion, namely that the Greeks, either as a whole or as individual cities, were fighting for their "freedom," is attested by two contemporary poems of Pindar. A fragment of a dithyramb, preserved by Plutarch,[40] praises "the sons of the Athenians" for having "laid the radiant foundations of freedom" at Artemisium; and in a poem celebrating Cleandrus of Aegina for a victory won at the Isthmian Games in 478 B.C., the "freedom" praised for its ability to cure the ills besetting mortals refers most probably to the outcome of the Persian Wars.[41]

Although there is no indication whether freedom is here predicated of Aegina or Greece as a whole, the passage confirms a political use of the concept shortly after the Persian Wars.[42] This meaning is further confirmed by two documents, which, though they have come down to us in fourth-century versions, are believed to contain a core of fifth-century language. The first of these is the so-called Themistocles Decree, found in Troezen in 1960.[43] Its lettering dates it to the end of the fourth century, but it purports to be a copy of the mobilization decree, moved by Themistocles a century and a half earlier, for the Athenian navy before the battles of Salamis and Artemisium.[44] If, though contaminated by fourth-century language, it retains some of the terminology of the original, it may well be that the injunction that "all other Athenians and foreigners of military age shall embark on the two hundred ships provided for that purpose and fight against the barbarian for their own freedom and that of the rest of the Greeks" (lines 12–16) derives from a version written c. 480 B.C. If so, we have additional evidence that the freedom of Athens as well as of Greece was already articulated as a war aim at the time of the Persian Wars.[45]

In addition, there is good evidence that cults of Zeus Eleutherios (Zeus guarantor of freedom) were established in several Greek states to celebrate the victory over the Persians. We noted earlier that a cult of this name is also attributed by Herodotus to Maeandrius of Samos, c. 522 B.C. to celebrate the establishment of internal freedom in Samos, brought about by the abolition of tyranny. This motive for establishing a cult and games in honor of Zeus Eleutherios can still be traced into the fifth century in Syracuse.[46] But a far greater number of cults of Zeus Eleutherios were established in the wake of the Persian Wars to celebrate the liberation of a city or of Greece as a whole from domination by an external power, Persia. The most famous case is the establishment of a panhellenic cult of Zeus Eleutherios at Plataea, the site of the last battle fought against the Persians on the Greek mainland;[47] but such cults are also attested for Troezen, Himera, and Athens—[48] at Troezen, interestingly enough, in honor of Helios Eleutherios rather than Zeus Eleutherios.[49]

The most striking and impressive proof that the Persian Wars were celebrated well before Herodotus as having brought "freedom" to all Greece comes from an eyewitness. Although Aeschylus's *Persae* was not performed until eight years after Salamis, its author himself had fought at Marathon and possibly at Salamis. Therefore, when he includes in the messenger's report on the battle of Salamis the Greek war-cry: "Forward, sons of Greeks! Free your country! Free your children, wives, the places of your ancestral gods, and the tombs of your ancestors! Now everything is at stake" (402–5), it would be churlish to doubt that these words reflect the actual language in which the events of the period from 490 to 479 B.C. were interpreted by their contemporaries.[50] We may thus conclude that "freedom" in its internal sense of "absence from autocratic rule" as well as in its external sense of "absence of foreign domination," in which it can apply both to individual states and to Greece as a whole, existed well before Herodotus and may have originated as a consequence of the Persian attacks on Greece.

There are two further political freedoms in Aeschylus. The prayer of Eteocles in the *Seven against Thebes* (468/7 B.C.) to Zeus, Earth, and the guardian gods of Thebes to keep the city "free and unfettered by the yoke of slavery" (74–75) in the face of his brother's aggression adds nothing new to what we have already learned about the concept. But a new twist is added to political freedom in the statement in *Prometheus Bound* (456 B.C.) that "no one is free except Zeus" (50): the "slavery" of a people under a tyrant is expressed in religious terms by the notion that freedom is confined to one person in a tyranny.

< IV >

Freedom and the Athenian Democracy

The thought that a tyranny deprives all citizens of freedom and leaves its enjoyment to one person alone is most likely to have arisen in a democratic form of government. This is possibly confirmed by the date of the *Prometheus*: it is said to have been performed first in 456 B.C., six years after the reforms of Ephialtes had put the coping stone on the development of democracy at Athens. But even without invoking the development of democracy as an explanation, it is remarkable that the problem of the degree to which an individual can be free is first posed in our record by Aeschylus. He is the earliest extant author to apply the notion of freedom to absence of human suffering: in the *Supplices*, death is praised for setting us free from ills (802), but it is also recognized that a destructive divinity "sets a transgressor free not even in Hades" (416).[51] His interest is focused more on the positive freedom of an individual than on absence of slavery. The Suppliant Women hope that their status as free persons will be recognized at Argos, and Danaus reports later that it has been confirmed (*Supplices* 221, 609); in the *Agamemnon* the Trojans' lament for their dead comes from "a throat no longer free" (328); Agamemnon's murder has stripped his marriage couch "of freedom" (*Agamemnon* 1494, 1518); fate knows no distinction between a "free person" and one who "has a master's hand over him" (*Choephori* 103–4); the end of the curse over the house of Atreus is envisaged as the "light of freedom" (ibid. 809, 863)[52]; and Orestes accuses his mother as having sold him, though he was the "son of a free man" (ibid. 915). But more significant for the development of political personal "freedom" in a democracy is the fact that Aeschylus is the earliest surviving author to conceptualize "freedom of speech" in the term *eleutherostomeō*, to which we shall now turn.

Herodotus credited the establishment of the "equal right of addressing the public" (*isēgoriē*) in Athens after the overthrow of tyranny and the subsequent reforms of Cleisthenes with a self-confidence born of freedom that enabled them to repel the onslaught of three external enemies on the same day in about 506 B.C. (5.78). If this is one way of celebrating what came later to be called "democracy," another was taken by Aeschylus in the *Persae*: "no longer is the tongue under guard among mortals: the people is liberated to speak freely (*eleuthera bazein*), because the yoke of strength is broken" (591–94). Eight years later, King Pelasgus proudly proclaims the decision of the Argive people to the Suppliants: "these matters are not inscribed on tablets nor sealed in the folds of books. What you are hearing comes clearly from a tongue endowed with free speech" (*ex eleutherostomou glōssēs*) (946–49). In the *Prometheus* (180), the chorus justifies Prometheus's punishment at the hand of "free" Zeus (50) by alleging that he "spoke too freely" (*agan eleutherostomeis*). The theme of the trilogy makes it clear that the audience was meant to see this description of the situation as an inversion: the free speech of Prometheus highlights the tyrannical conduct of Zeus.

The ideas of freedom we have so far discussed in this section unfolded along the lines already indicated throughout the second half of the fifth century. Few new dimensions were added in the domestic sphere, except that the development of democracy made for an increased interest in the individual in a number of ways. It is unlikely to have played a significant part in the careful distinctions drawn between slaves and free persons in the law code of Gortyn, usually dated just before the middle of the fifth century but including legislation that may go back as far as the seventh and sixth.[53] After all, many transactions and regulations require precision in distinguishing the legal and social relationships among the parties involved: in cases of seizure of a person, it does make a difference legally whether the person seized is free or a slave (Col. 1, esp. 15–18); similarly in cases of seduction, rape, and adultery (Col. 2); and in cases of inheritance it matters whether the father or mother were slave or free (Col. 6.56–7.10).[54]

We have no evidence to determine whether similar distinctions were made in written Athenian law. But we do have comments on the distinction between free and slave from a critic of the Athenian democracy writing c. 430 B.C. Usually referred to as the "Old Oligarch," he is the author of a *Constitution of the Athenians*, wrongly attributed to Xenophon. His main complaint is that freedom is running riot in Athens. The common people are reprimanded for not caring about the consequences of the freedom they seek (1.8–9); and slaves are getting so cocky that they dress like free men, and take advantage of the "equal right of addressing the public" (*isēgoriē*) against their free masters (1.10, 12). In tragedy, free speech, which we already noted as a positive quality in Aeschylus, becomes an increasingly important mark of a free man's self-assertion.[55] Not infrequently, "freedom" has a moral edge to it: it is independent thinking (Sophocles, *Trachiniae* 52–53, *Philoctetes* 1006) and telling the truth (Sophocles, *Trachiniae* 453–54); and it is honorable action: Electra rejects Chrysothemis's definition of living "free" as listening to authority (Sophocles, *Electra* 339) and substitutes for it avenging the death of her father and brother (970).

There is an increased awareness, partly no doubt engendered by the Peloponnesian War, of the difference in treatment of a slave and a free person, especially of a free person whom external circumstances, such as capture by the enemy, have reduced to slavery.[56] Frequently, the point is to illustrate the instability and brittleness of the human condition,[57] or to show that a status as free or slave is something accidental and not essential to being human.[58] In this respect, one might look on the evidence of fifth-century tragedy as prefiguring Aristotle's distinction between "natural" and "legal" slavery in the fourth century.[59] A rather whimsical use of "freedom" is Hippolytus's desire to live in a world "free" of women (Euripides, *Hippolytus* 624).

Some attention was also given to the freedom of social groups. Here Euripides's *Heracleidae* stands alone as predicating freedom of the land of Attica, as Solon had done.[60] Elsewhere in tragedy, we find, as expected, several allusions to the internal or external freedom of the city. Internal freedom is involved when Athens is praised as "a free city" in the *Heracleidae* (957) and especially throughout the *Supplices* (353, 405, 476), in which freedom is praised as the hallmark of democracy. Freedom from external control is an issue in Heracles's liberation of Thebes from the Minyans (*Heracles* 221), and in the liberation of Thebes to be brought about by Menoeceus's sacrifice (*Phoenissae* 1012). Finally, the contrast between "free" Greeks and "slave" barbarians is a theme in *Iphigeneia at Aulis* (1273, 1401).[61] This brings us to the last major Greek contribution to the concept of a "freedom," which is also political in nature.

≺ V ≻

Freedom and Empire

Thucydides is our most important source for the great paradox in Greek history, namely that the state most devoted to individual freedom was also the state which first enslaved other Greeks. The paradox is eloquently stated at the very first occurrence of *eleutheria* in his work: Thucydides has the Corinthians urge the Spartans to take action against Athens by blaming them for having permitted Athenian power to grow after the Persian Wars: "you have deprived of their freedom not only those whom they have enslaved, but by this time even your own allies; for a state that enslaves others is less correctly regarded as the perpetrator than a state which, though capable of stopping it, sits idly by, even if it enjoys the reputation of excellence for having freed Greece" (Thucydides 1.69.1). The remarkable feature here is that the freedom from (or perhaps better: prevention of) Persian rule over Greece has now changed into the advocacy of the freedom of Greek states from the dominion, actual or threatening, of another Greek state, Athens. With the creation of the Delian League in the wake of the Persian Wars and its subsequent development into an Athenian Empire, Athens sees herself and is seen by others as exercising tyranny over other Greeks,[62] despite the fact that she had herself been liberated less than a century ago from the tyranny of the Peisistratids.[63] By far the most common use of *eleutheria* and its cognates in Thucydides describes that which the so-called "allied" states of Athens have been deprived of, frequently accompanied by expressions of "slavery" as the status to which they have been reduced. Since "freedom" and "slavery" are applied to external political conditions only in a metaphorical sense, it does not surprise us to find them mainly, but not exclusively, in speeches.[64]

There is some scattered evidence from sources outside and earlier than Thucydides that the dominion of Athens over her allies was regarded as "slavery" from which those affected by it wanted to be "free." For example, Pindar's prayer, written in 446 B.C., that Aegina "should conduct this city in its voyage of freedom with the help of Zeus, mighty Aeacus, brave Telamon, and Achilles," may well reflect hopes for freedom from Athenian control kindled in Aegina by the news of Athenian reverses in Boeotia. Similar motives may perhaps also underlie an appeal of the people of Cos to the Thessalians—which may not be historical and for which we have no date—to help them in their struggle for freedom from Athenian slavery.[65]

In line with this, the liberation of "the Greeks," which had been written on the banner of the united Greek forces in the Persian Wars, now became freedom from Athenian control; it is found in speeches as well as in narrative as the professed war aim of the Spartans throughout the Peloponnesian War,[66] an aim strengthened by the Spartan claim of freedom in internal matters as one of their own characteristics.[67]

Further, the relation of Athens to her subject-allies is generalized into an opposition between "freedom" and "empire" *tout court*.[68]

More significantly, the new coinage *autonomia* enters the Greek language to articulate independence in the sense of freedom in internal affairs, originally perhaps as a demand on the part of Athenian subject-allies to respect a state's internal integrity in cases where the imposition of tribute and other controls was regarded as deprivation of *eleutheria*.[69] A shift in the political meaning of *eleutheria* begins to appear: it focuses on absence of foreign domination and tends to cede the field of internal freedom to *autonomia*. But this phenomenon is confined to cases in which a weaker state feels its internal institutions threatened by a stronger state or confederation of states; strong states do not tend to pride themselves on their *autonomia*.[70]

Thucydides is the earliest author in whom we find *autonomia* and *eleutheria* conjoined to describe the complete freedom of a city, that is, independence in both its external and internal affairs.[71] The coupling of these two terms became the rule in alliances contracted by Athens with other Greek states in the fourth century, especially in the charter of the Second Athenian League in 377 B.C.[72] Evidently, Athens had learned a lesson from her experience with her subject-allies in her fifth-century empire: freedom from external domination means little unless it is accompanied by non-interference in internal affairs of a weaker state. Needless to say, the principle of *autonomia* is indifferent to the form of government prevailing in the weaker state; it does not care whether a given state is democratically or oligarchically governed.

≺ VI ≻

Freedom in the Fourth Century

Debates about "freedom" reached a crescendo in the period from the last years of the Peloponnesian War to the death of Alexander the Great, that is, roughly from 415 to 323 B.C. This is the period that encompasses not only the works of the great orators (Antiphon, Lysias, Isocrates, Demosthenes, Aeschines, Isaeus) but also the works of Plato and Aristotle. The flood of relevant passages far exceeds that of earlier periods. However, we find few, if any, new substantive contributions to what had been said about "freedom" earlier; it is rather that earlier views are spelled out in greater detail. Accordingly, we shall confine ourselves to broad outlines of what aspects of "freedom" received consideration, and in what directions older concepts of "freedom" were expanded.

Let us begin with what we hear about the freedom of the individual. Here the oldest and most basic use of *eleutheros* identifies the status of a free man and differentiates it from that of a slave. Curiously enough, this usage is confined in Thucydides exclusively to narrative;[73] but in view of the appearance of forensic oratory from the late fifth century on its very frequent appearance in speeches and legal texts does not surprise.[74] Of special interest are a number of passages in which distinctions between free and slave are specified: free men cannot be imprisoned without due process, but slaves can;[75] there are different forms for the interrogation of free and slave;[76] their testimony has to be evaluated differently,[77] but that does not mean that a free man is more truthful than a slave: on the contrary the fact that a slave's testimony is given under torture may make it more credible.[78] Moreover, we learn from Aeschines that legislation existed to protect free young men from seduction and sexual violence.[79]

Much more frequent than in earlier literature is the notion of pride a given person takes in being a free man or woman. The conscious or unconscious basis for this sentiment is best expressed by Aristotle: "a free person exists for himself and not for another" (*Metaphysics* A, 982b25–6). Usually the assertion of freedom takes the shape of claiming some privileged treatment or objecting to not receiving it.[80] But it is also treated comically in the contention that a free whore is superior to a slave whore.[81] Moreover, moral overtones similar to those encountered in association with free persons in the archaic period appear again in the fourth century. A free man is moderate in his conduct; he has an inner nobility which prevents him from excessive indulgence in sex, food, and games, and he shows his mettle in war.[82] His opposite is often called *aneleutheros*, who solicits sexual favors from another.[83] Further, the adjective *eleutherios* as well as the adverb *eleutherōs* is frequently used in the same sense of "generous," "liberal," "uninhibited" in which we have met it before.[84] Aristotle regarded this quality, "generosity," "liberality" (*eleutheriotēs*), as sufficiently distinct from "freedom" *tout court* (*eleutheria*) to devote an entire chapter of his *Nicomachean Ethics* to it (4.1, 1119b22–1122a17).

Under the influence of sophists, there developed also what we should call "libertinistic" uses of "freedom": Antiphon praised "nature" as being "free" and contrasted it with the "constraints of the law," and Callicles in Plato's *Gorgias* equates "freedom" with a life of luxury, self-indulgence, and the license to do as you please.[85] These sentiments not only evoked reprimands from Socrates, Plato, and Aristotle,[86] but also made them design systems of education, which have been a lasting heritage from antiquity to our own time.

The idea that freedom is a property of the human soul is of long standing.[87] What Plato and Aristotle added to that was the conviction that the soul of a free person is amenable to reason, and that, therefore, a system can be devised to inculcate in it the kind of conduct that should characterize a free person.[88] Underlying this assumption is the belief articulated by Aristotle that there is a quasi-physiological ("natural") dimension to being "slave" or "free": he defines as a "slave by nature" a person who "has the capacity of belonging to another," and further asserts that "nature wants to make the bodies of free men <as well as their souls> different from those of slaves."[89] That it does not always succeed is shown in his recognition of the existence of "unnatural" slavery, to which a person who has the soul (and/or body) of a free man may be reduced by fortune, and in his statement that "convention" rather than "nature" determines the actual status of a person as a slave or as a free man.[90]

It is here that education becomes important: a free person must be brought up in the behavior of the free, and a slave in that of a slave. Different games are appropriate to each; dances which combine discipline with free and majestic movement form part of the education of the free; discipline is also inculcated by making the free rise early in the morning. This we learn from Plato's celebrated scheme in *Laws* 7 (794a, 795e, 796d, 808a), and the result is perhaps most graphically contained in Plato's distinction between the slave doctor, who blindly prescribes the kind of treatment he has been taught to apply and compels his patient to follow it, and the free doctor, who first tries to find the nature of the patient's ailment, discusses it with the patient and his friends, and prescribes nothing without the patient's consent (*Laws* 4.720a–e; 9.857c–e).

Aristotle left an even deeper imprint on the later history of "liberal" education with his discussion in the eighth book of the *Politics*.[91] It is predicated on his conviction that ideally only a person whose financial assets make him free to devote himself to public affairs should be admitted as a citizen; accordingly, industrial workers (*banausoi*), who have to work for a living, ideally ought to be excluded.[92] His educational program is, therefore, designed for those who enjoy this basic freedom.[93] How "useful" should their education be? "It is quite clear," Aristotle says

that whatever practical matters are indispensable must be taught, but not all of them. Since there is a difference between jobs suitable for free men and jobs suitable for unfree men, it is obvious that he should participate in such practical matters as will not make the participant an industrial worker. One should regard as proper to an industrial worker those jobs, skills, and studies which render the body, soul, or thinking of a free person unfit for the use and active exercise of moral excellence. It makes a lot of difference for what purpose a person acts or studies: it is not unfree to do so for one's own sake, for the sake of one's friends, or for the sake of being a moral person (*aretē*); but a person who does the identical things because of someone else is often thought to act like a laborer or a slave.[94]

"To look everywhere for what is useful is least fitting for magnanimous and freehanded men."[95]

With this we turn to the political uses of *eleutheria* in the fourth century. The association of freedom with democracy, which began in the fifth century, largely through the freedom of speech which democracy favors, becomes so common in all authors of the fourth century that it is fair to say that democracy is the only form of government of which freedom is predicated. Usually it is a positive association: paradoxically King Theseus proudly contrasts the freedom of Athens, the city where all citizens have an equal vote, and where the people rules in annual turns, with the tyranny which governs Thebes.[96] Lysias claims it for the Athenian democracy in his Funeral Speech (2.18, cf. also 18.24); Isocrates associates the two, as does Aristotle, especially in the fourth book of the *Politics*.[97] But there are also voices that condemn democracy for what they regard as an excessive love of freedom. The earliest of these is the Old Oligarch, who thinks that love of freedom goes in the Athenian democracy at the expense of orderly government. We also encounter the condemnation in Isocrates's two great Athenian speeches, the *Areopagiticus* and the *Panathenaicus*. In the former, he praises the good old times of Solon and Cleisthenes, when democracy was not yet indiscipline, freedom not yet lawlessness, political equality not yet license to say anything one pleased, and happiness not yet license to do as you please (4.20). Similar terms are used in the *Panathenaicus* (12.131). But Plato's attack on democratic freedom for its license to let a person say and do whatever he pleases, regardless of the consequences, which will lead to unfreedom under a tyrant, is the most ferocious in the fourth century (*Republic* 8.557b, 562b–564a).

And finally, the fourth century is rich in celebrating freedom from foreign domination. The encroachment of one city-state upon another, which characterizes the entire century, and the threat of Persian interference in Greek affairs, which came to a head after the King's Peace in 386 B.C., make us expect a preoccupation with freedom in the sense of political independence of one's own state.[98] But it is remarkable that the great majority of appeals are made to the "freedom of the Greeks" or to the "freedom of Greece," even where the enemy envisaged is not Persia in the past or in the present,[99] but another Greek state. In Lysias we find Athenian appeals against Spartan domination and against the Thirty who ruled Athens with Sparta's support, in the name of the "freedom of the Greeks,"[100] very probably as a propagandistic counterpoint to Sparta's professed aims in the Peloponnesian War. We find Demosthenes and Lycurgus invoke the "freedom of the Greeks" as well as the "freedom of Greece" against the encroachments of Philip of Macedon;[101] but we find both most significantly invoked as a rallying cry for Philip's campaign against Persia as a crusade to free the Greeks from barbarian rule.[102] The defensive slogan of the Spartan war aims in the fifth century has now become the parole of an aggressive imperialist policy of all Greeks against Persia.

≺ VII ≻

Epilogue

This does not end the story of the Greek foundations of freedom. The story we have outlined lived on through the Romans to European history in the Middle Ages and in the Renaissance; it was revitalized in the American and French Revolutions; it is embodied in our Bill of Rights; and it lives on in many problems that face not only us, but every generation. But as far as any specifically Greek contribution is concerned, it is fair to say that because of freedom's integral relation to the life of the Greek city-states, the developments we have tried to outline here came to an end with the conquests of Alexander the Great. These raised new problems, which received new answers, to which the heritage of nations that came to be dominated by Greek culture made fundamentally new contributions.

It is perhaps legitimate to conclude by asking whether "freedom" has any substance of its own or whether it is a term, in itself empty, which is infused with a polemical meaning by different generations and in different contexts. After all, as Aeschylus already recognized, no human being can enjoy freedom from suffering or death: everything that is freedom is of necessity circumscribed and conditional. Moreover, for the Greeks as for later generations, there are more freedoms "from" than freedoms "to": does this make "freedom" a predominantly negative concept?

An examination of the evidence presented here seems to me to show that for the Greeks the concept of "freedom" was not as hollow as it might appear. From humble beginnings which denoted merely an exemption from an official assessment, an *eleutheros* first came to distinguish an "ordinary" person from one who was not "ordinary" because he was or had become the property of another. Surely this was a substantive distinction, especially when certain characteristics of noble behavior or noble bearing came to be associated with a "free" person. If we can trust our fragmentary record, Solon will have been the first to extend personal freedom to social freedom, and to make the free man one who has been, and now is, emancipated from economic bondage to an upper class. Further, since land was involved in this emancipation, even the land could enjoy freedom. In its context, this "freedom," too, is something substantive: it is not merely liberation from indebtedness but an opportunity, even more fully realized after the liberation from tyranny, to play a full part in the life of society as a whole. It lays the foundation of the concept of a "free" society, despite the fact that the upper classes initially remain more "free" than the lower. Only after the development of naval power in connection with, and especially in the wake of, the Persian Wars did the lower classes gain enough freedom, through their right to hold all public officials

accountable for their conduct in office, to pave the way for the democratic freedom that was justly celebrated in the fifth and fourth
centuries.

While tyrannies and liberation from them made the Greeks create for the first time in human history the concept of internal political freedom, the Ionian Revolt, followed by the success the united
Greeks had in repelling the attack of the numerically vastly superior
Persian forces, created, again for the first time in human history, the
idea of freedom from control by an external power. The absence of
foreign domination makes this a negative kind of "freedom"; but it
has a positive aspect: it raised the self-confidence and self-reliance
of the Greek states to the point that it gave them a common cultural
identity which reflected also on the individual. This identity became important in the rallying cries of the fourth century, both
against one another and against the Persians.

But, beginning at the end of the Persian Wars and culminating in
the Peloponnesian War, this "national freedom," if we may anach-
ronistically call it that, also began the process of emptying "freedom" of substance by using it as a political football. There may have
been good justification for accusing the Athenians of having deprived their allies of both freedom and autonomy, because they had
tightened their network of alliances against Persia into an empire;
but that accusation came to be a propaganda tool, when the Spartans, whose grip on their own allies in the Peloponnesian League
was only a little less tight and who had prided themselves in being
the champions of freedom during the Persian Wars, proclaimed the
"liberation of the Greeks" as their war aim. As a result, "freedom"
became as much an empty slogan as it had been a reality. The facts
that it could be invoked by any city-state against any other in the
name of the Greeks as a whole, and that it could become a device to
create Greek unity against a Persia that, at the time, presented no
threat against the Greek mainland, cheapened the precious coin—
but not forever.

The idea of political freedom, the most singular Greek legacy to
us, neither requires nor excludes divine sanction in either internal
or external affairs; and since, further, it lent itself to describe substantive aspirations as well as vacuous propaganda, it could easily
be accommodated into almost any political situation in the course

of Western history. Monarchs could use it to defend the divine right of kings, tyrants could use it to annex lands in which members of their own ethnic group constituted a minority; but it was also used to rally the American and the French people to liberate themselves from oppression.

Freedom and the Medieval Church

BRIAN TIERNEY

A GREAT LEGAL HISTORIAN, Frederic Maitland, once wrote that, in the Middle Ages, "the church was a state."[1] Of course the medieval church was not—could not be in those days—a model of a modern liberal constitutional state. Some freedoms that later came to seem of central importance were nonexistent, hardly thought of then. The medieval church tolerated servitude and persecuted heretics. It would be wrong to ignore those negative aspects of medieval religious culture and we shall return to them; but this chapter is mainly concerned with a more positive theme. Its principal purpose is to explore the various ways in which the church played a constructive role in the development of Western institutions during the medieval era.

In the years around 1100 the church first shook itself free from the control of lay rulers, then began to reshape its own laws and institutional structure. For centuries the leaders of the church, both practical administrators and learned intellectuals, considered the problems of right order within a Christian society; and, in doing so, they created an array of ideas and procedures that were eventually assimilated into the theory and practice of Western constitutional government. This was the major contribution of the medieval church to the growth of modern freedom.

Medieval ideas on government were shaped partly by the real life circumstances of the age and partly by ideas derived from the ancient world. In the real world of the Middle Ages political life was marked by clashes of spiritual and temporal power and by the strivings of popes and kings to impose some degree of ordered peace on an inherently violent society. In the twelfth century a great new Christian civilization was growing into existence; but political development lagged behind cultural achievement. Unchecked feudal turbulence could produce conditions verging on anarchy; there was a need for strong rulers; but there was also a strong aversion to mere arbitrary government. The most obvious alternative to anarchy is absolutism; the achievement of the medieval era was to create effective governments that were still limited by law and by some acknowledged rights of their peoples.

The ancient sources that medieval writers turned to in reflecting on problems of governance included Roman law and Aristotelian philosophy. Also, around 1140, the canonist Gratian produced a great compendium of church law known as the *Decretum*, which included many early Christian texts; it provided for the first time a universally accepted corpus of canon law for the whole Western church. The assimilation of these early sources into the thought-world of the Middle Ages was a complex process. Medieval thinkers read the old texts in the context of their own newly emerging culture; they applied them to the problems of a society very different from that of the ancient world; and in doing so they were often led, by a sort of creative misunderstanding, to find in their sources meanings that the original authors could hardly have envisaged. Moreover, the sources themselves were ambivalent. In all of them, Justinian's *Digest* or Aristotle's *Politics* or Gratian's *Decretum*, one could find texts that might serve to justify either absolute rule or various forms of limited government.

The same is true of the most important of all the ancient sources known to medieval thinkers, the Christian scriptures. Christ's words to Peter at Matthew 16.19, "I will give you the keys of the kingdom of heaven," could (and did) provide a basis for theories of papal absolutism; but another text from Matthew, "If your brother sins against you . . . go tell it to the church," suggested that authority might inhere in the whole body of believers. And when the first council of the Church met in Jerusalem the apostles declared that the Holy Spirit had spoken through the assembled community.[2] There were always these two concepts of church unity coexisting in medieval thought, a unity maintained by subordination of all the members to a sovereign head, and a unity assured through a free association of the members, preserving an unfailing corporate life under the guidance of the Spirit. Moreover, while some texts defined the nature of the church as a corporate whole, a "mystical body" in medieval language, others stressed the value of each individual person in the eyes of God. There was ambiguity too in the idea of Christian freedom. When Paul wrote of "the freedom wherewith Christ has made us free" he was thinking of freedom from the bondage of the old law; but the words could be understood in a broad sense as implying freedom from all forms of ecclesiastical and secular tyranny.

Western ways of thinking about government entered a new era when medieval jurists, more concerned with practical problems of church governance than with theological nuances, strove to reformulate the old teachings of scripture in the language of constitutional law. In their works, and later in the writings of philosophers influenced by Aristotelian thought, a new language of discourse grew up. It was concerned with the interplay of spiritual and temporal power, with sovereignty and law, with consent, rights, and representation. A new vocabulary of words and ideas was created, at first concerned mainly with problems of right order in the church, but soon applied to secular government also. Then the medieval patterns of discourse, shaped at first by the distinctive needs of medieval society, persisted into the early modern era and in turn helped to shape the thought of a later age.

≺ I ≻

Church and State

Medieval discourse on government was persistently influenced by tensions between spiritual and temporal power. Indeed, the most obvious way in which medieval popes contributed (unintentionally of course) to the growth of modern liberty was by their insistence on the freedom of the church from control by secular rulers. In the Middle Ages there was never just one hierarchy of government exercising absolute authority, but always two—church and state to use the language of a later age—often contending with one another, each limiting the other's power. This duality of government was a rather unusual development in human history. In societies larger than a tribal unit or a city-state the most common form of rulership has been some form of theocratic absolutism. The Pharaohs of Egypt, the Incas of Peru, the emperors of Japan were all revered as divine figures. The order of society was seen as a part of the divine order of the cosmos; the ruler provided a necessary link between heaven and earth. But Christianity was different from the beginning. It grew up in an alien culture, the sophisticated classical civilization of Greece and Rome. To become a Christian or to persist in the religion was a matter of free personal choice, often involving considerable self-sacrifice; for early Christians the emperor was not a divine ruler but a persecutor of the true faith. The tension between Roman state and Christian church was expressed classically in the words of Jesus himself. "Render to Caesar the things that are Caesar's and to God the things that are God's."

After the conversion of Constantine and the establishment of a Christian empire there was indeed a possibility for a time that the church might become merely a sort of department of religion in an imperial theocratic church-state. But, as the imperial power crumbled in the West, the independent role of the church was vigorously reasserted by Pope Gelasius (492–96).

Two there are, august emperor by which this world is chiefly ruled, the sacred authority of the priesthood and the royal power . . . in the order of religion, in matters concerning the reception and right administration of the heavenly sacraments, you ought to submit yourself rather than rule.[3]

There were *two* authorities in the world; whole areas of religious thought and practice were excluded from the control of the temporal ruler. This text of Gelasius was incorporated into Gratian's *Decretum* in the twelfth century and was endlessly quoted and discussed in later disputes.

The problem of empire and papacy in its medieval form arose when Charlemagne sought to establish a new theocratic empire (c. 800), and his claims were reiterated by his successors of the Ottonian and Salian dynasties. By the eleventh century Charlemagne's empire had disintegrated into several separate kingdoms and the kingdoms themselves were divided into innumerable feudal principalities, often at war with one another. In such circumstances, strong monarchy seemed the only alternative to continuing anarchy, and churchmen again began to attribute sacred powers to their kings. In the coronation liturgies of the eleventh century a king was often compared to Joshua and David and Solomon; he was anointed with holy oil like an ecclesiastical prelate; he was hailed as a "vicar of God." And, as vicars of God on earth, the kings assumed the right to govern their churches; they regularly appointed bishops in the lands they ruled, and invested them with the ring and staff that were the symbols of spiritual office. When, from time to time, a German emperor invaded Italy and occupied Rome, he chose and appointed popes, just as he appointed other bishops.

The church seemed to be drifting into another form of theocratic monism. But a dramatic change came in the pontificate of Gregory VII (1073–85). Gregory condemned the whole existing order of society as radically contrary to divine justice. His declared objective was to restore the freedom of the church, a phrase he used like a kind of battle-cry. "It is better," he wrote, "to fight for the freedom of the church than to sink into miserable and devilish servitude."[4] In 1076 he forbade the practice of lay investiture (the appointment of bishops by kings) and so inaugurated a struggle that used to be called the Investiture Contest but that now is often referred to simply as the Papal Revolution. Henry IV, king of Germany and emperor-elect, refused to accept the pope's decree; instead he denounced Gregory as a pseudo-pope and a heretic. Gregory responded by declaring Henry excommunicated and deposed from his kingship. What had begun as a demand for the freedom of the church turned into a struggle for the dominance of Christian society.

To Gregory's adversaries, the pope's claims on behalf of the church meant simply an assertion of his own limitless power. Gregory always denied that he was motivated by personal ambition, but zest for power and zeal for the church were inextricably fused in his complex personality. In 1075, on the eve of his conflict with Henry, Gregory set down in his official register a series of terse propositions about papal authority known as the *Dictatus Papae*. They include the following claims: "That the Roman pontiff alone is to be called universal . . . for him alone it is lawful to enact new laws according to the needs of the time . . . his feet are to be kissed by all princes . . . he may depose emperors . . . he himself may be judged by no one."[5] In response to such claims Henry retreated somewhat from the ideology of royal theocracy; he asserted that Christ himself had separated the kingship from priesthood and that it was Gregory who sought to usurp both roles for himself. The fight that ensued between pope and king was both a war of propaganda and a real civil war in Germany and Italy. At one point Henry had to humiliate himself before the pope at Canossa and humbly beg his forgiveness; but later his armies occupied Rome and drove Gregory into exile. In the

end neither side could prevail and, after both of the original protagonists had died, a compromise peace was patched up in the Con-
cordat of Worms (1122).

The struggle between popes and kings was reenacted over and
over again in the following centuries. After denouncing the theocratic pretensions of kings, the popes were often tempted to assert a
similar role for themselves; sometimes they put forward extreme
claims to a kind of overlordship of Christian society in both spiritual
and temporal affairs. But the temporal claims of the papacy were
never fully accepted by medieval kings or their peoples. Moreover
the intellectuals in the universities were divided; throughout the
medieval era some canonists and theologians accepted the more extreme papal claims; others persistently argued against them.

The theocratic claims of the papacy reached a high-water mark
in Boniface VIII's Bull, *Unam Sanctam* (1302), with its uncompro-
mising declaration. "It is altogether necessary for every human creature to be subject to the Roman pontiff";[6] but Boniface was defeated
and humiliated in the struggle with the king of France that had
been the occasion of his pronouncement. Because neither side could
make good its more extreme claims, a dualism of church and state
persisted in medieval society and eventually it was rationalized and
justified in many works of political theory. The French theologian
John of Paris, for instance, writing in 1302 (the year of *Unam Sanctam*), wrote a treatise *On Royal and Papal Power* which presented
a carefully balanced dualism, assigning to each power its proper function. The priest was greater than the prince in spiritual affairs, John
wrote, and, conversely, the prince was greater in temporal affairs.[7]

In the circumstances that actually existed, it was impossible for
any ruler to consolidate a position of absolute power; and since, in
the conflicts between church and state, each side always sought to
limit the power of the other, the situation encouraged theories of
resistance to tyranny and of constitutional limitations on government. Already in the struggle between Gregory VII and Henry IV a
papal supporter, Manegold of Lautenbach, presented a primitive
theory of social contract. A ruler was bound to his people by a compact, Manegold wrote, and if the ruler broke the compact by becoming a tyrant and persecutor, the people were loosed from their allegiance to him.[8] Two centuries later John of Paris offered a more
detailed explanation of the right of resistance in church and state,

carefully demarcating the roles of pope, king, and people. If a king offended in some spiritual matter (by practicing simony say, or falling into heresy) the pope could excommunicate him; but the actual deposition of the king, if this was called for, had to be carried out by the nobles and people. Similarly, it was the duty of the cardinals or the fathers of a church council to restrain a delinquent pope, but a king could supply physical force to help them if necessary. Each power could use its own resources to check the abuses of the other.[9]

The most obvious significance of the medieval church-state struggle for the history of freedom is that it prevented rulers in either sphere from becoming absolute theocratic sovereigns. But there were other repercussions too. In complex ways that historians are still trying to understand the demand for freedom of the church encouraged a growth of free institutions in secular society.

The reforming popes insisted that bishops ought to be elected by the clergy and people of their cities, not appointed by some remote king or emperor. It seems more than a coincidence that, just at this same time, cities in many parts of Europe began to form communes that demanded the right to elect their own ruling magistrates. The Investiture Contest, it has been said, led to a kind of "disengagement" between the sacred and secular spheres of life. In the long run this made possible the emergence of a concept of the secular state, existing to serve human needs and regulated by human reason. But it also encouraged new ways of expressing the Christian ideals of love and brotherhood through various forms of corporate life in the secular sphere, outside the traditional ecclesiastical institutions. Among the laity innumerable fraternal associations grew up—craft guilds, charitable confraternities, city communes—formed not by compulsion from above but by free association of the members. They were like islands of self-governance in the surrounding hierarchical society. As Antony Black wrote, "Liberty of the church and communal liberty were related parts of the same movement for corporate self-determination."[10]

Moreover, as the church came to be recognized as a distinct estate in a medieval kingdom, with its own rights and privileges, it provided an example for other "estates of the realm"—first nobles, then commons—who eventually claimed analogous rights and demanded their own charters of liberties. The most famous such document, Magna Carta, declared in its first clause, "The English church shall be free and shall have all its rights entire," before moving on to consider the rights of feudal barons and free men in general.

The persistent dualism in medieval society that we have described was not a modern "wall of separation." In the Middle Ages the powers of church and state constantly overlapped and interacted and impinged on one another; but the church remained committed to a radical limitation of state power in the sphere of religion, and to that extent enlarged the sphere of human freedom. When this attitude was challenged by new forms of divine-right monarchy in the early modern world, the royal claims stimulated new forms of protest and new ways of asserting religious liberty—one of them eventually crystallized in the American First Amendment.

≺ II ≻

Ruler and Community: Sovereignty and Law

Along with the issues of church and state that we have considered so far, other problems arose concerning the balance of freedom and power in the constitutional structure of the church itself. If the claims of the *Dictatus Papae* had been realized in full and without qualification, Gregory VII's "freedom of the church" might have come to mean simply the subjection of all Christians to the untrammelled will of an all-powerful pope. But arbitrary rule is a negation of freedom. For a community to be free it needs to live under a rule of law—otherwise the strong could destroy the freedom of the weak—and under a law that reflects a consensus of the community and that is in some sense binding on the rulers themselves. These considerations gave rise to constitutional problems in the medieval church. If the ruler was a sovereign legislator how could he be under the law that he made himself? And if he was the supreme magistrate, who could be competent to judge him?

On an academic level the problems of sovereignty and legal restraint arose for twelfth-century jurists from an apparent conflict in the texts of Roman law. One passage of Justinian's *Corpus Iuris Civilis* asserted that "The Prince is freed from the laws," but another declared that "It is worthy of reigning majesty for the Prince to profess himself bound by the law."[11] In explaining these texts, medieval jurists commonly distinguished between an obligation to obey the law and the coercive sanctions that enforced obedience. The emperor was free from the law in the sense that he was not subject to the law's coercive sanctions. Since he was the supreme judge no one could judge him. But he was bound by the law in the sense that he had a duty to obey it of his own free will. Sometimes an analogy was drawn with Christ who, although he was above the law as a divine being, nevertheless voluntarily subjected himself to the law. This line of argument could resolve the verbal conflict of texts but it did not explain what remedy, if any, was available against a sovereign who in fact chose to rule lawlessly.

The English writer John of Salisbury carried the argument a step further in his *Policraticus*, a major work of political theory written in the 1150s. John sought to distinguish between fundamental principles of law that were always binding even on a king, and more flexible regulations that could be changed at the discretion of the ruler. He also discussed a simple remedy for tyranny—the assassination of the tyrant. John did not exactly recommend tyrannicide but he did remind evil rulers that God had a way of raising up avengers to punish them, and that tyrants were likely to come to an unpleasant end.[12]

The problem of defining a right relationship between ruler, law, and community arose in its most acute form for the medieval canonists and they were the ones who discussed it in the greatest detail. Their ruler, the pope, was the most exalted of monarchs; but their community, the Christian church, was a sacrosanct society, not just a worldly association, but a people of God, a mystical body of Christ. This gave rise to a persistent tension in canonistic thought. Some passages of the *Decretum* and the later volume of *Decretals* attributed an apparently unlimited power to the Roman pontiff, and the canonists seem sometimes to have pursued the implications of such texts with uninhibited enthusiasm. One of them wrote of the pope, "No one can say to him; why do you do this? . . . he can dispense above the law and against the law . . . changing the law and correcting it . . . and he holds a plenitude of power."[13] The canonists were indeed convinced that a strong, sovereign papacy was needed to uphold the freedom of the church—freedom from secular control and corrupt customs, freedom to institute reforms by enacting new legislation. But these same authors never forgot that the individual pontiffs who wielded such vast powers were mere human mortals, prone to sin and error like other men. A pope might conceivably become a criminal or heretic. He might use his power to injure the church. The canonists could not ignore this possibility if only because some passages of the *Decretum* referred to various early popes who allegedly had erred in faith. Moreover, while several of Gratian's texts asserted that the pope was immune from all human judgment, one of them added the reservation, "unless he is found straying from the faith."[14]

The canonists never doubted that the true faith would always live on in the church even under an erring pontiff. Here their doctrine of community came into play. The church, they said, could not err "in its whole body." Huguccio, the greatest canonist of his age, who wrote toward the end of the twelfth century, explained: "Although the Roman pope has sometimes erred the Roman church has not, which is understood to be not the pope alone but all the faithful, for the church is the congregation of the faithful." And again, "Wherever there are good faithful people, there is the Roman church."[15] This common doctrine of the canonists was incorporated into the ordinary gloss on the *Decretum*, a commentary read along with the text throughout the medieval era: "I ask of what church you understand what is said here, that it cannot err . . . certainly the pope can err. I answer the congregation of the faithful itself is to be called the church . . . and such a church cannot not be."[16] The canonists were opposing an unfailing Christian community to a possibly delinquent pope. Moreover they were trying to define the community in juristic language. One of them, drawing the usual distinction between the unerring church and an individual pope, even cited Roman corporation law to prove his point. "That is not said to be done by the church which is not done by the corporate whole (*ab ipsa universitate*), as we read in the Digest, *De regulis iuris, Aliud* (Dig. 50.17.160.1)." In such passages the old Pauline theology of the church as the body of Christ was being reshaped into an idea of the church as a juridical corporate structure in which the pope would rule as a presiding officer of the corporate community.[17]

But could he be bound by the laws of the community? Everyone agreed that the pope could not overturn the truths of Christian faith or the moral precepts of natural law. The more difficult question was whether he could be obliged by any humanly enacted laws. Could the Christian community articulate norms of faith and order for itself that were necessary for its preservation and well-being and that were binding even on the pope?

In addressing this question the canonists commonly appealed to the authority of general councils. And again they found support in certain passages of the *Decretum*. One of Gratian's texts, taken from Pope Gregory the Great, declared that the statutes of the first four councils were to be revered like the four gospels because they were established "by universal consent." Commentators on the text soon began to ask whether the pope too was bound by such statutes. Was there a kind of fundamental law of the church that obliged even its head? One problem was that the early councils not only had decided great issues of faith but also had pronounced on local and transient issues; it seemed clear therefore that not every detail of their legislation could be permanently binding on the pope and the church. Around 1160 two solutions were proposed. One commentator on the *Decretum* argued that the conciliar canons which not even a pope could violate were those concerning articles of faith; another held that the inviolable canons were those "promulgated with full authority to preserve the state of the universal church." From this time on it became common to combine the two formulas; it was widely held that the pope was bound by canons of general councils "in matters concerning the faith and the general state of the church."[18] By "state of the church" the canonists meant the fundamental constitutional structure of the church and the well-being of the whole Christian community. (A little later a similar phrase, "state of the realm," appears in secular constitutional documents with the same implications.) The canonists perhaps felt able to assert simultaneously the sovereignty of the pope and the overriding authority of a council's legislation because they held that a general council was normally convoked and presided over by the pope himself. They were arguing in effect that the pope was the sovereign head of the church but that sometimes he was more sovereign than others and that he was most sovereign of all when he was presiding over a representative general council. As one canonist put it, "The pope with a council is greater than the pope without one." It was an early formulation of a doctrine essentially similar to the later secular theory of the sovereignty of king-in-parliament.

There remained one difficult problem for the canonists. What could be done if a pope did indeed err in faith or abuse his power so as to endanger "the state of the church?" There were many answers to the question. Huguccio maintained that only the whole church was indefectible in faith but he would not concede that there was any juridical authority in the church competent to pass judgment on the pope. He held that, if a Roman pontiff publicly proclaimed his adherence to a known heresy or if he persisted in notorious crime, he could be removed from office without any need for a trial of the pope as such, because such a man would have already ceased to be pope. A person could not be a heretic and a pope at the same time. Moreover in Huguccio's view, notorious crime in a pope could be treated as equivalent to heresy because the pope's bad example might mislead the faithful and threaten the general state of the church.[19]

Huguccio's argument did not satisfy everyone. Some held that a pope could not be removed from office without a formal sentence of excommunication; but they avoided the need for an actual trial by suggesting that an erring pope might automatically fall under a sentence enacted by an earlier general council against anyone who violated its doctrinal decrees. This could follow from the widely held view that a council was greater than an individual pope. Other canonists insisted that some kind of due process was necessary to determine whether an accused pope was indeed guilty or innocent. One of them wrote, "A man is not a criminal when he is accused but when he is convicted." This writer suggested that a council should meet, not as a judicial body but as a deliberative assembly, to consider the pope's alleged error. If the council determined that the doctrine taught by the pope was indeed heretical, then it could be assumed that he had forfeited his office. Finally, a few opted for the simplest and most radical view that, in case of dispute between a pope and the members of a council on a matter of faith, the members held a greater judicial authority than the pope and were competent to judge him.[20]

The discussions of the canonists on these points, pursued in intricate detail in the years around 1200, anticipated nearly all the convolutions of later resistance theories that dealt with the relationship between kings and representative assemblies and with the various ways in which an oppressive monarch could be removed from office. Arguments about political freedom commonly involve a dialectic between sovereign power and community rights; the issue was never more subtly presented than by the medieval canonists.

≺ III ≻

Legitimacy and Consent

In a free society it is not enough that the community can in the last resort rid itself of an intolerable ruler. The question remains: how can we live under coercive government at all and still consider ourselves free? One part of the answer is that a government ruling a free people must govern for the good of the people, not for the selfish advantage of the rulers. And, above all, freedom is seen to be preserved when a people is ruled by its own consent.

Aristotle had emphasized the first criterion of legitimacy—rule for the common good—and his view was often echoed by medieval authors. Thomas Aquinas stated the doctrine specifically in terms of human freedom. "Authority which aims at the subjects' advantage does not remove their liberty," he wrote.[21] For Aquinas this was precisely the difference between a slave society and a free one. A slave was ruled for the sake of his master, but a free person lived for his own sake. Government over free persons was therefore just when it was directed to the good of all.[22] Probably no medieval author would have rejected this view; but in many of their writings there was at least an equal emphasis on the other criterion of good government, consent of the governed. This theme was pursued in various ways by Roman lawyers and canonists and political philosophers; they were concerned with consent to legislation and taxation and, more broadly, with consent as a necessary basis of all legitimate rule. As usual their thought was shaped in part by the realities of medieval life, in part by classical and Christian traditions inherited from the ancient world.

Medieval society provided many examples of consensual practices. Feudal contracts required the mutual consent of lord and vassal; urban communities in many parts of Europe routinely elected their mayors and other officials; and the two highest authorities in the Christian world, the offices of pope and emperor, were also elective dignities. On a theoretical level ancient Roman law provided a basis for doctrines of popular consent in a text asserting that the legislative authority of the emperor had originally been conferred on him by the people. "What pleases the Prince has the force of law because the people conceded to him all its own authority and power."[23]

It often happened that passages of Roman law that had been inert, lacking any real force in the Roman Empire itself, took on a new life and significance when they were reappropriated in the different society of medieval Europe. So it was with this text. From the twelfth century onward glossators began to ask questions that had never occurred to the jurists of ancient Rome. Did the people alienate their own authority when they instituted a ruler? Or did they merely concede the exercise of an authority that remained always inherent in the people itself? Such questions arose naturally in a society that was still permeated by the old Teutonic notion of law as an outgrowth of the whole life of a people, not just an expression of a ruler's will, and where the laws that men actually lived by commonly derived their authority from custom, from the usage of the people.

If a community did not alienate its own legislative authority it would seem that the people had a continuing right to make law for itself or to consent to laws proposed by the ruler or withhold consent. Some medieval jurists thought that such a situation was impossible. An emperor could not rule effectively if the subjects were not bound to obey his laws, they argued. But shortly after 1200 a Roman lawyer at Bologna, Azo, provided a very influential solution to the problem. He held that the Roman people conceded authority to the emperor but did not alienate it. Then, to explain how the emperor could be both an effective ruler and a minister of the people, he distinguished between the *populus* considered as a corporate whole and considered as a collection of separate individuals. The ruler was greater than each separate citizen and could command each of them individually; but he was not greater than the corporate body of the whole people.[24] Condensed into the epigrammatic phrase, *maior singulis minor universis* ("greater than each, less than all"), this argument was endlessly repeated in later discussions. During the conciliar movement of the fifteenth century it was used to prove that the whole church, or a general council representing the church, was greater than the pope.[25] Later on the argument often recurred in works of early modern political theory. Richard Hooker

wrote in the sixteenth century that, in countries like England where
the people freely assented to royal government, "It standeth for an
axiom in this case, the king is *major singulis, universis minor*."[26]

The medieval canonists also presented complex discussions
about popular consent and a ruler's legislative authority, often taking as their point of departure a text of Gratian's *Decretum*: "Laws
are instituted when they are promulgated; they are confirmed when
they are approved by the practice of those using them."[27] Early on
in the discussion Huguccio sensibly suggested that the necessary
approbation should be obtained *before* a statute was promulgated.
A new law ought to be considered long and carefully in the council
of pope or emperor, he observed, but once it had been "approved by
common counsel and consent" it was binding on all.[28] Often the
canonists presented the issue as one of popular custom versus enacted law. If a people adhered to a custom that was contrary to the
ruler's law—thereby in effect withholding their assent to the law—
should the custom or the law prevail? Thomas Aquinas, discussing
this question from the standpoint of a theologian rather than a jurist, held that, in a free community, the consent of the people was
of greater weight than the authority of the ruler.[29] The lawyers
themselves were always divided on this issue; in the fifteenth century they were still arguing about Gratian's twelfth-century text and
interpreting it in various ways. Some of them defended the overriding authority of the ruler. It would seem absurd, they held, that the
authority of a law should depend on the will of the subjects who
were bound by it. Others argued that, since a ruler would not wish
to impose a new law on an unwilling people, it could be presumed
that all laws were issued with the tacit condition that they found
popular acceptance. Jean Gerson, a leading theologian of the conciliar movement, cited Gratian's text to prove that the whole church
could limit and regulate the exercise of papal power. One persistent canonical argument distinguished between de jure and de facto
power. De jure, a ruler might promulgate what laws he pleased, but
de facto they would not take effect unless they were accepted by the
people.[30]

A similar problem arose in another major area of theory and practice involving consent—the right of consent to taxation. Medieval
kings who wanted to levy new taxes commonly negotiated in advance with their barons and the communities of their cities. What-

ever a king imagined his de jure powers to be, he knew that he could not de facto collect the tax effectively unless he first obtained the consent or at least the grudging acquiescence of those who were to pay. But, apart from such pragmatic considerations, there were issues of principle involved too. Medieval people did not feel obliged to pay arbitrary taxes because they had a strong sense of their own property rights, rights that were justified both by customary law and by the learned law of the civilians and canonists.

From the twelfth century onward Roman lawyers argued that the emperor's role as *dominus mundi,* lord of the world, did not make him the owner of his subjects' property.[31] The canonist-pope Innocent IV (1242–54) added that a city government could not arbitrarily deprive citizens of their goods because property was a right based on natural law. Then, in 1302, John of Paris gave a careful explanation of property rights in relation to governmental authority. In the church, ownership was vested in the whole Christian community and the pope was the principal administrator—but not the owner— of church property. In secular society a king did not have even this degree of authority; lay property did not belong to the community as a whole but to individual persons, who acquired it "through their own skill, labor and diligence" and, as individuals, possessed "right and power over it and valid ownership." A king had jurisdiction over disputes involving his subjects' property; but, John pointed out, jurisdiction was quite different from ownership.[32]

In these passages John relied in part on an earlier discussion by Godfrey of Fontaines, a Paris theologian who was writing in the 1280s. Godfrey's text included an explicit argument about the right of consent to taxation as an essential attribute of a free society. According to this author, when anyone ruled over free persons and not over slaves, and when he held the right of ruling by virtue of the consent of the whole community, he ought not to impose any burden on his subjects except with their consent. Because they were free persons the subjects ought not to be coerced. When they paid a tax they should do so voluntarily because they understand the reason for the imposition. It was not enough for the ruler to say that he was levying a tax for the common good or by reason of state necessity; if he did not seek consent of the subjects they were not obliged to obey.[33]

In the late Middle Ages the consensual practices that permeated the upper levels of medieval society were often transmuted into generalized theories asserting that all legitimate government must be based on the consent of the governed. One finds this doctrine diffused among many writers who, in other matters, sharply differed from one another—among radicals and conservatives, critics and defenders of the papacy. We tend to associate the idea of consent in this form with seventeenth-century theorists like Locke and Hobbes, but much earlier it had become a common topos of late medieval thought. Of course medieval authors believed that all authority came ultimately from God, as indeed did the seventeenth-century writers; the question at issue was how God's purpose was fulfilled on an earthly level. One writer of the early fourteenth century, Durand of St. Porçain, after asking how temporal power arose in the first place, responded that God had initially planted reason in man and that human reason then saw the need to institute governments.[34] And John of Paris summed up a common point of view in a succinct formula. Royal power, he wrote, came "from God and the people."[35]

The most noted consent theorist of the fourteenth century, Marsilius of Padua, associated his doctrine of consent with a radical secularism in the treatise *Defensor Pacis*, written in 1324. Blending together ideas derived from Aristotle and from the practices of contemporary city-republics, he wrote that there were two criteria of healthy government: the ruler must rule for the common good and he must rule over willing subjects. Then Marsilius added, "but absolutely and in greater degree it is the consent of the subjects which is the distinguishing criterion."[36] For Marsilius consent was the "efficient cause" of government.[37] Of course all power came ultimately from God as a remote cause, he acknowledged, but God operated through human minds and wills in establishing political authority.[38] The laws that guided a community's life were to be instituted by consent of the whole body of the citizens "or its weightier part." This was because the state was a community of free persons; they should not be subjected to slavish domination; but if one or a few citizens could impose laws on all the rest, such rulers would be acting like despots. Moreover, the people would more readily obey when each person seemed "to have set the law on himself."[39]

All this argumentation about political society was contained in Book 1 of the *Defensor Pacis*. In Book 2 Marsilius turned to the church. Here his views were revolutionary. All orthodox writers of the time agreed that Christ himself had conferred jurisdiction, the power to govern the church, on Peter and on future popes as Peter's successors. It was commonly held too that bishops and priests, as successors of the twelve apostles and seventy-two disciples, shared in a jurisdiction originally bestowed by Christ. Marsilius denied all this. The power that Christ conferred on Peter and the apostles was simply a power to administer sacraments, he held, and this power was equal in all priests (including the pope.)[40] Peter was not granted any coercive power over the church by Christ, and even if we were to assume that the apostles conferred power on him by electing him as their leader, this would not imply that his authority descended to later bishops of Rome. Indeed, Marsilius observed, scripture provided no evidence that Peter was ever at Rome at all.[41] Priests and bishops were subject to the coercive power of the government instituted by the people; and any coercive power they themselves possessed, like the power to excommunicate, came to them as a grant from the Christian community or from the government acting on behalf of the community.[42] In effect Marsilius was arguing that the ecclesiastical hierarchy was a human contrivance, not a divinely ordained structure, and that the church was essentially a department of the state.

Marsilius's ecclesiology was revived in the sixteenth century when his antipapal arguments appealed to some Protestant thinkers. In his own day his work was promptly condemned by the church. But it was only his specific teachings on church authority that were singled out for censure. The argument of Book 1 of the *Defensor*, dealing with consent to government in general, did not evoke any criticism. This is not hard to understand. In this part of his work, the part that most interests modern historians of political theory, Marsilius was expressing a commonly held opinion of his age, one that was shared by many orthodox thinkers. We can illustrate the point by turning finally to a contemporary of Marsilius, the Dominican Hervaeus Natalis. Hervaeus was a theologian of Paris who became master-general of his Order. He was an exceptionally staunch supporter of papal sovereignty in the church, the exact opposite of Marsilius it might seem. Yet, writing a few years before the *Defensor Pacis* appeared, he too presented a systematic argument that all licit government must be based on consent of the governed.

Marsilius has been called the most modern of medieval thinkers
but sometimes the arguments of Hervaeus seem to anticipate even
more closely the formulations of a later age. Hervaeus was perhaps
the first writer to divide explicitly the powers of government into
legislative, judicial, and executive functions. And, like John Locke
centuries later, he began his inquiry into the origin of government
by distinguishing between political authority and "the private jurisdiction that a father has over his son, a lord over a slave, a man over
his wife."[43] Public, or political, jurisdiction, he pointed out, was also
different from the authority of a teacher determining some matter
in the schools. A wise man could indeed give advice; but the essence
of a ruler's authority was that the subjects were bound to obey; they
were obliged by his decrees. How could such ruling authority licitly
arise, Hervaeus asked. He explained that it could not pertain to any
person by nature for by nature all were equal. If it were imposed by
violence on an unwilling people then it would not be a licit power,
for violent possession conferred no right. There remained only one
possible answer; legitimate ruling authority, Hervaeus declared,
came "only from consent of the people."[44]

Hervaeus went on to distinguish between the establishment of a
ruling office and the appointment of a particular person to fill the
office. In the one case of the papacy, the office was established by
Christ; but the institution of each particular pope rested with the
people or the electors to whom they had transferred the right of
electing. In the case of secular rulers both the office and the person
who held it derived their authority from the people.[45] Finally Hervaeus argued, like Durandus of St. Porçain, that a king's authority
came from God only in the sense that God had implanted in humans
a power of reason, through which they discerned the need to institute rulers. Such a position might have appealed to any seventeenth-
century opponent of the divine right of kings.

≺ IV ≻

Representative Government

The growth of political liberty is inseparably connected with the
rise of representative government; it is notable therefore that, from
the twelfth century onward, representative assemblies met with in-

creasing frequency, first in the church and then in the various monarchies of the West. In 1123, as soon as the Investiture Contest was
ended, Pope Calixtus II summoned a general council to meet in
Rome. Subsequent councils met at the Lateran in 1139 and 1179.
Then in 1213, Pope Innocent III convened the Fourth Lateran Council and summoned to it not only the great prelates of the church but
also ambassadors of kings, envoys from the Italian cities, and elected
representatives of cathedral chapters and other collegiate churches.
The assembled council formed a microcosm of medieval society. As
M. V. Clarke wrote, it "put the representative principle into action
on a scale and with a prestige which made it known throughout the
Christian world."[46]

Shortly after this, the Dominicans developed an intricate system
of representative government for their new Order. Each house of friars elected a prior. The priors of a province, together with an elected
representative from each house, formed a provincial chapter which
elected a provincial prior. Legislation for the whole Order was entrusted to a general chapter, which met in a triennial cycle. One year
it was composed of officials of the Order, then for the next two years
of elected representatives. Legislation had to be enacted in three
successive chapters to become binding. An enlarged general chapter—officials and representatives together—elected the master-general, the executive head of the Order.[47] This is only the barest outline of an intricate constitution, equipped with an array of checks
and balances that might have delighted the hearts of the American
founding fathers. It was the most sophisticated scheme of representative government that had so far been created; it provided an example of representation in action throughout the Western world.

Similar developments occurred in the secular sphere. In 1158
Emperor Frederick Barbarossa summoned a great diet at Roncaglia
attended by bishops, lay princes, and consuls of the Italian cities. A
Cortes of the Spanish kingdom of Leon in 1188 included bishops,
nobles, and "good men" of the towns. By the end of the thirteenth
century assemblies that included elected representatives had been
convoked by kings in all parts of Europe—in the other kingdoms of
Spain, in Sicily, Hungary, Germany, and Scandinavia. The French Estates General met for the first time in 1302. In England elected representatives were first summoned to a Parliament in 1265 during a
period of struggle between King Henry III and his barons. The next

king, Edward I, made a practice of summoning representatives from time to time, especially in the last years of his reign. In the fourteenth century representatives of towns and counties came to be included in all parliaments and, from 1343 on, they met as a separate group in their own "House of Commons."

The rise of medieval representative assemblies was of crucial importance for the future of Western government. It is a phenomenon that calls for an explanation. Some historians have seen the whole development as just a natural response to the practical needs of the age; medieval kings, they suggest, summoned representative assemblies simply because they found it "administratively convenient" to do so. This is certainly true so far as it goes. Medieval rulers in church and state did indeed convoke assemblies for their own purposes; when they wanted to win support for new laws or new taxes, one choice open to them was to summon representatives who could speak and vote on behalf of the whole community. But administrative convenience is hardly a complete explanation for the rise of medieval representation. After all, rulers always seek ways to implement their policies effectively; they have not usually chosen to do so by summoning representative assemblies. Indeed this might seem to be a risky expedient; it could easily give rise to constitutional argumentation—some of which we have already considered—about the relative powers of ruler and representatives. It is understandable perhaps that rule through representative institutions is a very rare phenomenon in the general history of human government.

Historians sensitive to this point have noted that, in order to understand what was unusual in medieval government, we must concentrate on what was exceptional in the structure of medieval society, and this has often led to comment on the unusual role of the church in medieval life. Otto Hintze wrote that, in studying representative institutions, "one faces a phenomenon that is characteristic only of the Christian West." Georges de Lagarde pointed out that general councils were conceived of as representing the whole church before any secular assembly assumed a similar role in the state. Ernest Barker discussed the Dominican Order as a possible model for English representative government. And Carl Schmitt held that all the significant concepts of the modern state were secularized forms of religious ideas, transferred from theology to political theory.[48]

These are significant observations, for the medieval church certainly did play a major role in the development of Western representative institutions. This came about mainly in two ways. In the first place, the church limited the power of kings so that they could not reign as absolute theocratic monarchs; they needed the consent of their people in order to rule effectively. Then the church developed its own practice of holding representative councils out of a deep-rooted conviction that the whole Christian community was the surest guide to right conduct in matters touching the faith and the well-being of the church. We need not suppose that any king deliberately set out to model his government on the example of church councils or the practices of the Dominican Order. It was more that administrators in church and state faced similar needs and drew on a common pool of ideas, often ideas developed in the first place by church lawyers. (The administrators of medieval kings were usually clerics and many of them were trained in canon law.) Sometimes a phrase of secular Roman law was taken up by the canonists, given a new scope and meaning in their writings on church government, and then taken back into the sphere of secular government through the clerics of royal chanceries. Thus the theory and practice of representation grew out of a complex interplay between ecclesiastical and secular elements in medieval culture.

This process has been traced in detail in two areas of legal thought that were of major importance for the growth of representative institutions. In order for such institutions to emerge there must be, first, an adequate technique of representation—a legal formula that enables one person to act on behalf of a whole community and bind the community by the decisions he takes on its behalf. Also there has to be a generally accepted legal doctrine that all those affected by a government's actions have a right to be consulted concerning them. In medieval jurisprudence these principles were expressed in two phrases that were taken from Roman law and that have been elaborately studied by modern historians—*plena potestas* and *quod omnes tangit*.[49]

The words *plena potestas* appeared in classical Roman law to define the scope of a proctor's authority when he appeared in court on behalf of his principal. But Roman law did not provide a really adequate doctrine of agency or representation—an agent could not enter into a relationship with a third party that created a legal obligation directly between the third party and the agent's principal. Perhaps this branch of Roman law remained relatively undeveloped because slaves could readily be used to carry through commercial transactions on behalf of their masters without any formal grant of authority. In the Middle Ages a different situation arose. The medieval church was honeycombed with corporate bodies—cathedral chapters, religious houses, colleges—that owned extensive property and were often involved in lawsuits. A corporation could only appear in court through representatives empowered to act on its behalf; and this practical situation led the canonists to formulate a sophisticated law of agency in which the term *plena potestas* played a major part. A proctor or representative equipped with a mandate of *plena potestas* could do all that his principal could have done if he (or they) had been present. The proctor could argue a case in court, accept a sentence, and even "transact," that is negotiate a compromise settlement with the opposing party. He did not have to refer back for further instructions; his decisions were binding on the person or corporation that had appointed him.

When medieval rulers summoned representatives of their towns to an assembly they wanted to be sure that the burgesses really would be bound by the votes of the persons they had elected; so gradually in the thirteenth century the use of *plena potestas* passed from canon law into constitutional practice. The first known example came in 1200 when Pope Innocent III summoned representatives of six cities in the papal states to appear at the curia with mandates of *plena potestas*. The elected officers of the Dominican Order were given "full power" from 1228 onward; in 1231 Emperor Frederick II summoned representatives of Italian cities to appear with *plena auctoritas*; and during the second half of the thirteenth century the use of mandates granting full power became common in both ecclesiastical and secular assemblies in various parts of Europe. In England the term *plena potestas* is first recorded in a writ of summons to Parliament in 1268 and it was regularly used from 1294 onward.

The second phrase from Roman law that was reappropriated by medieval jurists, *quod omnes tangit*, also occurs in the Code of Justinian, but again only as a technicality of private law. According to the Code, when several persons were co-guardians of a ward, they could not give up the joint administration without the consent of all of them, because *quod omnes similiter tangit ab omnibus comprobetur* ("what touches all similarly is to be approved by all").[50] The phrase *quod omnes tangit* was taken into canon law in Gratian's *Decretum*[51] and in a letter of Innocent III included in the *Decretals*.[52] It appears frequently in civilian and canonist writings of the thirteenth century as a maxim of private law, often with minor variations of wording. The canonists also made an important distinction between rights that were common to a group of persons as individuals (*ut singulis*) and those common to a group as a corporation (*ut collegiatis*). When rights belonged to separate individuals the consent of each one was needed; when they belonged to a corporate whole a majority would suffice. This was important when corporate communities came to elect members of representative assemblies by majority vote.

The decisive shift of *quod omnes tangit* into the sphere of constitutional law came in the work of a group of canonists working at the beginning of the thirteenth century. They maintained that, when a general council was to consider matters of faith, even lay people could be summoned to attend since the faith was common to all and "what touches all ought to be discussed and approved by all."[53] Subsequently, as with *plena potestas*, the phrase came into widespread use in the convoking of both ecclesiastical and royal assemblies. Pope Honorius II paraphrased *quod omnes tangit* when he convoked a council at Verona in 1222 and Emperor Frederick II quoted the phrase directly in his letters summoning an imperial council to meet in the same city in 1244. The civilian lawyer John of Viterbo, writing in 1261, cited *quod omnes tangit* in discussing the government of Italian cities. Then the maxim was quoted at Florence in 1284 in a speech urging that all classes of the city should participate in a discussion about an impending war with Pisa.[54] A particularly well-known example of the use of the phrase in a constitutional document occurs in a letter of King Edward I of England convoking a Parliament in 1295. This summons displayed both of the phrases we have discussed, *quod omnes tangit* and *plena potestas*. It was addressed to the Archbishop of Canterbury:

As a most just law exhorts and decrees that *what touches all should be approved by all* . . . we command you . . . that you be present in person at Westminster . . . [the cathedral chapter and the diocesan clergy were also to be represented] . . . the said chapter through one suitable proctor and the said clergy through two, having *full and sufficient power* from the same chapter and clergy.[55] [emphasis added]

Some historians have dismissed this use of *quod omnes tangit* as a mere rhetorical flourish, of no real significance in the emergence of parliamentary institutions. But Bishop Stubbs, the most eminent of nineteenth-century constitutional historians, held that King Edward had transformed "a mere legal maxim into a great and constitutional principle" by his use of the phrase. Stubbs was half right. There was a great principle involved here, but it was not invented by Edward I; the transformation to which Stubbs referred had begun a century earlier in the writings of the church lawyers. Of course medieval kings did not summon representative assemblies simply *because* a tag of Roman law, taken out of context, could be adduced in favor of such a proceeding. The important thing for a scholar seeking to understand the growth of representative government is not the raw material available in Roman law but the ways in which it was adapted to meet the requirements of medieval life. Kings summoned assemblies to serve their own ends; but they needed to do so because they lived in a complex society where rulers were powerful but not absolute, and where an idea of community participation in government had been nurtured by both Christian and Germanic traditions. The point of studying the mutations of our Roman law maxim is that by doing so we can gain a deeper insight into the whole mindset of the Middle Ages.

≺ V ≻

Ideal Government and Mixed Constitution

While lawyers and administrators were working out the technical details of medieval governing structures, philosophers and theologians sometimes considered the problems of authority and freedom from a wider perspective and on a more abstract level. One perennial problem of political theory concerns the best type of political regime. Granted that rulers ought to govern for the good of their subjects, what constitutional system is most likely to ensure that this desirable state of affairs will exist? When considering such questions the philosophers, like the lawyers, blended ideas from the classical past with their own medieval Christian concepts; and in doing so they established the foundation of much later political thought. In particular, Thomas Aquinas made a major contribution when he revived and reshaped the ancient doctrine that a mixed constitution, combining in some way the regimes of monarchy, aristocracy, and democracy, was the most perfect form of government.

In his treatise *On Kingship*, Aquinas wrote that "both the best and worst governments are latent in monarchy." On the analogy of the one God who ruled all the universe, he argued that the rule of one king was ideally the best form of government; but he added that a king might become arrogant, "exercising tyranny under the cloak of royal dignity." It was necessary therefore to arrange government in such a way that opportunity to tyrannize would be removed.[56] However, Aquinas left this work unfinished and did not explain here what kind of arrangement could achieve this end.

When he returned to the subject in the *Summa Theologiae*, Aquinas approached it in an indirect fashion. In a substantial treatise on the nature of law he discussed, among other varieties of law, the precepts that God had laid down for the Jews in the Old Testament and their relevance for Christians. An objection occurred to him about the governance of ancient Israel. The best form of government was kingship but God had not instituted a king over Israel from the beginning; therefore he had established an imperfect form of government for his chosen people. This argument was of course unacceptable to Aquinas. In responding to it, he wrote that two points had to be discussed in considering the right ordering of a state or nation. The first was that all the people should have some share in government, for this would ensure peace and stability. "All the people love and protect such a constitution," Aquinas wrote. The second point concerned the kind of regime to be adopted. Aquinas's exposition is very compressed but he seems to be presenting a consecutive argument. The problem was to define a regime in which all *could* have a share in government while still preserving the advantages of monarchy.

In typical fashion, Aquinas turned to Aristotle for help in advancing his scripture-based argument. Aristotle had written that the two best regimes were monarchy and aristocracy. It would seem then that the best form of government for any city or kingdom would be to have one man of exceptional virtue ruling over all and other virtuous men holding office under him. But, Aquinas concluded, everyone could have a share in such a government because the rulers could be elected from all the people and by all the people.

This is indeed the best polity, well mixed from kingship in that one rules, from aristocracy in that many hold office according to virtue, and from democracy, that is the power of the people, in that the rulers can be chosen from the people and election of the rulers belongs to the people.[57]

Then Aquinas argued that God had indeed established just such a form of government for Israel. Moses, ruling over all, represented monarchy; the seventy-two elders, aristocracy; but there was also an element of democracy in that the rulers were chosen from the people and by the people. This last conclusion required some rather creative exegesis of texts from Exodus and Deuteronomy.[58]

As Etienne Gilson pointed out, Aquinas claimed to derive his argument from Aristotle and the Old Testament, but the doctrine he formulated was really a new one.[59] Aquinas was the first Christian writer who derived a theory of mixed constitution from scriptural texts. Moreover his version of the doctrine was significantly different from Aristotle's. All classical accounts of the mixed constitution referred to the rule of a city-state, where the people could participate directly in government; but Aquinas was concerned with the best form of government for "any city or kingdom." Hence his version of democracy is a kind of representative system; the people all have a "share in government" in the sense that they can participate in choosing their rulers. Such a constitutional system could apply to a large kingdom or even (as Aquinas's successors pointed out) to the whole church.

Again, Aristotle was interested mainly in blending the interests of various classes in order to promote social harmony. Aquinas did not discuss social class; he was concerned more with checks and balances; for him the purpose of a mixed constitution was to temper the power of the king. In some contexts, as we have seen, Aquinas maintained that any government directed to the common good was compatible with the liberty of the people. But, in discussing the varieties of constitutions, he specifically associated a democratic regime with freedom, observing that "the end of democracy is liberty."[60] His underlying thought seems to have been that an admixture of democracy in a constitution would ensure that the ruler did in fact govern as a true king, ruling for the common good, and so the liberty of the people would be preserved.

Aquinas's argument became the starting point for a flourishing tradition of late medieval and early modern political thought; many later authors took up his theme and applied it in various ways to both ecclesiastical and secular government. John of Paris closely paraphrased Aquinas's account of mixed government in Israel and then took the argument a step further. This kind of government was not only appropriate for the ancient Jews, he held, but also for the modern church. "It would certainly be the best constitution for the church if, under one pope, many were chosen by and from each province, so that all would participate in some way in the government of the church."[61] Nicole Oresme (c. 1320–82) wrote extensively on the virtues of a mixed government for both church and state.[62] And Jean Gerson, speaking at the Council of Constance in 1415, maintained that the church assembled in a general council did indeed exemplify a mixed constitution. The pope represented monarchy, the cardinals aristocracy, and the other members of the council democracy.[63]

When Renaissance scholars rediscovered Polybius and other classical exponents of the doctrine of the mixed constitution there was already a flourishing tradition of discourse about the virtues of such a system; and in the seventeenth century the idea of mixed government persisted as a central feature of early modern constitutional thought. The writers of that period usually liked to quote classical authors rather than medieval ones in support of their views, but the doctrines they proposed were often influenced by the tradition that Aquinas had initiated. The very unclassical notion of an ideal constitution in ancient Israel, that could provide a permanent model of governance for both church and state, remained popular with seventeenth-century Puritans. The secular versions of the doctrine, in which a mixed constitution was taken to mean a representative government composed of king, lords, and commons, was closer to Gerson's pope, cardinals, and general council than to anything in ancient Greece or Rome. James Blythe hardly exaggerated when he wrote recently, "the origins of all the major ideas of Early Modern mixed constitutionalism were indisputably medieval and Aristotelian."[64]

≺ VI ≻

Natural Rights

So far we have discussed mainly the relationship between rulers and communities. Another major theme in the growth of modern freedom concerns the rights of individuals. From the seventeenth century onward the idea of natural rights became a central topic of Western political theory; and in this area too early modern theorists were building on a foundation of thought that was established in the medieval church.[65]

This fact has not always been appreciated in modern work on the early history of natural rights theories. Some scholars would place the origin of such theories as late as the seventeenth century itself, associating them with the nascent capitalism of the age or with the religious individualism of certain Puritan groups. Historians who have sought an earlier starting point for the idea of natural rights have usually found it in the work of the fourteenth-century philosopher William of Ockham. A doctrine of individual natural rights, it is argued, was a logical extension of Ockham's nominalist, individualistic philosophy. Michel Villey, who argued this thesis in many books and articles, maintained that Ockham introduced a radical novelty into Western thought—indeed a semantic revolution—when he defined the word *ius* as a "licit power" and so associated two concepts, *ius* and *potestas*, right and power, which, according to Villey, had hitherto been quite separate from one another.[66]

But this argument ignored a substantial body of earlier medieval material. For centuries before Ockham, both in formal jurisprudence and in everyday usage, the word *ius* was commonly used to mean a power or claim or liberty, often expressed in the plural form as *iura et libertates*, rights and liberties. Medieval society was saturated with a concern for rights and the concern was often reflected in the writings of the church lawyers—the ordinary gloss to Gratian's *Decretum* laid down that "No one is to be deprived of his right except for very grave cause."[67] The real problem is to determine when a doctrine of natural rights, inhering in all individuals, emerged from the medieval concern with the rights of particular persons and groups. On a semantic level we have to determine when the phrase *ius naturale*, which had traditionally referred to objective natural law, acquired a subjective sense also as meaning a natural right.

This development of thought occurred in the early commentaries on Gratian's *Decretum*. Gratian himself began his work by defining *ius naturale* as a moral precept, the Christian Golden Rule, "Do unto others as you would have them do unto you." But the authorities that he subsequently cited used the term in several different senses. To avoid confusion the canonists often made lists of all the various meanings of *ius naturale*, and among the meanings they sometimes included a subjective one that was not evidently present in Gratian's texts. One of the earliest Decretists, Rufinus (c. 1160), commenting on the first words of the *Decretum*, simply ignored Gratian's definition and gave a new one of his own. "*Ius naturale* is force instilled in every human creature by nature to do good and avoid the opposite."[68] Other canonists soon defined *ius naturale* as a "faculty" or "power" or "ability" associated with human reason and conscience and free will. Huguccio insisted that this subjective definition of *ius* was the primary and proper one, and that all other uses of the term, including Gratian's, were derivative from it.[69]

The subjective definition of *ius* as a kind of moral quality inhering in persons was not in itself a doctrine of natural rights but it could readily lead on to such a doctrine and it soon did so in the works of the canonists. During the thirteenth century they developed a considerable array of such rights.[70] There was a natural right to own property, a natural right to acquire the necessities of life, a natural right to self-defense. Spouses had natural rights in marriage. Even infidels had natural rights. From about 1250 jurists also began to argue that the right to due process in legal proceedings was a natural right, not simply a provision of human law.[71]

When William of Ockham came to consider natural rights in the fourteenth century there was a considerable body of sophisticated juristic material for him to draw on; so his role as an originator of natural rights theories should not be exaggerated. Still Ockham did make a substantial contribution of his own, not indeed through his nominalist philosophy but rather through a new kind of biblical exegesis. Ockham's original contribution was to take the scriptural teaching on evangelical liberty—Paul's "freedom wherewith Christ has made us free"—and use it to defend a doctrine of natural rights understood as freedom from tyrannical government, especially within the church. Arguing against a high papalist doctrine that attributed an absolute plenitude of power to the pope, Ockham maintained that Christ did not confer on Peter and his successors any power to injure the natural rights of Christians. The pope could not subvert "the temporal rights and liberties conceded to the faithful by God and nature."[72]

Along with Paul's text on freedom, Ockham emphasized especially the words of James on Christ's law as "a perfect law of liberty" (James 1:25). If the pope had the plenitude of power that his supporters claimed, Ockham argued, the law of the gospel would not be one of liberty but "a law of most horrible servitude," more oppressive than the Old Law of Moses. All Christian kings and prelates and clergy and layfolk would be mere slaves of the supreme pontiff. Such a claim, Ockham insisted, was not only false but heretical. The pope had no power to take away "the natural liberty by which men are naturally free and not slaves."[73]

Ockham died in 1347. Half a century later Jean Gerson took up his arguments and developed them further. Gerson gave a very influential definition of *ius* as "a power or faculty belonging to each one in accordance with right reason" and he maintained that, from *ius* so defined, it was possible to derive a whole theory of government and property.[74] In a striking and unusual fashion Gerson extended his conception of *ius* to include the whole of God's creation. Since *ius* was a power in accordance with reason, and the divine reason ruled universally, every creature had a right to its own characteristic activities. "The sun has a right to shine, fire to burn, the swallow to build its nest."[75] As regards humans, they retained many rights, even in a fallen state, including a right to liberty and a right to life, a right of self-preservation.

When Gerson, following Ockham, took up the theme of Christian freedom, he used the concept to argue for a radical reform of the law and practices of the church. Christ's law was a law of liberty, he wrote, but in his own day the Christian faithful were burdened by an intolerable weight of "human traditions," a maze of bureaucratic rules and regulations devised by the church hierarchy and imposed on pain of mortal sin. They were like snares and nets to trap the faithful; they were destructive of Christian liberty.[76] The essential obligation of a Christian was to obey freely the natural law that his reason and conscience could discern and the divine law revealed in scripture. Natural law led mankind to happiness on earth, divine law to eternal felicity. The God-given rights to life and liberty enabled humans to pursue these ends.[77] (If Gerson could have used the diction of a later age he might have written that God had endowed mankind with certain inalienable rights, among them life, liberty, and the pursuit of happiness.) Gerson's definition of a right remained well known in the sixteenth century; his work was one of the major channels through which medieval rights theories were transmitted to the modern world.

≺ VII ≻

Limitations on Freedom

There remain the two areas of life mentioned at the beginning of this chapter—human servitude and religious persecution—where the policies of the medieval church seem to have been merely oppressive. In both spheres the church nurtured doctrines that would eventually contribute to the growth of modern liberty; but this came about only in the changed circumstances of a later age. Medieval writers commonly maintained that by natural law all men were free,[78] and they commonly affirmed the authority of conscience in shaping individual beliefs. But they seemed blind to the implications of their own Christian psychology when they related these ideas to problems of servitude and religious freedom.

During the medieval period most of the peasants of Europe were semi-free serfs, and outright slavery never became extinct. The leaders of the church seem to have viewed this situation with equanimity. They were inhibited from any general condemnation of servitude most obviously by the fact that slavery was recognized as a licit institution in both the Old and New Testaments. Paul indeed wrote that "in Christ there is neither slave nor free," but the fact that all were equal in the sight of God was not taken to mean that all were equal in the ordering of human society. When medieval authors wrote that man was by nature free they meant only that slavery did not originate in the natural law that God had first instituted, but rather in subsequent human legislation. Slavery was not a necessary outgrowth of the human nature that God had originally established in Adam; it was rather a consequence of Adam's sin. If humanity had remained sinless men would never have enslaved one another; but, from a medieval point of view, the key fact was that humans were in fact sinners. Servitude followed as a regrettable but irremediable consequence. Even Ockham, amid all his rhetoric about Christian freedom, had to explain that he was not condemning slavery as such; he was only asserting that the law of Christ did not itself enslave anyone.[79]

Christian teaching perhaps mitigated the harshest consequences of servitude. Christian moralists always urged masters to treat their slaves with consideration, and in medieval Europe serfs were not regarded as just human cattle. In the eyes of the church they were persons, not things. Serfs could make valid sacramental marriages. A serf could rise to the dignity of the priesthood. (That required the lord's consent but it seems to have been commonly given; many village priests came from peasant families.) Moreover, Pope Gregory the Great had declared that, because men were by nature free, it was a meritorious act to manumit slaves and so return them "to the freedom in which they were born." This text was incorporated into Gratian's *Decretum* and duly commented on by generations of Decretists;[80] but none of them saw in it a possible argument for the abolition of all servitude. By the end of the Middle Ages serfdom had become almost extinct in western Europe, but this was due to economic causes rather than religious ones. And the end of serfdom was followed by the rise of new, harsher forms of slavery in the Christian world after the discovery of the Americas. As David Davis wrote, Christians readily perceived that sin was a kind of slavery; but they were slow to recognize that slavery was a kind of sin.[81]

The history of religious persecution provides a similar story; behavior that seems lamentable nowadays was taken for granted in medieval society. But here too there were elements of thought and practice that could have led on to a different tradition. Most importantly, medieval canonists and moral theologians often upheld the overriding value of the individual conscience as a guide to right conduct. Aquinas, for instance, held that a person was always obliged to do what his conscience discerned as good even though the conscience might be mistaken.[82] Among the canonists the same doctrine was vigorously expressed in the ordinary gloss to the *Decretals*. "No one ought to act against his own conscience and he should follow his conscience rather than the judgment of the church when he is certain . . . one ought to suffer any evil rather than sin against conscience."[83] Such texts were not concerned with a right to religious liberty but with a duty to obey one's own conscience. Still an emphasis on conscience was an essential element in the doctrine of religious freedom that grew up in a later age.

No such development took place in the medieval church. Every medieval writer who discussed the question saw heresy as a sin and a crime that was properly judged by the church and punished by the secular power. Gerson emphasized Christian liberty in his own way, but he had no conception of religious freedom as we understand it. Indeed he participated in the trial and burning of John Hus. He could defend the rights of Christians within the church but it never occurred to him to assert that heretics had rights against the church. Medieval people were so convinced of the truths of their faith that they could never see dissent from the faith as merely an intellectual error, a mistake of judgment. They thought that heresy must somehow stem from malice, from a perverted will that deliberately chose evil rather than good, Satan rather than God.

Even so, it is not self-evident to a modern mind that such personal deviance should be cruelly persecuted. Perhaps we can find a partial explanation of the medieval attitude in the remark of Maitland with which we began: "In the Middle Ages the church was a state." During the thirteenth century secular states were only just beginning to grow into existence; the principal bond of unity that held western Christian society together was the bond of a common religion. Nowadays the main focus of our loyalty is the state; we look to the state to protect our security and our liberty; to be a "stateless person" in the twentieth century is a most unhappy fate. The other side of the coin is that we do not tolerate people who are perceived of as traitors to the state. We charge them with treason; we inflict punishment on them, sometimes capital punishment in extreme cases. A plea of personal sincerity, that the traitor has acted from good motives, in accordance with his own conscience, is not a sufficient defense. Medieval people regarded heretics in much the same way; they held them guilty of treason to the church, and they treated them as traitors.

For people of our age such attitudes are hard to understand. And, even if we do succeed in understanding them, it will remain true

that in this area the stance of the medieval church was harshly antithetical to the growth of modern freedom.

≺ VIII ≻

Conclusion

During the Middle Ages, constitutional doctrines of church government were always opposed by more rigorous theories of papal absolutism. It was indeed the tension between the two doctrines that
gave rise to much of the argumentation we have discussed. In the
early years of the fifteenth century it seemed for a time that the
constitutional tendencies might prevail. A major schism broke out
in 1378. First two then three pontiffs claimed to be the true pope.
Finally a general council, meeting at Constance in 1415, removed all
three claimants and elected a new pope of unity.

To justify these measures, the council also published a decree,
Haec sancta, that defined its own authority. This declaration built
on the earlier arguments of the canonists discussed above, but carried them further:

This holy synod of Constance . . . declares that, representing the church
militant, it holds its power directly from Christ, and that all persons of
whatsoever state or dignity, even if it be the papal dignity, are bound to obey
it in matters which pertain to the faith, the rooting out of the schism, and
the general reform of the church in head and members.

The council further enacted a reform decree requiring that general
councils should meet at regular intervals in the future.

The significance of *Haec sancta* has been debated extensively
among modern scholars. Nearly a century ago John Neville Figgis
called it "the most revolutionary official document in the history of
the world." But the council fathers of Constance were not really
trying to establish a kind of revolutionary, republican government
for the church. They assumed that the reform councils of the future
would be summoned and presided over by a universally acknowledged pope. Their ideal was the kind of mixed constitution that Gerson, an influential leader of the council, described during the debates of 1415. Or one might say, borrowing the language used by the
English jurist Fortescue later in the century, that the conciliarists
did not want the government of the church to be a pure monarchy

(*dominium regale*) or simply a popular regime (*dominium politi-cum*) but rather a combination of both forms (*dominium regale et politicum*).

A new council did meet at Siena in 1423 and another at Basel in 1431. But this council soon quarreled with the pope, Eugene IV. After a few months the pope dissolved the council, but the council refused to accept his decree; then the council deposed the pope, but Eugene refused to accept its sentence. There was no longer a possibility of government by pope-and-council; it was a question now of pope or council. For a decade a war of propaganda was carried on but the princes of Europe—perhaps persuaded by the papal argument that conciliar doctrines might undermine the claims of all monarchies—gradually turned away from the council and threw their support to the pope.

If the ideals of the conciliarists had been realized, the papacy would have developed into a limited monarchy sharing power with a representative council. But by 1450 the conciliar movement was defeated and the popes were able to reassert their sovereign authority. The Roman church entered the modern world as a model of baroque absolutism. In later times the constitutional principles that had grown up in the church found their principal application in the theory and practice of the emerging secular states.

Rather paradoxically, this is especially evident in Protestant England, probably because the problems concerning the relationship between king and Parliament that arose there rather closely paralleled the earlier problems of pope and council. Earlier we noted that a vocabulary of words and ideas persisted from medieval discourse into early modern constitutional argument; seventeenth-century England provides many examples of such persistence. The doctrine *maior singulis minor universis*, asserting that the king was greater than each but less than all, was often quoted by parliamentary writers, and William Prynne noted that "the Papists were the first broachers of it long ago." Prynne and other writers also used the analogy of pope and general council in asserting that Parliament was superior to the king. (Such arguments led the royalist writer John Maxwell to complain that his adversaries had drawn their doctrines from the "polluted cisterns" of pre-Reformation Catholic writings.) The medieval mandate of "full power" was still used in seventeenth-century election writs and Henry Parker cited the maxim *quod omnes tangit* to establish Parliament's right to counsel the king and to represent the interests of the kingdom. In the 1650s George Lawson quoted Marsilius of Padua to prove that ruling authority resided always in the people or its weightier part.[84] King Charles himself, seeking a last-minute accommodation with Parliament, agreed that England was ruled by a mixed government of monarchy, aristocracy, and democracy, king, lords, and commons; and Puritan writers held up the supposed mixed constitution of ancient Israel (which Thomas Aquinas had first invented) as a model that England should faithfully imitate.

To understand the constitutional developments of the seventeenth century we need to study the real-life conflicts of that age; but we can only study them through the language that the protagonists deployed. Just as medieval writers had taken up classical and early Christian texts and adapted them in new ways by applying them to the problems of their own society, so too seventeenth-century constitutional theorists reappropriated medieval language and charged it with new meaning and power in the context of a different age. We can hardly understand the terms of seventeenth-century constitutional discourse and its contribution to the making of modern freedom without some awareness of this process.

To sum up then. The principal contributions of the medieval church to the development of Western freedom were these: a limitation of state power in matters of religion; a well-developed theory of consent as the basis of legitimate government; new techniques of representation; significant adaptations of the old idea of a mixed constitution; a nascent theory of natural rights. Some things were not achieved. Before the modern ideal of freedom could emerge there had to be an end to slavery and an end to religious persecution. These were tasks for a later age.

Medieval Urban Liberty

JOHN HINE MUNDY

THIS CHAPTER SKETCHES THE socio-political history and ideas experienced and expressed by western European townsfolk from the tenth century through the fifteenth. It is divided into four parts. Dealing with political history, the first part sets the stage for three other sections, two portraying the measure of liberty and equality hoped for and achieved, and one the degree of political participation attained by the population of city and town.

≺ I ≻

Historical Context

A vast expansion of agricultural settlement and town building began in western Europe in the late tenth century, and lasted until the mid-fourteenth century. By 1300 two areas boasted an urbanism almost modern in intensity. Grandest was that of northern Italy, enclosed in a circle from Genoa to Florence, Bologna, Venice, and Milan. The second area, centered on Bruges and Ghent in maritime Flanders, outstripped the urbanism on the Rhine and Meuse to become, with its export woolens, north Europe's largest industrial complex. Some great metropolises, including London, Paris, and Naples, lay in regions graced only by modest towns.

To economic expansion was added political revolution in the age called "Gregorian" after the radical pontiff Gregory VII (1073–85). From the mid-eleventh to the mid-twelfth century with violence peaking from 1073 to 1099, civil war weakened the Empire, Europe's greatest secular power, and consequently its rival, the newly liberated papacy, advanced to become Europe's ecumenical government. Paralleling Rome's rise was that of local centers of authority. Although several old monarchies remained vigorous, and all save the Empire were soon to be renewed, power everywhere devolved from the hands of the greater monarchs to regional princes, and, beneath these, to seigniories, petty states both rural and urban.

The cities or urban seigniories that are the subject of this chapter differed among themselves. In both north and south Europe, towns tried to dominate the countryside, and all had dependent villages. In either 1323 or 1324 little Provins in Champagne had eight, and Lorraine's Metz ruled no less than 168. In 1373 the episcopal principality of Liège's assembly had four canons, four nobles, and fourteen burghers, and the latter oversaw that body just as Bruges, Ghent, and Ypres did the estates of maritime Flanders. No northern town, however, could compare with Lombardy's Milan that by 1300 had extended its sway over whole provinces, towns and villages alike. Northern cities were also often split apart by princely power. By 1300 the new and larger part of Liège was ruled by magistrates (*jurati*) elected annually by its inhabitants, but the prince-bishop and his council of assessors (*scabini*) still governed the original small urban nucleus as well as the ambient countryside. Similar divisions elsewhere inform one that citizens in north Europe, south Italy, and much of Iberia, unlike their north Italian counterparts, rarely governed either the whole of their community or the countryside outside their walls.

The social groups housed in town provide another notable contrast. Artisans, merchants, knights, and titled magnates were and remained town citizens in Italy, much of southern France, and Rhenish and Danubian Germany. Nobles, in fact, were often forced to reside in Italian cities. Elsewhere this mixture was abnormal or did not persist, and magnates and knights were only infrequently urban citizens. One result was that the towers of noble and patrician lineages filled north Italian cities with skyscrapers, but north French and German ones had few or none. Another is that modern historians mistakenly have come to think of north Europeans as the founders of the bourgeois way of life.

The reasons for these differences are twofold. Much northern urbanism was new, and many communities were initially too small to produce the intermediary social grades that tied the nobility to ordinary townsfolk so successfully in Italy. This economic circumstance, however, is related to a political one. Only in those regions where central states were weak or absent did towns win great liberties, support the complex society described above, and successfully subject their surrounding regions. German towns joined Lübeck in building the Hanseatic League to govern North and Baltic sea commerce after 1300 when the Empire, on whose frontier they lay, was fading rapidly. Weightier was the French and German urbanism along the Empire's western boundary, extending from its northern heartland in maritime Flanders southward down the Meuse, Moselle, Rhine, Saone, and Rhone valleys. Towns there won much freedom and were able, as Metz above, to dominate rural circumscriptions. In the south, the Gregorian revolt and the Empire's rapid collapse from the Peace of Constance in 1183 to the death of Frederick II Hohenstaufen in 1250 made north Italy the seat of a true urban republicanism, the largest one in the Middle Ages. To this favored region may be added several adjacent territories where central states were nearly wholly absent in the 1100s, one reaching from Provence across Languedoc from Avignon on the Rhone to Toulouse on the Garonne, and the other including the small towns in Swabian or Swiss and other south German territories. Outside those areas lay firm unitary states with subordinate towns: England's sturdy monarchy to the north, for instance; and others along the frontier with Islam, such as the south Italian realm of Apulia, Naples, and Sicily, and, to the west, the Iberian kingdoms.

As exemplified by Marseille's "God alone rules this city" of 1218, a city's ultimate ambition was to be free to govern itself, or, as was said then, "to hold" of God and of no other. Only in northern Italy after the Peace of Constance, did many cities, as the jurists said, cease recognizing any "superiors on earth." Most towns had to be content with less. Like villagers, townsmen owed taxes to prince or lord and submitted to controls on marriage, inheritance, and residence, and hence strove for a customary law enshrining personal liberty and limiting their princes' military service, taxes, and judicial prerogatives. Most won only a share of such freedom; even great Milan never wholly obliterated imperial lordship, although it well-nigh vanished for a time.

Where towns gained a substantial measure of freedom, new types of elected magistracies arose. From the late 1000s, Italian and later southern French cities elected boards of consuls, their title a faint reminiscence of ancient Rome. Meaning both a jurisdictional area and its chief, the word "power" (*potestas*) early described an imperial governor; but after the Peace of Constance, Italian towns began to elect *podestàs* as presidents. Northern achievements were not so prepossessing. The consulate spread rapidly around the Mediterranean, in south France and elsewhere; but north of the Alps it was rarer, spreading to Germany, for example, only in the thirteenth century. The elected mayors and councils of northern towns, furthermore, had less power than their Italian equivalents.

Durability was another difference between the areas. Early linked to Byzantium, Venice was always free and remained so until 1797. After the Peace of Constance in 1183, Lombardy's cities, long led by Milan, threw off imperial power, and, followed soon by towns in Liguria, Romagna, and Tuscany, remained free for at least two centuries, and often longer. Elsewhere, republics were short-lived. In Languedoc Toulouse's liberty lasted from 1189 to 1229, but thereafter faded, being all but extinct when the Capetians inherited the town in 1249. Marseille's citizens replaced its lords from 1212 to 1220, governed a republic for almost two decades, but then submitted to the Angevin monarchy in 1245. The difference between Italy and the rest provoked thought. A later Dominican political thinker, Ptolemy of Lucca (d. 1327), opined that cities, by their very nature, were everywhere self-governing. Villages were too small for independence, he thought, and kings were best for regions too large for the easy accommodation of differences.[1] Theory aside, he went on, the free towns were in Italy; elsewhere freedom was limited by princes.

Republican government suited cities, then, but what groups controlled the republic was the touchy question. By around 1200 many towns had been led to victory by the well-to-do. Where princes were weak and urban growth rapid as in Italy, the martial and administrative nobility joined rich business folk to provide leadership. Where princes were strong, the martial cadre often split, part becoming a largely rural nobility and part assimilating to the bourgeois. Even where the latter pattern held sway, however, patricians boasting both lineage and wealth emerged to lead in time.

The real threat to oligarchy or plutocracy was the rise of the "people" or popular party in the 1200s, or, to state it theoretically, the devolution of power from the few to the many. Modest or humble individuals could neither protect themselves economically nor impress their will on government, but the corporations they formed could. Necessarily seeking both objectives, the "people" created the first age of gild expansion. The results were spectacular: by about 1300, gilds almost dominated towns both north and south. Ghent was a one-industry town: in 1300 its 50,000-odd inhabitants included 5200 weavers, a number to be multiplied by their families and other clothmakers. In 1379 gildsfolk constituted 62 percent of Hamburg's population.

The rise of the many was linked to the relationship of princes to towns. Where princes were strong, they sponsored gilds in order to weaken the patricians under whom town self-government had grown. By 1204, the lords of Montpellier in France's Midi saw to it that its constitution was corporative, wholly fusing the gild organization with government. Such was not true of Italy's self-governing industrial cities until after 1250. Class conflict also helped princes overthrow town independence. Around 1250 the patricians of Paris lost control of government, and the statutes of 101 gilds were registered by royal order. The French royal governor Philip of Beaumanoir (d. 1296) endorsed graduated taxes on property against the sales taxes favored by the well-to-do, and claimed that the rich wantonly monopolized town office. The abolition of town self-government, in fact, was sometimes a popular cause. At Provins in the early fourteenth century 96 percent of the voters favored replacing elected magistrates with royal officers.

Even in free towns, however, gilds grew. Organized around 1250, Italy's masters and laborers began to gain political power. As they built gilds, however, others did also. Entrepreneurs founded publicly chartered commercial, banking, and industrial companies. An example is the Florentine *Lana* gild that oversaw all aspects of woolens manufacture and even policed the crafts in the industry. Legal and medical professions created colleges to regulate and monopolize their functions. Founded by merchants, crafts-, and tradesfolk, the gilds had engendered widespread corporatism.

Corporatism also formalized social divisions. In Italy and elsewhere where nobles were town citizens, the law came to define as magnates those from lineages having knights as members or among their ascendants, as well as patrician commoners who "lived nobly." At Toulouse around 1220, literature and law divided the citizenry into "knights, bourgeois and the people" or "knights, bourgeois and artisans." In 1247 the Aragonese custom of Huesca defined the bourgeoisie by saying: "they do not work with their own hands, but have masters and workers through whom they exercise their professions," adding that merchants, moneychangers, lawyers, and medical doctors also counted as bourgeois.[2] Although these assessments took time to spread throughout Europe, the divisions of early modern society had already been limned.

The Florentine constitution exemplifies the political expression of corporatism. By 1250 the greater gilds, those of the entrepreneurs in the woolens and silk industries and the literate and legal professions, had pushed into government, creating a second if lesser head of state, the people's captain, to stand beside the *podestà*. In the 1280s and 1290s, the middle gilds of artisans and shopkeepers acquired office and made the republic hydraheaded. Led by a banner-bearer of justice, gild priors or "ancients" became the republic's highest magistrates. Partial analogs to people's captains were also seen in northern latitudes: a gild *Obermeister* first appeared in Basel in 1280, and the office spread thereafter in Rhenish and Danubian Germany. Social struggle punctuated the rise of the gilds. After see-saw battles in the early 1300s, the crafts at Liège overthrew the prince-bishop and patricians in 1343, eliminating the latter altogether in 1384. This "democratic" constitution was not destroyed until the all but regal duke of Burgundy, prince of the Low Countries, overwhelmed the town in 1468.

Gild power was lessened by the division between entrepreneurs and artisans. The businessmen of the *Lana* mobilized the whole woolens industry in Florence behind the Guelph popular party in the late thirteenth century. No matter how militant, the wool carders of the revolutionary *Ciompi* of 1378 were financially a minority in the cloth industry, and demographically a minority of the population. Movements such as theirs therefore never retained power for long, and rarely gained it. Although the gilds continued to regulate professions, businesses, trades, and crafts, division gradually robbed them of political force.

Echoing Aristotle, many believed that a republic should rest on the middle range of the population. The famed jurist Bartolo of Sassoferrato (d. 1357) repeated Ptolemy of Lucca's argument on this point. If in power, Ptolemy said, the lower classes or plebs straightway "democratize" everything.[3] The Austin friar and political theo-rist Giles of Rome (d. 1316) pointed out an innate "flaw" in democ-racy, namely that what begins as a drive for political participation ends up as one for economic equality.[4] His prayer that the many might restrain their passion to hit the rich by leveling wealth was contradicted by those who claimed that such was democracy's in-evitable result. This put iron into the spines of the upper and middle classes. If sometimes shaken by the roars of their humbler fellow citizens, they usually managed to muffle their voice.

Equally disruptive of political harmony, according to Bartolo and Ptolemy, was that the very powerful and wealthy always wish to "tyrannize over" a community.[5] The result was that popular legis-lation often attacked magnates. From 1250 to 1350 as Italian democ-racy reached its apogee, an air of social war marked the republics. In the early years, the Franciscan chronicler Salimbene (d. c. 1290) re-marked that expelling the magnates from town led to her cities be-coming like French ones, empty of nobles.[6] In the two years after 1293 just under half of the noble and great popular families were exiled from Florence. From the 1280s on Italian popular parties of-ten insisted that only those who worked with their hands could hold political office. In reality, however, save momentarily, the well-to-do were not disfranchised, probably because a literal application of blue-nail (from the dye used in clothmaking) legislation would have extinguished popular leadership itself. Education and leisure had trained or engendered those idealistic or profit-seeking upper class deviants who found empire in the rise of popular parties: in 1292, a knight, Giano della Bella, led the middle gilds to power in Florence. The patrician Artevelde family directed Ghent's popular party in the fourteenth century.

Reservations aside, however, around 1300 Italian democracy (moderately oligarchic as will be seen) attained its apogee. The mon-archist Giles of Rome stated that "in Italy, the many or the whole people normally rule. Although a *podestà* or lord always rules the city, the people rules more than he does because it elects and can reprimand him and also because it issues the laws beyond which his government cannot go."[7] This peak was represented in grand politi-cal theory, Marsiglio of Padua (d. 1342) expressing its politically moderate ambitions in a style that still convinces. Echoing the

Hohenstaufen Frederick II, Frenchmen like Beaumanoir and Peter Dubois (d. 1312) cursed the Lombards for "inventing" republicanism. A half century later when a similar movement triumphed in the Low Countries and west Germany, northern conservatives were forced to turn their worried eyes homeward.

After centuries of growth, things fell apart. For upwards of two hundred years following the early 1300s, economic troubles, foreign war, social struggles, and the plague became endemic in town and countryside, spreading from Italy and France to almost all of western Europe. Similar ages had been seen before, especially during the Gregorian civil wars. The two periods, however, differed significantly: in the earlier troubles, the ecumenical church together with the towns and rural seigniories won liberty, while population increased; in the later one, the church declined, towns and seigniors lost liberty and population decreased. Warfare also changed: cannon were used in sieges early in the 1330s, and were soon capable of subduing lordly fortresses and breaching town walls. Possessing a tight cohesion lacking in the mounted and foot militias of divided local society, companies of mercenary or professional soldiers appeared everywhere. Late medieval society, it seemed, could attack but was incapable of defense.

In this context, class conflict, intensified by economic crisis, rent Italy's republics. The Florentine carder Ciuto Brandini was executed in 1345 for plotting a workers' uprising. His followers were told not to summon foreign help. This seemed wise: with artisan aid three years before, a foreign tyranny had almost been established. In earlier times, in fact, to judge from the Torre family's role in leading Milan's popular or Guelph party, temporary dictators aided the rise to power of lesser social groups. By this time, however, they were invited to serve, but remained to rule. Brandini's carders also indulged in revolutionary preciosity, suicidally rejecting alliance with the Florentine magnates. Past experience of gaining ever broader political participation, however, prevented the excluded from eschewing hope. A result was that revolts like that of Florence's *Ciompi* punctuated late medieval Italian town life.

However troubled, these were nevertheless real republics. Later on, in 1393, even after the final defeat of the lesser gilds, the two Florentine legislative assemblies numbered 700, and no councilor was allowed to sit after his year for up to three years. With the population approaching 70,000, Florence's executive and judicial officers were about 150 in number, holding offices for terms of from two to four months elected from about a quarter of the adult male population. Few modern republics equal this measure of popular participation.

A curious feature of these republics is that they witnessed the atrophy of the party system. In the mid-1200s, there were two already bitterly hostile parties: the Guelphs favored the popes and republicanism; and the Ghibellines, the Empire and monarchy. A century later, no significant republic with two parties was to be found. What caused this change is hard to fathom. As in the church, perhaps, difference of belief was viewed as heresy. By 1290 no Florentine public figure could be Ghibelline, only a Black or White Guelph. As a White Guelph, however, Dante Alighieri (d. 1321) was philosophically a Ghibelline. Another reason was that the rise of the "people" made society so corporative that politics was reduced to determining what gilds, colleges, and social orders would share government. Not that parties disappeared: they remained to describe diplomatic alignments. Florence's rivals in Tuscany were Siena and Pisa; Florence being Guelph, Siena and Pisa were Ghibelline. But party meant little ideologically, and Bartolo rightly taught that, were a tyrant Guelph, the good man's duty was to be Ghibelline, and vice-versa.[8]

Limited to terms of six months or a year and circumscribed by constitutional and personal limitations, the office of the *podestà* was designed to prevent a restoration of monarchy. In the later time, such restrictions were no longer wanted. Instead, committees and individual magistrates were granted extraordinary powers to make sure that their party's program was enacted into law by any and all means. Emergency committees or officers were authorized to wield free power (*potestas absoluta* or *liberum arbitrium*) within a certain sphere. The spheres themselves were gradually enlarged and the duration of office extended until an individual was granted full power over a republic for life. In 1299 at Mantua a lifetime captain was endowed "with freedom of will to rule as seems best to him, with or without advice." He was also authorized to make war or peace, raise taxes, appoint or remove all other officers, and summon any

public assembly according to "his own unlimited and sufficient discretion and will, nor shall he be bound by any law, custom, edict,
decree or statute."[9]

It took time to convert such extraordinary magistrates into real
princes: they could only be abstracted from society's classes when
succession was vested in a particular family. At first this was assured by electing a scion during the incumbency of such an officer.
Even when hereditary right was admitted, however, ruling clans
lived by private law, opening the door to conflict by partitioning at
death their territories among the heirs. Although precocious Milan
achieved it as early as 1396, undivided inheritance spread in Italy
only during the fifteenth century.

Not every city underwent the same evolution. Progress was rapid
in some, slow in others: if Milan led the way to princely power,
Florence lagged behind. The initially covert principate of the Medici
was enthroned as hereditary by the emperor Charles V between
1512 and 1531, leaving behind memorials to inspire the republicanism of later ages. Florentine history itself demonstrates, however,
that evolutionary patterns varied. Before the Medici acquired lordship with popular backing in 1434, a limited group had constituted
an oligarchy, ruling by means of secret councils. Much the same was
true of Siena before 1487.

The most splendid oligarchy was Venice. Although temporally
broadening it, the cloture of 1296–97 froze the group participating
in government, abolished the general assembly, and created a secret
supreme council. The excision of the *doge's* power and the defeat
of popular and patrician risings in the early fourteenth century cemented the oligarchy. Why Venice and, to a lesser degree, Florence
and Genoa were able to build stable oligarchies when elsewhere this
effort failed as the principate rose is a mystery. Perhaps it was because these cities enjoyed uncommonly strong international connections. Both Genoa and Venice had maritime empires governed by
their oligarchs. The Florentine merchant-bankers, richer than those
of other cities and closely linked to papal finances, constituted that
city's oligarchy. Florence's financial power, however, did not prove
as durable as the others' thalassocracies, and, as noted above, she
soon became a principality.

At this time, Bartolo of Sassoferrato examined oligarchy. He sur-
mised that town republics of modest size were best ruled by the

multitude, excluding troublesome elements, however, namely the very rich and very poor. Larger communities should be ruled neither by a prince nor by the multitude

but instead by a few, that is, by the well-to-do and learned. Both Venice and Florence are ruled in this way, and sedition plays no role in these republics. For although they are ruled by the few, they are few only with respect to the multitude contained in these cities, but many with respect to other cities. Since they are many, moreover, the multitude does not object to being ruled by them, and also they cannot easily be divided against themselves because many middling folk participate and uphold the law of the city.[10]

Popular government had, in short, been demolished. Although oligarchy persisted, the principate normally triumphed. Its power was circumscribed: specializing in diplomacy, war, and social police, it rarely disturbed private business and property law. Brigaded in gilds and economically protected by them, the mass of the population largely ceased participating in political life. The wealthy increasingly centered around the prince's court, where privilege and nobility were granted as rewards for service. Enhancing quiescence, this polity was advantageous for both prince and society. It reduced governmental councils to an "aristocracy" separated from the people and viewed by them with misgivings: increasingly rhetorical, the remnant institutions of the republican tradition had become unpopular.

In areas where monarchy did not have to be reinvented, so to speak, the analog to the Italian principate was the development of royal power at the expense of the liberties and self-government attained by towns in the past. The mechanisms were similar: social conflicts between the popular and upper classes invited arbitration, and, as usual, the prince was opportunist. At Sens in 1320, France's king intervened to protect the poor on their invitation; at Amiens in 1383, the reverse was true. Monarchy's impartiality was also shown by tax policy. The poor wanted graduated taxes on property, but the rich favored market tolls. Arbitrating such disputes, royal officers first "reformed" the system and then happily collected both imposts.

Like southern cities, the northern town resisted the imposition of princely power, and also tried to create a semblance of the Italian principate. James of Artevelde's dictatorship at Ghent lasted eight years before his assassination in 1345, and social trouble resulted in the lifetime dictatorship of a mayor at Zurich in 1336. At no time, however, were northern towns as free from great princes as were Italian ones, and hence the local principate never took root there. Ghent's last Artevelde captain-general was crushed in 1382 by the Burgundian ducal prince. Northern towns fought hard to retain the liberties they had once gained. Victories in the 1200s and 1300s gave way to defeats in 1452 and 1492, yet Ghent's self-rule was abolished by Charles V only in 1540. Tumultuous Liège rose again in 1603, being finally vanquished by its prince-bishop in 1684. In the meantime, urban liberties and even republics both survived and flourished in the interstices between expanding regional states and nations, especially in the Empire from Amsterdam to Hamburg and thence down the Rhine to the Swabian and Swiss towns. An example is Cologne on the Rhine, whose prince-bishop had surrendered all but criminal justice in 1288, and whose relatively popular fourteenth-century constitution remained in effect until 1796.

<< II >>

Liberty

The sources for the next parts of this chapter are mainly Italy's civilian jurists together with ecclesiastics, also largely Italian, who wrote treatises on politics. The reason Italians are overrepresented here is that intellectuals and lawyers elsewhere in western Europe were little attracted to republican political thought. Sparked by Italian-style Roman legal studies, schools of jurisprudence developed as early as the twelfth century, and hence learned lawyers and judges were soon seen in England, France, and elsewhere; but almost all were monarchists. Northerners who favored republican government—and there were not many—were usually influenced by Aristotle (d. 322 B.C.) as taught by the schoolmen. An Austrian abbot, Engelbert of Admont (d. 1331), lauded Italian republicanism, for example, and a canon, John of Hocsem (d. 1348), condemned monarchy and applauded true democracy in his history of Liège's popular risings. Ideologically like those in Italy, political parties likewise existed up north. In Flanders during the early 1300s, one party (*Leliaert*) favored the French monarchy and defended oligarchy, for example, and another (*Clauwaert*) applauded democracy and Flemish particularism. Speaking comparatively, however, these parties were transitory.

Sometime between 1257 and 1300 a law book of Magdeburg on the Elbe river defined freedom as "the natural liberty of a man to do what he wants, unless prohibited by force or law."[11] This law circulated widely and was translated into Latin, Czech, and Polish. Seeing this, one might believe, as did Milton, Montesquieu, and Jefferson, that freedom had its origin in Germany's forests. That even before Tacitus (d. c. 120 A.D.), the antonomastic popularizer of Teutonic myths, Germans had thought about freedom or felt its urgings is almost surely true if only because all men want to do what they want to do. But what makes one look beyond Magdeburg is the brisk economy of the formulation recorded in its book. It comes as no surprise to find that contemporary Italian jurists used the same sentence, and cited their source, the second century Roman lawyer Florentinus.[12] Nor was Florentinus inventive: the Roman jurists borrowed from Stoic thought, and even Cicero (d. 43 B.C.) once defined personal freedom as "the power to live as you please."[13]

As Magdeburg's good lawyers also did, Florentinus had gone on to say that "slavery is a definition of practical law [ius gentium or ius civile] by which a person is subjected to the ownership of another against nature." Both ancient and medieval lawyers certainly believed that, since the loss of the primal bliss described in Roman law and Christian Scripture, slavery marked society.[14] More subtle but also more ambiguous was the statement of the civilian Accursius (d. by 1263), who conjectured that natural law grants an individual the "possibility" of doing what he wants, unless "prohibited by force, that is, by the practical law that has been introduced by man's needs."[15] What, in Florentinus, was almost a capacity had been reduced to a mere possibility. And because human need can never be sated (if the poor always *need* more than they have, for instance, oncoming death always makes the rich *want* more), natural law was perhaps mere theory and the only true law was practical. Surely repelled by all the pious blather about natural law, the jurist Placentinus (d. c. 1192) flatly stated that "although unjust in natural law, slavery is just in practical law," and hence contended that practical law had actually abolished liberty.[16] In fact, limited only by protection accorded the life and religion of those in that condition, slavery was licit throughout the Middle Ages both in town and in countryside.

Placentinus's harsh opinion was, however, that of a minority. The greater Azo (d. c. 1230) stated that, "although it can be obscured by civil law, the liberty derived from natural law cannot be removed." He then promptly allowed one to sidestep the law: "natural laws are called immutable," he said, "because they cannot be wholly abrogated . . . but they can nevertheless be modified."[17] This being said, it is also sure that, as in antiquity, it was praiseworthy to "restore" persons to their natural liberty by means of emancipation. This vision beguiled everybody, presumably because the credulous believe, or cannot but hope, that nature is kindly. A celebrated Florentine law of 1289 illustrates this by forbidding the acquisition of power over the "liberty or person" of another. Putting aside the real motives for the law, and they were decidedly self-interested, its prologue defined liberty in these terms: "Decorated in many ways by natural law, liberty—by which each man's will depends on his own judgment, and not on that of another—is that by which cities and peoples are defended from oppression and their laws protected and improved."[18] Freedom, the magistrates fondly thought, is profitable for human society.

When the Bolognese Odofredo (fl. 1228–33) reviewed Florentinus's definition of freedom, he cited an earlier jurist, Irnerius (d. *ante* 1118). This founding father of Bolognese studies had gone beyond the text to assert that "each and every man has free will by the law of nature" and that it is "licit for him to do what pleases him" simply because of that endowment.[19] Although the contention that free will has a knowable relation to doing what one wants to do is hardly demonstrable, this supposition led some to quite other definitions. In Dante's *On Monarchy*, the desire to do what one wants is in danger of being reduced to mere appetite, and, borrowing from his theological sources, this poet and political activist went on to say that "if antecedent appetite should move a man's judgment in any way, he cannot be free because he is dragged as a captive by another and not by himself."[20]

If purged of appetite, Dante found freedom beneficent. To him it was best guaranteed by a world monarch who, because he had everything and wanted for nothing, would "greatly love mankind and [hence] wish all men to become good, which cannot happen" under any other kind of government.[21] He therefore condemned the Florentines, who, impelled "by the fearful gluttony of cupidity," had rebelled against the emperor. Believing that "they would be protected by the false robe of liberty, [they have] fallen into slavery's prison." To restore "enslaved Italy," the poet wished to replace the capacity to do what one wants with the tranquil acceptance of the will of an ecumenical monarch who rules for mankind's good.[22]

Fired by his Ghibelline passion, Dante was really attacking the measure of democracy achieved at Florence. Nor was he the first to scorn democracy's inescapable materialist gluttony. Lamenting the fall of the Empire, Alexander of Roes of Cologne conjectured in the 1280s that the "republic of the Christian faith" had three manifestations: government, religion, and learning. The first was the German sphere, the second the Italian, and the third French. Each nation had distinct mores. The main German quality was the "love of ruling," that of the French the "love of knowing," and the Italian the "love of acquiring." In Italy, the people rule, in Germany, the soldiery, and in France the clergy, and their vices fit their leaders. The Germans were given over to "rapacity and discord," the French to "lust and pride," and the Italians to "greed and envy."[23]

Apart from theory that, with little difficulty, led one far away from nature's freedom, liberty was impeded by practical impediments. One was the slavery mentioned before. Excluding rural and occasional urban serfs, privately-owned slaves were rare during much of the Middle Ages. After 1300, however, Italian mariners imported expensive domestics with a high percentage of women from the eastern Mediterranean. In the fifteenth century, slavery, increasingly male and black, spread to mines and agriculture, at first in the Aegean islands, then in Sicily, and finally in Andalusia and the Algarve in Iberia. This novelty was noted by the French historian Philip of Commynes (d. c. 1511), who sourly commented that the sale by Africans of slaves to the Portuguese exemplified man's misuse of man.[24]

Knowing that medieval communities usually merely enjoyed some privileges and were not really free, some scholars have conjectured that their inhabitants lacked an understanding of freedom. Perhaps so, but "understanding" may differ from wanting to do what one wants—which medieval townsfolk did understand. This chapter earlier touched on Toulouse and other communities that, after brief periods of independence and self-government, had been subjected to the Capetian house of France and lost their freedom. Such towns, one may say, remained privileged with many rights, but were now subject. Two points may be made about them, however, and may be extended fairly to communities that had never obtained more than a small measure of liberty. The first, and most basic, is that the people always want to be free. In 1040, when the citizens rose in Milan, they fought, the chronicler says, "to acquire liberty."[25] Later, in the Renaissance under the principate, the Milanese were doubtless proud of their liberties, and that they were no longer free in the sense of being self-governing cannot be shown to have voided their minds of the conception of freedom. Second, privileges or partial freedoms were real liberties. Winning tax reductions or predictability, lessening military obligations, protecting rights of property and movement, and gaining jurisdiction over civil or criminal cases were and are meaningful. A small privilege, furthermore, sometimes grew into a large freedom. In 1282 the federated towns of Tangermünde, Osterburg, and Stendal in the Saxon Altmark won from their lord the right to secede from obedience if he diminished their rights. The fact that one frequently settles for a slice does not mean that one cannot envisage a whole pie.

Speaking about taxes reminds one of the tithe and therefore of ecclesiastics. Although the church weighed on medieval people it nevertheless defined the *respublica Christiana*, that is Latin Western culture at this time. Except for permitted exceptions, the Jews and, far less durably, the Muslims, all were members of that republic until after the Reformation or Europe's sixteenth century religious division. Not that its subjects were always happy: peaking at certain times, dissent was characteristic of medieval life. The tithe was frequently protested, especially when it spread from crops on land to manufactures in town. This heavy tax is a measure of the problem, however, because laymen from landed gentlefolk to town moneylenders either sometimes "usurped" it, or served as profit-seeking collectors.

Tithes aside, the church impinged on the town dwellers' desire to do what they pleased by prohibiting usury. Churchmen were of two minds about the marketplace. On one hand, they tolerated it because commerce was a risky service to society and deserved remuneration. On the other, they favored economic brotherhood, recommending that landlords and businessmen follow Scripture: "Love your enemies, do good and lend, hoping for [no profit] therefrom."[26] Other than the later literate secular professions, scribes, lawyers, and medical doctors, the clergy's main social rivals were soldiers and merchants. Not themselves shedding blood or lending money, at least not directly, the clerks claimed moral superiority. Gregory VII expressed this in 1078: "If a soldier or merchant or one in any profession that cannot be exercised without sin should come to penitence, let him know that he cannot obtain eternal life unless he leaves business or gives up his profession."[27]

Although traditional, this moral rigor was not popular until the Gregorian "reform" excited the clergy. Before that time, churchmen were themselves in business: monasteries lent money by mortgages until the mid-twelfth century, sold entry to their houses, and concocted many fraudulent property charters. Although not wholly, the moralizing polemics of the Gregorian age planed away the rough edges of this "economism," partly by reviving another viewpoint. Scripture had praised the communism of the apostolic community: from each according to his means, to each according to his needs.[28] Monastic and even some lay groups therefore tried to convert the people into Christian brotherhoods in which all was shared and all worked with their hands. In 1213 Cardinal Robert of Curzon urged the convocation of a council of bishops and princes, there to instruct all "to work either mentally or physically, and to eat only the bread won by their own labor, as the apostle commanded. Then will all usurers and robbers be removed, charity flourish and all be brought back to its pristine state."[29]

Long since justified in Christian doctrine and protected by Roman law, however, private property could not be abolished. Cleansing the marketplace by attacking usury was therefore less thoroughgoing but also far less revolutionary. Arguments from Scripture and pagan learning, notably Aristotle's celebrated "barren money" theory, were marshaled to defend this position. Why the clergy liked it is worth investigating because to require an investor to forgo gain is to demand the impossible. But, although this demand is the kind of usury that moralizers often exact from those living in the world, it also happened to suit the social evolution of the age.

From late Roman days princes had limited usury, but, as moral rigorists railed, were always happy to accommodate it for a fee. As long as the state was the senior partner, the clergy could do no more than grumble, but the Gregorian reversal changed things in two ways. One was that the crusades launched by the papacy—peace at home; war abroad!—required the regulation of crusaders' debts, and hence a law of enforcement appeared early in the 1100s. The other was that, given the erosion of state controls in a decentralizing world, a kind of "economic individualism" had emerged in both town and countryside, wherein usury in the form of mortgages and loans at interest abounded. As this "capitalist" ethos grew, so also did its opposition. In towns, the trades- and craftsfolk in the tumultuous first efforts of gild growth described above were for a time allured by the seductions of economic brotherhood. Moved by a similar ideal, churchmen partly replaced state officers in regulating the marketplace. Not only did it take time to elaborate usury law, however, but enforcement always fell far short of what rigorists wanted.

This was perhaps because, without a wholesale redistribution of property which few recommended, the obvious impracticality of economic brotherhood made concessions necessary. Curiously, usury law did not much harm business. Derived from Roman law, a penalty medieval men called "interest" sidestepped condemned usury and accented instead a lender's intention. The principle that law requiring the impossible should be mitigated flourished anew, and risk was sometimes said to allow profit. As long as usury was not explicitly defended (declared heretical in 1312), some clerks bowed to the world by easing austerity and some even defended business practice. Giles of Rome opined that merchants may profit from their insider's knowledge of market practice. Peter John Olivi (d. 1298) noted that "capital had a certain seminal quality of generating gain," and hence, when risk was shared, this Franciscan radical allowed investments or loans to be returned with increase.[30]

Rigorists only grudgingly bowed to reality, however. In a letter of 1236, Gregory IX refused profit to those who lent money to merchants even if they shared the risk.[31] Again, although the prosecution of usurers really depended on marketplace consensus, the pressure on businessmen was penitentially omnipresent. If, being a deceitful gift during an unrepentant life of continued crime, philanthropy was damned by rigorists, it was nevertheless frequently blessed by popes. More demanding was the obligation imposed on businessmen of placating the deity in a deathbed testament. Ideally, the penitent was to "restore" directly to those from whom usury had been wrung, but, if impossible, the church could be given a sum for good works. John of Joinville, writing a canonized French king's history in 1309, caustically called such "uncertain restitution" the devil's way of corrupting churchmen.[32]

To these sources of income may be added obligatory penance. Evolving out of crusade financing, the sale of indulgences (partially graded according to wealth) for remission of sin's temporal penalty brought in rich revenues. The keystone of this program was confession to, and assignment of penance by, a priest, a practice made mandatory in 1215. By 1229, moreover, charitable giving on the deathbed was demanded of all. Once churchmen had surrendered business and become rentiers, the expanding penitential system was advantageous. Rentiers are hard put to keep pace with rising economies, but penance grew with, or even outgrew, the economy, and therefore aptly typifies the apogee of ecclesiastical power.

When the tithe is added to the above, "spiritual" taxation explains how the churches and monasteries that covered Europe were financed. Huge and beautiful buildings of little practical use were constructed on a scale so vast that they stun modern economists. Part of the take, however, went for practical things, building bridges, for example, and schooling. Most schooling was to recruit and train ecclesiastics, but the growth of legal and medical studies shows the significance of this endowment for layfolk. What this meant for towndwellers may be seen at Carcassonne, a substantial south French town in an area well served by universities (Montpellier and Toulouse). In 1304 the population was about 9,500 and included 43 nobles, 12 Lombards, and 30 Jews. Law and government were represented by 63 notaries (solicitors), 15 advocates (barristers), and 40 soldiers and police. Religion, medicine, education, and charity were served by 9 university-trained medical doctors, the same number of parish priests and 250 other persons under canon law, including a bishop and cathedral chapter, monks and friars, servitors and oblates in hospitals, and schoolteachers. Of this population, the notaries, advocates, medical doctors, parish priests, and upper clergy and monks had both Latin and the vernacular. Christian merchants, some artisans, Jews, and most nobles, furthermore, were literate in the vernacular, and the merchants and a few nobles probably had some Latin.

Happy though the results may sometimes have been, the clerks' teaching weighed on merchants and investors. Successful business-folk invariably assure themselves of a profit disproportionate to that of their humbler economic brothers, but, instead of being congratu-lated on making money, they were (as were soldiers for their booty) ordered to make restitution. A commentator on Dante's *Comedy*, Benvenuto of Imola (d. c. 1387 or 1388) expressed their dismay some-what artfully: "He who practices usury goes to hell; he who does not, to poverty."[33]

< III >

Equality

The Magdeburg law did not mention equality, but the lawgivers who wrote it were doubtless familiar with natural law theory. The basic teaching was that of the Roman Ulpian (d. 228): "in civil law, slaves have no stature; not so in natural law, because, as far as pertains to it, all men are equal."[34] Churchmen had commented on this idea from antiquity on, and Ulpian's sentiment had also been emascu-lated or made practical by thinkers such as Gregory I (d. 604). This pontiff had proposed that, because individuals differ in their capaci-ties or perhaps social role, divine dispensation "constituted distinct grades so that, while inferiors revere their betters and the betters in turn love their inferiors, a cohesive concord shall be made from di-versity."[35] This attitude elicited adhesion thereafter. Noting that Ar-istotle had said that someone must always lead, Ptolemy of Lucca agreed that "the government of man over man is natural; it was so among the angels and before the Fall, and is so even now."[36] Like liberty, equality had invited redefinition, and had been shorn of part of its glory.

Within towns, noncitizens were not equals. Having defined citi-zens as the active population, Marsiglio excluded women, children, foreigners, and slaves from their ranks. Curiously, the great Paduan failed to mention Jews. The ordinary glosses of both civil and canon law asserted that Jews were Roman citizens, and Bartolo of Sassoferrato summed up juristic doctrine by saying that "Jews have all that Roman citizens have."[37] This teaching was somewhat fictional: even male Jews were citizens only in the passive sense of being protected. In happy moments, they were well-to-do in comparison with their Christian neighbors, and their communities were usually self-governing and settled their own disputes unless these involved crime. Although local practice varied, the Roman law principle that "the plaintiff pleads in the court of the defendant" ordinarily applied to litigation between Jews and Christians.[38]

Jewish citizens were nonetheless not equal. They were excluded from the professions (although Jewish medical doctors were employed by Christians) and never held magistracy over Christians. Their real liberty was the permission to practice Judaism, western Europe's major exception to the Greco-Roman and Christian idea of social harmony through obligatory integration. They were not, however, always spared. During the Gregorian revolution when ideas of Christian citizenship overwhelmed secular notions, Western integration insisted on conversion or death in the Rhine valley. Jewish testimony reports that, although the numbers involved were small, whole communities were extirpated. After that awful moment, peace reigned until the beginning of the fourteenth century, when another popular wave of Christian integration led to renewed massacres. During this difficult age, Jews were largely expelled from England, northern France, western Germany, and parts of northern Italy, lasting as large and well-to-do populations only on the German-Slavic frontier and in Iberia. Between these two extremes, the impoverished Jews were reduced to marginal and unpopular economic activities. Increasingly denigrated in both law and letters, this minority came to be viewed by both ideologues and poor Christians (who rarely dared attack their own rich) as demoniacally exploitative, filthy, and even cannibalistic. In sum, lacking equality with their Christian neighbors, Jews (and Muslims, for that matter) were not true citizens.

To turn to the Christians, all citizens were supposed to be equal, at least in the sense of being equally protected by the republic. A passage from the statute book of Viterbo in 1251 affirmed that a *podestà* was to "maintain the whole people, each and every one . . . in person and property."[39] Because "person" meant both life and status, a citizen's "life, liberty and property" were here guaranteed.

And property was also sanctified by function. The judge Alberic of Rosate (d. 1360) found that "statutes are made for reason of the public good, namely for the dignity and memory of families which wealth conserves and want diminishes."[40]

To effect this end, children depended on adults until majority—ranging from twelve for girls, to fourteen for boys, up to twenty-five years of age. They were protected even against themselves, against, for instance, contracting debts. They also lacked rights. Indigent parents were allowed to sell infants and the well-to-do often pushed surplus children into monasteries. Parents nevertheless had obligations. Where dowries were customary, for example, a young woman was owed one for her marriage, that or a smaller endowment to enter a nunnery. The civilian Albert of Gandino (d. c. 1310) reviewed a Florentine statute reducing to age eighteen the time during which a parent was obliged to educate a child. Many applauded the law, "but I believe," said Albert who favored Roman law's twenty-five, "that the education of children is an immutable part of natural law."[41]

Women had more rights. Citizenship inhered in their persons: princes normally granted liberties to the "men and women" of a community, and women could be citizens in places where their husbands were not. A woman's passive role had the considerable advantage of freeing her from military service, but she also suffered disabilities. Although frequently given a fair share of family wealth for their dowries and commonly active in crafts, trades, agriculture, and business, women were poorer on average than men. Offered less education, even wealthy women were not as literate as their men. They were largely excluded from the liberal and legal professions and from the clergy, save for a modest number of scribes, primary school teachers, and religious (far fewer than monks). In political life, an occasional princess without brothers or a princely widow held office by virtue of family, but no elected magistrate of significant grade was female. Exceptions to political exclusion, however, exist. In the Provins plebiscite several times cited above, almost 14 percent of the voters were wives, widows, and unmarried women from every element of the population: farmers, artisans, tradesfolk, and bourgeois. To sum up, the famed English lawbook bearing Bracton's name (composed from 1220 to 1234) copied a truthful opinion from the great civilian Azo: "Women differ from men . . . because their condition is worse than theirs."[42]

Countryfolk were also denied equality. In antiquity, those who lived in the city of Athens and those in Attica were all Athenian citizens, and such was sometimes the case in the Middle Ages. In 1256 and 1257 Bologna's magistrates inserted in the citizens' *Book of Paradise* the names of six thousand rustics, and Italian and other communities awarded citizenship to foreigners and yeomen, enlisting them as soldiers or allies. Nearby villages and small towns were often part of a political community. At Provins villagers constituted about a third of the voters. Generally, however, both in Italy's republics and those of the north, rural folk were ruled from town but were not citizens.

Townsmen often believed that they liberated rural populations, but by that they really meant making them adhere to their interest. In Italy, for example, Guelph towns obliged nearby small towns and villages to be Guelph, and town fathers everywhere, north and south, subjected rural seigniors and communities. Probably rightly, the preacher James of Vitry (d. 1240) complained that they crushed their neighbors, recommending that "if robbers and usurers are held to restore [their ill-gotten gains] how much the more should these violent and pestiferous communities that weaken and oppress neighboring lords and destroy their jurisdictions be held to restore [rural] liberties."[43] Overlooking the plains outside its walls, San Gimignano's handsome towers housed rival patrician and noble families whose members were moneylenders and lawyers profiting from the circumambient villages. The question is nevertheless a difficult one. With town aid, farmers often gained freedom from their lords, but their liberty necessarily destroyed the petty seigniorial states in which they lived, leaving them open to urban exploiters.

Could villages in fact pass laws contradicting those of cities? Albert of Gandino asked this question about a village in the district of Brescia, and read in Roman law that "any people or *universitas* can make law for itself."[44] In fact, the real answer was "no, not usually." The famed jurist Baldo de Ubaldi (d. 1400) echoed reality when he distinguished between city people possessing real liberty and "a people that has no jurisdiction, as in unfortified and fortified villages that are wholly subject to a city or lord . . . or a community that has a jurisdiction limited to civil cases or light crimes, as is the case of many [villages] in the March of Ancona."[45]

Small towns and villages nevertheless evolved in ways similar to cities. A measure of judicial or executive power sometimes fell to villagers, who entrusted it to elected officers bearing titles similar to those in town. Countryfolk published law codes, often adapting customs from nearby towns. Communities leagued together to attain or defend freedom. A renowned example is the action of the Swiss forest cantons in 1291 from which the enduring confederation was to grow. Small towns also sometimes equaled large cities. Forty years after the rise of self-government at Toulouse, nearby l'Isle-Jourdain won the right to elect its consuls. In 1230 these officers were empowered to eradicate onerous customs, written or not, and issue new laws at will. No single document in Toulouse said quite so much so bluntly. Thereafter, it was all down hill, and by 1275 liberty's cause had been compromised at l'Isle. New law was no longer mentioned, and electoral liberty had faded. The lord and outgoing consuls were together to choose forty worthies from among the knights, burghers, and those living in the suburbs, from whom seven consuls were picked by lot. The electoral pool of the forty, moreover, was to be chosen from among both the *maiores*, the greater, and the *mediocres*, the lesser. Typical of princes, this was a way in which town liberty was diminished by empowering the people, the many, against the few, the well-to-do who had headed most independence movements. All told, however, l'Isle did better than Toulouse even in the retreat: if political liberty is what one loves, her single trumpeter had sounded a clearer clarion than had the brassy choir at Toulouse. Size is not everything.

By and large, however, villages and small towns acquired less freedom and self-government from their lords than did towns. Contemporaries wondered why, and Ptolemy of Lucca answered that villages were too small for independence because they lacked sufficient specialized services for a good or rounded life.[46] Villages and small towns, in fact, never boasted a law or medical faculty, and rural nobles held their tournaments or assemblies in fields near cities. Although many had walls, village and small town defenses were limited. Alberic of Rosate wrote that "a fortified or unfortified village and a hamlet are not honored by the dignity accorded a city . . . because they are unwalled."[47] These and other insufficiencies obliged farmers to rely on lordly families, church institutions, or nearby cities for technical leadership. Although elements of self-government were everywhere present, the basic political form of village govern-

ment was consequently the petty seigniorial monarchy, and the freedom achieved by its inhabitants was usually expressed in social
terms—freedom of marriage, inheritance, and movement; and abate-
ment of services and taxes—rather than political ones.

From antiquity on, these differences had engendered condescen-
sion toward rustics. In the fourth century Vegetius had waxed po-
etic: "In the earliest time, the creation of cities first distinguished
the rude and uncultivated life of man from the communion of dumb
animals or beasts."[48] This idea was conjugated curiously. Other ancients had noted that men first lived in forests and then built houses
and finally cities. Giles of Rome, who served both kings and popes,
remarked that the intelligent are to rule the stupid, especially the
"barbarians who live in the woods," and went on to assert that
townsmen, "who have more prudence and intelligence, may wage
just war against rustics if they refuse to submit."[49] Others argued
that humanity lives by the sweat of farmers, and discovered virtues
peculiar to rustic life. Besides, countryfolk were useful in internecine urban struggles. Italian proto-tyrants swamped town assemblies
with discontented rustics, and Burgundy's dukes supported the rural
Franc of Bruges in order to balance the Flemish Parliament's three
great cities.

Even if rural subjects of cities were not equal, town citizens
were, and had an equal right to the protection of law. The law on
this point was sacrosanct. Boncompagno of Signa (d. *ante* 1250)
called secular judges "priests who are seen to provide something sacred because they conserve each man's right unimpaired."[50] This
popular writer for notaries and lawyers here drew on Roman law
wherein justice, described as sacred, was said to "attribute to each
man his right."[51]

Sometimes, however, public power overrode individual rights.
Public officers, for example, could breach the Roman legal principle
that "no one should pronounce judgment in his own case."[52] Cino
of Pistoia (d. 1336) correctly observed that those, from emperors to
barons, who recognize no earthly superiors could nullify a citizen's
right.[53] As the later Baldo perceived, furthermore, because its elected
priors enjoyed the same "full, free and general will" as did a prince,
the republic of Perugia could do the same.[54] For treason, violent
crime, or heresy, also, both Roman and church law abrogated a citizen's right to counsel. Some civilians, however, were of two minds

about that. Alberic of Rosate summarized the opinions favoring legal representation, saying that "advocacy is a public function and publicly useful . . . [and] defense should not be denied to an excommunicate . . . or to a [layman] exiled" for treason or other high crime.[55]

Weightier were social and economic hindrances. As soon as trained advocates appear in the courts around 1100, the texts begin to allege that the poor suffer because they could not afford lawyers. Leaning on Roman law, the civilians favored the principle that, if one party, for fear or poverty, lacked advocatorial help, the judge was to balance the scales.[56] A good principle, perhaps, but the well-to-do saw no reason to pay for it. Azo remarked that he had never seen a judge actually balance advocacy when "one party had many and good lawyers, and the other only few and inexpert." He went on to define what everybody knew to be the cure by saying that in antiquity "advocates received a public salary."[57] Hurriedly embracing equality, princes often used this defect to rally the discontented poor against patrician town government.

Social reality also curtailed equality. Because the poor lacked regular employment and residence, some of them lived "disordered" lives. Following Roman law, the civilians therefore proposed that, since they had few means, the best way to punish them was physical. "Those of greater dignity," Azo said, "should be punished more gravely financially, and more gently physically"—save in the case of high crime.[58] In law, then, the various strata of purportedly equal citizens were treated by society's police and judges in vastly different ways. Luckily, in Italy, thirteenth century jurisprudence eased physical punishment by developing exile, which Alberic of Rosate defined as an "ejection from the public good and therefore a kind of secular excommunication."[59]

The historical introduction to this chapter stated that political thinkers followed Aristotle in favoring rule by the middle range of the population. A reason given for excluding the very poor and the very powerful was that both shared a violent style of life. Boncompagno of Signa remarked that magnates were generous, improvident, lubricious, drunken, litigious, and given to violent contentiousness.[60] He might have added that their young rode as fast as possible even in town, and, worst of all, that their old were rich in land and armed retinues, thick as flies in the legal and ecclesiastical professions, and closely linked to patrician commoner families and merchant-banking firms. Popular parties often leveled their towers, proud symbols of huge extended families and nobles' associations that, until well into the 1200s, had handled litigation within their class. Exile was a favored method of controlling patricians and nobles (an example is Dante's nineteen-year exile from Florence that started in 1302), but there were other ways, and they are less attractive.

Since notables had much power in both the economy and the courts, popular legislation tried to balance the scales. At Parma in 1316 a law forbade magistrates from hearing charges against those who had accused a magnate, and Baldo recorded a statute from Ancona forbidding gentlemen from litigating against any "popular person" unless proof of damage to person or property could be adduced. The same civilian also recorded statutes punishing magnates, their children, and their grandchildren with greater penalties than those meted out to *populares*.[61] So far so good, perhaps, but, as always, social conflict prompted enthusiasts to step over the line. A Parmesan statute of 1316/17 ordered that the *quaestio* (judicial torture, that is, introduced by Italians early in the age of the popular republics) was to be employed only by magistrates in the presence of five of the *populares* who served as the republic's priors or "ancients." The presence of these worthies was to obviate torture that weighed especially on "*populares* and other small persons." The magistrates, however, were permitted to "torture magnates . . . without 'ancients' [being present]; against others of whatever condition, however, they should proceed rationally and with such moderate torture that no one should fall into danger of death." Things went so far that, in popular legislation at both Bologna and Pisa in 1282 and 1286, suspect magnates could be judged guilty "as if the crime had been fully proved."[62]

≺ IV ≻

Political Participation

Deleting the numerous exceptions seen above, all citizens were to participate in political life. Their executive and judicial magistrates therefore voiced a law emanating from them, the people. The civilian John Bassiani (d. 1197) was forthright: "The vigor of both law and custom is the will of the people . . . laws bind us for no other reason than that they have been received by popular judgment . . . Law depends solely on the will of the people."[63] For Alberic of Rosate two bodies created law, the councilors in their assemblies and the magistrates in their courts. Even professional judges derived from the people, "for what these magistrates do," he remarked, "is done with the authority of the people who elected them, and thus the people does it."[64] In short, as Ptolemy of Lucca observed when describing Italian city republics, "republican rectors are bound by the laws, and cannot go beyond them in administering justice. This does not suit kings and other monarchs because they find their laws in their hearts . . . and what pleases the prince has the force of law, but this is unsuitable for republican governors . . . because they dare not do anything new that is not found in the written law."[65] Italian townsmen usually examined their magistrates' judicial actions and their councils' new legislation in annual public reviews (*sindicationes*).

England's judges and French governors were professional officers, but differed from Italian ones because, being royal servants, they were not elected by the communities in which they served. In his *Treasure* of c. 1264, the Florentine Brunetto Latini observed that this lack, together with the sale of offices, typified monarchy's inherent corruption.[66] Professionalism also reached greater heights in Italy. From 1250 to 1296, the knight Matthew of Corrigia from Parma was elected *podestà* fifteen times in eleven communities for annual terms. Such technicians were bound to be literate, but in what tongue? Many knew Latin; some did not. Proud of his Latin, learning's language, the university-trained jurist Roffredo of Benevento (fl. 1215–43) complained that persons ignorant of that tongue "are often elected *podestà* and deliver judicial sentences. Such individuals should have assessors literate in the law by whose advice they are ruled."[67] Town statutes, in fact, often insisted that assessors sit with their judges.

The learned, however, only partly got their way. A common method of legislating, Alberic of Rosate noted, was that "a university or its councilors elect experts to whom they give the power of issuing legislation." He then quoted the admission of Albert of Gandino that, while such persons "ought to be jurists . . . layfolk ignorant of the law are usually chosen."[68] Enthusiastic exponents of the vernacular, gentlemen sometimes thought learning Latin beneath them. Writing in 1288, the schoolteacher Bonvesino della Riva cited the example of William della Pusterla, a Milanese knight who, although without Latin, was superior to all because of "natural wisdom." "When," Bonvesino reported, "William was *podestà* there among the jurisconsults at Bologna, they, perceiving a man without Latin to be so wise, called him paradigmatically 'the wise layman.' "[69] William, in fact, had busied himself in town government from 1180, and was *podestà* sixteen times in nine cities from 1190 to 1224, including four terms at Bologna. Jurists like Odofredo not only knew of him, but also respected his ability.[70]

Social motives also played a part here: judges and lawyers were often allied to the magnates, from whose ranks indeed many were drawn. Worse, such experts were rightly suspected of obstructing popular lawgivers. Boncompagno of Signa's harangue for a model statute reads: "Because the immensity of jurisprudential learning unsettles not only questionable propositions but also valid cases and reasons of the most manifest solidity, we compose this statute for the common good. To it, we permit no exception or interpretation, insisting that the words of the whole statute are to be taken literally (*ad litteram*) without gloss or modification."[71] Jurists torpedoed this kind of legislation. Alberic of Rosate records that Jacob Butrigarius (d. 1348), a teacher of Bartolo of Sassoferrato, enjoyed rehearsing a story about Bologna's Most Sacred Statute of 1282. Among other things, this renowned monument of popular legislation forbade shedding anyone's blood in the town palace under pain of execution. Should then, Jacob asked, a doctor who there phlebotomized a patient be beheaded?[72]

Although, other than princes and lords, laymen rarely served as judges, they were elected to legislative councils. Methods of election varied widely. Especially oligarchic, at Ghent in the mid-1200s, the outgoing councilors chose their successors, continued to participate in their work for two years after holding office, and were then reelected. In more democratic places, councilors and magistrates were elected by town quarters, gilds, councils, and even sometimes by the people at large. The latter expressed themselves by public acclamation, and hence, except in moments of much passion, their elections were not free. In small or executive bodies, elections and votes were often determined by lot with secret ballot (depositing colored beans, as in Italy). In such bodies, and sometimes even in large ones, such as the three divisions, or "members," of the eighty-six councilors of Ghent after 1360, individuals or specific groups could veto the action of the whole, following the Roman law principle that all, each and everyone, must approve what touches all.[73]

Once elected, councilors legislated in various ways, of which Alberic of Rosate identified three. One of these, by a designated board of experts, has been seen above. Another, equally frequent method was that, after the councilors "who have the administration of the city" have assembled together with the *podestà*, the new law was proposed, debated, and passed [*propositio, consultatio,* and *reformatio*]. Least common was to assemble "the people or the whole body of the city in a public parliament," and there handle the matter.[74] It was commonly esteemed that in sizable communities, the people had best elect a council or commission to legislate and/or review judicial sentences for them. General assemblies were held up to four times yearly, but were really for public education in the law or building solidarity in crises, such as wars. Small in comparison with assemblies of all adult males, working councils were often large by modern standards. Odofredo laughingly remarked that "Rome was ten times larger than Bologna, but only had a hundred senators. Without counting the doctors of law, Bologna's council has two thousand."[75] This jurist was nevertheless not hostile. He claimed to have derived from the famous law *Humanum*, wherein Theodosius II vowed in 446 A.D. to consult the senate, an "argument against those who say that a university cannot consent . . . Although it cannot easily do so, it nevertheless can if all, congregated by trumpet or bell, should cry *fiat! fiat!*"[76]

All citizens not only should be eligible for councils, but should also speak up in them. This theory reflected a measure of reality. Refuting the tag "there are as many opinions as there are persons," Alberic of Rosate favored wide counsel.[77] So did an earlier manual on government called the *Shepherd's Eye*, maintaining that "truth is better discovered from many because there is safety where council is broad [*multa consilia*]." The same tract also observed that, unlike princes, "communities elect many to their councils, perhaps adhering to the rule that what touches all ought be approved by all . . . and that, as Scripture says, omnipotent God sometimes reveals to the humble what he hides from the powerful."[78] The Franciscan Salimbene not only recommended that the Italian system of short-term office be adopted by the religious orders, but also recorded the two mutually contradictory scriptural opinions on counsel: "For if 'the number of fools is infinite,' so also is the 'multitude of the wise the health of the earth.'"[79] Others stressed the danger of giving power to small groups, however experienced or learned. Following Aristotle, Marsiglio of Padua argued that public well-being requires balancing the self-interest of small groups by the whole citizenry's judgment: "for the few will not discern or desire the common good as accurately as would the whole multitude of the citizens."[80]

For the many to participate the poor must be able to serve as magistrates or councilors. Always conservative, Ptolemy of Lucca turned to Aristotle to distinguish between types of poverty. Voluntary poverty is good; poverty derived from want, however, is mere appetite prompting individuals to "fill their bellies and purses." Executive or judicial office should therefore be entrusted to the poor only if their "poverty is placid."[81] Like Dante, Ptolemy dreamt that antiquity's noble Romans had served for pure love of the republic, and looked down his nose at the salaries given Italian professional officers. He also weaseled, however, admitting that, since salary and employment were their objectives, "mercenary" officers were more gentle in their judgments than princes, as was suitable for the naturally free Italians.[82] A similarly moderate position was taken by John of Viterbo (fl. 1240s). This manualist of town government proposed that "it is better to elect a wealthy man, if competent, since a poor one may be easily corrupted." He nevertheless allowed that, if tested, a good person without means was wholly satisfactory.[83]

Such exceptional individuals appeared during the rise of the popular party in the thirteenth century. Salimbene tells of the Guelph leader John Barisello, "a poor man and wise discovered" in Parma, "who liberated the city by his wisdom," defeating the dreaded Ghibellines. A peasant's son and tailor, John was rewarded by his city in ways that sound only too familiar: "he, who had been poor, was made rich, [and was given] a wife of noble birth."[84] One who shared Dante's distaste for popular government, the jurist and poet Cino turned this coin over. At Lucca, he said, he saw a people's captain who sat in the communal palace "selling himself like a whore in her brothel."[85]

Salimbene affirmed that Barisello, the Parmesan leader of the popular party, had "much common sense and a gift for public speaking." The latter gift was rare among the humble because of lack of education, and for a poor man to be praised for it was even rarer. Barisello had luckily ridden a wave of wide popular support strongly propelled by the papacy. In ordinary political life, however, the modest faced their "betters" (read "employers"!) without such reinforcement. Alberic of Rosate asked, for instance, whether a *podestà* could call together both the council of the people's captain and his own larger council, that of the 600, to vote on a major statute. The *podestà's* council, he noted, contained the "most noble and powerful" persons of the town. He then adduced the opinion of the earlier Bolognese jurist Martin Silimani (d. 1306), who had determined that "the *podestà* had done badly because, when the two councils were mixed together, the people's councilors would not dare speak as freely as they would were they alone, and are often drawn to follow in the wake of the opinion of the councilors of the council of the 600."[86]

Because the self-confidence and competence of the rich depends on their capacity to buy time and assistance, a solution was to endow the poor by sharing the wealth. Communist teaching modeled on the famous passage in the Acts of the Apostles mentioned earlier in this chapter was much discussed, and even flourished for a time among the laity because the early stages of the gild movement reinforced the notion of economic brotherhood. Usually, however, only monks in the monastery and friars in the hermitage were thought able to live up to this ideal. The utopian urge was therefore largely removed or withdrawn from the world, being witnessed there only among a few deviants, often heretical.

Found in Roman law and reinforced by Scripture, the notion that natural law did not laud private property was disturbing.[87] If nobody could be dispensed from obeying all-encompassing nature, many worried if all humanity was living in sin. A Bolognese canon lawyer, Simon of Bisignano (d. 1215), comforted the fainthearted by asserting that such an opinion was absurd. "Natural law," he contended, "is expressed in three ways: commands, prohibitions and demonstrations. In the first two it cannot be dispensed from, but in the third it can. Natural law does not command or prohibit the common ownership of property or unimpaired [personal] freedom, but only shows that it would be good if men could be in that state."[88] Better than this covert lamentation that heaven is not for this earth was a positive, if brazen, note sounded by the civilian jurists. Rehearsing other Roman passages, they found that private property guaranteed freedom by limiting princes and government. Although applauding the famous *Lex regia* which says that "what pleases the prince has the force of law," Odofredo trumpeted that "the emperor cannot take *MY* property from *ME*."[89]

A fragment of nature's brotherhood necessarily persisted. Could one say that, asked Alberic of Rosate, "if someone stole bread during a famine," he should always be punished by the harsh statutory penalty? In his *Questions about Statutes*, Guy of Suzzara [fl. 1250–92] said yes! Relying on Roman and canon law and a mendicant theologian, however, Alberic said no! "because in time of need all things are in common."[90] Although, occult or overt, such compensation helps in emergencies, the many cannot participate equally in political life unless wealth is leveled, and hence these republics were, if sometimes moderate, always oligarchies.

Exceptions apart, medieval republics and self-governing towns were not the direct progenitors of Europe's modern governments. The reason for this is obvious: the measure of republican liberty and even democracy attained in medieval communities around 1300 weakened irreparably in the late Middle Ages or Renaissance. Not only were once-independent towns absorbed and their liberties suppressed by renascent monarchies, but also most large urban republics were transmuted into principates. These events seem related to the innate advantages of monarchic government in ages suffering social and economic disruption. Society then calls for a government capable of favoring its own growth by arbitrating and stilling the conflicts of all warring social groups. Opportunist self-interest makes kingship's divine spark manifest: as long as they serve, princes do not much care from whence their servants come. A second advantage of this way of ruling is that, as medieval commentators often perceived, monarchy was better able to harmonize many differing and conflicting regions than were local urban states. It is noticeable, moreover, that, even in divided Italy and Germany, the size of political entities grew steadily as Europe approached modern times. Lastly and most crucially, monarchy rose as the church faded. The people increasingly adhered to majestic royal and princely absolutism in order to plough under the tired mysteries of priests and popes.

Change apart, medieval town liberty left tracks that were followed again in modern times, ones ineradicably imprinted in historical and legal studies and in philosophy. Although grudgingly succumbing to Humanist and scientific attacks, medieval Aristotelian thought and Bolognese jurisprudence were never wholly erased. The path was also partly institutional. If democracy had all but vanished, not a few oligarchic republics persisted. The best example was Venice, although large northern towns like Hamburg were nearly as noteworthy. That these meant much to late medieval or Renaissance thinkers is easy to show. A French gentleman, Commynes, lauded Venice as a model "aristocratic regime," and he was but one among many.[91]

The city was not the only agency transmitting medieval republican traditions or limiting monarchic absolutism. Others were the parliaments in southern Italy and Sicily, Iberia, England, Scandinavia, and Germany's increasingly free provinces, in all of which bourgeois representation was significant although not dominant. Initially almost wholly composed of farmers, the famed Swiss confederation of rural counties and small towns has already been mentioned. Renowned for religious tolerance was the electoral monarchy of Poland and Lithuania, an oligarchy of country squires whose parliaments flourished for over two centuries. And a similar time span was granted to that other oligarchy, the successful wedding of Amsterdam's mercantile urbanism to the small towns and rustic provinces of the Netherlands.

Since humans cannot but believe themselves capable of self-government, antiquity had taught and medieval thinkers had reinforced the notion that the republican form of government is better than monarchy. Although this teaching almost vanished as monarchy became the dominant form of rule in early modern times, its subterranean memory surfaced again when, as the church was overwhelmed by secular philosophy and science in the seventeenth and eighteenth centuries, kings no longer seemed useful. Like those of the church, their pompous rites became silly or inconsequential in the eyes of intellectuals and the people. The revolutions of modern times had therefore prepared the way for the oligarchic republics, sometimes moderate ones, in which most west Europeans and North Americans live today.

Parliaments and Estates

H. G. KOENIGSBERGER

HENCE, TO CONTINUE MY ARGUMENT, is there a king or other lord who has power, outside his domain (private lands), to levy even a penny on his subjects without the grant and consent of those who have to pay it, unless it were by tyranny or violence?[1]

Thus wrote Philippe de Commines (c. 1447–1511), a man who had been an active politician in the service of both the duke of Burgundy and the king of France, and one of the most intelligent observers of his contemporary political scene. Commines did not mention the word freedom; but in fact he had defined it as the Greeks had defined *eleutheria*, the opposite of rule by tyranny or violence. For Commines, the touchstone of this freedom was the need for the ruler to obtain consent to taxation. Such consent Commines and his contemporaries expected to be given by a parliament or assembly of estates. Not that this was the only function of these institutions, nor had they been originally created for this purpose. But, from their origins, representative institutions, whatever their shortcomings and limitations, had been regarded as bulwarks against tyranny of the ruler and as a defense of the subjects' property.

At the end of the fifteenth century, there were representative assemblies everywhere in Catholic Christian Europe, from England to Hungary, from Portugal to Poland, from Sicily to Sweden. They had many names: parliaments and estates, Cortes and Reichstage, diets and sejms. They also had many and varying powers, but these nearly always included the power which Commines had seen as all-important: that of giving consent to taxation by the ruler. They were regarded as representing the community of their country, and their composition varied even more than their names.

What they never were was democratic. The Greek notion of equal citizenship had survived only in some of the city republics of the period, and it was precisely in these that representative assemblies had not developed. This is an important point which I shall come back to, for it throws light on the nature of representation. Medieval society was highly stratified. It was the function and aim of parliaments and estates to represent this society, not to change its basic structure. Medieval and early-modern parliaments were never—and certainly never in the consciousness or intentions of those who served in them—the forerunners of modern parliamentary democracy. That they could become this was the unexpected result of the history of some of them in the sixteenth and seventeenth centuries.

And yet, there was already in the Middle Ages a real connection between parliaments and liberty: there was a need for consent between governors and governed. Basically, this idea was, like democracy, a Greek invention. It was the Greeks who, with their polis (city-state) invented the idea of citizenship, the active participation of the citizen in the making and enforcing of laws, in the taking of decisions about war and peace, and in the defense of the polis. This was done through dialogue, the dual activity of speaking and listening, and through the acceptance of rational conclusions which emerged from this dual activity. It was a dynamic relationship, open-ended and uncertain in its conclusions, and it formed the basis of both the rights and the obligations of the individual citizen. In other words, it was the basis of freedom.[2]

What parliaments and assemblies of estates came to do in the Middle Ages was to adapt the Greek practice of "speaking and listening" in order to arrive at consensual conclusions in a structured society outside cities, or in greater political units which might or might not include cities. This was not a conscious or purposeful adaptation, even though some knowledge of Greek political ideas and practice certainly existed among educated Europeans, especially after the rediscovery of Aristotle's *Politics* in the twelfth century. It was rather the outcome of specific political needs with historically developed and developing social attitudes.

≺ I ≻

The Origins of Representative Assemblies

In the first five or six hundred years after the collapse of the western half of the Roman Empire in the fifth century, Europe was an economically poor and backward continent. The vast majority of its inhabitants lived as peasants, able to produce little more than what was needed for a bare subsistence. What little surplus they managed to produce would be wanted, not in the neighboring village—which was probably producing the same commodities—but in much more distant areas. Medieval trade was therefore small in volume but tended to cover long distances. It needed a group of professional merchants who spoke an internationally comprehensible language, mostly Latin, and who, if possible, could buy, sell, and travel under the protection of a political authority with power over a wide geographical area. Later in this period, protection might also be provided by internationally accepted commercial and legal codes.

What was true of commodities and trade was true of all specialized skills. Cathedral builders, bell founders, forgers of fine weapons, and even the most skillful wielders of these weapons would not be able to make a permanent living in their home districts but needed to travel, often over long distances, to where their services were required at particular times. The same pattern held for the church and its institutions. Learned men—and practically all learned men were churchmen—and skilled church administrators, fluent in Latin, would travel to take up the most attractive jobs and careers all over Christian Europe—just as in our own time scientists and other scholars take up jobs in universities and institutes wherever English is spoken.

This then was the nature of early medieval society: a vast mass of peasant communities, speaking their own languages and clinging tenaciously to their traditional ways of life, and a thin layer of educated and skilled persons who could provide Europe with the commodities and services which it wanted but which could not be provided locally. All this goes a long way to explain the otherwise puzzling phenomenon that, after the fall of the Roman Empire, Europe did not simply dissolve into a mass of small political units. The successor states, on the contrary, were large kingdoms covering varied geographical areas, or even huge empires, like those of the Franks and Danes.

The problem was to control such large kingdoms or empires for longer periods of time. It was at least in part to solve this problem that feudalism developed. Psychologically, feudalism was grounded on the much older idea of the loyalty of a free warrior to his leader.

While in practice often flawed by the even more basic emotions of selfishness, greed, ambition, and fear, the concept of loyalty between lord and vassal, ruler and ruled, remained the most consciously taught manly virtue in the Middle Ages and the psychological cement of medieval society. It was signalled by the vassal through his oath of loyalty or fealty and by the ruler through the bestowal of protection together with a *beneficium*, an honor, an immunity, but most especially a grant of land. The land was called a fief and its holder, the vassal, obliged himself to serve his lord or ruler, especially in war. The great vassals, in their turn, could attach lesser men to themselves with very similar benefits and obligations; or, alternatively, free men would ask for lordship from their most powerful neighbors on similar terms.

This system of political and military organization was admirably flexible and effective. In the ninth, tenth, and eleventh centuries it spread from the Frankish Empire in varying forms to England, Italy, Germany, and the Slavonic kingdoms of eastern-central Europe. Its hold on Scandinavia and Spain was much weaker; and even in central and western Europe there were areas, such as Friesland and some of the Alpine valleys, where it never appeared at all.

From about the year 1000 A.D. onwards Europe became richer, partly at least thanks to the effective services provided by the small international group of experts. There were now sufficient surpluses for European society to afford a growing number of experts with specialized skills. For another two hundred years, at least, the international part of European society continued to expand. This was the period when the church built up its international organization and pushed the claims of its head, the pope, to unprecedented levels. But the expansion also benefited the regions of Europe. Skills now became available regionally; experts could find careers nearer home. This development could be seen in the growth of regional cultures: towns and cities were founded, or refounded on old Roman sites; written literature appeared in English, French, German, Italian, Icelandic; Gothic styles of church building, while still showing some basic similarities, differed much more from region to region than the earlier Romanesque style had done. By the fourteenth century most of the larger countries were founding their own universities.

The history of political organization followed a similar pattern. Feudalism, while a very effective method of political organization when it first appeared, was not a stable system. Fiefs tended to become hereditary and their owners tried to set up as independent rulers. In this they were often helped by their own vassals, who preferred loyalty to their immediate feudal overlord to loyalty to a distant and sometimes ineffectual emperor or king. The history of these developments was uneven in different parts of Europe and over different time periods; but the days of loosely-ruled large kingdoms and empires, built up in the lifetime of a single conqueror, were over. Everywhere new and more efficient regional organizations had to be found to provide the new regional rulers with effective control over the resources of their states; for they had to survive in the fierce military competition with their neighbors and rivals and at the same time provide their subjects, whose greatest fear was anarchy and lawlessness, with more effective administration of justice and internal peace-keeping. Such developments did not so much replace the earlier feudal relationships as supplement and transform them.[3]

These were the historical circumstances in which parliaments had their origins, nor can they be understood apart from these circumstances. Yet there was nothing inevitable about the development of representative institutions.[4] The Islamic world of the early Middle Ages, like Christian Europe a direct successor of the Roman Empire, had, for all the important differences in detail, a similar history: huge empires, the caliphates, were ruled by a small, educated elite speaking an international language, Arabic. From the tenth century the great Abbasid caliphate disintegrated, to be replaced by regionally based states. But none of them developed representative institutions. No more did the Christian Byzantine Empire, nor the new Russian principalities, Christianized and civilized by the Orthodox Church from Byzantium. The origins of parliaments will therefore have to be sought in the quite specific circumstances of Catholic Christian Europe in the later Middle Ages.

The various Germanic peoples who set up the successor states on the ruins of the western half of the Roman Empire had traditions of mass meetings of free men. In Italy in the seventh and eighth centuries the Longobard kings used such meetings, among other things, to publish their royal laws.[5] During the same centuries the Franks had similar meetings which took place regularly. These were always assemblies of free warriors, and their most important, although not their only, business was to give their king advice (con-

silium) and help (*auxilium*) for his military campaigns. These two functions were to remain central to the role of medieval assemblies and parliaments.[6] By themselves, however, they do not explain the appearance of representative institutions. Where political units and the numbers of free warriors remained small, as for instance in some Alpine valleys or on the coast of Iceland, such "direct assemblies," a kind of limited democracy, could persist for centuries, or even into our own times, as effective guardians of the law or even as repositories of sovereignty. They were the nearest any rural part of Europe came to Greek democracy.

But in most of Europe the political units were too large, and their organization was becoming too complex, for such arrangements to survive. A second characteristic of the Germanic assemblies therefore came to predominate. This was the prominence enjoyed from earliest times by great and powerful men, heads of clans, owners of great stretches of land, effective leaders in war. These were the men on whom the king was bound to place most reliance. The development of feudalism institutionalized this practice and, equally, it institutionalized the obligation of the king's chief vassals to give him advice and military help, as well as support on other specific occasions, such as the knighting of his sons or the marriage of his daughters and the providing of their dowries. Thus the German emperors Frederick I and Frederick II, in their great struggles with the papacy in the second half of the twelfth and the first half of the thirteenth centuries, summoned their principal vassals to meetings or diets, in Italy, to obtain their support for their campaigns, but also to impress both their own subjects and their opponents with the might and magnificence of their following.

The vassals, for their part, found that giving advice and help to their feudal overlord was a most useful activity for furthering their own interests. Gradually therefore, the feudal obligation of giving advice came to take on the coloring of a right which the king's magnates would demand.[7] With the realization of the opportunities which assemblies afforded to a king's vassals there also crept in ambivalent feelings between rulers and such assemblies, for the aims of the two sides did not always coincide. Kings naturally wanted the maximum support from their vassals. The vassals might or might not approve of the king's aims and they would certainly want rewards for services which went beyond their purely customary obligations. Above all, they would want to safeguard their rights and privileges and perhaps also extend them. This ambivalence remained a basic fact in the relations between princes and their parliaments, whatever either side might say on specific occasions.

Apart from advice and help there was another reason why kings summoned assemblies, and this was their need for information. How effective was the king's rule on the ground? Were his orders obeyed by his subjects or, indeed, by his own officials? The feudal ruler was held to be the ultimate source of justice and, as such, responsible to God. Were his magnates providing justice for their own vassals who were, after all, also the king's subjects? How effective were the royal courts? A king's subjects could petition him on failures of justice, or on other matters affecting them, and this right was generally recognized and continued to be used throughout the Middle Ages and beyond. Saint Louis (King Louis IX of France, 1226–70) was famous for his readiness to accept petitions:

In summer, after hearing mass, the king often went to the wood of Vincennes (near Paris), where he would sit down with his back against an oak . . . Those who had any suit to present could come to speak to him . . . The king would address them directly and ask: "Is there anyone here who has a case to be settled?" Those who had one would stand up,

and the king would then hand the case to one of his councillors.[8]

Admirable as this practice was, it was also haphazard and it could deal with only a few individual cases of those who happened to live near where the king stayed. Kings therefore traveled, like the Anglo-Saxon king, Edgar (957–75)

who winter and spring went everywhere within the realm . . . diligently seeking out how the rules of the law and the provisions of his decrees were kept by the chief men and whether the poor suffered the oppressions of the mighty.[9]

Alternatively, kings could send out agents to provide them with the required information. William the Conqueror, for instance, did this in 1086 for the famous Domesday Book, the most detailed description of property and property relations in any country during this period. But it was also a highly unpopular exercise, possible only for a very powerful ruler shortly after the conquest of his country. It was never repeated, at least on such a comprehensive scale, although kings would send out agents to investigate specific problems or judges to hold court in different parts of the country. Or again, kings could ask their local officials—in England it would usually be the sheriff (not a policeman, as now in the United States, but the highest royal official in the county)—to send him information obtained from men knowledgeable about the local communities, the villages, the hundreds, or the whole shire (county). In a sense, such men represented their community. This was not a formal or regular representation by elected delegates but a highly flexible and practical arrangement which suited both the king and the local communities.

The concept of actual representation first grew up in Roman and canon law. The jurists developed two important principles—that a community could grant plenary power to a representative who acted on its behalf, and that all those whose interests were involved in a given matter should be consulted before a decision was reached. (The technical language in which these doctrines were expressed, *plena potestas* and *quod omnes tangit*,[10] has been discussed in an earlier chapter.) By the fourteenth century we find these principles in use all over Europe, both by rulers when they request counsel and aid, and by the governed when they have doubts about the policies pursued by their rulers.

But what was a community? In England, a country with a strong monarchy and an advanced judicial administration since Anglo-Saxon times, it was a hierarchy of units, from the village to the hundred, the shire, and the kingdom as a whole. Englishmen were accustomed to assemble regularly in the sessions of the shire court and meet with royal judges. The tone, as also everywhere in Europe, was set by the richer landowners. In towns and cities the feeling of community was obviously strongest within their walls. This was especially so in the twelfth and thirteenth centuries, an age when cities were founded or refounded and expanded rapidly. Many obtained charters from their kings and developed into self-governing corporations. Soon their rulers found it convenient to summon the representatives of these cities together with the great magnates to their feudal assemblies. They could certainly be asked to give help, even if one spurned their counsel. Gradually it was accepted that the principle of "what concerns all" might apply to townspeople as well as to the feudal nobility.

In this respect, the history of Italy is particularly interesting. At a great feudal assembly, or diet, at Roncaglia, in 1158, the emperor Frederick I (Barbarossa) obtained the consent of his feudal magnates to the imposition of *regalia* in the Italian cities of his dominion. *Regalia* were tolls and taxes on specific types of trade, minting, or mining rights, all traditionally regarded as part of a king's prerogative. But the emperor had neglected to get the consent of the cities to these impositions. The cities responded by forming leagues against Frederick and fought him successfully until they obtained virtual independence from his authority. Having effectively become city-states, the cities of Lombardy and Tuscany—characteristically, they were called communes—experimented with various forms of government, much like the Greek city-states, and just like these they felt no need for representative institutions. The essence of a commune was that it could enjoy government by consent through a general assembly of citizens (which, of course, meant males) or through other methods of citizen-participation in government. So powerful did some of these communes become that they conquered neighboring cities and established territorial states like those of the greater princes. Their motivation was also very similar: the desire to expand the territory from which they could levy taxes or obtain soldiers, and the necessity, in a fiercely competitive and militaristic world, to deny such territories and resources to their rivals.[11] Just occasionally, cities such as Siena summoned the nobility and the representatives of subject towns to a *parlementum*. But such assemblies never became regular institutions.[12]

The unwillingness of the Italian city-states to summon representative assemblies from their *contados*, their subject territories, throws an interesting light on the nature of representative institutions as they developed in the later Middle Ages. While the relationship of a commune with the feudal nobility in its *contado* was an essentially feudal one, it did not have to rely for its government on a council of feudal magnates, as kings had to do. There was no point in summoning a nobleman from the *contado* except when his services were required as an individual. More important still was the problem of the subject cities. It could never be in the interests of Florence to summon the representatives of the Tuscan cities together and thus provide them with the opportunity to cooperate against herself. This anti-estate tradition was so strong that it prevented the development of representative assemblies even in those

states which had been transformed from city republics into principalities, as happened to Verona, Milan, and many others.

It is clear, therefore, that neither a feudal relationship nor the
revival of Roman law and the growth of canon law—both particularly evident in Italy—were by themselves sufficient to account for
the appearance of representative institutions. What was so often
lacking was the element which, as we have seen, was inherent in
the very idea of representation: a feeling of community in the whole
of a given political structure. Such a feeling could appear only when
economic, social, and intellectual development had proceeded sufficiently from the early-medieval condition of needing an international elite to survive. Two examples, in very different parts of Europe, will make this clear. What both Sicily and Flanders had in
common, and what makes their history particularly illuminating for
the problem we are considering, was that the feeling of community
in each was only just strong enough to prevent the country from
breaking up into a multiplicity of city-states during a succession
crisis in the ruling princely house.

The kingdom of Sicily, comprising the island itself and mainland
southern Italy, had been established by the Normans in the eleventh
century, and its throne had been inherited by the German Hohenstaufen dynasty. After the fall of the Hohenstaufen the French dynasty of Anjou ruled the kingdom and did so despotically, setting
aside the rights and privileges of nobles and cities. In 1282 the
island-Sicilians overthrew the French ("Sicilian Vespers") and the
kingdom split into two at the Straits of Messina. At first the great
cities of the island were inclined to proclaim their independence,
like the city-states of northern Italy. But a feeling of community had
begun to develop, helped no doubt by the geographical position of
Sicily as an island, and strongly reinforced by the fear of reconquest
by the Angevins, still firmly entrenched in Naples. King Peter of
Aragon claimed the crown of Sicily by inheritance through his wife;
but it was a Parliament which he summoned to Palermo and which,
for the first time in Sicily, included representatives of the cities, that
effectively transferred the crown to him. It seems that this Parliament represented only western Sicily for, a few months later, King
Peter summoned another one, to Catania, on the east coast of the
island. The Sicilians prided themselves on the voluntary transfer-
ence of their crown to the house of Aragon, and Sicilian parliaments

would never allow their Aragonese (and, later, Castilian) kings to forget this fact. King Peter's third Parliament, in Messina, in 1283, voted him a money subsidy for the war against the house of Anjou in Naples. It comes as no surprise that Peter III also found it necessary to summon a Cortes of his own principality of Catalonia, in 1283, to obtain support for his ambitious Sicilian policy. The prelates, the nobles, and the representatives of the towns jointly demanded and obtained the confirmation of their privileges and the king's promise that he would issue no new laws without their consent.

By 1296, when the third Aragonese king, Frederick III, succeeded to the throne of Sicily, the Parliament of that kingdom was firmly established. It insisted on the reissue of the kingdom's privileges and charters—those privileges and charters which the Angevin kings had abrogated or ignored. It obtained a promise that the new king, unlike his predecessor, would live in the kingdom and that he would not make war or conclude peace without the consent of Parliament. The king and his agents would be subject to the laws of the kingdom and Parliament should elect a committee of twelve to supervise the administration of justice.[13]

What had happened was that the leading groups of the whole country had cooperated to install a new ruling house and to confirm their own charters and privileges in the course of a succession crisis and foreign intervention. This was done through a representative assembly, a Parliament. Or, put differently, a prince whose succession was contested, in this case by the former ruling house, had needed to get the cooperation of the most powerful elements of his new country and to get it quickly. What better way than to summon these elements together in a Parliament?

Our second example, the county of Flanders, was one of the successor states of the great Carolingian Empire. The counts, originally Carolingian officials, had made themselves hereditary rulers, virtually independent of their feudal overlord, the king of France. In 1127 the reigning count was assassinated in a conspiracy of some of his nobles. He had no direct heir nor close relatives. There followed a period of confusion, during which members of the nobility and several of the cities formed leagues based on special oaths. In 1128 representatives of the nobility and of the major cities, notably Bruges and Ghent, met on their own initiative, deposed an interim count, and elected Thierry d'Alsace as their new count and made him swear to observe the laws and privileges of the country.[14]

Was this a Parliament or, as has been suggested, a pre-parliament? There is no point in answering this question, for in 1127–28 no one in Flanders was thinking of later developments. It is unlikely, even, that at this early date anyone had the what-concerns-all-maxim in mind. It was rather that the conditions of the crisis imposed it as a practical necessity. A succession crisis was nothing new. What was new was that the cities of Flanders had already at this date grown so much in populousness and wealth that they had to be associated with the process of election, if the election was to stick—a point admitted even by the ultimate suzerain (feudal overlord) of Flanders, the king of France. And, again as in Sicily a hundred and fifty years later, there was already a sufficiently developed feeling of community for barons, clerics, and cities to act together; but, again as in Sicily, only just. For centuries to come, the great Flemish cities, Bruges, Ghent, and Ypres, behaved almost like the independent Italian city-states, imposing their authority on the smaller towns and lordships around them and exploiting them like an Italian *contado*.

For the rest of the twelfth century, however, the cities played no part in the government of Flanders. In 1157 Count Thierry arranged the succession with the sole collaboration of the barons. From the end of the twelfth century and throughout the thirteenth, when the newly revived French monarchy attempted to reintegrate Flanders into the kingdom of France, the counts were driven to seek the support of the cities and to associate them again with their government.[15] Again, just as in Sicily, the history of representative assemblies did not develop in a closed political system but was crucially influenced by the actions of outside powers. This was to be a permanent characteristic of the history of parliaments everywhere in Europe, though the nature, extent, and ultimate importance of such outside influences would vary from case to case.

This holds good also for England, the other great European island with a distinguished parliamentary history. In contrast to Flanders and Sicily, England did not have great corporate cities apart from London; and even London in the twelfth and thirteenth centuries, with the royal fortress of the Tower just outside its city walls, was not as independent of princely power as Palermo and Messina, let alone Bruges and Ghent. But in England, just as on the Continent, the rulers needed the support of the most powerful forces of their country, and especially at moments of political crisis.

The crisis of King John's reign was brewing for some time. The country had had to pay heavily for Richard I's participation in the third crusade and then for the heavy ransom which the emperor Henry VI demanded when Richard became his prisoner on his return from the Holy Land. Richard's successor, King John, continued to make heavy demands on his subjects to pay for his campaigns in France and Wales. Opposition from the barons and the higher clergy grew apace and some of them conspired to murder the king. In August 1212 and again in 1213 John issued general writs to the sheriffs of all English counties to send "six or more lawful and discreet knights" to meet him, probably to inform him about the rumored conspiracy and also "to do what we shall tell them." In return, the king promised concessions to all who owed debts to the Jews.[16] No doubt there had been demands for such a move and, equally without a doubt, John knew the old ploy of gaining credit by being generous with other people's property.

The baronial movement against John, however, continued and was supported by the citizens of London. In 1215 he was forced to sign Magna Carta. This most famous of medieval charters confirmed the nobles' rights and privileges, but also included all free men in the right to trial by their peers according to law. A council of twenty-five barons, together "with the commune of the whole land" was to have the right to enforce the provisions of the charter, even if it meant waging war on the king. John repudiated the charter, but he died in 1216. The civil war which had broken out continued during the regency for the boy-king, Henry III. The rebellious barons obtained help from Prince Louis (later Louis VII) of France who himself had claims to the throne of England. Faced with this formidable alliance and in order to gain adherents, the regency government reissued Magna Carta three times, in 1216, 1217, and 1225, each time with some different details, according to the needs of the current political situation. Copies were always sent to the county courts. In the last issue, what the government wanted was no longer support in the civil war which it had already won; but financial help, a traditional feudal tax of a fifteenth part of the value of all moveable property.

Magna Carta was a feudal document imposed on the king by a

group of magnates who saw themselves as acting for the community of the realm. This was certainly the way in which Magna Carta came to be interpreted. It was reissued by successive kings and, what was more important still, it was successive parliaments which insisted on these reissues. The reputation of parliaments and the reputation of Magna Carta as a safeguard of the basic rights of Englishmen reinforced each other and grew together to form the characteristic symbiosis of the notion of government under the law, the rights and privileges of the ruler's subjects and the representation of the whole community.[17]

It took another half century to establish regularity in the royal summons of Parliament and in the election, or simply appointment by the sheriff, of the knights of the shire in the county courts. Nor was it immediately clear that these knights represented the community of the shire, let alone the community of the whole realm. The king would still summon specific groups of his subjects in separate assemblies, sometimes even the Jewish communities from the towns (1231 and 1241). But more and more often the royal writs spoke of "men to be elected by the whole community of the county." It meant that these men represented the county in Parliament as they traditionally represented it in the county courts.

But it was also becoming evident that both the king and his opponents were using this tradition to drum up support in the country as a whole or rather, just as they were doing on the Continent, from the most powerful men or groups of men in the kingdom. Again it was a political crisis which highlighted many of the issues in men's search to combine ambition with good governance and which drove them to extreme actions. Henry III had gradually made himself more and more unpopular with his autocratic methods of government and his reliance on relatives and advisers from Poitou (southern France) and Savoy. These practices antagonized many of the magnates who, in traditional feudal terms, thought of themselves as the king's natural advisers and, of course, as the principal beneficiaries of his patronage. At the same time the king's government offended the growing feeling of community of the kingdom of England. This was still an ambiguous feeling, far from modern nationalism. Language was one, but not necessarily its most important, unifying element. English (Middle English as against Old English, Anglo-Saxon) was spoken by the common people (although in mutually only barely comprehensible dialects) and was spreading to the educated. But, since the Norman conquest of 1066, the court and the ruling elites spoke French. Official documents were mostly in Latin, which was also the language written by those most vociferous patriots and xenophobes, the monastic chroniclers. Conversely, a common language did not necessarily make for a feeling of community. It did not do this between the English and the Lowland Scots, any more than it did between the Flemings, Brabanters, and Hollanders, or between the Sicilians and the mainland Italians. In Flanders, as in England, the nobility spoke French; but in both cases it was beginning to see itself as part of a community with vertical links to members of other classes.[18]

The ambiguity in the concept of community was demonstrated by the leader of the baronial rebellion against Henry III in 1258. Simon de Montfort was a Frenchman who functioned in England as earl of Leicester. His baronial and knightly supporters formed a league, rather like the Flemish leagues of the previous century. Their communal oath was similar to that taken by the barons of the crusader kingdom of Jerusalem in 1231, which Montfort, a former crusader, was likely to have known.[19] (It is also just possible that there is a link with the Sicilian events of 1282; for in 1231 the emperor Frederick II was king both of Sicily and of Jerusalem and it is not unbelievable that Sicilian baronial families had links and family memories with the events in the crusader kingdom some fifty years earlier.) Henry III was forced by the Provisions of Oxford to send his relatives and officials from Poitou and Savoy out of the country and also to accept elected noble councillors and regular meetings of a "parliament" three times a year. It was to "review the state of the realm and treat of the common business of king and kingdom."[20]

Here was an attempt to create a permanent constitutional machinery to limit the powers of the monarchy, something that Magna Carta had not done. Henry III certainly saw it in this way and so did his fellow monarch, Louis IX of France, to whom both sides had appealed. This time, unlike 1216–17, French intervention helped the royalist side.

Civil war followed. Montfort, for all his constitutional ideas, acted more and more dictatorially, thus losing the support of the community for whom he claimed he was acting. In December 1264 he summoned representatives of the boroughs, as well as the knights of the shires, to a Parliament in January 1265. In the nine-teenth century historians saw this action as the origin of the House of Commons and hailed Simon de Montfort as the founder of the modern English Parliament. In fact, he was rather desperately trying to gain support in a civil war which, in spite of some tactical victo-ries, he was losing. But while Henry III certainly won the civil war, he and his successors also found it convenient to continue to sum-mon representatives of the English boroughs. If one leaves aside motivation and recognizes historical irony, the nineteenth-century historians were not altogether wrong.

But it was only gradually that the knights of the shires and the burgesses came to assemble together regularly as "the commons" in order to represent the community of the "commons" at the king's court, that is, Parliament; for this was what they had done regularly, and continued to do, in the county courts in order to assess and collect taxes, and to deal generally with the business of local gov-ernment and more especially the administration of law and the pres-ervation of the privileges and liberties which had been won since Anglo-Saxon times and which were being extended in the thirteenth century. These liberties and privileges had often been won from a reluctant king or, like Magna Carta itself, by openly fighting him. Parliament, as a representative assembly, did not grow in this way, but rather grew as a means of cooperation between the ruler and the local communities. When the representatives of these communities were assembled together, whatever the original reason for doing this, they gradually came to be seen as representing the community of the realm. Since it was the ruler who needed their help and co-operation they were in a strong position to defend the privileges of the whole community and, if occasion arose, to extend them.

≺ II ≻

Representative Assemblies Become Regular Institutions

From the late thirteenth century on, representative assemblies spread all over Catholic Europe. They appeared in nearly all inde-pendent kingdoms and principalities because in all these the ruler needed counsel and support. The principle of "what touches all must be approved by all" progressed in its triumphal march through

Europe precisely because it put into words a common feeling and defined courses of action which everyone regarded as both reasonable and, with some early romantic idealization, as an ancestral tradition. Its implications for the nature of government and authority had been debated, as Brian Tierney has shown in chapter 3, by theologians and canonists, with both passion and high philosophical arguments, since the eleventh century. The inherent dualism of royal power and representation had therefore become thinkable throughout the European educated elite. There remained the question of counsel and support: by whom and how? and closely related, the further question: who were these "all" who were touched or concerned and what was it they were approving?

Rulers were counselled by their *curia*, their court of magnates, lay and ecclesiastical. From the eleventh to the thirteenth century government became more complex and, consequently, the court became professionalized. Lawyers, administrators, and accountants had to supplement the advice given by the feudal magnates. It was still necessary, however, to have both counsel and support from those who had independent power and could command obedience locally.

These were, in the first place, the great barons. When it gradually dawned on them that, at least in western Europe, they could no longer hope to set up as independent rulers, they came to see that the best opportunities for their personal and family ambitions lay in increasing their influence on the government of their ruler. There were two ways of doing this: the first was by direct personal service to the ruler, in his council or in his army; the second, by using the newfangled institution of representative assemblies to defend and perhaps to increase their rights and privileges. Such action by the barons required cooperation. One could form leagues or brotherhoods, usually short-term associations for some specific tactical purpose, such as the resolution of a disputed royal succession or the winning of an important charter from the ruler; or the cooperation could take the less dramatic, long-term form of intermarriage among the baronial families and the patient construction of family and clientage networks. Thus the great feudal vassals of a king became a nobility, a self-conscious estate, which could speak with one powerful voice in the assembly.

It was a slow process, proceeding at different speeds in different

parts of Europe and leading to different results. Even in France some
of the greatest magnates, if they were also royal princes, could still
become virtually independent rulers. Members of a younger branch
of the ruling house of Valois became dukes of Burgundy in the second half of the fourteenth century and over the next hundred years
acquired a clutch of duchies and counties in the Netherlands. In
Germany the greatest barons, even when not royal princes, became
independent rulers of their duchies and principalities when imperial
power collapsed in the thirteenth century. But it took a long time
before the legal status of even the greatest of these princes, joined
by several bishops and archbishops, was fully established. From the
middle of the fourteenth century seven of these princes were recognized as the sole electors of the king (who received his imperial title
from the pope). While they were a most exclusive group, a college
as it was called, they did not evolve into an estate. Indeed, each one
of them called himself an estate of the Holy Roman Empire, and this
appellation was used also for all those other German princes who
could claim that they had no feudal superior apart from the emperor.
The semantic confusion of this appellation mirrored the legal and
power-political confusion in the later Middle Ages.

It was in the great principalities, such as the Austrian duchies,
Bavaria or Saxony, that the nobility formed itself into estates, with
sufficient feelings of community to act together in representative
assemblies which, from the fourteenth century, were appearing in
these principalities.[21] Yet here, too, there were complications which
distinguished the estates of the German nobility from estates of the
nobility in southern and western Europe. The most important was
that in Württemberg and in several ecclesiastical principalities, the
lower nobility opted out of allegiance to their prince, maintaining
only their allegiance to the emperor as "imperial knights." In the
assemblies of these principalities there was therefore never an estate
of the nobility. In Württemberg, a country without great monasteries and therefore without an estate of prelates, the result was a representative assembly confined to one socially homogenous estate of
patricians and local officials, the *Ehrbarkeit*. It proved to be one of
the most effective and long-lived of German parliaments.

The development of the estate of the clergy proceeded along lines
similar to those of the nobility and with similar variations from
country to country. All rulers needed the services of ecclesiastics in

their councils; they also needed bishops in their dioceses, both as controllers of the parish clergy and, together with the heads of monastic houses, as great landowners who were personally and financially the equals of the high nobility from whose ranks they had frequently been chosen. Ecclesiastics developed a feeling of community of a separate estate and this development was helped by their dual allegiance to the king and to the papacy. In representative assemblies they could be overwhelmingly important, as they were in Bavaria where, collectively, they owned nearly half the land of the duchy; or they could virtually disappear from the assemblies, as they did in neighboring Württemberg and in Holland and Flanders, where there were no cathedral chapters, few rich monasteries. Except in Sweden, the humble parish clergy were rarely represented at all or only indirectly, through their bishops.

Rulers had for a long time employed commoners in their councils. But the "commons" as the "third estate" developed in most of Europe with the growth of corporate towns. For this estate, too, as we have seen in the histories of Sicily and Flanders, it was necessary for a feeling of community to develop between the ruling groups of the cities, as well as, vertically, between the different social strata of prelates, nobles, and commoners. In most countries' parliaments the third estate came to be limited to representatives of several quite specific cities. These cities were originally chosen by the ruler and were usually the richest and most populous cities, although, as the examples of Flanders and Sicily show, the great cities could also take matters into their own hands. But, once admitted to the assemblies, it proved difficult to change the pattern, even when some declined in population and wealth and others rose. Where cities became completely independent, as in Lombardy and Tuscany, or virtually so, as in Germany, they did not develop into an estate at all or, again as in Germany, only very tentatively and late.

In any case, there were wide variations. In England where the cities outside London had remained small, the earlier medieval shire organization prevailed. Here "the commons" came to be a mixture of landed gentry (roughly the equivalent of the continental lower nobility) and the burgesses, the representatives of those boroughs which were summoned to Parliament and of which there was a far greater number than in any continental kingdom except France. In England this left a numerically quite small titled nobility who joined with the bishops to form the "upper house" of Parliament, the House of Lords. The English clergy met as an estate in a separate assembly, convocation. They were anxious to keep this privilege of separateness intact, only to find that, in the long run, they had sidelined themselves from the real centers of power, the monarchy and Parliament.[22]

Historians have often made rather too much of these differences between England and the Continent. It is better to see them simply as among the many variations in the development of representative institutions in medieval Europe. Something very similar to the development of the English commons happened in Flanders with the Franc of Bruges, a fourth "member" of the Third Estate—the other three were Bruges, Ghent, and Ypres—created specifically as a counterbalance to the three great cities by the count and comprising representatives of the lower nobility and castellanies. In some parts of France, especially in the south, and in some parts of southern Germany, even village communities came to send representatives to local assemblies. While they did not become a separate estate, some village communities developed corporate institutions and considerable degrees of self-government in the control of local courts, the need to assess and collect the ruler's taxes, and the need to protect themselves by collective action against neighboring robber barons.[23]

For all their variations in structure and self-perception, all representative assemblies began in some ways as extensions of the ruler's council, and their early history shows them as having retained many of the characteristics of the princely *curia*. Once institutionalized, their duty of giving counsel came to be seen as a right. This was a gradual process, and there were great variations in the rights which the assemblies claimed. But the process was an all-European phenomenon, and in the later Middle Ages it had its parallels in the general councils of the church. It involved having access to the ruler and his principal ministers, perhaps also some influence over decision-making—that was, after all, what counsel was about—and certainly the opportunity to present petitions, urge him to remedy abuses and to respect and reaffirm previously granted freedoms and privileges and, if the opportunity arose, to extend them.

It was in the nature of such relationships that they should become linked with the ruler's other great need and the subjects' and vassals' other great duty, that of *auxilium*, giving support. Originally, this support had been mainly military, and the military aspect of *auxilium* remained paramount throughout the Middle Ages. But quite early it had become clear that vassals were not always able to follow their overlord into battle. They might be too old or too young or sick, or they might be women or ecclesiastics. They could provide substitutes; but soon it became more convenient for all concerned to provide money. Kings needed to hire professional soldiers or they had to pay their feudal vassals for service in campaigns which lasted longer or were conducted outside the boundaries of the vassals' traditional obligations. From the twelfth to the fourteenth centuries the western European monarchies engaged in increasingly elaborate and increasingly expensive programs of castle building; and rulers with sea coasts or overseas dominions, such as the kings of England or of Aragon, needed navies.

All this required much more money than rulers could raise from their domain lands or from their *regalia*. In 1308 Philip IV of France demanded from his subjects an "aide pour fille marier," a feudal payment in money, really a tax, for the marriage of his daughter Isabelle, to Edward II of England. Philip sent his agents into the provinces to collect this payment and, not unnaturally, they met with great reluctance.[24] In the provinces of Saintonge, Périgord, and Quercy, southern-central France, the ecclesiastics, the nobles, and the towns decided to send representatives to Paris. When they arrived, they found representatives of the Normans already there, about the same business. Negotiations, both about the *aide* itself and about the powers of the proctors to take decisions which would bind their principals, continued until the spring of 1310.[25] In this case the initiative for these meetings had come from the king's subjects and he had to accept it—a very different situation from the famous occasion of 1302 when Philip IV had summoned representatives from his whole kingdom to associate it with his quarrel with Pope Boniface VIII.[26] This assembly used to be hailed as the first Estates General of France; but it was really little more than a grand assembly in which the king proclaimed his policy.[27]

When the kings of England wanted to tax the export of wool, the most valuable commercial activity in their country, as a regalian right, they found it most convenient to make a voluntary agreement with the wool merchants. From 1294 onwards assemblies of merchants granted the king *maltolts*, taxes on the export of wool, for limited periods of time. Characteristically, this tax took the form of a bargain. The king's part was that the merchants received the right to form a monopoly cartel. They claimed that the tax fell on the foreign consumer. In fact, it soon became clear that the tax fell mostly on the English sheep farmers in the form of lower prices for their wool. Not unnaturally, Parliament, representing mainly the landowners, many of whom were sheepfarmers, objected to this tax. But more important than economic grievances was the fact that the *maltolt* was really a public tax, paid by an influential section of the community. Parliament therefore claimed that it should be levied only with its consent. In 1351 the House of Commons asked the king to abolish the grants of the merchants, but "in case it pleased the king in this his great necessity (the war with France) to have the forty shilling subsidy (that is, the *maltolt* on each sack of wool) for half a year or a year, let him show his wishes to the lords and commons."

By the middle of the fourteenth century the kings of western and southern Europe were regularly asking their parliaments to grant taxes. This practice was justified by the feudal obligation of *auxilium*, now more and more converted into money payments, and also by Roman and canon law principles that subjects had to support their rulers in cases of "necessity." In this way the individual feudal obligation of the vassal was generalized to apply to the whole community. And this community had, more and more frequently, come to be "represented" by parliaments. A treatise of 1321 on the functions of the English Parliament, the *Modus Tenendi Parliamentum* (the way to run a Parliament), stated that its business was, first, war and the king; second, the concerns of the realm such as judicial matters and legislation; and third, the business of private members.[28]

It was not held to be the business of parliaments to deny the king's requests, and outright refusals of granting financial aid were rare, anywhere in Europe. But parliaments could and did require the king to explain and justify necessity. Normally this meant the defense of the realm. But what was defense? Was it still a "necessity" when there was a truce with the enemy? And did the king have the right to go on collecting the taxes which had been granted for the actual fighting or to make preparations for the future resumption of the war? In England Edward III managed to persuade Parliament on several occasions that the French were planning to restart the war and therefore to continue the taxes they had granted.[29]

In France it proved more difficult. By the fourteenth century France had a large number of representative assemblies in a rich and bewildering variety of shapes and forms, depending both on the political history of the different parts of France and on the local social structures. There were assemblies for the bailiwicks (*bailliages*), seneschalcies (*sénéchaussées*)—very roughly like English counties— and whole provinces—much larger than any English units of administration. They represented geographical-social units, each with their own feelings of community. A sense of community for the whole kingdom of France was certainly gradually developing, but local patriotism and local interests often overrode it. Loyalty to the king was still largely feudal. His wars in distant parts of the kingdom often did not seem to present the necessity which required aid, might indeed drain away resources that might soon be needed to defend one's own region; for the war record of the French monarchy during much of the fourteenth century did not inspire much confidence in a central direction of a war. At the very least, one felt justified in refusing aid when there was no actual fighting.

By contrast, England had been unified much earlier than France and since the twelfth century had enjoyed a common law. When Edward I's wars in Scotland, at the end of the thirteenth century, resulted in a permanent French-Scottish alliance, it became obvious to Englishmen in both the north and the south of the country that the king's wars concerned everyone. Or rather, they were approved of by most of the English nobility who found fighting in France congenial and profitable, provided, of course, the fighting went well. Edward II's military failure in Scotland cost him his throne and his life. But the war in France, up to the treaty of Brétigny in 1360, did go remarkably well, on the whole. And it was the militarist nobility who enjoyed this war who set the tone in Parliament. Cooperation between king and Parliament on a national level was, in consequence, working well.

It was not as if the French failed to see this point. In 1339, for instance, Philip VI's advisers produced a memorandum on the relative merits of a central assembly, regional assemblies, and negotiations with smaller local assemblies. They thought the latter were the least desirable, as being too time-consuming, expensive, and likely to lead to too many, and to too many different, concessions to powerful local persons, groups, or corporations. In an Estates General, a national assembly, in 1343, a time of truce but with renewed war looming, the king promised to redress grievances, especially about the debasement of the coinage; in return he received at least the tacit backing of the kingdom for a sales tax and a *gabelle*, a tax on salt, which the Crown had previously imposed without asking for consent.

In 1346 the English war resumed and the French suffered disastrous reverses in the battle of Crécy and in the loss of Calais. The initiative for a new Estates General now came from the king's subjects. They demanded a reform of the personnel of the king's court and, again, a reform of the coinage. In return, they promised a huge contribution to the war effort of apparently nearly three million pounds *tournois*. It was to be raised by a sales tax, or in ways to be determined by the local bailiwick assemblies, and it was to be collected by *élus*, tax collectors chosen by the local estates. It looked as if cooperation between monarchy and a representative assembly was working as well in France as it was in England. At this point the unexpected happened. The Black Death, the epidemic of bubonic plague, hit western Europe and very little of the agreed tax could be collected.[30]

After King John II's crushing defeat and capture in the battle of Poitiers (1356), the Estates General voted the necessary taxes for the war and for the payment of the king's huge ransom. They also attempted to reform the central government; but these attempts foundered in faction fights to a background of peasant revolts. The new king, Charles V, saw little point in working through general assemblies. Taxes were now well established, the *élus* came to be appointed by the Crown, and gradually an extensive organization or, rather, a number of organizations of royal financial officials was spread over France. As tax collecting organizations they were complex and not particularly efficient; but they enabled the Crown to raise a number of important taxes at will and without having to ask the consent of representative assemblies. It has sometimes been argued that the French financial officials were paid and could therefore be controlled by the Crown, whereas the English sheriffs and, later, the justices of the peace were unpaid and were therefore more independent of the Crown. In fact, the French monarchy could not easily dismiss its officials, for the practice of selling public offices as private property became more and more common. Wholesale dismissal of recalcitrant officials could therefore have been done only at ruinous expense. It was rather that the French *baillis* and seneschals enjoyed a higher social status, with important judicial rights, than the English sheriffs and were therefore less dependent on local good will.[31]

The Hundred Years' War between England and France set the history of their monarchies and assemblies onto divergent courses. The early political unification of England and the very strength of its monarchy made for cooperation between Crown and Parliament in a prolonged war. Since this war was being fought overseas, and was therefore not causing deep geographical and social divisions, it led to a further strengthening of the feeling of community in England and hence of the body which, together with the monarchy, came more and more to represent this feeling: Parliament. Politically and constitutionally, it was the community feeling of the privileged and propertied sections of society, exemplified, for instance, in their easy cooperation in the enactment of the Statute of Labourers in Parliament, in 1351, which was designed to keep down the wages of a labor force depleted by the Black Death. There was a similar easy cooperation during the Peasant Revolt of 1381, the popular rebellions against a new poll tax.

By contrast, France was much less unified than England. The English invasions, the shifting loyalties of cities and magnates, the rivalries between different branches of the ruling house, all against the background of much more frequent and terrifying peasant revolts than in England—these were not conditions which made for a growth of effective community feeling. In the long run, the French monarchy, for all its weaknesses, appeared to be the only force capable of rescuing the country from invasion and of restoring order. To this end, Frenchmen were willing to allow their monarchy to impose certain taxes: a sales tax (*aide*), a hearth tax (*fouage* or *taille*), and a tax on salt (*gabelle*). These taxes were the more acceptable to the privileged classes as they became exempt from the *taille*. The king could also issue ordinances, that is legislate without asking for the consent of those who would be affected. In England, too, the king could legislate by ordinance; but precisely because laws and ordinances were more likely to be obeyed if issued with the consent of the community, it gradually became the custom for the kings of England to legislate through Parliament, although without giving up non-parliamentary legislation altogether. In France royal legislation was restricted by existing law and was subject to approval by the *parlement* of Paris, a court which still had some of the characteristics of a representative assembly. At the same time, the monarchy continued to summon the local and provincial estates, to obtain consent for taxation, and to deal with local and private grievances. It managed these assemblies not by confrontation but by bribery, by sharing the proceeds of the taxes voted by these assemblies with the local nobility.

All over Europe it was the crystallization of powerful social groups into estates or other self-conscious units which came to determine the form of representative assemblies, and it was the rulers' need for consent to taxation which was the most important element in shaping the relations between rulers and parliaments. As a result, representative assemblies, parliaments, became regular institutions; and like all regular institutions, they began to develop a life and an ethos of their own. In many continental countries the grant of a tax became a kind of contract between ruler and Parliament, a contract in which both sides were bound by quite specific obligations: providing money, on the part of Parliament, and the redress of particular grievances or the grant of certain rights or privileges, on the part of the ruler. Powerful rulers could afford to have powerful parliaments and use them for their own purposes. Where royal power was weak or fragmented, as in fourteenth-century France and in fourteenth-century Sicily, parliaments were likely to be weak, too. It was not until the fifteenth and sixteenth centuries that they were sufficiently developed as institutions to provide an alternative unifying force for a whole country.[32]

Yet even in the fourteenth century this was attempted, with at least temporary success, in the economically and socially highly developed duchy of Brabant. The occasion was a series of succession crises, the classic point of weakness in all medieval and early modern monarchies. A statistical study for the sixteenth century has shown that, at the death of a ruler, there would be at least a 50 percent chance of a disputed succession, with the immediate likelihood of foreign intervention; or of succession by a woman or a child, with a strong chance of civil strife for the control of the regency.[33] The chance of a ruler's early death from disease and a problematic succession was certainly not less in the fourteenth century. In Brabant succession crises occurred in 1248, 1261, 1312, 1356, 1406, 1415, and 1430. Just as in neighboring Flanders in the twelfth century, the cities felt it necessary to intervene in these crises and large sections of the nobility followed their lead. Many nobles had intermarried with the rich patrician families of the cities or they had become "foreign citizens" of the cities in order to enjoy their privileges and perhaps have careers in the town councils. In the crisis of 1312 the estates forced the duke to grant them the Charter of Kortenberg. They won another charter in 1314 and then in 1356 a comprehensive one, the *joyeuse entrée*, the oath which every duke had to take on his first "joyous entry" of the duchy on his accession. The charters stipulated that all public offices were to be reserved for natives, that no Brabanter was to be judged by a court outside the duchy, and that the duke must obtain consent for all taxation, for the striking or devaluing of the coinage, and for the waging of war.[34]

Magna Carta had been imposed on a king by a group of feudal magnates and only later came to be identified with the primary concerns of Parliament. The *joyeuse entrée* of Brabant was imposed on their rulers by the estates, with the towns in the forefront, and it was concerned with both individual liberties and the actual government of the state.[35] During successive regencies the estates imposed their own nominees on the councils of regency, significantly with as many members from the towns as from the nobility, and they set up councils to control the taxes they had voted. In 1415 they actually created a council of regency which was directly responsible to the estates. The duke tried to repudiate these arrangements, but after several further confrontations, in 1420 and 1421, he had to acknowledge the principle that the estates could refuse him obedience and elect a regent in his place if he infringed their rights and privileges. The Burgundian duke, Philip the Good (1430–67), reestablished ducal control over the government of the duchy. But the attempt by the estates to control the actual government of their country had contributed to a slowly developing myth of the estates of Brabant and of the States General of the Netherlands. The *joyeuse entrée* became a battle cry in the constitutional conflicts of the later fifteenth and of the sixteenth century.[36]

≺ III ≻

The Fifteenth Century

In most of central, eastern, and northern Europe it was only in the course of the fifteenth century that assemblies of estates began to be summoned as regular institutions. In Germany, much of which was economically not very far behind western Europe, the reason was the weakness of the central monarchy and the splintering of political authority into local units. Most of the larger towns became virtually independent, as they did in Italy, and the estates of the separate German principalities therefore lacked the initiative and drive which the cities of Flanders and Brabant gave to their estates. Characteristically, it was in the kingdom of Bohemia, part of the Holy Roman Empire, where the cities did not become independent, that the estates developed earlier than in most of the German principalities.[37]

The German princes summoned their estates for the classic reasons: their need for money because of the heavy debts they incurred in their frequent wars with each other and, closely connected with this problem, the frequent crises of princely succession. These were even more intractable in Germany than elsewhere in Europe because of the German tradition of dividing the principality between brothers, who would then fight each other. The estates were therefore frequently concerned with damage limitation: trying to separate princes' private property from public finances. In the process they often took over the administration of the taxes they had voted; imposed conditions on the princes' freedom of action, especially the waging of wars; and sometimes insisted on nominating the members of their councils and on the unity of the principality. For this purpose they also sometimes met as assemblies of the whole principality when it had been divided among two or more branches of the princely family.[38]

Unlike Germany, the kingdom of Poland did not disintegrate in the later Middle Ages. In this vast and sparsely populated country the towns had remained small and a large part of their populations consisted of German immigrants or their descendants. They took little part in politics. Only in western Prussia ("Royal Prussia"), acquired by the Polish Crown in 1466, did the towns, and especially the patricians of Danzig (Gdansk), dominate the estates. They met regularly, often several times a year, for the usual purposes of taxation and the defense of their privileges. Their feeling of community was a regional, German-speaking feeling, entirely at ease with its Polish king, provided he respected the local privileges and traditions.[39] In the rest of Poland only the nobility attended the assemblies (sejm) and it was only at the turn of the fifteenth century that they became definitely organized in two chambers, of the magnates and the lower nobility (szlachta).

In Sweden the institutional development of representative institutions was even slower. Sweden was throughout most of the Middle Ages still at the stage of development at which western Europe had been before the eleventh century: small isolated settlements of peasants or miners, often with huge empty spaces between them. There was a not very numerous landed nobility, and a latinized church provided what written culture there was. Foreign trade was in the hands of Germans settled in towns which were even smaller than those of Poland. Local government was carried on by small local assemblies, usually dominated by the richer landowners. The king was advised by his council of magnates and churchmen but would summon different groups of the population, burghers and free peasants, to get support for his policies or help against rival claimants to the throne. He was not above using annual fairs for such political purposes. A feeling of community of the whole kingdom was slow in growing. Even for the nobility and clergy the identity of Sweden was not clearly defined beyond the person of the king; and throughout the fifteenth century the Crown was united to the culturally and linguistically closely related kingdoms of Denmark and Norway (Union of Kalmar, 1397–1523). It was only among some members of the nobility, supported by miners and peasants in some central regions of the country, that a feeling of Swedish nationality grew sufficiently strong for Gustavus Vasa, the leader of the anti-Danish nobility, to be able to summon a national Parliament, a riksdag, at Västerås in 1527 and to have himself proclaimed king.[40]

Representative institutions had appeared in the later Middle Ages mainly in medium-sized and smaller states, especially the dukedoms and counties into which the great successor states of the Roman and Carolingian empires had splintered. In the fifteenth century two further developments took place or became common. The

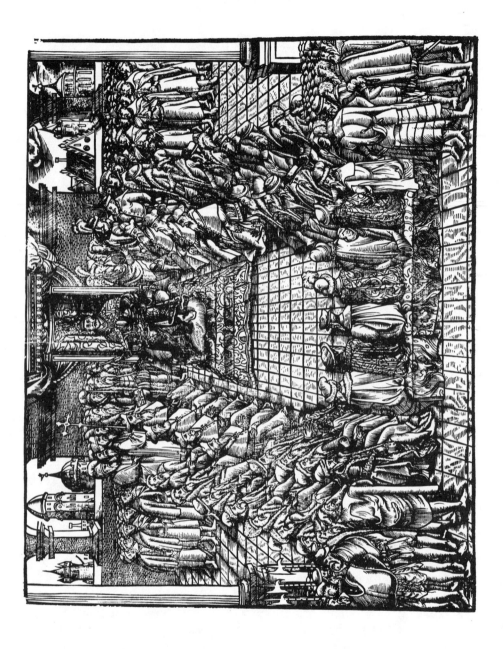

first was an increasing number of confrontations between rulers and their parliaments; the second was the appearance of composite monarchies.

Parliaments had originated in rulers' need for support and thus they had often developed as extensions of the prince's council. Their value to the prince depended precisely on the fact that they commanded a degree of independent authority within the country. They could expect obedience and support in their own right. The form this took would vary a great deal. Bishops could most obviously expect it from their clergy; feudal lords, from their vassals and tenants—as indeed could bishops and abbots, since the institutions they headed were also great landowners. Further, through family alliances and patronage, the local authority of magnates could encompass half a province or parts of several provinces.

As corporations with considerable, if varying, judicial independence, cities and towns also commanded authority and obedience. Even where there were no fully formed corporations, village communities were often developing considerable degrees of self-government. Even the most powerful and self-confident governments had to rely on the village communities to assess the incidence of the taxes they had imposed or agreed to with their parliaments. In England the urban corporations were weak, compared with many of their continental counterparts, and many local government functions were performed in the county and hundred courts. There was, however, no basic difference in the principle of representation: what was represented was the local communities, however they were structured.

Since the end of the thirteenth century the English Crown had insisted that the members of Parliament should have *plena potestas*, full powers to take decisions and to bind their constituencies to these decisions. On the Continent the town councils usually insisted on an "imperative mandate," a strict limitation of the powers of their representatives; sometimes the councils insisted that the deputies refer back to their constituencies.[41] This difference, however, was not as clear-cut as it appears; for in England, too, members

---

Opposite: Sigismund II Augustus of Poland (1548–72) and the sejm. Engraving. From A. Guagninus, Sarmatiae Europae Descriptio, Spira 1581. By permission of Count Adam Zamoyski.

of the House of Commons could not simply take arbitrary decisions but had to take account of the interests and views of their local communities.[42]

The result of this pattern was an underlying tension between rulers and their parliaments; for in the long run their interests could not always be identical nor reconcilable. It is perhaps best to visualize this with a geological metaphor. People or states lived on a fault line; they might do so peacefully for several generations, but internal tensions would rise and, sooner or later, they would have to be resolved. This could happen through a long series of rumbles and minor adjustments, or through a sudden and violent earthquake. In either case the outcome would depend on the interplay of the forces involved, and these were neither uniform nor fully predictable.

Most frequently it was the perceptions and actions of the rulers, rather than the ruled, which led to increasing tension. For had the ruler not sworn to observe his subjects' rights and privileges and did these not often curtail his authority? There were always lawyers at hand who told the ruler, more and more persistently, that he was above the law—in Roman law the term was *legibus solutus*—or, at the very least, that he was allowed to legislate. Men, even when they are quite willing to cooperate, do not gladly give up authority which they have enjoyed and which they feel they are entitled to. The dukes of Brabant often resented the *joyeuse entrée*, and the Brabanters, having forced its conditions on their dukes, were unwilling to give up what they had gained. The kings of France would not accept the authority which the Estates General had arrogated to itself when, at least according to its own claims, it had saved the kingdom from falling apart when its king had been taken prisoner in the battle of Poitiers. Ferdinand of Aragon and Isabella of Castile had to fight a civil war to secure Isabella's succession to the Castilian throne. Her succession was confirmed by the Cortes, the Castilian Parliament; but, having achieved this confirmation, Isabella did not summon another Cortes for eighteen years. Henry VII of England won his throne by rebellion and civil war against the reigning king, Richard III, and had his crown confirmed by Parliament. After that he summoned Parliament only rarely and between 1497 and 1504 not at all.[43] This contrasted with fifty meetings of Parliament between 1377 and 1422.[44]

Louis XI of France went so far as to propose a specifically antiparliamentary alliance to the dukes of Milan and Piedmont-Savoy in order to break the considerable power of the latter prince's parliaments. In 1471 the French ambassador to Savoy informed his Milanese colleague that

His Majesty, the king of France, has given him to understand that . . . they should wait until they had all their troops together in order to reduce this state of Savoy to the condition and form of that of France and that of His Serene Highness (the duke of Milan). The duke and duchess of Savoy—(the duchess was Louis's sister)—should then be able to manage their subjects, (and) keep them on a rather tighter rein . . . For, since His Majesty, His Excellency and the House of Savoy are at present united and allied, this would greatly enhance the security and stability of the state of each one of them, for they could help each other with their troops.[45]

The rulers of Savoy and Milan politely declined this ride on the tiger of the mighty French monarchy. But Louis XI had spelled out the uncomfortable fact that relations between a prince and his Parliament were unlikely to remain matters of purely internal concern and that the use of force in this relationship was not ruled out.

For the historian this means that an analysis of the internal forces alone will not provide a sufficiently accurate model for any prediction or retrodiction of the eventual results of the tensions or the earthquakes in the relations between rulers and their parliaments.

The second important development of the fifteenth century was that of the spread of composite monarchies. In the composite monarchies the constituent parts always antedated the union as developed political and institutional entities. Sometimes the unions were the result of conquest, but most unions were voluntary. A country might choose a foreign prince, as the Sicilians did in 1282; or agree to have a single king, as Denmark, Norway, and Sweden did in the Union of Kalmar. Most commonly, however, two or more countries were joined by marriage or inheritance. In all these cases the prince swore in his coronation oath to uphold the existing laws, customs, and privileges of his newly acquired state. And this state would almost always already have a Parliament, a representative assembly of one form or another, with a living tradition of defending these laws, customs, and privileges.

Provided these ground rules were observed, this system worked remarkably well. A prince could add province after province, kingdom after kingdom to his realm and rule each as its own prince, under different laws and with varying powers. Prerogatives which he had in one dominion he did not necessarily have in another, and the same was true for his subjects' rights.

Nevertheless, this was not the whole story. The ruler of a composite monarchy, by virtue of his very position, was bound to pursue political aims which could not be harmonized with the interests of his subjects in each one of the constituent parts of his monarchy as conveniently as they could be when he was the ruler over only one country with only one representative assembly to bother about. An immediate point of friction was often the prince's reliance on advisers from his original state whom he would wish to employ in his newly acquired or more outlying dominions. He would be inclined to favor his old friends and original compatriots when he dispensed patronage; and even if he was not so inclined, he would find it difficult to persuade his subjects of this fact. His different dominions would try to defend themselves with the privilege of the *ius indigenatus* by which they reserved public offices and ecclesiastical benefices to natives of their province. They were not always successful and quarrels over this point were common, although by themselves not usually serious enough to lead to major political crises.

A more serious problem was to get the support of all his dominions for particular policies. The most logical way to achieve it was by summoning a States General, a composite representative assembly, representing all his dominions or, at least, their separate assemblies. The grandest and most ambitious attempt to do this was the summoning of the general councils of the whole Catholic church in the first half of the fifteenth century; for, as a political structure, the church was the biggest of all composite monarchies. The councils of the fifteenth century are discussed in chapter 3. Here it is only necessary to point to two characteristic features of their histories. The first was that the councils tried to limit the absolute power of the head of the church and subject it to the will of the council. The second was that the interests of the delegations from the four corners of Europe were too diverse and contradictory to make possible a consistent common front against the papal monarchy. By skillfully playing on these divisions the popes were able to defeat the conciliarists.

These two features of the history of the general church councils appeared, in varying degrees, also in the history of the secular states generals. In contrast with the general church councils, it was very rare that states generals included delegates from an overseas dominion. The kings of Aragon occasionally summoned a combined Cortes of their three Iberian states, Aragon, Catalonia and Valencia; but they did not attempt to combine them with the Parliament of Sicily. The nearest secular analogies to the general councils of the church appeared in the two largest composite monarchies of Europe whose component parts were contiguous, France and Germany.

In France the monarchy's unhappy experiences with its Estates General inclined it to do without this institution unless it could absolutely not be helped. The elaborate financial administration which had been built up and the pause in the war with England until the Agincourt campaign of 1415 made it easier for the monarchy to dispense with formal consent to taxation. Characteristically, it was a question of the succession to the throne which brought the Estates General back on to the scene. In the treaty of Troyes (1420) Henry V of England was recognized as heir to his father-in-law, Charles VI of France. Both parties to the treaty felt it necessary that the estates of both kingdoms should swear to uphold this extraordinary agreement, and Henry specifically promised to respect the rights and privileges of "all peers, nobles, cities, towns, communities and individuals" in France.[46] Henry V and, after his early death, the regents for the infant Henry VI regularly summoned the estates of Normandy and Guyenne. They provided the English kings with considerable support during the continuing war. Until it was finally driven from France in 1453, the English monarchy was therefore effectively ruling over a composite state.

These circumstances also forced the dauphin (later Charles VII) to summon, in his turn, both the provincial estates of those provinces of France which were not occupied by the English and the Estates Generals of Languedoil (roughly the provinces north of the river Loire) and of Languedoc. When the English were in retreat, after 1436, Charles VII simply ceased to summon the Estates Generals. There was little demand for them from the country. The support of the estates of Normandy and Guyenne for the king of England demonstrated how weak French national feeling was as yet and how far the kingdom of France was still a composite monarchy. Since the turn of the fourteenth century the monarchy had regularly bribed the nobility, the corporate towns, and its own officials with a part of the taxes which it levied without the consent of the estates. These taxes therefore came to fall more and more on those who had no political organization and no political clout. The privileged and now increasingly tax-exempt classes could defend their privileges more conveniently in their local and provincial assemblies than in the Estates Generals.[47]

In the second half of the fifteenth century the central government summoned an Estates General only once more. In 1483 Louis XI was succeeded by his minor son, Charles VIII. A regency council was headed by his sister and her husband, and they needed wider support. There were many who wanted to use this opportunity to limit the authority of the monarchy. But, just as in the general councils of the church, it proved impossible to reconcile regional and class differences in this very large and only recently united, really still composite kingdom. The regent successfully played the different parties against each other. In the end, the French monarchy emerged with undiminished authority and did not feel the need to summon the Estates General for another seventy years.

The case of Germany was different. Here was a large kingdom which had become a kind of composite monarchy in the thirteenth century, not by the accumulation of states and provinces under the Crown but by the catastrophic weakening of the monarchy during its century-long struggle with the papacy for the control of Italy. It was essentially a feudal situation. The great lay and ecclesiastical vassals still acknowledged the overlordship of the king (the Holy Roman Emperor) but left him with the barest minimum of effective authority. From time to time he would summon his immediate vassals to diets (*Reichstage*) but these were feudal, rather than representative, assemblies. As in western Europe, but here as late as the fifteenth century, cities and smaller princes formed leagues for mutual protection and the preservation of peace. Throughout the fifteenth century people talked about a constitutional reform. In 1495, at the diet of Worms, the princes, led by the archbishop-prince elector of Mainz, Berthold von Henneberg, granted the emperor Maximilian I an annual tax on all imperial subjects for four years. In return, he had to agree to annual meetings of the diet, the setting up of a supreme court, the Imperial Chamber, whose judges were chosen by the diet, and the organization of an Imperial Council (*Reichs-*

regiment) with powers over war and peace, made up of representatives of the imperial estates, that is the princes.

This radical constitution would have transformed the Holy Roman Empire into a constitutional monarchy. In the prevailing circumstances, however, it was a quite unrealistic plan. Maximilian was most unwilling to accept such limitations of his imperial powers, just as he had been unwilling to accept such limitations when he was regent of the Netherlands, ten years earlier. The *Reichstag* was even less able than the French Estates General to commit the whole kingdom to the payment of a common tax. Unlike France, there were in Germany not even the beginnings of a royal financial administration. The annual tax, the "common penny," had to be left to the good will of the princes and their own assemblies of estates. The role of the cities and even their representation in the diets had not been clarified, yet the princes expected the cities to pay the bulk of the common tax. Perhaps most important of all, the German estates were as unwilling to see a strong parliamentary government, dominated, as it would be, by the six prince-electors—Bohemia, the seventh, had been left out of the proposals—as they were to see the return of a strong traditional monarchy.[48] In the event, both the Imperial Chamber and the Imperial Council were actually set up and survived, but with much reduced powers. For the next hundred years the diets met frequently, although not annually, and they were to play an important role in German politics during the Reformation. The Holy Roman Empire continued to function as a composite monarchy with an active but limited representative assembly—but not nearly as effectively as the reformers of 1495 had hoped.

Where composite monarchies were not even notionally one kingdom, the effect of their union produced much more complex relations between their rulers and their assemblies. The most obvious effect was a drastic change in the balance of power, in favor of the ruler; for now, in case of a quarrel with the Parliament of one of his states, he had the resources of all his dominions at his disposal. In the fourteenth century Sicily was ruled by kings of a younger branch of the house of Aragon. The line died out in 1412, and the new king of Aragon, from the Castilian family of Trastámara, refused to continue the previous arrangement, and from then on Sicily was governed by viceroys sent from Spain. At a stroke, and without any overt coup in the island, the Sicilian Parliament lost half its power;

for all important decisions, especially on matters of war and peace, had now been removed to the court in Barcelona.

Having firmly established its own position of ultimate power and decision making, the Aragonese monarchy was careful not to repeat the mistakes of the French in the thirteenth century of riding rough-shod over the customs and privileges of Sicily's ruling elites. The kings of Aragon continued to summon the Sicilian Parliament, with its classic structure of three estates—prelates, nobles, and towns—every three years for the grant of the "donative," in return for which the monarchy accepted most of Parliament's petitions. By the name of *capitoli* these were a form of parliamentary legislation, although the monarchy reserved the right to veto specific proposals, just as the English monarchy did until the end of the seventeenth century. This system continued to work for three hundred years and gave rise to the Sicilian legend that their Parliament and the British Parliament were the only surviving parliaments in Europe.[49] When kings neglected the fundamental rule of respecting parliaments in outlying dominions, the results could be catastrophic, as the Spanish monarchy was to find in the seventeenth century in its relations with the Catalans, and the British monarchy, at just about the same time, in its relations with the Scots.

After the union of the crowns of Aragon and Castile, in 1479, Ferdinand and Isabella concentrated on establishing their authority in the larger and richer of their two kingdoms, Castile, and treated the Cortes of Aragon, Catalonia, and Valencia with the same benign neglect that they treated the Parliament of Sicily. They never attempted to summon an Iberian Cortes. In Italy the dukes of Piedmont-Savoy also made no attempt to summon a combined assembly of their two contiguous principalities, probably because they were afraid of increasing the power of the already powerful Parliament of Piedmont. A prominent Piedmontese parliamentarian, Luigi Talliandi, told the ambassador from the autocratically governed duchy of Milan, in 1476,

that although they (the Piedmontese) have a prince, nevertheless, in every important case, it is the three estates which deliberate, make decisions and govern the country.[50]

In the Netherlands the situation was different again. Over a period of some forty years, from 1384, the house of Burgundy had ac-

quired dominion over a dozen or so duchies and counties with varying social structures and speaking several different languages. All of
them had assemblies of estates, again with varying structures: from
the classic three estates, in Brabant and Hainault, to the single-
chamber assembly of Holland, in which the six towns normally summoned had six votes, the nobility one; and the clergy no separate
representation at all. But since medieval institutions were rarely rigidly defined, there were occasions when up to another dozen of the
smaller towns of Holland were also summoned. The most singular
assembly, however, was that of Flanders, which had three dominant
cities, Bruges, Ghent, and Ypres, and a fourth "member," the *Franc
de Bruges*, which was the representative of a mixed area of lower
nobility and castellanies between Bruges and the sea; some of the
other small towns were summoned on occasion. After 1430 the
dukes were able to command vastly more powerful resources than
their predecessors had been able to when they were rulers of just one
or two duchies or counties. They demonstrated this superior power
when they defeated rebellions of individual cities, even of populous
and rich Ghent with its history of successful popular revolutions—
though it took Philip the Good six years (1447–53) to do so.

But the dukes still needed to demonstrate their newly won authority to their whole composite monarchy and to establish a convenient venue for getting the financial help they needed. The cities
and provinces, for their part, were anxious to cooperate with each
other and with the duke on such matters as monetary policy or a
common front against their commercial partners and rivals, the English. Between 1384 and 1506 the estates of Flanders, for instance,
met over 4,000 times, on average for three to nine days, and mostly
to discuss economic matters. From the 1420s onwards the dukes
summoned combined assemblies of the estates of several provinces
and they did this with everyone's approval. In 1463 the estates issued their own invitations to a States General in order to discuss a
family crisis in the ruling house. Philip the Good, outraged by their
initiative, quickly issued his own summons—for the same deputies. Both he and his estranged son (later Charles the Bold) found it
convenient to use the States General as mediators, and this body
emerged from what had been a mainly dynastic crisis with a greatly
enhanced reputation.

From then on the States General was summoned regularly and

soon found itself objecting to Duke Charles the Bold's authoritarian methods of government and his expensive aggressive foreign policy. In the 1473 session the chancellor, Guillaume Hugonet, tried to justify government policy in terms of principle. Human society, he declared, was both natural to man and a part of the divine hierarchy of the universe. There were three forms of government: monarchy, aristocracy, and democracy; and of these monarchy was the best and most natural, like the human body in which the head controlled the members. Monarchy and subjects should therefore cooperate for the common good of the state. Hugonet's arguments were the common coinage of Aristotelian ideas as they were expounded by rulers or their chancellors to parliaments all over Europe. Thus Henry VIII of England assured Parliament in 1543 that

we at no time stand so highly in our estate royal as in the time of Parliament, wherein we as head and you as members are conjoint and knit together into one body politic.

Such addresses were no doubt gratifying to the deputies or members of Parliament, but they were not something one argued about. Hugonet, at least, seems to have been aware of this, for he went on to make a much more relevant propaganda point. The Netherlands had developed free institutions, he said, especially under the house of Burgundy, whereas the French had to live under heavy exactions which their king imposed on them. The States General should therefore help the duke to defend their country against France.[51]

But relations between Charles the Bold and the States General continued to deteriorate. A crisis was triggered by outside events. On 5 January 1477 the duke was killed in battle against the Swiss. Louis XI of France immediately sent his troops into the duchy of Burgundy and into the provinces of the southern Netherlands. The government of Duke Charles's heir, his young daughter Mary, summoned the States General and was immediately forced to sign the *grand privilège*, a charter for all the provinces of the Netherlands. Basically, this was the *joyeuse entrée* of Brabant writ large and extended to the whole of the Netherlands. Its clauses dealt with immediate grievances, such as the late duke's disregard of provincial and urban privileges, with the confirmation of the *ius indigenatus*, reserving public offices to the natives of each province together with the right to conduct public business in the language current in each province. This was not so much narrow provincialism as a way of assuring a reasonable distribution of patronage in a multilingual, composite monarchy. As to the States General, it won the right to assemble without being summoned by the duke. No wars were to be waged without its approval and, if the duchess and her prospective heirs failed to observe these conditions, the subjects were released from their duty of obedience.[52]

The *grand privilège* was not a deliberate step towards a parliamentary monarchy, nor were its clauses designed to sabotage "state formation" or dissolve the union of the provinces of the Netherlands. The limitations it tried to impose on the monarchy were neither new in 1477 nor unique in Europe. Of the central institutions of government the recently established supreme court in Malines (Mechlin) and the central treasury, the "chamber of accounts" in Lille, were abolished. The functions of the supreme court and its judges were taken over by the duchess's council and soon the judges returned to Malines. The functions of the chamber of accounts reverted to the council. Government and States General had been spurred to their extraordinarily fast agreement by fear of popular revolts in the big cities. In vain! In mid-February 1477 such rebellions broke out in the great cities of Flanders and Brabant. The revolutionary new council of Ghent took the lead in persuading the States General to negotiate with Louis XI—rather ineptly, as it turned out. In Ghent itself they arrested and executed not only several of their own magistrates but also the chancellor Hugonet and another hated member of the late duke's government. They tried them for alleged treason and forced Mary to sign their death warrants (4 April). There is a striking similarity with the impeachment of the earl of Strafford and the act of attainder passed against him by the English Parliament, in 1641. In both cases a representative assembly forced its ruler to authorize the judicial murder of a minister accused of leading his prince into tyranny. In both cases this terrible humiliation of the ruler meant the collapse of trust between prince and Parliament. In both cases this collapse led to civil war.

In the Netherlands this happened when Mary's new husband, Maximilian of Austria (later Emperor Maximilian I) refused to acknowledge the validity of the *grand privilège* and tried to return to Charles the Bold's policies and methods. Mary died in 1482 and Maximilian claimed to exercise all ducal powers, as guardian for his

children. At war with France over his claims for the return of the
duchy of Burgundy, he now found himself involved also in a civil
war with Flanders, which, at times, managed to obtain the support
of the other provinces of the States General against Maximilian. The
civil war was not settled until Charles VIII of France, in order to
have his hands free for his campaign to Naples in 1494, gave up his
support for the Flemings. Ghent lost many of its privileges, but cooperation between ruler and States General was restored by Maximilian's son, Philip I, "the Handsome."

For the first time a representative assembly had disputed the actual government of its country with its prince. It was not a premedi-
tated parliamentary policy. The long, destructive, and confused civil
war saw magnates, cities, and whole provinces change sides and
German and French armies invade the country. Its outcome had
been quite unpredictable. In the end, it satisfied both those represented in the provincial estates and in the States General and also
Maximilian. His court memoirist, Olivier de la Marche, quotes the
advice which Maximilian gave to his son, after all his bruising experiences in the Netherlands:

To tell you the truth, I am giving you this rule: never give authority over
yourself to those who live under your rule. But I advise you, for the conduct
and execution of your great affairs, always to ask their counsel and help.[53]

Maximilian may or may not actually have said this; but the ethos
of late-medieval kingship could not have been put more succinctly.
Too succinctly; for it left hazy a distinction that had become very
clear to many at the end of the Middle Ages. This was the distinction between autocratic rule and rule by consent, consent given
in nearly every European monarchy by a representative assembly.
Commines had centered it on taxation; Hugonet on the rights and
privileges of the estates. Talliandi had included in the estates' rights
of decision making, "every important case." Chief Justice Fortescue
said categorically:

The statutes of England . . . (are) not enacted by the sole will of the prince,
but with the concurrent assent of the whole kingdom, by their representatives in parliament.[54]

He distinguished between *dominium regale*, an autocratic monarchy as in France, and *dominium politicum et regale*, the limited
monarchy of England. The results of these differences of regime, he

claimed, were abject poverty in France and the inability of the French to defend their country, whereas in England

the people thereof be not in such penurie . . . but they be wealthy and have all things necessary to the sustenance of nature. Wherefore they be mighty and able to resist the adversaries of this realm, and to beat other realms.[55]

Freedom and military greatness were often equated at that time, even by republicans such as Machiavelli.

It is not necessary for historians to agree with all the consequences which Fortescue ascribed to the differences of the two regimes, nor to accept his patriotic machismo. After all, he himself had lived through the most decisive defeat England has ever suffered in a major war, when the despised French (at one time led at least symbolically by a woman!) pushed the English out of France. But the distinction between *dominium regale* and *dominium politicum et regale* was real enough and was recognized to be so.[56] A few years into the sixteenth century, the Venetian ambassador to the court of France reported King Francis I recounting a joke, told to him, he asserted, by the emperor Maximilian: the king of France was a ruler over beasts, because everyone had to obey him like a beast; the king of Spain was a ruler over men, because his subjects obeyed him only when they thought this right; but the emperor was a king of kings, because no one ever obeyed him: in our terms, *dominium regale*, *dominium politicum et regale*, and virtual chaos in a monarchy which had splintered into its feudal components.

Personal Liberty
under the Common Law
of England, 1200-1600

J. H. BAKER

LIBERTY AND FREEDOM WILL not be found as titles in the books of common law before 1600. "Liberties" and "franchises"[1] are met with often enough, but only in a narrow technical sense; they are specific privileges or exemptions, treated in effect as forms of property. It was not the usual technique for the medieval common law to deduce answers to particular problems from broad general principles such as freedom or freedoms. The nearest we get to it is in the fine phrases of clause 39 of Magna Carta (1215):[2]

No free man shall be taken or imprisoned or disseised or outlawed or exiled or in any way ruined, nor will we go or send against him, except by lawful judgment of his peers or by the law of the land.

The same sentiment is echoed in Edward III's statutes of due process.[3] But these enactments were regarded by medieval lawyers as mere declarations of the previous common law, and they did not lay down any particular remedies in case of infringement. Such legal remedies as were developed were not, until the sixteenth century, derived directly from the legislation, although theoretical links began to be made in the Tudor period. Moreover, clause 39 referred only to "free men," thus explicitly indicating that there were also the unfree who were not within its spirit or its letter. Those unfree were, in 1215, largely outside the common law. Even when they were brought within the scope of the due process legislation in the fourteenth century, it made no difference to their unfree status; that was itself part of the "law of the land."

< I >

Freedom and Due Process of Law

If a typical Englishman were asked in 1215, or even in 1415, what it meant to be free, his answer would most probably have been given in terms of bondage. Freedom was not yet conceived of in terms of parliamentary representation, let alone in terms of written pronouncements: Magna Carta itself did not extend freedom to anyone who was not already free. Freedom was rather the antithesis of bondage, of villeinage, and therefore the first part of our study will be the treatment of villeins under the common law and the disappearance of villeinage for all practical purposes by the end of the sixteenth century. As villeinage disappeared, Englishmen may have thought about their freedom more expansively. This is evident from the beginning of Henry VIII's reign (1509–46) in a current of cases in which subjects asserted freedom from coercion and unlawful constraint by the government of the day, such as imprisonment by order of the ministers of the Crown. It is from these cases—some of them still unpublished—that the law of liberty as debated in 1627–29 largely grew.

The precondition of all these developments was acceptance of the principle that everyone is subject to the law of the land: even the king, because it is the law which makes him king.[4] The king's own judges would ensure that the king observed the law, by requiring that any grant or acquisition by the king, and any act of constraint against a subject, be carried out in a procedurally correct manner and duly recorded. This policy would in the fifteenth century gain expression in the courteous fiction that the king can do no wrong;[5] anything done unlawfully in the king's name is void, because the king cannot have authorized it. By the middle of the fifteenth century the king's judges would say that the king himself may not commit subjects to prison, even for good cause, because there would be no way of challenging the cause in the courts. All imprisonment belongs to the king's authority,[6] but that authority must be exercised by due process of law.

However, although the importance of due process was frequently asserted in legislation, it would not be realistic to think of it as a specific doctrine suddenly generated by Parliament like a piece of Victorian law reform. Its origins are beyond easy reach. It was a notion preceding Parliament, precarious in reality and therefore re-asserted as a principle to be personally acknowledged by king after king, lest it should be forgotten or laid aside. The repetition of the principle by Parliament was doubtless of great importance, but the guardians of due process in reality were the judges and juries who decided the fate of real people. In the seventeenth century, the jury would be associated with the "judgment of his peers" in chapter 29 of Magna Carta. This was an anachronistic interpreta-tion, but telling nevertheless; the jury was perceived as being, in a crisis, the main bulwark between government and subject. No man could be tried for his life save by twelve good men and true. We shall see that the jury played a leading role in the ending of villeinage.

Another precondition of freedom under the law, as was also per-ceived very clearly in the early seventeenth century, was an indepen-dent judiciary. In the 1630s the reputation of the judges was to reach its lowest ebb; very likely they had never before been put under such intense political pressure. But for most of the preceding three centuries the judicial tradition had been one of growing indepen-dence. Although the judges were appointed by the Crown and held office during pleasure, they were sworn to do justice according to law, and the common law was a sophisticated, independent science taught in the great law school housed in the inns of court. It was this independent spirit which enabled the Tudor judiciary to react to autocratic tendencies in government by encouraging the devel-opment of habeas corpus[7] into a remedy whereby the humblest subject could challenge the greatest ministers of the Crown in the courts.

It could not be claimed, and it is not a necessary part of the ar-gument, that the judiciary always stood firm in the face of pressure, or that juries were always right. All human institutions, including courts of law, suffer from weaknesses and are susceptible to failure. The essence of the argument is that in the longer term, as adminis-trations came and went, the English judiciary nurtured a continuous tradition of obedience to a system of law which bound the rulers as well as the ruled.

≺ II ≻

The Common-Law System

The common law, a body of law common to the whole of England as opposed to variable local custom, was necessarily a product of centralization.[8] The centralizing influence was the royal court, which began to expand its activities in the twelfth century, especially under King Henry II (1154–89), as it became established that the king might delegate his authority to royal judges (called *justiciarii*). Royal justices might sit in the king's presence, or in the king's palace when the king was absent, or in particular localities; or they could travel on circuits through the country. Their principal concern at first was the king's own concern with public order and revenue, the pleas of the Crown. But experience taught that peace and order are heavily dependent on the final settlement of disputes over land, and so pleas of land soon became an equally important aspect of royal jurisdiction.

It was probably never anyone's intention that royal justice should supplant or stifle older ways of proceeding in the ancient local courts. But the existence of a centralized body of courts, in which one uniform law was dispensed throughout England, and effectively enforced through the king's sheriffs, ineluctably diminished the Englishman's perception of all inferior forms of jurisdiction. At the very least, the latter had to be subject to the king's courts and the common law. Feudal jurisdiction was drastically circumscribed by the writs and assizes which enabled tenants to assert proprietary and possessory rights to land in the king's court. The ecclesiastical courts were kept in check by the writ of prohibition, which could be issued by the king's court to prevent litigants overstepping the accepted boundaries of Church jurisdiction. Then again, any decision in a court of record, such as borough court, was subject to review in the king's court by writ of error. And any other jurisdiction was subject to similar scrutiny by the writ of false judgment. Anyone who exercised private jurisdiction, or had some executive authority, such as keeping a jail, executing writs, keeping a market or fair, or imposing tolls,[9] was liable to justify that authority before the king's justices by showing some lawful warrant for it (the procedure called *quo warranto*). Anyone who injured or imprisoned another person, albeit under color of official authority, could be required to justify himself before the king's justices in a writ of trespass. No one, therefore, not even the king and his servants, was outside or above the common law.

Such was the activity of the central royal courts in the thirteenth century that a legal profession came into existence to service them.[10] The advocates in the principal court, the Common Bench (later called the Court of Common Pleas), were a select guild of experts in law and pleading, known as "serjeants"; from them alone were the judges chosen. The more numerous "attorneys" were general practitioners whose services enabled a litigant to be represented in a faraway royal court at all stages in his case without the need for personal attendance. Between these two extremes there was an innominate body of intermediate practitioners, many of whom gave counsel and performed the same kind of function as the serjeants but in other courts.

Already by the 1260s there was a law school to train this profession. It was attached in some way to the court itself, and its students were known by 1280 as "apprentices of the Bench." Around the 1340s this law school developed a collegiate system, and the teaching passed (as to a lesser extent it did in the universities) to the colleges.[11] These colleges, called "inns" (*hospicia*) were in two tiers. In the fifteenth century a young student would generally spend two years in one of the lesser inns, called inns of chancery, to learn the writs and other rudiments of legal knowledge. If it then seemed appropriate for him, he would gain admission to one of the four "inns of court," where lectures (called "readings") were given on the old statutes. The course began with Magna Carta, and the members took part in elaborate disputations called "moots." Students were also expected to attend Westminster Hall, where the principal royal courts were held, to learn by watching the serjeants argue in real cases.

The law taught in the inns of court was of homespun origin. Roman law, though taught at Oxford and Cambridge, had little or no relevance to the law of England, which was so inextricably enmeshed in the complex procedure of the king's courts, as it had developed since the twelfth century, that it was hardly comprehensible in the abstract. Nor was the law of England written down, though it was augmented at various points by statutes, and it was illustrated by real cases, reported since the thirteenth century in the Anglo-French dialect of the men of court. It could not simply be "read"; it could be learned only by personal discussion, by immersion in the tough educational routine of the inns of court. Not surprisingly, the two degrees taken in the inns, that of barrister (one who argues at the bar in moots) and that of bencher (one who sits on the bench at moots), became necessary prerequisites for practice as counsel and for advancement in the law.

These institutions provided the foundations for the tradition of governance according to law. Again, that is not to say that they always worked perfectly, without let or hindrance; but without an institutional framework to produce a tradition of law, and a means of enforcing legal rights against powerful officials and even against the Crown, freedom could have little practical significance. It would be patently absurd to argue that the common lawyers invented liberty. However liberty is defined at a particular time, the connotation of the word is such that everyone has a sense of what it is and wants to have it. In the real world, of course, the desire for liberty is not always matched by any real prospect of gaining it. The legal concept of freedom was concerned with the reality, with the practical achievement of such aspirations through parchment and wax and motions in court. It was less an abstract concept than the tradition of legality, what fourteenth-century lawyers called the "due process of law." That tradition grew in the small world of Westminster Hall and the inns of court chiefly because those who advised subjects on their rights and liberties were educated and taught in the same school of learning as those who advised the government, most of the officials of government, and those who sat in judgment in the king's courts. They argued together, ate together, and shared a set of common assumptions. Those whose liberties developed latest were those with the most limited access to this world.

We have seen how Magna Carta, in speaking of freemen, was deliberately excluding the unfree, and it is with the latter that we shall start. We shall nevertheless see that even the villein came to owe his practical extinction to the common-law system rather than to parliamentary institutions. The way in which unfree status disappeared illustrates very neatly how liberty in practice owed more to the common law's ability to enforce popular notions of fairness than to political theory or to the rise of Parliament. Parliament, in fact, played virtually no part in the story—indeed, in one of its very few enactments touching upon free status,[12] it actually introduced slavery as a punishment.[13] It has still not seen fit, or found it necessary, to abolish villeinage.

≺ III ≻

Villeinage

The common-law term for unfree status—as opposed to unfree tenure[14]—was villeinage "by blood" (*de sank*).[15] But the status was in existence before the common law. Indeed, the Anglo-Saxons had known other forms of bondage, such as serfdom. The word serf derives from the Latin word for slave (*servus*), and the Domesday survey of 1086 recorded more than 25,000 of them in England. Exactly what this status meant is less than clear, and it may have varied according to local custom, but it was assuredly a miserable plight. The word villein had originally meant simply a peasant villager (*villanus*), and the adoption of this word in the twelfth century may indicate a softening of attitudes towards the unfree.[16] At any rate, there was a blending of social categories in that century.[17] The villein was not a slave in the Roman sense, nor was he owned by his lord, except in the sense that the lord's rights over him were usually annexed to real property and could pass with it. Nevertheless, the villein was under a considerable degree of subjection to his lord. He could own property, but only at the will of the lord; therefore whatever he acquired could be seized by the lord at any time. The lord could discipline the villein by corporal punishment. And the villein could not leave his tenement, even to work, without the lord's consent; escape could be prevented with force.

The common law of the twelfth century recognized this condition as an existing fact of life, and also protected the lord's rights. The lord could recover the body of a villein straying from his native manor into another manor by the action of naifty (*de nativo habendo*), brought against the rival lord. The villein could not bring an action of trespass against the lord for mistreating him or taking his property away. The earliest author on the common law, at the end of the twelfth century, taught that villeinage was an indelible status inherited from either parent; even if the lord granted a villein his freedom, he became free only as against the lord.[18]

Within fifty years a rather different view of villeinage was becoming established, and was first expounded in the treatise called *Bracton*. The guiding principle, it seems, was that the law leaned in favor of liberty.[19] The original sense of this principle may have been that the law should guard against the wrongful deprivation of a free man's liberty rather than that it should make it easier for villeins to become free;[20] but its effects in the longer term were to weaken the bonds of servitude to the point of dissolution. *Bracton* devoted much space to villeinage. Pursuing an abstract lawyer's logic which treated liberty as a right akin to property, it asserted what became the three principal characteristics of villein status at common law. The first was that there was only one kind of unfree status: all villeins were equally unfree. The second was that villeinage was relative; reversing the earlier view, *Bracton* held that a villein was unfree only against his own lord, and free as against the rest of the world.[21] There was even a presumption against villeinage; in the absence of proof, a man was to be presumed free, "in favor of liberty."[22] A consequence of the relativity theory was that manumission by the lord freed the blood absolutely. Moreover, a villein was perfectly entitled to sue anyone other than his lord in the royal courts: another concession "in favor of liberty."[23] Indeed, a villein who was violently mistreated by the lord could bring an appeal of felony against the lord himself.[24] The third principle (established by 1219) was that tenure of land by villein services did not make someone a villein *de sank*.[25] Unfree status could only be inherited in the blood-line; and here *Bracton*, again departing from the older learning, took the more generous view that it descended only from the father, except in the case of an illegitimate birth, when it could descend only from the mother.[26] By the early fourteenth century, the analogy with real property led to the abandonment even of this latter exception. A bastard was the child of no one (*filius nullius*); he could not inherit land, and on the same principle he could not inherit disabilities either.[27]

In reality the lot of medieval villeins was not normally one of abject oppression. The tax laws assumed they would have money, and they were indeed often allowed to retain earnings, even to pursue professions. The bonds which tied them to their lords were often little different in practice from those which bound low-born free men to lords or masters. Most important of all, the villeins' exclusion from the common-law courts did not exclude them from manorial justice. By the customs of manors, villeins enjoyed rights analogous to those of free men at common law; for instance, they might make wills of their chattels and hold lands heritably. Under manorial custom a lord's rights were typically limited to the accustomed services, an annual tax payment, and a payment on marriage of the villein's children (the merchet, or "ransom of flesh and blood"). Custom frequently fixed the sums payable, thus limiting very considerably the lord's de facto sovereignty. It was, in any case, in the lord's own interests to maintain a productive workforce. Treating villeins badly, by excessive taxation or confiscating the means of livelihood, was bad husbandry;[28] and if it drove away men in times of labor shortage, it was regarded in law as an injury to the inheritance.

If a villein's life was hard by modern standards, it was not necessarily much worse than that of his free neighbor. Yet villeins were more vulnerable to exploitation than free men.[29] The status of being free affected a person's security, sense of dignity, and social standing, and claims to villeins were frequently disputed in the royal courts. The most direct means of challenge was the action of naifty. When used to recover a villein straying from his "nest" (place of birth), along with his "brood" and chattels, this took the form of an executive command to the sheriff, who would decide between competing lords. But if the alleged villein claimed to be free, the case had to be removed before royal judges, "in favor of liberty."[30] The defendant was allowed to prove his liberty "by all the ways he knows how, and that in favor of liberty."[31] If his claim succeeded, he was free for ever: as Serjeant Herle said in the Common Bench in 1310, "In the beginning every man in the world was free, and the law is so favorable to liberty that he who is once found free in a court of record shall be held free for ever."[32]

By 1300 the action of naifty was normally brought against the alleged villein himself with the object of initiating a trial of status in the royal court. According to one writer, not more than two villeins could be claimed in one writ, because of the odium of bondage.[33] The plaintiff had to make out title by showing possession, which required proof of "tallaging high and low at his will, and taking ransom of flesh and blood," the proof to be made either by record or by producing the bodies of two male villeins of the same blood.[34] Its cumbrous nature, and the fact that jurors tended to favor claims to freedom, led to its decline in the later medieval period.[35]

≺ IV ≻

The End of Villeinage

It was established at an early period that villeins could achieve their freedom in a number of different ways: for instance, by manumission (a grant of freedom by the lord); by estoppel or implication from conduct (where the lord acknowledged the person to be free by dealing with him as if he were);[36] by residing in a privileged city or borough (or in the ancient demesne of the king) for a year and a day without adverse claim;[37] by ordination, profession in religion, or knighthood;[38] or by marriage.[39] The doctrine that unfree status could not descend to a bastard offered another means of escape: if an alleged villein could prove that his parents or ancestors were unmarried, he was necessarily free. This became a regular means of enfranchisement in the fifteenth and sixteenth centuries,[40] by which time it was established that a certificate of bastardy from the ecclesiastical court was binding on the lord even when he was not a party to the proceedings.[41]

These rules invited collusion.[42] It is evident from the plea rolls that some episcopal courts would routinely certify bastardy in cases of disputed villeinage, and we may reasonably guess that this was a form of pious mendacity rather than a reflection on villein morality. Moreover, if some dioceses were known to be sticklers for the facts, resort could be had to a further fiction; the alleged villein would simply plead his birth in a diocese (such as Norwich) known to be more cooperative.[43] This procedure can be shown in some cases to have been the outcome of a composition between lord and villein to obtain a formal manumission; a judgment recorded on the plea rolls of the king's courts was the most secure conveyance of liberty, and such security was advisable where (as must often have been the case) the lord in possession did not have an absolute title.[44] Collusion may explain the predictability of the outcome in such suits;

the ecclesiastical judges could with some semblance of good conscience avoid looking too closely into the facts of suits which were uncontested.

The other principal means of escape was the jury, which could give effect to popular attitudes even when they were at odds with strict law. By the fifteenth century, at the very latest, there was no socially identifiable villein class; unfree status had become more of a legal anomaly than a social reality.[45] Both villeins and free men could be found in the same families, and free countryfolk regularly married their villein neighbors. Men of villein stock could reach high places: even the chief justiceship of England.[46] Doubtless many families genuinely did not know for sure whether they were free or not; such uncertainty was itself tantamount to being free, since a lord would find it difficult in practice to resurrect a dormant claim.[47] Villein status seemed to most people outmoded, and it had actually disappeared in many parts of the country, especially the north.

These attitudes were shared by the common lawyers. Sir John Fortescue, a former chief justice of England, writing in the third quarter of the fifteenth century, remarked that:

A law is necessarily adjudged cruel if it increases servitude and diminishes liberty, for which human nature always craves. For servitude was introduced by men for vicious purposes; but liberty is implanted in human nature by God. Hence freedom, when taken away from a man, always wants to return, as is always the case when natural liberty is denied. So he who does not favor liberty is to be deemed impious and cruel. In considering these matters, the laws of England favor liberty in every case.[48]

John Fitzherbert, in the 1520s, said villeinage was the greatest inconvenience then suffered by the law, because of the possibility of abuse.[49] At much the same period, in a Gray's Inn moot, it was said that it was "an odious thing in law and not favored, for it is absolutely contrary to liberty, and liberty is one of the things which the law most favors."[50]

In this context, it is not surprising that juries provided a more or less uncontrolled means of declaring people free in cases of dispute. There were several ways in which this could be achieved, after the desuetude of the action of naifty. The most obvious was for the alleged villein to bring an action against the lord, such as an action of false imprisonment for an actual past detention,[51] an action of trespass for lying in wait and threatening to seize him as a villein,[52] or (if the lord was currently detaining him) an action to replevy his person (*de homine replegiando*).[53] This latter was an important remedy, because it required the plaintiff's liberty and goods to be restored pending trial of the issue; without it, lords might have prevented men from suing them by taking their substance and locking them up. By what seems to have been an act of judicial legislation in 1498, the King's Bench decided that the procedurally less cumbrous action of trespass could be used in the same way as *de homine replegiando*, so that the plaintiff's goods would be returned to him pending the outcome, even when the plaintiff himself was not in custody.[54] After 1510, the nascent action on the case for defamation was also used in respect of verbal assertions of unfree status, obviating the need for proof of any physical threat or restraint.[55] But any action would do, since the defendant would plead villeinage against the plaintiff and issue would be joined on the status, leaving the jury to decide conclusively whether the party was free or unfree. Although these were only personal actions for damages, the courts by 1500 held the jury's verdict on the status to be decisive.[56] This above all rendered the older action, which was conceptually closer to the actions for real property, obsolete. There was no longer any need for proof by kin, or any of the antiquated technicalities. The records show that nearly all verdicts went in favor of liberty, and large sums were sometimes recovered in damages, especially against prosperous defendants.[57]

The attitude of juries, perhaps more than any other single factor, is what seems to have dissuaded even the more conservative sixteenth-century lords from trying to preserve villeinage. Lords who were determined to insist on their rights—and prominent among them were abbots and priors devoted to preserving the temporal wealth of their religious houses—might cut their losses by selling manumissions and abandoning the capital asset; others just gave up their position as uncharitable and obsolete. The Crown effected a general manumission of most of its own remaining bondmen (at a price) in the 1570s. This was achieved by granting the profits of the enterprise to a courtier, Sir Henry Lee, who thus had a financial incentive to seek out and bargain with villeins.[58] Some quite substantial men were enfranchised, including an ecclesiastical judge.[59] From time to time a "general manumission" by act of Parliament was discussed or demanded, and a bill to that effect reached its third reading in 1536,[60] but no such legislation was ever passed. No doubt a good many villeins, especially the poorer ones who could not afford to compound for their manumission, therefore remained technically unfree. But the prevailing sentiment rendered their formal enfranchisement unnecessary. Sir Thomas Smith, writing in the middle of the sixteenth century, said he never knew any villeins in gross[61] in his time, and of villeins regardant to manors said, "so fewe there be that it is not almost worth the speaking."[62] He thought they had been kept mainly by religious houses, because abbots were not willing to impoverish their churches.[63] He nevertheless attributed the final disappearance of villeinage to its perceived inconsistency with Christianity.[64]

This was not, of course, the end of the story. The failure to abolish villeinage left open the question of captive slavery. A contemporary of Smith, the Rev. William Harrison (d. 1593), went so far as to say that, not only were there no bondmen in England, but "such is the privilege of our countrie by the especiall grace of God, and bountie of our princes, that if anie come hither from other realms, so soone as they set foot on land they become so free of condition as their masters, whereby all note of servile bondage is utterlie remooved from them."[65] There are no cases in the law reports concerning imported slaves before the later seventeenth century, and the question doubtless did not arise because the few Negro servants brought to England before then were not treated differently from other servants.

The common law at the end of our period could be said to have an open mind on the possibility of slavery. Prisoners of war may have had a status akin to slaves,[66] and were certainly pressed into galley service by the Council in the sixteenth century. The Star Chamber recognized punitive slavery also, when in 1548 it sentenced Edmund Grimston to be in the king's galleys "as a slave" for life, for a scandalous libel against the city of London and its recorder.[67] Later generations would choose the less emotive term "penal servitude" for punishment involving hard labor; but slavery was evidently not too emotive a term to use for a deterrent punishment in the sixteenth century. Punishment, nevertheless, was considered a far cry from a status inflicted by birth. In the case of Negro slavery, eventually abolished by Parliament, the most effective arguments in the courts were derived from the common law of villeinage and the near impossibility (in later times) of proving villein blood. Slaves, if permitted at all in England, could not be worse off than villeins.[68]

≺ V ≻

Arbitrary Imprisonment

Villeinage, however qualified, was a permanent lack of freedom. But even free men might suffer a temporary lack of freedom if someone with power over them put them (rightly or wrongly) under a physical restraint. The other principal achievement of the common law in the sphere of personal liberty was the establishment of the principle that no one may be imprisoned without lawful cause. This was no mere abstraction but was realized through the provision of practical remedies for those imprisoned without lawful cause.

Imprisonment, in the language of the common law, is not confined to putting people in jail. Any physical restraint of liberty—for instance, by putting someone in the stocks, or confining him in a private house,[69] or seizing him in the street, or (at any rate in later times[70]) arresting him by mere words—is in law an imprisonment which requires justification. The justification is needed not only by the person who first lays hands on the prisoner, but also by the servant who turns the key and the jailer who keeps the key.[71] The general principle governing imprisonment has usually been traced, since the seventeenth century, to chapter 29 of Magna Carta: "no free man shall be taken or imprisoned except by the lawful judgment of his peers or the law of the land." What, in real life, did this import in medieval England?

It is well known that in the seventeenth century chapter 29 came to be loaded with far more weight than its words will bear in their original context. In 1215, trial on a criminal charge was by ordeal rather than jury, and habeas corpus was used to put people into jail rather than to help them out of it. The uncertainty of the charter's broad phrases was to be its strength in later times, but readers (lecturers) in the fifteenth-century inns of court took the words very narrowly indeed: "peers" meant lords of Parliament in case of felony,[72] "take" meant arrest by writ of *capias*, "right and justice" (at the end of the chapter) meant writs of right and *justicies*.[73] There was little here in the way of broad principle. Moreover, no remedy was laid down by the statute for dealing with cases of abuse. The 1368 statute of due process, mentioned by some of the readers on Magna Carta, merely provided that whatever was done contrary to these enactments should be void; but that was rather a negative remedy for someone who had been harmed or was currently being deprived of liberty. The remedy most discussed by the readers was the common-law action of false imprisonment, to which we shall turn in a moment. It was occasionally debated, however, whether a special action might not be founded on the legislation itself.[74] By the beginning of the sixteenth century such actions are indeed found in the plea rolls,[75] chiefly in respect of irregular suits before individual royal councillors or conciliar committees. There is no reported example, and so we do not know the nature of any underlying debates, but the actions (always against the opposing party rather than the minister himself) were sometimes successful[76] and the precedents were known to later generations.[77]

In addition to these means of challenging an irregular deprivation of liberty, such as unwarranted incarceration on the orders of the king's council, remedies were also needed for the improper use of regular forms of imprisonment. Imprisonment by regular legal process was effected by a sealed writ, usually addressed to the sheriff of a county, containing the command to "take" someone (*capias*). The common-law procedure for the "return" of writs required the sheriff to report what action he had taken on every writ received, by an appointed day (the return-day of the writ), so that prisoners were not simply forgotten. Bail was widely available by the end of the thirteenth century in both criminal and civil proceedings; except in those cases where the law classed the accused as "irreplevisable" (for instance, in cases of treason or homicide), the sheriff was bound to release a prisoner who offered good sureties for his appearance to answer the charge against him.[78] A sheriff or bailiff who arrested someone lawfully, but then detained him unlawfully, for instance by returning the writ late, or by returning that the person had not been found, or by wrongly denying bail, was liable to an action of trespass.[79] Actions could also be brought for abusing a prisoner whose original arrest had been lawful.[80] The substantive law of imprisonment is not easily separated from these remedies, the principal of which we may now examine in outline.

⪻ VI ⪼

The Action of False Imprisonment

Around the time of Magna Carta a wrongful imprisonment could be made the subject of criminal or civil proceedings.[81] Appeals of false imprisonment are found early in the 1200s, and civil actions of false imprisonment constituted the commonest category of trespass actions later in the century.[82] Many of these proceedings resulted, as we have noticed above, from villein claims. The next commonest subcategory was the action against a public official such as a sheriff, bailiff, or constable, for exceeding or abusing his authority.[83] But it had wider uses as well. It was sometimes used in jurisdictional disputes, as when it was brought against the earl of Arundel in 1319 to challenge his power to imprison at Clun,[84] or in the case of 1495 (known to Coke and Dyer) when it was used to challenge certain aspects of ecclesiastical jurisdiction over heresy.[85]

To illustrate the range of false imprisonment, we may take a series of challenges to civic authority. In the fifteenth and sixteenth centuries there are a number of cases in the year books in which false imprisonment actions were used to challenge the validity of alleged municipal customs to imprison. The Common Pleas under Chief Justice Bryan (d. 1500) showed considerable hostility towards such customs. Thus, in 1481, Bryan held that a mayor could not prescribe to imprison an affrayer until he found surety to keep the peace; even the Common Pleas could not do that, and such a power could not rest on usage.[86] The following year, a defendant in false imprisonment pleaded a custom for the mayor of a borough to arrest anyone on suspicion of felony and imprison them for three days in the town jail before taking them to the nearest king's jail. Bryan retorted: "You cannot have this prescription, for it is completely against common right and all reason," in that it did not allow for any means of release within the three days, or for bail, and if one could prescribe for three days (as in this case) another might prescribe for three weeks or three years. The case was adjourned without known result.[87]

Four years later, two defendants pleaded a custom of London for parish beadles to arrest people found in adultery, take them to the

Counter (a city prison), and leave them there with a warden. Bryan was against the plea because they had not said how long they left the plaintiff in the Counter; but the judges were divided as to whether the prescription was in principle good, the main doubt being that adultery was a "spiritual" matter beyond the cognizance of the temporal authorities. No judgment was given.[88]

Despite the absence of judgments, which is a common feature of year-book cases, these doubts stood in the books and had their effect on later opinion. There was a similar group of cases challenging civic authority a century later. In 1579 the judges ruled against a "general warrant" issued by the recorder of London, holding that a warrant to arrest someone must specify the cause.[89] In 1587 they held that a mayor could not commit someone to jail for calling him a fool, unless he was sitting as a justice of the peace at the time.[90] A few years later it was held to be contrary to Magna Carta for a town, which had power to make ordinances, to imprison a resident for not paying a charge levied by ordinance; they could enforce payment by distress, or action at law, but could not give themselves a power to imprison.[91] Already, then, before 1600, Magna Carta was being pressed into new forms of service.

≺ VII ≻

Shortcomings of Trespass Actions

It cannot be pretended that the action of false imprisonment, and the other actions of trespass, were a perfect guarantee of freedom from restraint. For one thing, they were retrospective; they could only be brought after the event, by someone who had regained sufficient freedom to be able to launch an action, against someone whom it was practicable to sue; and they gave a successful plaintiff monetary compensation, not liberty. The rule that they could not be brought against the Crown itself was not a serious obstacle, insofar as the king did not personally lock up his subjects; there was always an agent who made the arrest or kept the keys, and he could be sued.[92] At the lower levels of authority, this did not present a problem. But where the arrest was ordered on high by the king's council, or by a justice of the peace, or some other authority closely associated with governmental power, the efficacy of a common-law action which required the cooperation of the sheriff (as all actions of trespass did) was limited.

The worst case was someone kept so closely and for so long that there was no practicable recourse to justice. But many others who were abused by public authority would probably have been advised that a suit would not succeed. Before the development of habeas corpus to fill this gap, the only recourse was to petition the king's council itself. And we find that, at any rate by Tudor times,[93] the Star Chamber could be sensitive to complaints of injustice committed by others. The original records of the court are lost, but Sir Thomas Egerton (later Lord Ellesmere, lord chancellor 1603–17) at the end of the sixteenth century collected the following three precedents (1488, 1520, and 1529) from the early registers:

Decembr. anno 4 H. 7 Pylkington fyned in 10 marks and imprisoned in the Fleete for imprisoning a pore man. 13 Febr. 11 H. 8. Sir John Townley to the Flete for attaching one who had a cause here agaynst hym. 27 Maii 22 H. 8, ten poundes awarded to Bennet Tracy for wrongfull imprisonment 3 quarters of a yere in the castell of Jersey by Sir Hugh Vaughan.[94]

Not long after this, we learn from Sir John Spelman (d. 1546), that Sir Humphrey Browne, a king's serjeant at law, was incarcerated in the Tower of London in 1540, apparently for giving advice which would have undermined the feudal revenue of the Crown; Browne complained to the Star Chamber after his release, and the legality of his imprisonment was discussed. Although no resolution in favor of liberty was arrived at, the case is of great interest as showing that the serjeant placed reliance on chapter 29 of Magna Carta.[95] Browne would himself become a judge; and the judicial tradition of which we have spoken may have been influenced by the fact that even eminent lawyers were not immune from high-handed action.

A particularly notable case occurred in the Star Chamber in 1577. One Simon Harcourt, a justice of the peace, had taken a prisoner to his own house and kept him there lying on his back for three or four hours with his legs in a pair of stocks, before taking him to the "common cage." For this offense he was fined £200 by the Star Chamber, imprisoned, and put out of the commission of the peace.[96] This shows how effectively the king's representatives could be brought to heel by the Council for acting improperly and without authority; but by this date the writ of habeas corpus was coming to provide a more routine means of challenging an imprisonment, or of obtaining bail, even in the case of an imprisonment by members of the Council itself.

≺ VIII ≻

Habeas Corpus

The writ of habeas corpus, as the name suggests,[97] was designed for moving bodies into the king's court.[98] It can be traced to the early thirteenth century,[99] and was at first chiefly used for executive purposes. In the fourteenth century, versions of it came into regular use as part of the process of the courts: the *habeas corpora* to secure the presence of unwilling jurors, the *corpus cum causa* used by the Chancery to review local (especially urban) courts, and the writ of privilege used by the common-law courts to protect persons attending the court as attorneys or litigants.[100]

None of the cases so far discovered before the sixteenth century clearly represents the general writ used to secure a release from imprisonment, though Coke and other later writers detected the underlying principle in some of the early precedents. Thus, Edward I issued a writ to free a monk from imprisonment by the bishop of Durham, and when the messengers were also imprisoned the court ordered the seizure of the bishop's liberties, and the arrest of his person, for contempt; according to Hale, this case established the king's authority to require cause to be shown for the imprisonment of any of his subjects, even in a palatinate.[101] In 1351, we find a writ addressed in French to the chief justice of the King's Bench to examine some poor prisoners in the Tower and certify the causes of their imprisonment, so that right could be done.[102] It seems from subsequent proceedings that this was at the instance of one of the prisoners; but the writ did not require the body to be sent, and it seems to have been an unusual procedure of an equitable character. Both Dyer and Coke attached importance to a case of 1465, which showed the use of *habeas corpus cum causa* to deliver a prisoner

---

Opposite: The Court of King's Bench, Westminster Hall, London, c. 1450. Miniature cut from law book. Reproduced by permission of the Masters of the Bench of the Inner Temple, London; photo courtesy of Inner Temple.

from the archbishop of Canterbury's prison at Maidstone; but this was a writ of privilege, the prisoner being a litigant in the King's Bench, and there was a jurisdictional dispute with the Audience Court of Canterbury.[103]

In the absence of privilege, then, the writ does not seem to have been generally available before the sixteenth century, as of right, to all persons who wished to challenge their detention. There is some indication, mentioned below, of the use of such a writ in the fifteenth century, but its establishment as a general remedy belongs to the Tudor period.

In the reign of Henry VIII we see the development of the remedy in its later form, the *habeas corpus ad subjiciendum*,[104] an innovation probably to be associated with a strong reaction against the abuse of conciliar authority in the later years of Henry VII.[105] In 1518, we find one Thomas Aprice, detained by command of Cardinal Wolsey, being released by habeas corpus in the King's Bench because the attorney general would not support the detention.[106] Aprice may have been implicated in the feud between Wolsey and Sir Robert Sheffield, whose habeas corpus in the same roll is returned "by command of the king alone."[107] The precedent was collected over forty years later by Chief Justice Dyer, when marshalling authorities on the scope of the remedy, and the Sheffield dispute was also known to Coke.[108] Another of Dyer's precedents was from 1546, when John Hogges and Thomas Heyth, after being committed to the Tower "by order of the king's council," were removed into the King's Bench by habeas corpus and committed to the marshal there.[109] They seem to have been common criminals; at any rate, they were sentenced to death the same term for receiving a thief.[110] But that was not the cause stated in the return, and (as Dyer noted) the legal significance of these precedents was that they established the authority of the King's Bench to examine the cause of imprisonment of any prisoner in the realm, and to commit, bail, or enlarge him as they thought expedient. Dyer also recalled how, when he was a student, the judges of the Common Pleas had disallowed a general return of a committal to the Tower by the mighty Thomas Cromwell as a member of the council.[111] Other uses of habeas corpus to secure the release of prisoners are known from this period.[112]

In Elizabethan times, the extent to which extrajudicial imprisonment—for instance, by command of the queen, or of privy councillors—could be judicially reviewed by means of habeas corpus became a familiar issue before the courts, and it is to this period that the final recognition of the remedy seems to belong.[113] Early in the new reign the judges were confronted with the case of Alexander Scrogges, an attorney of the Common Pleas who had become embroiled in controversy over an office in that court. The office had been unlawfully granted to a layman while the chief justiceship was vacant in 1558, but the court had rejected the grantee and admitted Scrogges. The earl of Bedford and Lord Robert Dudley used their influence at court to procure a special commission to determine the title, with power to commit Scrogges if he refused to answer. Scrogges demurred to the bill of complaint, and was committed to the Fleet prison for contempt. He then applied to the Common Pleas for his release, and Chief Justice Dyer considered using a general habeas corpus, which he considered could be issued under the court's inherent jurisdiction;[114] but it was decided instead to rely on Scrogges's privilege as an attorney, and to release him on a writ of privilege (which was a special form of habeas corpus laying stress on the need for his attendance to serve his clients).

Scrogges was immediately committed again by the commissioners, "to be kept in close prison": which was, as Dyer put it, "a check to the law." He remained in the Fleet for five weeks and more before he was released by Lord Keeper Bacon, who intervened to end the dispute; Scrogges kept his office, but had to pay a composition for it. The judges regarded the commission's behavior as a major affront, and (according to Chief Baron Saunders) actually held the commission void in law, so that everything which the commissioners did was *coram non judice*. Saunders wrote with some feeling about the case, concluding that "all suche of the justices of the Commen Place as did learnedlie and willinglie agree to the awarding and executing of the same wryt of pryvilidge deserved the imortall fame of honorable and good judges."[115] Nevertheless, the incident had brought home to them how troublesome it might be to give effect to the law in the teeth of powerful courtiers who cared little for due process. This may be one of the reasons why, as early as 1562, Dyer was collecting pertinent precedents of general habeas corpus, and these are of considerable interest, since they were overlooked by Selden (when collecting similar materials in 1627[116]) and are not noticed by modern writers either.[117]

Two important cases occurred in 1565. First, there was the case of John Lamburne (or Lambert), imprisoned by the Council of the North at York. The sheriff made his return to the writ of habeas corpus, in the Queen's Bench, that he had sent his deputy to York Castle to have the body, and was told by the jailer that he would not release the prisoner without leave of the archbishop of York, president of the Council, and the other members of the Council. The sheriff thereupon went to the archbishop, who told him that the prisoner was "incarcerated by command of him the said archbishop and others of the lady queen's Council and that he was not the prisoner of me the said sheriff," that he had written to the queen for a pardon, and that until he heard from the Privy Council concerning the pardon he would not release him; the archbishop then sent his secretary to the jailer, commanding him not to deliver the prisoner on receipt of the king's writ. The Queen's Bench not only ordered an *alias habeas corpus*, but (on the motion of a queen's serjeant) ordered a writ of attachment against the archbishop as well as the jailer.[118]

Secondly, Dyer provides in 1565 the first reported instance of habeas corpus for a prisoner of the High Commission.[119] The prisoner (a papist) was released, but promptly rearrested, on the footing that the commissioners had power to imprison at their discretion, without bail. This example of high-handedness was "much debated," but apparently without a resolution. Twelve years later the judges showed more boldness in rejecting a general return "committed by command of the high commissioners"; and it was on that occasion that Dyer recalled the case concerning Cromwell.[120] The court said it would allow a general return only in the case of a committal by the whole Privy Council, which might have secret reasons which it would be unsafe to make public; but an individual privy councillor had no power of committal without express cause, and no more did the High Commission. Even in the case of committal by the whole Council, the King's Bench would allow bail.[121]

Dyer further noted that in 1573, when a justice of assize, he followed a precedent of 1523 authorizing a habeas corpus to remove the body of a prisoner attainted of felony before the chief justice at his house in the country during the vacation; the reason for doing this is not stated, but the precedent was of value as showing that the writ could be used out of term or in chambers. The controlment rolls suggest that the practice of returning habeas corpus before individual judges in vacation became quite common at this period. Many of the examples were routine criminal cases, but the principle was of constitutional importance: liberty was not to be constrained by the calendar of Westminster Hall.

We have seen that imprisonment had been the subject also of jurisdictional and procedural wrangles, and by the 1570s (at the latest) habeas corpus was being used in such disputes as an alternative to false imprisonment. Thus, it was used to challenge customary claims by municipal authorities to imprison for disciplinary purposes, as being against Magna Carta.[122] It was used to challenge, with success, a novel clause in a royal writ of protection authorizing imprisonment for infringing its terms.[123] In the 1590s it came to be used to examine the orders of justices of the peace.[124] It was even invoked to check the jurisdiction of conciliar courts, such as the councils of the North and the Marches,[125] and the Court of Requests.[126] The way was already well cleared for Coke and Selden.

< IX >

Conclusion

The two aspects of liberty discussed above were not exhaustive of the categories of freedom recognized by the common law before 1600, but they were probably the two aspects most likely to spring to the mind of any contemporary asked about the state of liberty in England. And in practice they could not be divorced from the character of the legal system which gave them meaning. Admittedly, lawyers cannot claim responsibility for the idea of liberty, which as an abstraction is never very precisely defined; but in practice only they were able to invent, improve, and defend the means of securing it. As we have seen, liberty was not a heading in their books, with subdivisions and elaborate ramifications. Indeed, it was not built into the common law from the outset, but developed through the cumulative effect of decisions which were not widely known to outsiders and became unknown to posterity save through laborious research. Once taken, however, each of these decisions made an irreversible step "in favor of liberty."

That is the way the common law characteristically grew: not

through the vision of individuals of genius, but through the mediation of a learned profession which knew the wishes of its clientele and understood the mindset of the judges by whom those wishes had to be turned into reality. To be sure, every step might be opposed by lawyers of equal skill, and the path of development might therefore be long and tortuous. But the golden thread which no generation of judges ever lost from sight was that running from the great charter and its more expansive progeny: the principle that no one should be outside, beneath, or above the law of the land. "The law is the greatest inheritance that the king has," said Chief Baron Fray in 1441, "for by the law he himself and all his subjects are governed; and if this law did not exist, there would be no king and no inheritance."[127] The same law, as it developed in the centuries between Magna Carta and the end of the Tudor period, also gave the king's subjects in their turn a fair measure of personal freedom, and provided the doctrinal ammunition for the constitutional struggles of the seventeenth century.

Liberty in the Renaissance and Reformation

WILLIAM J. BOUWSMA

AFTER MUCH DEBATE , historians are now in general agreement that the Renaissance and Reformation, though differing in emphasis, were parallel and complementary expressions of a major shift in Western culture toward a world view more recognizably modern than anything that had preceded them. This was so, among other ways, in their contribution to modern conceptions of liberty. Major developments in this period included an assertion of the rights of particular polities to self-determination (that is, sovereignty), the claim that such polities should be governed by legally established bodies of their own citizens ("republican liberty"), and assertions (less securely established) of the rights of individuals to freedom of belief and expression. Even more fundamental in this period, however, was a shift, perhaps unique to Western culture, in the perception of freedom itself. It ceased to be viewed as intrinsically disorderly, indeed as a violation of the order of the universe as well as the order of society; it could now be seen instead as a positive good and essential to a fully human existence.[1]

≪ I ≫

Towns and the Emergence of a New Culture

No single cause can account for these developments. They undoubtedly included the emergence, from about the tenth century, of increasingly populous, well-organized, and assertive towns in some parts of Europe, whose claims to autonomy were problematic within an established feudal and hierarchical order in which every entity was theoretically subject to some superior. The rise of free towns was made possible by their growing wealth and power, but it was facilitated by the disintegration, increasingly apparent from the fourteenth century, of a traditional culture that had justified the feudal order and was therefore inimical in principle to freedom.

According to that traditional view, all that exists—in Christian terms the whole of creation—constitutes an ordered whole, a *cosmos*, whose immutable structures include all things within a single, integrated system. This system was generally described as "nature" and believed to be ruled by "laws of nature" ordained by God himself and accessible to human reason. Non-human nature was thought to obey these laws out of necessity, but human beings were believed to have some degree of freedom. This freedom, however, was not absolute; it was to be exercised in accordance with both divine and natural law.

Internally, as in the structures of feudalism, the cosmos was thought to be organized throughout as a hierarchy, every entity within it subordinate to the one above and the whole subject to God. Thus the heavenly bodies, themselves hierarchically ranked, were believed to influence things on earth, with some exception to accommodate the freedom of the human will. One expression of this conception was astrology, which was no mere superstition but considered a true science based on the orderly principles at work in the universe. Liberty was thus rejected on both physical and metaphysical grounds.

The extent to which the heavenly bodies limited the freedom of human beings was much debated. For the human personality was itself conceived as a "microcosm," a little world organized by the same principles as those at work in the universe, the "macrocosm." Thus human being too was understood as a hierarchy properly governed by reason, which was more or less identified with the soul. The will, the passions, and the body were believed to owe it obedience. "True liberty" for human beings, in this perspective, was identified with the rational acceptance of their place within the system as a whole.

Societies and governments were supposed, from this standpoint, to be similarly organized. In this view self-determination presented itself as rebellion against a divinely decreed order implicit in the whole of created reality and, indeed, visible in the orderly motions of the heavenly bodies. This meant in the first place that the realm of politics, like the cosmos it properly mirrors, is ideally a unity, commonly referred to as the "*respublica Christiana*," under a single "head," the emperor (or in other versions the pope), who presides over a hierarchy of lesser rulers: kings, princes, and the various ranks of feudal nobility. The controlling principle here was what Walter Ullmann has called the "descending theme" of political authority, in which every rank and person is ruled from above. In this system there could be no *citizens*; no person could be anything but a *subject*.[2] The emperor (or pope) was himself subject to God. The persistence of this scheme into the Renaissance is exemplified by the insistence of the Florentine Ambrogio Traversari that "true liberty consists in true subjection."[3]

Basic to the entire scheme was a remarkable optimism about the capacity of the human mind to grasp the patterns of order governing all things. The emergence of modern conceptions of liberty thus depended to a large degree on the replacement of a conception of human being as essentially rational, and realizing itself best in contemplating the divinely constituted order of things, by a far more complex image of the human personality as a bundle of unpredictable impulses, passions, and needs primarily oriented to action in society. Before the realm of politics could be regarded as of major importance in human existence, the old optimism about the human mind that had been fundamental to classical philosophy had to give way to a very different understanding of human being; *homo rationalis* had to be replaced by *homo socialis*. This was an essential prerequisite to a positive estimate of liberty.

Large cultural shifts are among the most difficult events for historians to explain. Nevertheless the erosion of what I have described as "traditional culture" was probably closely connected to a series of terrible disasters that afflicted the peoples of Europe in the fourteenth and fifteenth centuries: conflicts within towns, prolonged and destructive wars, and epidemic diseases; the shrinking of Christendom under pressure from the Ottoman Turks in the eastern Mediterranean; the collapse in Germany and Italy of the effective power of the two great agencies of universal authority, the Holy Roman Empire and the papacy; and the exile of the papacy in Avignon from its "true home" in Rome, which was followed by the division of the supposedly universal church into two, and for a while three, segments under rival popes. These terrible events cast doubt on the fundamental order and rationality of the world, or at least on the ability of human beings to grasp them. The actual condition of the world, practically if not necessarily in theory, belied the supposed order of things.

In addition, before the end of the thirteenth century some Christian thinkers had already begun to realize that the considerable naturalistic determinism implicit in this traditional world view was antithetical to a biblical understanding of the world and the human condition; and the authority of Aristotle, for some time considered "*the* philosopher" by many European intellectuals, was opposed not only by the papacy but even at the University of Paris. By the fourteenth century two movements of thought, both largely religious in inspiration, were directly challenging the traditional rationalism and the view of the human personality and its powers that accompanied it. One was nominalism, a development within later medieval philosophy and theology;[4] the other was Renaissance humanism.[5] Both movements expressed a growing sense of the limitations of the human intellect and thus increasing reservations about the comprehensibility of nature as traditionally conceived. Nature now seemed less and less promising as a source of reliable guidance for human behavior or for the structures of society and government. The result was a growing challenge to human beings to invent for themselves, on the basis simply of their own needs, such institutions and ways of life as best suited them.

≺ II ≻

Renaissance Humanism and Italian Republicanism

The skepticism underlying both nominalism and humanism deeply influenced the Reformation in northern and central Europe. In Italy, however, nominalism had little influence; and for the Renaissance understanding of liberty humanism was more important. This movement had its origins in the arts curriculum of the Italian universities as a rebellion against an emphasis on logic, the fundamental art for the rationalism of the traditional culture, in which it was considered the key to laying bare the underlying order of reality.[6] Early humanists (this name is derived from the noun "*umanista*," an arts student) instead emphasized rhetoric, the art of persuasive communication in society, and therefore an essential instrument of moral and spiritual improvement. In order to develop this art, humanists studied the classical Latin (and eventually Greek) orators, poets, ethical writers, and historians, rather than speculative philosophy, a shift that also reflected a changing conception of the human personality.

Humanistic rhetoric found fertile soil in the towns of Italy, whose inhabitants experienced the world less as a coherent system of intelligible and dependable regularities of the kind to which logic could give access, than as a succession of novel, often unpredictable, ambiguous, and even contradictory experiences, in the rough-and-tumble of social existence, whose meaning was perhaps best grasped immediately, imaginatively, and emotionally, but intellectually perhaps only secondarily. In cities ordinary people conversed and corresponded with their friends and neighbors, and businessmen sought to persuade their customers and associates. Governments negotiated with one another, sent out embassies, and appealed to local or foreign opinion.

The political status of the Italian town was of special importance for the history of liberty. Imperial control even in medieval Germany had rarely been practically effective, and in Italy it was, with rare exceptions, even more precarious. In an otherwise largely feudalized Europe, northern and central Italy was unusual for its concentration of towns that aspired to rule themselves. As early as the twelfth century they were described by Otto of Freising as "so desirous of liberty" that they chose "consuls" as their rulers in order to maintain "the freedom of the people."[7] A century later the Florentine Brunetto Latini, a scholar active in the affairs of his city, remarked in commenting on Aristotle's *Politics* that governments "are of three kinds: one is of kings, the second is of the aristocracy, and the third of the people, which is the best of the three."[8] And rhetoric proved especially useful for the needs of such self-governing republics as Florence. Their citizens had to win the agreement of peers on questions of public policy, and ruling bodies had to persuade their citizenry to support them. Latini had also recognized the political value of rhetorical skills; he himself studied the rhetoric of Cicero so that he could teach his contemporaries, as the fourteenth-century chronicler Giovanni Villani reported, "how to speak well, and how to guide and rule our republic according to policy."[9]

Republicanism was also allied with the scholarly side of humanism, which investigated and idealized republicanism in antiquity. It was well known that Roman law had, at least in theory, seen the community as the only source of political authority.[10] There were already hints of the idealization of republicanism in Francesco Petrarch (1304–74), the "father" of Renaissance humanism, whose admiration for the Roman republic was central to his epic poem *Africa*, and who was excited by the prospect of its reconstitution in his own time, a possibility suggested to him by a revolt in Rome in 1347 led by Cola di Rienzo.[11] Humanists not only idealized the Roman republic; at times they even glorified tyrannicide.

But although they commonly praised government by "the people," this did not, in the Renaissance, mean democracy, but—a quite different matter—government by those duly designated as citizens. Citizenship was variously defined in Renaissance Italy.[12] But it was usually confined to a relatively narrow group, and the words *"populus"* or *"popolo"* generally referred to what was considered the politically competent minority, Aristotle's middle party of practical order, indeterminate in size, between a small group of powerful men who aspired to rule from above and the politically incompetent masses. This often meant, in Florence and elsewhere, something closer to oligarchy than to democracy; the idealized political discussion of Renaissance republicans generally ignored the disenfranchised masses, who were regarded as dangerous to the order of the state. Machiavelli would note in his *Florentine Histories*, of a period particularly dangerous for the survival of the Republic, the existence of three interest groups: one of "the great," another of "the people," and a third of "the artisans."[13]

Yet a greater degree of egalitarianism was sometimes suggested in republican writings. The distinguished Florentine humanist Leonardo Bruni (1369–1444) had suggested that the liberty he praised so highly was rooted in equality, and civic humanists generally subscribed to the view that "true nobility" is a function rather of virtue, which is possible for everybody, than of birth. The idea was not new, and it was not immediately applied to politics; but it was potentially significant for the future extension of political freedom.

Although we encounter it in other places in Italy—notably Padua and Milan, occasionally in Rome, and finally in Venice—the alliance between humanism and republicanism was most conspicuous in Florence. Several distinguished humanists served as chancellors of the Florentine republic during the later fourteenth and fifteenth centuries, employing in this capacity their considerable rhetorical skills to supervise the correspondence of the government and to write and speak on its behalf.[14] The first of these, Coluccio Salutati (1331–1406), was deeply convinced that a republic, in which decision-making rested ultimately with the whole body of citizens, was the kind of government most acceptable to God. He modeled the style of his official letters on the classics, and his eloquence was famous; he made the pen seem, for the first time in European history, mightier than the sword. The duke of Milan, at war with Florence, admitted that Salutati's writings were worth more than a thousand of his own horsemen. Against despotic Milan Salutati celebrated the freedom and—for him they went together—the virtue of Florence, heir to the admirable values displayed by the Roman republic.[15]

The leading humanist-chancellor of fifteenth-century Florence was Bruni. An even better classicist than Salutati, Bruni exploited analogies from Greek and Roman history to display both the effectiveness of rhetorical eloquence and the moral values inherent in republican liberty. Republics, he believed, provided a uniquely favorable environment for the productive use of human energy and the realization of the highest possibilities of the human condition. "Once the sweetness of liberty was tasted, and the people itself was lord and bestower of honors," he wrote, "[men] applied themselves with all their strength in order to merit the respect of their peers." These were major themes in his *History of the Florentine People*, itself a notable example of rhetorical art.[16] Following directions laid out by Salutati, this work provided a historical justification for Florentine republicanism. Bruni traced the origins of Florence back to the time of the Roman republic rather than (as previously done) to that of the Empire. He saw the establishment of the Empire as the beginning of Rome's decline, "for liberty [then] gave way before the imperial name, and as liberty disappeared so did virtue." The collapse of the Roman Empire, however, provided, he argued, the opportunity for a new birth of republicanism. "Little by little," Bruni wrote about later imperial rule, "the Italian cities began to want liberty and to acknowledge the empire's authority [only] nominally rather than in practice. The city of Rome received respect for its ancient power rather than for its present awesomeness . . . Meanwhile those Italian cities that had survived the various floods of barbarians began to grow and flourish and to regain their original independence."[17]

In various writings Bruni praised Florence, especially because Florence was a republic. A notable example was a funeral oration he composed for a Florentine contemporary in 1428 on the model of the famous oration of Pericles given by Thucydides:

Equal liberty exists for all . . . the hope of winning public honors and ascending is the same for all . . . provided they lead a serious-minded and respected way of life; for our commonwealth requires *virtus* and *probitas* in its citizens. Whoever has these qualifications is thought to be of sufficiently noble birth to participate in the government of the republic . . . This, then, is true liberty, this equality among citizens before the law and in the participation in public office . . . But now it is marvelous to see how powerful this access to public office, once it is offered to a free people, proves to be in awakening the talents of the citizens. For where men are given the hope of attaining the highest honor in the state, they take courage and raise themselves to a higher plane; where they are deprived of that hope, they grow idle and lose their strength. Therefore since such hope and opportunity are held out in our commonwealth, we need not be surprised that talent and industry distinguish themselves in the highest degree.[18]

The importance of Florentine republicanism for the history of European liberty, especially as it was articulated by Bruni, has been widely discussed by historians during the last few decades. The discussion began with the publication in 1955 of a major work by Hans Baron, *The Crisis of the Early Italian Renaissance*.[19] Most historians now agree with Baron on the significance of the development of the Florentine republican consciousness for European political discourse and historiography. But Baron's explanation for it has been much disputed. In his view, it was stimulated by a prolonged confrontation between despotic Milan and republican Florence which, he argued, acutely threatened Florentine liberty, especially between 1400 and 1402, when Florence was nearly conquered by a Milanese army led by Duke Giangaleazzo Visconti.

This "crisis," Baron believed, produced a great wave of patriotic fervor, articulated by Bruni and other humanists, that made Florentines fully conscious of their republican values. Their love of Florence awakened, Florentine humanists were also able to move from the limited historical perspectives of an earlier classicism that idealized the Roman Empire to a novel admiration for independent and self-governing states like their own. For a model of political perfection they no longer looked, as Dante had done, to the universal state constructed by imperial Rome, which had given the world the benefits of unity and peace, but to the self-governing republics of antiquity: that of Rome, but also of Periclean Athens. For Baron, then, Bruni's writings were the first significant result of this shift, and he was followed by other "civic humanists" in a rich tradition that reached a climax in Florence with the great political and historical compositions of Machiavelli and Guicciardini. Florentine republicanism was thus eventually crucial for modern political thought and especially for the democracies of the Atlantic seaboard.

For Baron's critics, however, this contrast between fourteenth and fifteenth-century Florence is too extreme. Above all it seems unlikely that so basic and momentous a shift in attitudes could have occurred in so short a time. Gene Brucker, for example, perhaps Baron's most balanced critic, while accepting his argument for the importance of Florentine republicanism, prefers to account for it in terms of general features of Florentine society and politics, long at work, that had "facilitated communication between intellectuals, merchants, and statesmen, and provided a unique forum for the spread of new ideas and opinions." The result was a peculiarly Florentine "symbiotic bond" between "the worlds of thought and action" that gradually shaped a distinctively republican consciousness.[20] Quentin Skinner, on the other hand, has pointed out that Florentine republicanism was nourished not only by Renaissance humanism but also by scholastic thinkers, mostly followers of Thomas Aquinas, so that in this respect too it does not make so radical a break with the past as Baron believed.[21]

It is also important to recognize limitations in the republicanism of Salutati and Bruni, whose thought remained, in at least one major respect, traditional. They were, as their writings reveal, idealists who viewed politics, in the words of J. G. A. Pocock, as "the assertion of values, or virtues, by individuals, in public acts." A state, in this conception, both is maintained by the virtue of its citizens and provides opportunities for its expression. In this perspective, the state is above all "a moral community," indeed an instrument for the salvation of its members; and it is endangered chiefly by the possibility of degeneration or corruption. This view of the state was also essentially static; it recognized change only in the decline or the renewal of a moral ideal.[22] This idealized politics infused, for example, Bruni's explanation for the decline of the Roman Empire. "Liberty ceased with the emperors," Bruni wrote, "and with liberty, virtue departed. For previously the way to honors was through virtue." But under the Empire virtue was no longer valued; thus "the government of things passed to the worst elements," and this gradually destroyed the state.[23] In the words of another fifteenth-century Florentine humanist, "Virtue is the quality by means of which it is possible to maintain a stable and lasting political society."[24] The moralism and the timelessness here both suggest the persistent influence of traditional conceptions of politics. But in spite of these reservations, Baron's views continue, however modified, to stimulate lively debate.[25]

But the survival of the Florentine republic was precarious. Although the forms of republican government endured, Florence in the later fifteenth century was increasingly controlled by the Medici, a prominent and politically active banking family, who eventually dominated the city somewhat like modern big-city bosses; and their autocratic direction steadily reduced the active participation of the whole body of citizens in public affairs. And before the end of the century Italy had become a battlefield for foreign armies. A French invasion of Italy from the north in 1484 was met by Spanish forces in the south; and the two great powers fought each other for the control of Italy until 1530, after which most of Italy was dominated by Spain. The unsettled condition of Italy made possible the restoration of the Florentine republic from 1494 to 1512 and again, more briefly, between 1527 and 1530. But with Italy increasingly subjected to great outside powers, Florence could no longer effectively control her own destiny. Republican liberty, both as independence and as self-government by citizens, was doomed; and the fully autocratic rule of the Medici was effectively restored through the collaboration of the Holy Roman Emperor (who was also king of Spain) and a Medici pope.

During the temporary revival of the Florentine republic, however, Florentine republicanism found its most mature and articulate spokesmen. Between 1494 and 1498 the Dominican friar Girolamo Savonarola preached charismatic sermons that combined republican fervor with calls for moral and spiritual reform.[26] He was followed as an exponent of republicanism by Niccolò Machiavelli (1468–1527), who served the restored republic after 1498 as a secretary and diplomat. Machiavelli lost his position with the demise of the republic in 1512; but during his enforced retirement, he reflected about the tragic events that had destroyed the liberty both of Florence and of Italy. The result was a number of works, especially *The Prince, Discourses on Livy,* and *Florentine Histories,* which constitute the fullest and most sophisticated discussion in the Renaissance of republican liberty, its benefits, and the dangers to which it was exposed.

Machiavelli thus brought the Florentine republican tradition to a new stage in its development. He had studied and was influenced by Bruni and other civic humanists. Like them he was concerned to persuade his contemporaries to support the values, and devote themselves to the service, of their community; and although he wrote in the vernacular rather than in Latin, he too was a distinguished rhetorician.[27] He also shared and gave further impetus to the cultural assumptions underlying the rhetorical tradition, especially its indifference to grand speculative systems of thought. But his perspectives on politics differed from those of his predecessors in one important respect. Where they had been idealists, he was a realist.

His views were radically secular. Thus, instead of looking above for guidance, to the abstract principles of nature, to reason, or even to Scripture, he studied the world around him, seeking guidance through the tangle of contemporary events in political experience, both his own and that of the past as recorded in histories. And the conclusions he drew from experience seemed to him utterly at variance with the old idealism. The chief motives of political behavior, experience taught him, were simply ambition and greed. For Machiavelli, as for St. Augustine, human beings are sinners; and they come together in societies not, as Aristotle taught, because they are by nature social or, as for Bruni, to exercise virtue, but the better to defend themselves against other predatory human beings. For the same reason the ideal of an enduring order and peace in human affairs was for him an illusion; history, given the restlessness and undependability of human nature, always has been and always will be a record of conflict and change and of human efforts to cope with them.

Machiavelli valued political liberty as deeply as his Florentine predecessors, and like them he believed that its preservation depends to a substantial degree on the deliberate choices of human beings. He recognized that freedom to make wise choices in politics is not absolute, but always limited by immediate circumstances, by historical conditions, and by unpredictable events; fortune, he admitted, rules half our actions. But this also meant that we can control the other half; and he insisted that this substantial if limited area of freedom makes possible both morality and human dignity.[28] As he put it in the concluding chapter of *The Prince*, "God does not want to do everything, in order not to take free choice from us and the part of that glory that belongs to us." The exercise of such choices was, for Machiavelli, a particular obligation of political leadership; he condemned the indecisiveness of Florentine rulers in the past and was generally sickened by the passivity and irresolution he discerned among the princes of his time, which he blamed for the woes of Italy.[29]

His insistence on this basic dimension of human freedom underlay his more particular conceptions of liberty, which again he described much like earlier Florentines. For him too political liberty consisted first of all in freedom from external control, the right of states to self-determination, in a word sovereignty. He followed Bruni in viewing the breakup of the Roman Empire in the West as an opportunity rather than a tragedy, elaborating on the idea: "There was so much bravery and intelligence in some of the new cities and governments that afterward sprang up," he wrote of this event, "that, even if one did not dominate the others, they were nonetheless harmonious and ordered together so that they freed Italy and defended it from the barbarians."[30] He believed in general that "where political powers are many, many able men appear; where such powers are few, few."[31]

But on this matter Machiavelli's vision went beyond Bruni, who was chiefly concerned with Florence. Following a tradition that can be traced back to Dante and Petrarch, but above all deeply disturbed by recent events, he applied the idea of self-determination to the whole of Italy, domination over which had been contested in earlier centuries between emperors and popes, and in his own time by the ravaging armies of France and Spain. He compared the subjugation of Italy by foreign powers to the enslavement of the Israelites in

Egypt; and, exploiting an analogy that would be often invoked by later liberation movements, he compared the emancipation of Italy for which he yearned to the Exodus.[32]

A corollary of the autonomy of states was, for Machiavelli, the balance of power to regulate their relationships with one another. So often blamed for the disorders of modern history, this principle seemed in the Renaissance, in the absence of a single overarching power that could control the entire political universe, the only means of preserving peace. In fact this notion had been articulated first in fifteenth-century Venice.[33] But during the prolonged crisis in Florentine affairs set off by the French invasion of 1494, young Florentines began to analyze the troubles that had followed this event; and one of Machiavelli's friends, Bernardo Rucellai, explained the relative peace in Italy that had preceded the invasion by the conception of an equilibrium maintained among its major powers.[34] Machiavelli drew on the conception in his own description of the peace that, as he believed, had followed the disintegration of the Roman Empire.

But liberty conceived simply as sovereignty is also consistent with despotism, as Jean Bodin and Thomas Hobbes would demonstrate; and a second and equally important aspect of liberty for Machiavelli, as it had been for the humanists of the previous century, was self-government by citizens in a republic. Like them he idealized the Roman republic and contrasted it with the Empire. "The peoples of old," he wrote, "were so fond of liberty and held the word in such esteem that they detested tyrants and gave them no peace." He condemned the Roman Empire for its destruction of free republics, at the same time noting that it found the conquest of free peoples especially difficult.[35]

There was thus something like a moral dimension to Machiavelli's republicanism. Republican government, in his view, is superior to all other forms of government because it alone can be depended on to serve the common good.[36] Fidelity to this purpose was, for him, the essence of justice. He also saw it as the basis of personal freedom, for him essential to the good life, which he defined as the ability of a man "to enjoy freely his property without fear and to have nothing to fear for the honor of his wife and daughters or for himself."[37] Freedom from fear loomed large for Machiavelli and his contemporaries; not the least among the advantages of a republic, in which no single person had a monopoly of power, was personal security.

Machiavelli thought a republic superior to any other kind of government. Republics, he believed, are likely to be wealthier and more populous. Their citizens are more stubborn in defending themselves and support their leaders more effectively. Agreements with republics are more trustworthy than those with princes. Since a prince is likely to be "more ungrateful, changeable, and imprudent than a people," republics last longer than principates. Princes may be better at imposing order—a sentiment that helps to explain the place of *The Prince* in Machiavelli's thought—but a people is far superior in maintaining it once established.

At times Machiavelli also suggested an egalitarianism more radical than that of any of his predecessors; that his sentiments were more democratic than theirs was implicit in his writing in Italian rather than Latin, the language of scholars. In his *Florentine Histories* he attributed to a figure whom he praised as "one of the most daring and experienced" of the Florentines a remarkable exhortation to his upper-class colleagues to respect those below them on the social scale: "Strip all of us naked, you will see that we are all alike; dress us in their clothes and them in ours, and without a doubt, we shall appear noble and they ignoble."[38] Social inequality, in short, was for him as arbitrary as the clothes we wear. He also recommended the enlargement of the Great Council, the most democratic of the Florentine governing bodies, to include all citizens.[39] It is hardly surprising, then, that the voice of the people, for Machiavelli, was like the voice of God.[40]

But he also recognized that the stability of a republic depended on an appropriate institutional framework; institutions, he believed, are in the long run more important—because they outlive them— than men.[41] He recognized that, unless regulated by laws, government will necessarily be arbitrary and incapable of promoting the common good.[42] Above all, he was convinced, a republic needs a constitutional framework, another lesson he learned from republican Rome. The best arrangement, he believed, again following Bruni, is a mixed constitution, in which the principle of balance, so useful for regulating the relations among states, would also operate within them.

Machiavelli's constitutional thought was thus based on a charac-teristically realistic recognition that the common good will always be endangered by the efforts of special interests to manipulate the power of government to their own advantage. But he saw that, given the plurality of such interests, the danger from one can always be balanced and neutralized by the combination of the others. Thus self-ish special interests, however reprehensible in themselves, should never be permitted to eliminate each other entirely; this would be even more dangerous.[43]

The constitution of the United States would eventually adopt this Machiavellian principle in its provision for the separation of powers. Modern constitutionalism would have other sources be-sides Florentine republicanism, including the Roman and canon law traditions, Thomism, and conciliarism, a movement of the period that envisaged the church as a constitutional monarchy.[44] But Ma-chiavelli would be more widely read in later centuries than the rep-resentatives of any of these currents of thought.

The reciprocal checking and balancing of competing particular interests may also suggest still another dimension of freedom that is at least implicit in the Renaissance civic tradition: freedom of thought and expression. The deliberations of citizens in their assem-blies would be profitable only if contrary views could be freely ex-pressed. Machiavelli recognized this too. He described Roman an-tiquity as a "golden age when everyone [was] free to hold and to defend his own opinion," and he denounced episodes in Florentine history when Florentines were forbidden to speak freely.[45] The move-ments of the Reformation in northern and central Europe would add urgency to this dimension of liberty.

Although Florence was the most notable example of Renaissance republicanism, it was not alone in Renaissance Italy. Venice was at least as important politically and commercially, if not culturally; and after the demise of the Florentine republic, when the rest of Italy was largely controlled by foreign powers, the Venetian republic remained free, both from Spanish control and as a state ruled by her own citizens under a constitution that was admired in much of Eu-rope. And the fear of her great neighbors, together with the central-izing pressures of the Counter-Reformation papacy, stimulated in Venice, during the later sixteenth and early seventeenth centuries, reflection about republican liberty comparable to what we have observed in Florence. The result was a kind of delayed flowering of Renaissance republicanism in Venice that made a powerful impression on Europeans elsewhere.[46]

The most important exponents of Venetian republicanism were Paolo Paruta (1540–98), a cultivated Venetian statesman and historian, and the Servite friar Paolo Sarpi (1552–1623). Paruta composed an extended dialogue *On the Perfection of Political Life* (1579) that idealized Renaissance republicanism and the active life of civic responsibility in ways reminiscent of Florentine civic humanism; and his *Political Discourses*, published in 1599 after his death, suggests the realism of Machiavelli. The interest of this work in the decline of the Roman Empire, which he attributed to its excessive size, also suggests one of the concerns of Florentine republicanism.

Sarpi served as legal adviser to the Venetian government during an interdict imposed by the pope in 1606–7, which was resisted by Venice on the ground that papal claims to supervise aspects of Venetian social and religious life infringed on Venetian sovereignty. Here we again encounter, in a new context, a fundamental concern of civic humanism, although Sarpi's treatment of the subject also drew on the more radical position associated with Jean Bodin and the divine right theories of the seventeenth century. Sarpi wrote widely in support of Venice. His *History of the Council of Trent* (1619) deserves special notice as a vehicle of the Italian republican tradition for Europeans of the seventeenth and eighteenth centuries. A sustained criticism of the papal monarchy over the church from the perspective of Renaissance republicanism, it was widely translated. William Brewster, the spiritual leader of the Plymouth colony, carried its English translation to the New World.[47]

Through the writings of a series of Renaissance republicans, the advantages of republican liberty were widely publicized throughout western Europe.[48] The relative merits of princely and republican rule became a favorite topic for displays of rhetorical virtuosity even at princely courts: a sign, perhaps, in an age of princely absolutism, that, except briefly in England, republicanism was no longer much of a threat to European establishments. A debate on this subject figured in Baldassare Castiglione's *Book of the Courtier* (1528), in which princely rule is predictably the winner, though only after a Venetian had been allowed to praise republican liberty in conventional terms.[49] More surprising was the endorsement of republics by Giovanni Botero (1544–1617), who spent most of his life as a publicist for the ideals of the Counter Reformation and whose works were widely read. Botero wrote:

From good government derive all those good qualities in subjects that belong to civil and virtuous life, every means for doing good things, all the arts both of peace and war, of acquiring and saving, all polite customs, all noble manners, every honored form of politeness. For this reason free cities of great size surpass those that are subject to princes, at once in magnificence of buildings and in beauty of streets and squares, in multitude of people, in variety of arts, in refinement of manners, and in every kind of polity and humanity. Venice and Genoa prove it, and Florence and Siena did so in their time.[50]

The contributions of Renaissance republicanism to liberty were not forgotten in later centuries.

_{≺ III ≻}

Liberty and the Reformation

Because Protestantism varied widely, the contribution of the Protestant Reformation to modern liberty was more complex than that of the Renaissance, which had been essentially a function of urban republicanism, especially in Florence. Each of the main Protestant leaders and groups conceived of liberty in different ways. We must therefore look in turn at the movements led by Martin Luther (1483–1546), Ulrich Zwingli (1484–1531), John Calvin (1509–64), and Heinrich Bullinger (1504–75), all representatives of what is sometimes called the "magisterial Reformation" because the churches they founded were officially established by the governments of princely states or towns and usually given a monopoly over religious life. But another element in the Reformation was a sectarian movement that rejected such collaboration with worldly government. Sometimes identified (inaccurately) with "Anabaptism," sometimes described collectively as the "radical Reformation," this movement raised the issue of religious toleration.

A major similarity between the Reformation and the Renaissance was that both were largely based on self-governing (or "free") cities: Protestantism, especially in Germany and Switzerland, was a

phenomenon of cities that, like those in Italy, obeyed no superior
and were governed by their own citizens.[51] Machiavelli had heard
enough about the free German cities to believe that they were republics after his own heart. Only in Germany, he believed, were
there still republics "in the full enjoyment of liberty, observing their
laws in such manner that no one from within or without could venture upon an attempt to answer them." They obeyed the emperor,
he thought, only "when they chose," and they did not "fear him or
any other potentate." He attributed this, among other matters, to
the "perfect equality" that prevailed among them and to their hostility to the German princes.[52]

Machiavelli was not entirely wrong; citizens of the German
towns resembled those of the Italian republics in some respects.
They too were patriots, proud of their communities and concerned
to define and promote the common good; and, as in Italy, their values were sometimes articulated in the writings of local lay humanists. The free cities of Germany also resembled the republics of Italy
in that they were more oligarchic than democratic. There were differences among them; democratic tendencies were stronger in southern Germany and Switzerland than in the north. A series of guild
revolts in the later Middle Ages had slightly broadened political participation; and there were growing tensions between rich and poor
in the towns on the eve of the Reformation, accompanied by growing pressure for reform on the part of the lower strata of society,
some of it articulated by humanists.[53]

Nevertheless German towns differed in one significant respect
from those in Italy, if only in degree. In their unusual emphasis on
its religious dimension, they departed from Machiavelli's ultimately
secular model of political community; and this difference helps to
explain why Protestantism had little impact on Italy. German and
Swiss towns saw themselves as sacred communities, instruments of
collective salvation, ruled at least ideally by the Gospel. In them the
language of brotherly love was commonly used to describe the relations among their inhabitants.[54]

One expression of this conception was the close supervision of
churches by town councils;[55] well before the Reformation civic authorities in northern Europe sought to enforce Christian morality
by laws against prostitution, adultery, gambling, and—most important—blasphemy. As the great northern humanist Erasmus of Rot-

terdam (c. 1469–1536) asked rhetorically in a letter of 1518, "What else is a city but a great monastery?"[56] The implications of such legislated morality for individual freedom were hardly positive.

But the cultural changes that underlay the development of political freedom in Italy were also at work in northern Europe, though they may have worked more slowly; and northern humanists were in some cases more directly concerned with religious reform and readier to defy ecclesiastical authority than those in Italy. Erasmus, scholar and religious thinker, was the great spokesman for this concern. His many publications—lucid and witty religious writings, editions of classical and patristic works, biblical commentaries, and even a Greek New Testament—gave him an international literary reputation. He also corresponded with other scholars in every part of Europe.

Erasmus's contribution to the history of liberty consisted partly in his dissemination of attitudes destructive of traditional culture and favorable to liberty similar to those in Italian humanism, partly also in an insistence on the individual appropriation and inwardness of Christian belief that was ultimately subversive of institutional authority. Skeptical of the rationalizing scholastic theology of the time, his most famous work, *The Praise of Folly* (1509), identified Christianity not with what passed for wisdom in the world but with its opposite. Erasmus sought to substitute, for a Christianity that has been described as 80 percent moralism, 15 percent sacramental observance, and 5 percent dogma,[57] a more personal and inward religion of the heart, based on individual study and appropriation of the Bible, that would find expression in practical piety and works of love. For Erasmus Christianity was both a way of life for the individual and the means to reform a deficient world. It is hardly surprising that ecclesiastical authority took a dim view of Erasmus; it was a common saying of the time that Erasmus had "laid the egg that Luther hatched."

Luther's challenge to the papacy in 1517 over the question of indulgences is generally taken as the beginning of the Reformation. His own contribution to the history of liberty was, however, ambiguous. To be sure, his revolt against an authoritarian papacy, the spiritual representative of traditional universalism, encouraged the rebellion of others; and his theology—though in part misunderstood—helped to set off a broader though ultimately unsuccessful "revolt of the common man" against political and social injustice. But Luther's absolute distinction between the all-important realm of the spirit and the institutions of this world, which he considered spiritually indifferent, meant, for him, that Christians should submit to authoritarian governments; it was therefore generally inimical to political freedom.

Nevertheless the central importance Luther attributed to justification by faith was a major contribution to the value of the individual and of individual experience that is basic to the history of liberty. And his doctrine of Christian liberty helped to establish freedom as a central value of human existence. This doctrine was based on another absolute distinction: between the merely external virtue that results from obedience to law, rendered out of fear and self-concern, and a free, cheerful, and spontaneous goodness that resulted, for Luther, from a faith which consists in a whole-hearted trust in God that liberates the believer from self-concern. "This freedom," he wrote, "consists of taking pleasure simply by doing good, or in living uprightly, without being constrained to do so by the law. This freedom is therefore a spiritual freedom; it does not abolish the law; rather it supplies and furnishes us what the law lacks, namely willingness and love."[58] "Thus," he declared again, "a Christian living in this trust in God knows everything, is capable of everything, and dares to do anything that is to be done, and does everything joyfully and freely, not in order to amass merits and good works, but because it is a pleasure to him to please God in this way; and he serves God wholly gratuitously, content that it pleases God."[59] For Luther any other conception of freedom only enslaves human beings to their own anxieties; like Machiavelli, but in a more general way, Luther was concerned to liberate his contemporaries from fear. His loyal lieutenant Philip Melanchthon also suggested the relation of this doctrine to the new Renaissance conception of human being; Christian freedom meant, for Melanchthon, not the rejection of the law, "but that we will and desire spontaneously and from the heart what the law demands. This no one could ever do before."[60]

Another expression of Luther's meaning, possibly developed under his influence,[61] was the idealized Abbey of Thélème depicted by François Rabelais, one of Erasmus's most famous followers, in *Gargantua* and *Pantagruel*. Its name derived from a Greek word meaning free will, the abbey had only one rule: "Do What You Will [Fay

Ce Que Vouldras]." Its residents included both men and women, whose lives were "laid out not by laws, statutes, or rules but according to their free will and choice. They got out of bed when they saw fit, drank, ate, worked, slept when they felt like doing so."[62]

Since the freedom of the Christian was an individual freedom and accessible to every individual, it was also subversive of the principle of hierarchy, so often used to justify political domination. "There is no superior among Christians," Luther asserted, "but Christ himself and Christ alone."[63] Other aspects of his thought also defied the hierarchical principle. Thus he denied that any good work is superior spiritually to any other. For if a man's heart "is assured that it is pleasing to God," he wrote, "the work is good, even if it is as small as picking up a blade of straw."[64] His doctrine of the priesthood of all believers, too, was an assertion in principle of human equality. So was his doctrine of the calling, which was basic to his respect for political authority. He believed that every occupation, every station in life, is an assignment by God, and that every worldly status is equal before God: the emperor is thus no greater than the humblest artisan, peasant, or housewife.[65] Lutheranism did not overtly threaten power and dominion, but it profoundly altered the way in which they were regarded.

Luther's early followers were attracted by his doctrine of Christian liberty. But they tended to understand it only negatively, as freedom from a wide range of obligations enforced by the church: among others confession and penances, fasting and pilgrimages, and the obligation of celibacy for the clergy. Protestant rejection of clerical celibacy had implications, too, for the dignity of women. The rule of celibacy had been widely violated in the later medieval church, especially in rural areas, where priests often entered into illegal but stable family relationships. The freedom of a Christian, for Luther personally but also for others, allowed the clergy to marry; and the "priest's whore" was thus promoted in Protestantism to the honorable status of priest's wife.

But the positive implications of Luther's doctrine of Christian freedom, as Melanchthon recognized in retrospect, proved "hard to comprehend."[66] For Luther it meant, to be sure, freedom from self-concern, but only for service to God and neighbor.[67] Here we can discern, in a new form, another motif of civic humanism: a conception of the religious life as active service on behalf of the community. For Luther too a human being not only best serves God but also best fulfills the deepest needs of his spiritual nature by service to others. "A man," he wrote, "does not live for himself alone in this mortal body to work for it alone . . . he lives only for others and not for himself . . . He cannot ever in this life be idle and without works toward his neighbors, for he will necessarily speak, deal with, and exchange views with men, as Christ also, being made in the likeness of men, was found in form as a man and conversed with men."[68]

The Reformation in the urban republics of Switzerland and southern Germany was more directly relevant than Lutheranism to the history of liberty. We have noticed above that the self-image of these towns as sacred communities combined with growing social tensions to make them unusually receptive to calls for religious change; but they rejected Luther's radical distinction between the spiritual and worldly realms. For many townsmen the Reformation presented itself as an opportunity to bring this world into conformity with the Christian values of love, equality, and brotherhood and thus to bring it fully under God's rule. Thus they interpreted the spiritual egalitarianism in Luther's doctrine of the priesthood of all believers as requiring an attack on social injustice. So in 1525 large numbers of discontented townsmen joined depressed rural communities in a widespread revolutionary movement that has come to be known as the revolution of the common man.[69] Before it was suppressed, it badly frightened the ruling classes of central Europe; it was rumored that the revolution aimed to destroy the entire German nobility and to create a popular republic on the model of Venice or ancient Greece.[70]

In fact the aim of the movement was rather to reorganize the municipalities of southern Germany on the model of the Swiss Confederation. This would have removed them from the supervision of any superior authority, whether prince, emperor, or imperial diet, a condition largely realized by the towns of Switzerland.[71] One of the results of the movement was also to compel the ruling groups in the towns, traditionally conservative and tied to the old church, to abolish whatever remained of Catholicism. Among its other expressions, this meant the abolition of special privileges, both spiritual and temporal, for the clergy. But the results were meager and temporary; the old ruling circles generally remained in power.

In a number of towns, nevertheless, Protestantism had significant political consequences. Historians have given particular attention to three of these: Zurich under the humanist-reformer Ulrich Zwingli (1484–1531) and later Heinrich Bullinger (1504–75); Strasbourg, whose Protestant leader was Martin Bucer (1491–1551), a former Dominican friar; and Geneva under John Calvin (1509–64). Although Calvin finally emerged as the most influential, all were in their own time figures of international importance who, in works that were widely read, modified along Protestant lines the conception of the town as a sacred community. They also contributed, if somewhat ambiguously, to the modern conception of liberty.

The earliest of these to achieve a position of political leadership was Zwingli in Zurich. He believed strongly in the duty of the spiritual and political authorities to collaborate in expanding God's rule over the world. This required the rule of godly men. "He who rules with God alone has the solidest and best empire," Zwingli wrote, "while he who rules according to his own whims has the worst and most unstable one."[72] Such rule was to be guided by Scripture as interpreted, in the case of Zurich, by Zwingli himself. On the other hand this conception also required self-government; Zwingli was utterly opposed to the traditional feudal regime in which every political entity had to be subordinated to some overlord; his ideal was a free community governed by its own godly citizens, Christian, but also, to a degree unusual in the communities of his time, democratic.[73]

Bucer, as an urban reformer in Strasbourg, shared many of Zwingli's views, though he was somewhat closer to Luther in distinguishing between the urban community and the church; as a result he imposed more limits on the civil power.[74] But he adhered closely to the ideal of the sacred community, which should be modeled, he believed, on the church, which is "the most perfect, most friendly, and most faithful brotherhood, community, and union." Like the church, the political community, for Bucer, was to be governed by love.[75] He also believed that service is of greater importance within a community than status, and he advocated congregational election of ministers. In Strasbourg as in Zurich, the ministers were expected to instruct the magistrates on God's will for the community as revealed in Scripture.

Bucer's influence expanded after he was driven from Strasbourg by political changes in 1549 and took refuge in England. There he taught at Cambridge and wrote his *De regno Christi*, dedicated to young King Edward VI to promote "the fuller acceptance and re-establishment of the Kingdom of Christ in your realm."[76] As this language suggests, he aimed in this work to apply the same princi-ples he had developed for Strasbourg to a national monarchy. This pointed to the reform of a very traditional social structure; Bucer summarily rejected the hereditary basis of political authority.

But if Bucer, by attacking one kind of authority, contributed in the long run to the limitation of monarchy, he proposed to substi-tute for it a new authoritarianism. He insisted on the duty of a re-formed royal government, as he had on that of the urban magistracy, to supervise the administration of true religion, to suppress impiety, to impose at least an external religious conformity on the commu-nity, and to supervise the conduct of every subject, "since there is no one who does not need a watchman, monitor, and overseer of piety and virtue." It was the responsibility of all governments, he proclaimed, to do everything possible so that "from earliest child-hood everyone is formed and led toward a responsible and happy way of life." He spelled out what this meant in considerable detail, and he was emphatic that no Christian community, of whatever magni-tude or however organized, could permit religious toleration.

John Calvin, who was more deeply saturated in the attitudes of Renaissance humanism than any other Protestant reformer, sought to combine an unusually clear understanding of classical republi-canism, much like that of the Florentine civic humanists, with the establishment of a godly rule over the city of Geneva like that of Zwingli and Bucer over Zurich and Strasbourg.[77] Because of his larger influence over Protestantism elsewhere, however, he is better known than they; and his significance for the history of liberty, though largely unintentional, was greater because Calvinism largely shaped the Protestantism of England and Scotland (and therefore of New England), of the Netherlands, and of some parts of Germany and central Europe. Calvinists also participated in the revolutionary movements of the later sixteenth and seventeenth centuries and found nourishment for their political programs in the thought of Calvin.[78] For Calvin produced a huge mass of writings that touched on numerous matters of interest to his followers throughout Europe.

In an age when freedom was still widely suspect, he praised it, though cautiously, as became a strong believer in original sin. "As I freely admit that no kind of government is more happy than one where freedom is regulated with becoming moderation and is properly established on a durable basis," Calvin declared, "so also I reckon most happy those permitted to enjoy this state."[79] He detested slavery; and although he thought the subordination of some persons to others useful to maintain order in human society, he rejected the traditional assumption that hierarchical authority is rooted in the nature of things. In principle he believed, like Luther, in the equality of all human beings. He liked to castigate the wickedness of the great, and he sometimes proclaimed the superior virtue of the lower classes. In an eloquent tribute to the achievements of human beings, he was unusual in praising the practical as well as the liberal arts. "Artisans of every sort who serve the needs of men," he proclaimed, "are ministers of God and have the same aim as other ministers: namely, the conservation of the human race."[80]

Like other republicans he detested world empires and indeed all large concentrations of power. He thought the very idea of universal empire absurd, on the ground that no one person is competent to rule the whole world. He also shared the hatred of the Florentines toward the Roman Empire because it had destroyed the republic. And although, like Machiavelli, he was flexible about the forms of government, he thought a citizen-republic best in principle. It is "safer and more bearable," he thought, "for a number to exercise government, so that they may help one another, teach and admonish one another." At the same time, like Machiavelli, he favored a mixed constitution. "I will not deny," he wrote, "that aristocracy, or a system compounded of aristocracy and democracy, far excels all others." In any case he thought it a primary duty of magistrates "to apply themselves with the highest diligence to prevent the freedom (whose guardians they have been appointed) from being in any respect diminished, far less violated. If they are not sufficiently alert and careful, they are faithless in office, and traitors to their country."[81]

He frequently denounced tyrants; and it is notable that his own version of the mixed constitution omitted Machiavelli's monarchical component. Although he rejected any general right of rebellion on the part of private persons, he did allow it, in the case of a ruler who "goes beyond the limits of his office," if led by lesser magistrates, those authorized by their office to take political initiatives. "I am so far from forbidding them to withstand the fierce licentiousness of kings in accordance with their duty," he declared, "that, if they wink at kings who violently fall upon and assault the lowly common folk, I declare that their dissimulation involves nefarious perfidy, because they dishonestly betray the freedom of the people, of which they know that they have been appointed protectors by God's ordinance."[82]

But Calvin was also as concerned as Zwingli and Bucer to establish God's rule over the community for which he was responsible, and this aspect of his program was less clearly on the side of freedom. In the case of Geneva, community discipline was imposed by exiled French ministers on a native population that stubbornly resisted such regulation; and, though he paid lip service to Luther's spiritual understanding of Christian liberty and what it implied for government, Calvin attributed major religious responsibilities to the secular ruler. Among his other duties, it devolved on the ruler, for Calvin, "to cherish and protect the outward worship of God" and "to defend sound doctrine of piety and the position of the church." In practice this meant not only the enforcement of orthodox belief but also surveillance over and enforcement of public morals. It also implied the effective subordination in important respects of the state to the church, magistrates to ministers.

Because of the insecurity of Geneva, whose liberty was threatened by outside forces, Calvin was able, within some limits, to enforce this program on Geneva. He did so by means of a "consistory" of ministers who met regularly to discuss and discipline the behavior and beliefs of the people. For Calvin, though not rejecting it in principle, did not share Luther's belief in the priesthood of all believers. He believed strongly in the authority of pastors, an authority enforced by the power to excommunicate offenders. For Calvin too the community must be kept holy.

In one particular, however, the "order" Calvin sought to impose on Genevan society, since it was based on a conception of justice, favored a kind of freedom unusual in his time: the liberation of women. Calvin insisted on the equality of the sexes before God, and on this ground he called for the religious instruction of women equally with men. Their equality notably applied to the sexual relationship; husband and wife, Calvin declared, "are equal in bed," a pithy pronouncement with broad implications. By the same token he rejected the venerable double standard that punished only women for adultery.[83]

Calvin's place in the development of modern liberty, like that of the other Protestant reformers, was thus ambiguous. Its ambiguity is especially evident in his conception of the deity. For in spite of his republicanism, he conceived of God as exercising an absolute and unrestricted monarchy over the whole of existence, a monarchical conception that found expression in his doctrine of predestination. According to this teaching, God has freely (that is, arbitrarily) "elected" every person to either salvation or damnation. This belief was evidently in some tension both with his republicanism and with his concern to enforce Christian behavior within the community, a demand that appeared to assume, in a typically Renaissance manner, freedom of the will. For this and other reasons, he was himself, therefore, cautious in discussing predestination, which he considered a great mystery. But many of his followers were prepared to spell out its most extreme implications in the ensuing age of absolutism.

But Protestantism varied on such matters, and a much less ambiguous contribution to the history of liberty came from Heinrich Bullinger, Zwingli's successor as leader of the church in Zurich. Bullinger, in other respects one of Calvin's allies, found in the Old Testament idea of the covenant a very different conception of the relationship between God and his people. Bullinger was not original on this matter; his understanding of the biblical covenant can be traced as far back as the ancient church fathers. But he introduced it into the Protestant world of thought, in which it eventually had major political and social consequences, partly perhaps because the relation between God and his people on which it rested seemed plausible in societies in which personal and commercial relations were increasingly defined by contracts.

In fact the Calvinist conception of a unilateral imposition of God's will on human beings suggested again the determinism of traditional thought against which Renaissance culture had reacted. But the idea of a covenant implied that the relation between God and his people is to some degree reciprocal. In Bullinger's view, which was based on his reading of the Old Testament histories rather than on dogmatic considerations, the various covenants between God and his people were agreements freely proposed by God and freely accepted by them, though not without God's help. The ultimate covenant, in Bullinger's view, was contained in the New Testament, in which Christ, as representative of the whole human race, freely suffers on its behalf. Bullinger was hesitant to attribute freedom of the will explicitly to human beings, but it is at least implied by the notion of a covenant. He was eventually cited in favor of it by later Protestants who rejected the more extreme versions of predestination.

The covenant idea would be important for politics because it defined not only the relationship between God and individuals but above all the relationship between God and the whole community of believers. In this way it eventually became a model for the relation between polities and their secular rulers. Applied to governments, the covenant idea points to the notion of a contract between ruler and ruled, with limitations on the power of the former and responsibilities on both sides. It became a common theme of seventeenth-century political discussion, and eventually it was a major element in the background of the constitution of the United States.[84]

< IV >

Religious Toleration and Freedom of Expression

The Protestant movements so far considered were alike in their insistence on established and exclusive churches coterminous with their respective communities. In this they were also in agreement with Roman Catholicism and Anglicanism. To some extent all of them accepted, and accommodated themselves to, this world and its institutions, however fallen and sinful, which they aimed to control and redeem. In all of them, too, citizenship and church membership were coterminous. Just as an infant did not choose to be born into a community, so also he became as an infant, through baptism, a member of an established church. Both church and state, in this conception, enforced the unity of the community, especially its unity of belief, by a variety of officially sanctioned and coercive instruments. Deviation and disobedience were subject to a variety of disabilities. Thus one might be expelled from any of these established churches by excommunication (except in Zurich, which was in this respect exceptional); and excommunication was often accompanied too by civil penalties.

There was, however, one group of religious movements associated with the Protestant Reformation that differed from all those so far considered. They varied widely, and their members have been variously described: as the "radicals" of the Reformation, or its "left wing," or, because some of them rebaptized converts from other Christian groups, as "Anabaptists." They are called "sects" here because their only common characteristic was their detachment from established churches. Although the Christian Church had from the beginning insisted on its unity, sects had emerged very early in its history, breaking away from the larger body of Christians on various issues, but in general because they could not tolerate any imperfection in what should, they believed, be a community of the perfect. A church coterminous with social and political communities could obviously not meet this standard.

In response to the uncertainties about religious matters during the Reformation and emboldened by its challenge to religious authority, sects of many kinds proliferated, withdrawing from established churches to form small holy communities, entrance into which required repentance and a mature and voluntary choice for a new and pure life. In this respect the sects carried to an extreme the individualism already at work in the teachings of Erasmus and Luther.

Some sects, to be sure, practiced excommunication; and they could be quite as dogmatic and intolerant as the established churches, sometimes enforcing standards of behavior even more rigidly. Nevertheless their very existence made possible a degree of individual choice impossible when the spiritual and political authorities collaborated closely. Finally, although sectaries withdrew from the established churches, they were likely still to reside in their old communities, and thus they raised the issue of religious freedom, for dissident groups if not always for individuals. By the same token sectarianism pointed to the separation of church and state, in the long run so important for religious liberty.[85]

But except among the sects, which rejected in principle the coercive power of the state over religious belief, religious toleration was almost unthinkable during the period with which this chapter is concerned. The skepticism about human claims to knowledge

that underlay Renaissance humanism may have pointed to toleration, but certainty about Christian belief was thought to be assured
by the authority of the Church for Catholics and of Scripture for
Protestants. There were doubts among the followers of Erasmus
about the dogmatism that resulted; Erasmus himself had written,
not long after the emergence of Luther, "The essence of our religion
is peace and unanimity. We shall preserve these values only on condition of being voluntarily very hesitant to define [dogma] and of
giving up numerous questions to the free judgment of each one."[86]
But such views were exceptional.

There were political as well as religious motives behind the enforcement of unity of belief. Thomas More, Erasmus's old friend, is
instructive on this point. In 1515, two years before Luther's challenge to the old church, More described in his *Utopia* as "one of the
oldest rules" of the place "that no one should suffer for his religion."
Its king, he continued, had decreed "that every man might culti-
vate the religion of his choice, and proselytise for it too, provided he
did so quietly, modestly, rationally, and without bitterness towards
others . . . because he suspected that God perhaps likes various
forms of worship and had therefore deliberately inspired different
men with different views."[87]

But the religious controversies of the sixteenth century stimulated increasing insecurity on all sides, and as a result growing mili-
tancy, rejection of dissent, and religious persecution. By 1528 More
himself had recognized, in his *Dialogue Concerning Heresies*, that
"heresies breed disorders, and fear of these has been the cause that
Princes and peoples have been constrained to punish heresies by terrible death." The problems caused by religious differences were, in
short, as much political as religious in societies where political and
religious unity were so closely intertwined. One of the speakers in
More's dialogue therefore argued that "princes are bound to see that
they shall not suffer their people to be reduced and corrupted by
heretics, since the peril shall in short while grow to as great, both
with men's souls withdrawn from God and their goods lost and their
body destroyed by common sedition, insurrection and open war,
within the bowels of their own land."[88] Similarly, Erasmus, though
deploring the persecution of Protestants (chiefly because it was in-
effective in stemming Protestantism) approved the persecution of
sectaries, not on religious but on political grounds: because of their

refusal to recognize the authority of secular rulers deemed essential to maintaining order in society.

One event, however, the burning of the free-thinking Spaniard Michael Servetus in Calvin's Geneva in 1553, produced a major protest against the prosecution of heresy. This incident was scarcely unusual; it was a result partly of Calvin's need to demonstrate that he was no less zealous on behalf of the true faith than the Catholic authorities who were taking similar measures against his followers in France. The execution of Servetus was applauded by other religious leaders, including even the moderate Melanchthon.

But it also inspired Sebastian Castellio, a former associate of Calvin in Geneva, now resident in Basel, to publish *On Heretics and Whether They Should Be Persecuted* (1554). This work, which owed much to Erasmus, condemned the execution of Servetus and pleaded for tolerance. It was mainly an anthology of learned opinion in favor of toleration in matters of belief, but Castellio stated his own views in a preface and epilogue. His main argument was that true religion consists in godly living rather than in correctness of belief. Belief itself, he argued, is an individual matter and essentially subjective. "To force conscience is worse than cruelly to kill a man," he concluded, "for I must be saved by my own faith and not by that of another."[89]

The plea for freedom of conscience did not immediately prevail. The later sixteenth and seventeenth centuries, which would be known by church historians as "the age of confessional orthodoxy," was one of the most rigid and intolerant ages in European history. It was a period when it was dangerous to be identified with minority views, whether one was a Jew in Spain, a Catholic in England, or a Protestant in France and Italy; survival depended on external conformity and dissimulation in religion.[90] Castellio had sounded a note that would only much later be generally welcome, and even then only in some parts of the world and under special conditions.

≺ V ≻

Conclusion

The progress in the various sorts of freedom during the period of the Renaissance and Reformation should not be exaggerated, and the emphasis here on its positive contributions to modern liberty gives a somewhat misleading impression of the general character of the age. However much they were admired in later centuries, its achievements did not last. They reflected for the most part the conditions and needs of the independent urban republics of Italy and Germany, areas that lacked effective central authority. But the future of Europe did not belong to small polities of this kind. During the sixteenth century an age of cities was giving way to an age of princes: in Italy, where only Venice survived as an independent republic, decisively; and also in Germany, where the Protestant free cities suffered badly from decades of religious conflict with a Catholic emperor who had previously been their ally against lesser princes whose own position was now strengthened by control over their state churches. The future belonged increasingly to such princes, but above all to the royal monarchs of France, Spain, and England, where assertions of liberty had been in any case less effective.[91] Europe was moving into an "age of absolutism." This meant not only that the political freedoms of the Renaissance and Reformation were largely eroded, but also that there was a resurgence of authoritarian attitudes as absolute in their demands as those that had been challenged by the more open culture of the Renaissance—and enforced more effectively. Nevertheless the more liberal impulses released by the Renaissance and Reformation, however distasteful to the authorities of church and state, survived in uneasy tension with the absolutist claims of philosophy, science, and the state, to become attractive again in a later age of revolutionary change.

Kingship and Resistance

DONALD R. KELLEY

"THE EAST KNEW AND to the present day knows only that *One* is free," wrote Hegel; "the Greek and Roman world that *some* are free; the German World knows that *All* are free."[1] Slavery and mastery, subjecthood and rulership, citizenry and civil government, resistance and kingship: these are all governing dualities of Western social experience and political language, and the one thing on which each of them turns is the concept of liberty. In the national states of early modern Europe "liberty" signified in general the ability to exercise one's will without interference and within the confines of law. Viewed in these terms, Western society was a battlefield of "wills" within an institutional framework that was still essentially corporate, ecclesiastical, partly feudal, and, at least in northern Europe, ruled by monarchy. In this context liberty was a highly ambivalent concept—the sovereign liberty of the ruler being defined and realized in large part at the expense of the social, economic, and religious liberties of the ruled.

In effect free will was thus a political as well as a theological concept. According to the ancient formula often invoked by champions of the European monarchies, the will of the prince is law (*Quod principi placuit legis habet vigorem*),[2] while the wills of subjects all too often represented a contrary sort of "liberty" that led to subversion of this law. Early modern kings were sworn to uphold the traditional, "ancient liberties" of their subjects; yet behind the term the conflict of wills repeatedly threatened the social order promised by law. As one sixteenth-century French historian wrote in the light of recent historical experience, "This specious word 'liberty' is the most beautiful, sweetest, and most deceitful thing in the world. It is a brew that poisons the minds of men."[3]

This is a statement on which celebrators of kingship and defenders of resistance could agree. When only one is free, can there be anything but tyranny? When all are free, can there be anything but anarchy? This political paradox set the terms for one of the most fundamental debates in Western history.

The themes of kingship and resistance, which run contrapuntally through early modern history, cannot be understood apart from a third term of political and social interaction, namely, the law. Law was at the same time a framework for liberties of all sorts, a justification for resistance under certain conditions, and a defining trait of kingship (*rex a recte regendo*, according to the old etymology); and as such it embodied another enduring political contradiction. This was especially the case with Protestants, for whom, as for St. Paul, law was identified with bondage and so opposed to true liberty. This "Christian liberty" was of a spiritual nature of course, but in the wake of Luther's biblical usage the term was also employed in secular expressions of hostility to ecclesiastical authority, and under conditions of persecution and civil war Luther's spiritual concept of "liberty of conscience" was progressively politicized. The ambiguities in the ideas of liberty and law are nicely captured by Thomas Cooper, who gave the following definition to the Latin term *jus*: "Law: right: Authoritie: Liberty: power." What more explosive set of identifications (or confusions) could be imagined in a society torn by confessional as well as social and political divisions?[4]

In general ideological conflict can be seen as a struggle to monopolize the vocabulary of legitimacy. Kings claimed not only to rule within but also, as the "living law" (*lex animata*), to embody the law; opponents of kingly rule likewise claimed legitimacy under the law, rightly understood; and both parties claimed loyalty to principles of true liberty. An understanding of the twin topics of kingship and resistance must make its way through these semantic thickets of ambiguity, equivocation, and dissimulation.

≺ I ≻

The Idea of Kingship

Kingship at the end of the Middle Ages had many layers of meaning; but it could be defined most concretely in terms of those concrete "liberties"—royal prerogatives, preeminences, and regalian rights—

which it had accumulated in its struggles over the centuries with various rivals and with its own feudal and ecclesiastical subjects. It was in this sense that the beleaguered Gregorian papacy took up its war-cry, *Libertas Ecclesiae*, against the oppressions of the medieval emperors; and it was in this sense that the "liberties of the Gallican church" were asserted, often in the French king's name, against the intrusions of the Roman papacy.[5] The first of these traditional Gallican liberties, according to a sixteenth-century legist, was "that the popes can order nothing . . . concerning the temporal things in the lands within the obedience and sovereignty of the Most Christian King" of France.[6] In this way "liberty" was identified with one of the first principles of kingship.

Yet kingship was also a prehistorical institution, possessing a religious as well as a political character and a sacramental as well as a patriarchal foundation; and it claimed legitimacy through both divine origins and family connections. The Latin *rex* (related to *regere*, to rule) was a term with religious overtones from the beginning;[7] the Germanic *king* was chosen by kin-ship and blood-right; and the confluence of these two traditions (along with more practical acquisitions of political and military power) lay at the roots of all the early modern Christian monarchies. To this was added the "mystical" notion of the "king's two bodies," which (on the analogy of the two natures of Christ) distinguished between the body natural of the king and the supernatural body politic of the kingdom.[8]

The image of the father-priest-king was further enhanced by accumulation of fabulous genealogies linking the European dynasties to the Hebrew patriarchs and to the Trojan heroes. Overlaying these "origin stories" were other constructions—"the legend and the memory of Charlemagne," the Arthurian mythology devised in opposition to Norman domination, the dim recollections of the Visigothic heritage in Spain, and the stories of Arminius and other champions of Germanic liberty against the Romans—which all emphasized the cultural identity of the European states ruled by hereditary monarchs.[9] Such mythical constructs have been significant and even foundational for the early modern theory of kingship and were celebrated by early modern historians and jurists as well as poets.

Kingship in the sixteenth century was still surrounded by myth, then, and still embellished in popular opinion with fiction and fantasy. Kings, "twice-born with greatness," were portrayed as saints and scholars, full of piety and learning, sacrificing themselves for their people, endowed with magical abilities, including the thaumaturgical power to cure scrofula,[10] and in general appearing in official propaganda and perhaps popular imagination as earthly gods (*deus terraneus*). These images were enhanced by some of the more sensational happenings, such as assassinations—attempted, successful, and imputed—and the death of kings in battle, including Charles the Bold of Burgundy in 1477, James IV of Scotland in 1513, Louis II of Hungary in 1526, and Sebastian of Portugal in 1578. According to popular belief several of these kings indeed "never died," living on in hiding, according to rumor, or reappearing in the form of impostors. As Yves Bercé has shown, the "hidden king" often continued to reign in popular imagination and to add further luster to the cult of kingship.[11]

The marvelous and mythological dimensions of kingship were illustrated, too, by the attribution of symbols, insignia, and magical powers to their medieval and modern successors, who happily preserved these trappings and superstitions of royal authority. The sacramental attributes of the king were displayed and dramatized in countless spectacles—from princely cradle to royal grave and in between in coronations, royal entrees, and marriages.[12] In 1486, to crown his recent victory, coronation, and marriage, Henry VII began a great Progress through his kingdom; and his triumphal entry into York illustrates the images which kingship called up. "Was the king Noah returning from the flood?" asked the janitor of the city in his welcoming speech. Was he Jason bringing the golden fleece or Julius Caesar coming in triumph? Other parallels with King David, Scipio, and of course King Arthur further inflated the transcendent status of the new Tudor king.[13]

In France such ceremonial propaganda was even more spectacular. The coronation and entry ceremonies of Charles VIII in 1484, for example, featured representations of the three stages of French history: the legendary Trojan origins (the eponymous Francus, son of Hector, who married the daughter of Remus, king of the Celts and founder of Reims); the legal tradition of the monarchy, beginning with Pharamond, first king of the Franks, seen in the company of the four compilers of the ancient "Salic Law," that is, the law of the Salian Franks (often confused with the modern prohibition of women from royal succession in France), and Samothes, grandson of Noah and first king of the Gauls; and the establishment of the "most Christian" kingship (the baptism of Clovis and the legend of the Holy Ampulla brought down from heaven by a dove).[14] In France, in significant contrast to England, such spectacles were increasingly penetrated and colored by the influence of Humanism. In 1549, for example, Henry II made his royal entry into Paris not like a descendant of Clovis but like a triumphant Roman emperor. As Ralph Giesey summed up the contrived scene, "The spirit of the late-medieval *joyeuse entrée* has been transformed into an ancient imperial *adventus.*"[15]

These legends were taken up by the various hired apologists of the monarchy, including historians, some of whom subjected this tradition to scholarly criticism, while yet preserving the ideas of sacral and immortal kingship. For Charles Dumoulin the French monarchy was not only the best but also the oldest monarchy in the world—indeed twice as enduring as the empires of Israel and India.[16] In 1570 the royal historiographer Bernard du Haillan followed ceremonial imagery in celebrating the "fortune and virtue" of France and its superiority to all national traditions, including that of ancient Rome;[17] and of course such expressions of national sentiment were reinforced by a royalist ideology based on ideas of divine right, the priestly office of the king, and the supernatural powers of the anointed ruler. Even for Guillaume Budé, the greatest of French humanists, the king of France was a veritable god in human form (*quasi Deus; imago Dei*) and more than the equal of the emperor.[18] The old formula "the king never dies" (*le roi ne meurt jamais*) captured this mystical notion—as well as accommodating modern ideas of kingship as a public office.

The English and Spanish monarchies made similar efforts at constructing and embellishing their images through Trojan myth (associated with Brutus, another son of Hector) and sacramental attributes. Throughout its whole history England had never been ruled by government either "Aristocraticall" or "Democraticall," declared Sir Thomas Smith, "but onely the royall and kingly majestie," which was first divided among several kings "until at last the realme of England grew into one Monarchie."[19] Similar claims were made for the "most Catholic kings" of Spain (so-called from 1494), whose rule likewise emerged from a plurality of crowns until the

Jean Cousin, *"Enfant de Ville" in Henry II's 1549 Parisian entry*. Woodcut. Reproduced from Lawrence M. Bryant, *The King and the City in the Parisian Royal Entry Ceremony* by permission of Librarie Droz S. A.

fifteenth century, when the marital union of Ferdinand of Aragon and Isabella of Castile and more especially the joint inheritance of their grandson Charles gave some institutional plausibility to the medieval notion of a "Spanish" monarchy. But of course the young Habsburg prince, Charles, ended up with many crowns; and to them he added the imperial dignity, which further enhanced his already impressive claims to majesty (*Sacra, Cesárea, Católica, Real Magestad*).[20]

Charles was not alone in invoking connections with classical ideas of sovereignty—for in vernacular languages this was exactly identified with "majesty." To the medieval cult of royalty the recovery and teaching of Roman law brought more secular and "political" conceptions of office and of legislative authority. The locus classicus, invoked by royal legists of all nations, was the famous two-part formula of Ulpian which made the will of the prince absolute law by virtue of an original popular concession. "What pleases the prince has the force of law," runs this foundational claim displayed prominently in Justinian's *Digest*, "because by a regal law [*lex regia*], which establishes his authority [*imperium*], the people confer all authority and power on him."[21] To Justinian's Byzantine compilers of classical Roman law this formula, hyperbolic and without historical basis, was meant to reflect the new state of affairs in the sixth century—that beginning with Justinian's legislation the emperor himself would be the exclusive source of law, thus superseding the enactments of the senate, the decisions of the jurisconsults, and the customs of the people. In other words sovereignty—the "majesty" of the Roman people, which through the legendary *lex regia* had passed to the prince—was essentially legislative in nature and identified with the emperor's will.

Such was the political model which it pleased the European kings of the later Middle Ages, and their Romanizing and modernizing legists, to follow. Each of them claimed to be, in the famous formula derived from canon law, "emperor in his kingdom" (*rex imperator in regno suo*), with "no superior in temporal matters" and even throne-worthy of the imperial crown.[22] According to the Romanoid *Siete Partidas*, the Spanish king—*Rex Hispaniorum* or *totius Hispaniae Rex*—had the same authority in the temporal sphere as the Roman emperor: *Quanto en lo temporale, bien asi como el emperador en su imperio.*[23] And this conception of kingship transcended cultural boundaries. As Charles Merbury put it, the king had "that Power which the Greekes call *Akron exousian*: the Latines *Maiestatem*: th'Italians *Signoria*: the French *sovverainete*: that is, Power full and perpetual over all his subiectes in generall, and over every one in particular."[24]

Both medieval and humanist "mirrors of the prince" (*Specula principis, lunettes des princes; Fürstenspiegel* etc.) carried on the idealization of kingship; but they were more likely to emphasize the human virtues and lawfulness of rulers. There are many types of authority, wrote Erasmus, "man over beasts, father over children, husband over wife, yet Aristotle believes that the rule of king is finest of all and calls it especially favored of the gods because it seems to possess a certain something which is greater than mortal." Yet it was not enough to possess kingship. "Never forget that 'dominion,' 'imperial authority,' 'kingdom,' 'majesty,' 'power' are all pagan terms, not Christian."[25] Moreover, Erasmus continued, the king's authority was like that of the mind over the body; and for this reason wisdom represented the true crown of kingship and peace its primary goal.

This leads to one other ingredient of kingship that went into the eclectic mixture of Renaissance monarchy; and this was the belief, derived from antiquity and transmitted through scholastic philosophy, that "kingly rule" (*potestas regia*) was based on natural law, which required that every natural body needed a single head—not two heads, "like a monster," as Boniface VIII put it in his *Unam Sanctam*.[26] Unity, as Gierke remarked, was "the Constitutive Principle of the Universe."[27] So God had designed his Creation, and kingship followed the same model as providential and paternal rule. Needless to say, this model was exclusively masculine; for so were conceived God, pope, priest, king, magistrate, preacher, and most other public roles.

What about queenship? Even for the liberal-minded Erasmus the inalterable pattern of kingship was fatherhood. It was possible for queens, such as Isabella of Spain and Elizabeth of England, to assume all the attributes and authority of kingship and so to override the masculine prejudice inherent in Western political thought, classical as well as Christian, from Aristotle to the kings of Israel; and of course queens were also crucial in dynastic strategies of state-building and in the government of regencies. Yet the assumptions of early modern rulership were largely antagonistic to female rule, and sixteenth-century political literature is filled with vituperation against the rule of women—with Catherine de Médicis and Mary Tudor becoming the blackest symbols of this calamitous situation. The most doctrinaire expression of this male monopoly (aside from the Roman hierarchy) was the famous "Salic law" of the French monarchy, which was fashioned by jurists in the early stages of the Hundred Years' War and, as Claude de Seyssel and many others argued, guaranteed that the crown "cannot fall into the hands of a woman."[28] In general, notions of sacred, hereditary kingship, whether absolute or limited, were tied to equally mystical notions of paternalism and what Sarah Hanley has called the "seminal theory of kingship," with royal "birth-right" (suitas) passing on the eternal power of the king's second body.[29]

≺ II ≻

The Institutions of Kingship

If the locus classicus of the European idea of kingship was the formula of majesty applied to Justinian, the locus modernus was, and is perhaps still, the famous formula of Sir John Fortescue, chief justice of the King's Bench, in which a distinction is drawn between absolute and limited monarchy—dominium regale and dominium politicum et regale.[30] The former rested on a literal construction of the Quod principi placuit formula and was best illustrated by the French monarchy, or rather Fortescue's caricature of it. The latter was the view of English monarchy taken by common lawyers like Fortescue and, over a century later, by Sir Edward Coke, representing their political tradition as government by consent and solicitude for the legendary "liberties" of Englishmen which, according to the coronation oath, the king promised to respect and preserve. To any who argued that the king was above the law, Merbury answered "that our Prince is subiect unto lawes both civill and common, to customs, privileges, covenantes, and all kinds of promises, so farre forth as they are agreeable unto the lawe of God."[31] It is no longer fashionable to speak of Tudor despotism or even a "new monarchy" (in the famous phrase of J. R. Green), but it is undeniable that English ideas of kingship under Henry VIII often went beyond Fortescue's and Merbury's benign views and toward the Romanist notion of "empire," which was invoked in the opening of the Act in Restraint of Appeals, drafted by Thomas Cromwell. The break with papal Rome obviously enhanced this imperialist conception of sovereignty.

Yet Fortescue's stereotypical view of France as a state in which the king had no respect for private liberties or property, however plausible on the surface, hardly corresponded to the realities or ideals of French kingship. In fact French political tradition also portrayed kingship as limited, at least in practice. A generation after Fortescue, Claude de Seyssel represented the French monarchy as a mixed constitution because, he argued, "it partakes of all three forms of political government."[32] Theoretically, the king had "complete power and authority to command and to do whatever he wishes," but in practice he was limited by certain "fundamental laws." In his *Monarchy of France* Seyssel celebrated the special virtue of French government produced by three essential "bridles" on kingly power, namely, the principles of religion, justice, and police. This secular trinity represented not only natural and moral restraints but also institutional dimensions of kingship—that is, the hierarchy of the Gallican church, the jurisdiction of the parlements and other "sovereign courts," and the administrative structure of the Crown. In Seyssel's proto-constitutionalist view, then, "the things necessary for the preservation and augmentation of the monarchy" included not only royal power but also an institutional structure which bound the king to all the estates of the realm and which in turn enhanced the *grandeur* of the "grand monarchy of France." Seyssel's main purpose was to show not only "how this bridling of the absolute power of kings is to their own great honor and profit" but also how, like the English constitution, it contributed to the liberties of all the estates, including the lesser folk (*le peuple gras*), and even made it possible to move from one to another.

This was the general pattern of royal government, which never in this respect wholly extricated itself from medieval political traditions. The kingdoms of Spain, too, had traditions of liberty counterbalancing assertions of royal power. Although the famous Aragonese oath to the king ("We who are worth as much as you") was probably a sixteenth-century fabrication, it reflected a genuine tradition of aristocratic "liberties";[33] and so did the noble leagues (*herman-dades*) of Castile, which were formed to guard against excesses of monarchy and which characteristically did so by invoking what R. B. Merriman called "the magic words 'liberties' and 'fueros' [charters]."[34] In Aragon the coronation oath, which survived in the meeting of the Cortes, was reciprocal and required not only the estates to obey the king but also the king to uphold their "fueros." In the sixteenth century even Philip II (his "black legend" notwithstanding) regarded it as his royal duty to respect the fueros and liberties of his subjects—although this did not include the Dutch "Beggars" who protested against the violation of their "liberties" by the oppressive Spanish government in the Netherlands. It was in this connection that the "defense of liberty against tyrants" led to ideas of active resistance.[35]

In the early modern process of state-building kingship was an essential ingredient to the exercise of full "sovereignty." The aims of two remarkably successful dukes—Giangaleazzo Visconti of Milan and Charles the Bold of Burgundy—were finally frustrated, at least in part, because of their failure to gain a royal title. By contrast the long efforts of the house of Hohenzollern, against the liberties first of the Church and then of the nobles, was crowned finally with success and high legitimacy when Frederick William, the Great Elector, assembled his scattered possessions into a modern state, and when his successor Frederick III received permission from the emperor to assume the title of King in Prussia.

The last quarter of the fifteenth century saw the emergence of the "national monarchies" familiar to modern political experience—although the force of nationality was marginal and in fact dynastic and local interests prevailed in most arenas of political action.[36] France under Charles VIII, Louis XII, Francis I, and Henry II; Spain under the "Catholic kings," Ferdinand and Isabella, Charles I, and Philip II; and England under the Tudors, especially Henry VII, Henry VIII, and Elizabeth I, marshalled their forces, devised their strategies, and played out their hands in the game of international power politics according to the new "vision of politics" emerging in the tumultuous age not only of Machiavelli but also of Luther.[37] "Peace and justice" was—again following Roman precedent—the declared aim of these states, but in fact the main business of European kings was war and, to that end, the extension of their territories, the consolidation of their institutions, and the calculated exploitation of their resources. Royal administration enhanced by a national church, a unified system of laws, a docile Parliament, a full treasury, a standing army, and an expanding bureaucracy (including legal counsel, record-keeping, formal procedures, and specialization): though never fully achieved, these were the constant aims of monarchy from start to finish.

In general kingship cannot be understood merely as a sacrament, an office, an "estate," or as a product merely of "virtue and fortune"; it was also the nucleus of a complex administrative network involving various medieval institutions and modern alterations and additions designed to give practical effect to theoretical sovereignty. In human terms, then, kingship became institutionally remote, as the legalistic language of its pronouncements illustrated. No longer did the kings of France, like Louis IX, dispense justice under the oak in Vincennes; no longer even, or seldom, did they, like Louis XII, participate frequently in the gatherings of the "sovereign court" of the Parlement of Paris. In Spain, although Philip II tried to revert to a more personal style of governance, in fact his authority had to be exercised through an astonishingly extensive system of administrative councils which often detached him from the concerns of his subjects.

Here we move from the theoretical to the practical side of kingship, which involves the whole career of medieval monarchy over several centuries and which centers on the royal domain and the fisc, which—subject like kingship itself to mystical interpretation and consecration—became (in the words of Ernst Kantorowicz) "the hall-mark of sovereignty."[38] In 1372 a summary of the king's special powers and "liberties" was drawn up and inserted in the registers of the Parlement of Paris. According to this list of twenty-seven "sovereign rights and legal resources" (*les droits de souverainetez et de ressort, et autres droits royaulx, au roi notre seigneur*), the king enjoyed not only control (*garde*) over particular churches, which was one expression of the "Gallican liberties," but also exclusive authority in a growing number of public areas, including the crime of treason (*lèse-majesté*), appointment to royal offices, coinage, letters to ennoble or to legitimize persons, pardon for crimes, imposition of new taxes, permission for fairs and markets, and other special rights belonging "to the king and no other."[39] By the sixteenth century these *regalia*—secular and ecclesiastical—had multiplied enormously, making the French king to some degree practically as well as theoretically "emperor in his kingdom."

In the sixteenth century such collections of *regalia* became at once more common and more systematic—and of course more "public," in the sense that they were featured in commissioned and published contributions to the ideology of French kingship. Jean Ferrault, Barthélemy de Chasseneux, and Charles de Grassaille all produced variations on the theme of the autonomy, uniqueness, and superiority of the French monarchy and, in Grassaille's words, the "liberty of the most serene crown of France" (*libertas serenissime coronae Franciae*), combining the various prerogatives with the honorific and holy insignia of theocratic kingship.[40] According to this royalist liturgy, the king was "vicar of Christ" and "most Christian"; he "recognized no superior in temporal things," had innumerable ecclesiastical privileges, and was the sole source of law (*Solus Rex facit constitutiones seu leges in regno Franciae*). For these and many other reasons, historical, natural, and supernatural, he was "above all other kings." His sacral powers, moreover, could be used to benefit his subjects; for not only did he have the thaumaturgical power to cure scrofula but, according to one of the regalian rights, "Praying for the king opens heaven's gates."

Despite their constitutional traditions the English were second to none in their admiration for the institution of kingship. "The dignitie Royall, is so great and holy," wrote George Whetstone in 1586, "as kings that are protectors and defenders of human society, imitates the providence of God, whose office & action is to govern all things."[41] Invoking the same trinity that Claude de Seyssel had used seventy years earlier to describe the "grand monarchy of France," Whetstone went on to argue that these god-like kings "should imitate God, whose lieutenants they are: in their religion, Justice and government." As Frances Yates has shown, England also had an increasingly "imperial" image and pretensions.[42] Drawing on a variety of classical and Christian motifs, royalist apologists represented Queen Elizabeth as the virgin "Astrea," who was last of the immortals in the Ovidian pantheon, was associated prophetically with the virgin Mother of Christ, and was also "empress of the world, guardian of religion, patroness of peace, and restorer of virtue." Like her continental rivals, the English queen was glorified politically, ceremonially, iconographically, historiographically, and poetically, and was graced with solar imagery, classical affinities, and divine attributes. For Edmund Spenser, Elizabeth was "the enthroned imperial virgin" and in no way inferior to her masculine counterparts on the Continent.

The history of the Spanish monarchy was much more complex, and indeed the title itself does not appear until the fifteenth century; for as all observers and chroniclers insisted, the Iberian peninsula was dominated by "diverse kingdoms"—conventionally by the "five kingdoms." Yet from the fifteenth century learned historians found a central heritage of "Spain" (*Hispania*) in the history of Castile, especially because of its "divine war" against Islam, the *Reconquista*.[43] As French legists argued for the Carolingian origins of their monarchy, so advocates of the "neo-Gothic" thesis in that period represented the Castilian monarchy as the legitimate heir of the Visigothic kingdom and so its ruler as king of Spain (*rex totius Hispaniae*). The imperial themes, according to which Spanish monarchs were "emperors in their kingdom," were reinforced by the election of the Habsburg Charles I of Spain as Holy Roman Emperor as well as by the actual extent of his political claims in the worlds both old and new. "Sire," wrote one apologist to Charles V, "now that God in his prodigious grace has elevated your majesty above all Kings and Princes of Christendom, to a pinnacle of power occupied by none except your mighty predecessor Charlemagne, you are on the road toward Universal Monarchy and on the point of uniting Christendom under a single shepherd."[44] So Charles affected to be not only "emperor in his kingdom" but also king in his empire.

≺ III ≻

King and Counsel

Central to royal (and imperial) government in all of the European monarchies was the royal council, an institution which was as ancient as kingship itself and which was the root of more specialized offshoots, administrative, judicial, and parliamentary, that at once strengthened and limited the king's will. A separate tradition was the administration of the king's own household, although it was only in England under the Tudors, especially through the work of Thomas Cromwell, that these personal servants acquired a large public significance and bureaucratic organization.[45] The growth of bureaucracy was a general pattern in the sixteenth century—with university-trained secretaries (*letrados* they were called in Spain) and notarial experts being added to the old administrative and conciliar bodies and providing institutional memory.

In France the most direct expression of the royal will appears in the royal ordinances, which commonly began by stating that "The king wishes and orders" (*le roi veut et ordonne*) something—*si veut le roi, si veut la loi* is another old maxim—but in fact such legislation depended on one other essential ingredient of kingship, which was the support and instruction which he received from his counselors. In sixteenth-century political thinking the "problem of counsel" was hardly less prominent than celebrations of royal authority. Seyssel's *Monarchy of France*, Erasmus's *Institution of a Christian Prince*, Guillaume Budé's *Institution of the Prince*, Thomas More's *Utopia*, Baldassare Castiglione's *Courtier*, Thomas Elyot's *Boke of the Governor*, and Machiavelli's *Prince*—all published in the first quarter of the sixteenth century—are concerned centrally with the problem of counsel and the aims and values of kingship. Counsel is, said Elyot, "the end of all doctrine and study." About his own advice Seyssel remarked to the new king, Francis I, "[T]ake what seems good, and supply the rest by your sound judgment and prudence and by the counsel of men of the better sort . . . [and in this way] you can render this your realm the happiest and most renowned that ever has been."[46] Counsel also provided a standard of judgment and a way of understanding the motives of rulers—government depending vitally on "good counsel" and misgovernment being commonly blamed on "evil counsel," partly as a way of protecting "his majesty" from personal culpability.

Most prominent in the process of counsel was the presence of ministers who acted and often spoke for their royal masters, and in the sixteenth century this process included a number of extraordinary figures with the characteristic title of chancellor or secretary. In England there were Cardinal Wolsey and Thomas More, both lord chancellors, and Thomas Cromwell and William Cecil, principal secretaries; in Spain Cardinal Ximenes, Francisco de los Cobos, and Mercurio Gattinara, grand chancellors; in France Antoine du Prat and Michel de l'Hôpital, also chancellors. These men were in effect prime ministers and as such prepared the ground for even more powerful statesmen such as Richelieu, Olivares, and other architects of absolute monarchy who were entrusted with the practical tasks of kingship.

In all of the national monarchies the royal council, in its various forms, was the vehicle for the most direct expression of the king's will. According to an ordinance of 1526, the English king required that "a good number of honourable, virtuous, sad, wise, expert, and discreet persons of the Council shall give their attendance upon his most royal person."[47] The council was the source of a large body of royal proclamations which constituted a sort of extra-parliamentary legislation, though valid only during the reign of the current king. The council had a judicial as well as a deliberative function, and from 1494 the Court of the Star Chamber became an independent institution. Under Henry VIII conciliar functions were in many respects superseded by single ministers, especially Cardinal Wolsey and Thomas Cromwell, who gathered a number of offices under the function of principal secretary. Whatever the procedure, however, the only authority exercised by these advisers was the royal prerogative.

In France the council, consisting of princes of the blood and holders of high office such as the chancellor, was divided into a *conseil secret* or *des affaires* for major issues, and a larger *conseil privé* for lesser matters; in 1497 a separate judicial branch called the *grand conseil* was formed.[48] Under Henry II four principal secretaries of the council took responsibility for relations between the Crown and certain foreign states as well as the provinces. Through these and other offices the king's policies were translated into formal "acts" of legislation and command in all areas of political, social, and economic activity. Theoretically, the king's authority did not extend into the area of private law; and yet even here, most obviously in the sixteenth-century movement to reform provincial customs, the king could make his "will" felt.

In Spain royal government was impeded by divisions between the particular Crowns; but between the time of Ferdinand and Isabella and that of their great-grandson Philip II important steps were taken toward political unity, religious uniformity, and administrative efficiency; and again conciliar organization was the key. The Council of Castile (also known as the *Consejo real*) was reorganized by Isabella; and a Council of Aragon was instituted by Ferdinand in 1494, both of them to be in close attendance on the Catholic Kings. Under Charles I this device was expanded into an extraordinarily comprehensive conciliar system which came to include councils of state and war and separate councils for the Inquisition, the old military orders, the crusade, financial matters (*Hacienda*), and all the far-flung territories of the Spanish Empire, including the Indies, Italy, the Netherlands, and Portugal.[49]

Even the Holy Roman Empire of the German Nation (as it was called from the fifteenth century), though rent by chronic conflicts between the emperor and the independent principalities, made some effort to emulate the French model of kingship.[50] The constitutional reform attempted at the Diet of Worms in 1495 proposed a general public peace, a general tax (*Gemeinpfennig*), and a unified legal system, which was to be employed in the highest imperial court (*Reichskammergericht*) and which was based on a "reception" of Roman law. Later the empire was divided into ten administrative circles under a new governing council (*Reichsregiment*) to reinforce these efforts at imperial administration. This effort at reorganization failed, however; and if the kings of France, Spain, and England could plausibly claim to be "emperors in their kingdoms," the elected emperor was finally unable to make himself king in his empire—in part because of the elective character of the title (and the need to make a formal "election-capitulation" to the princes making up the electoral college), in part because of the spiritual resistance arising in the wake of the Lutheran scandal which was brewing even before the election of Charles V in 1519.

A unified structure of monarchy, though on a dynastic rather than a national basis, was thus the common aim of the sixteenth-century rulers of the great states of western Europe. In France this goal was expressed by the old Gallican motto "One king, one faith, one law" (*un roi, une foi, une loi*), which the king's legists pursued against all threats, external and internal. In Spain Philip II was also told that his inheritance was based on "one monarch, one empire, and one sword."[51] In England Elizabeth was represented as a female Augustus, presiding over a land blessed with peace and about to enjoy a golden age graced with renewed Christian piety. Charles V continued to pursue his political dream, but in the end it was the

German princes who displaced their imperial overlord in the enterprise of state-building—though under the most destructive conditions of internal and international war and religious schism.

≺ IV ≻

The Theory of Resistance

Resistance was inseparably bound to kingship in Western legal tradition in the sense that it represented the opposite side of the coin
of royal sovereignty—majesty being challenged by "lese majesty."[52]
Derived from the ancient Roman *populus* and transferred to the
prince, majesty was claimed by European kings as their own; and it
contributed directly to the sacral character of their office, making
them literally "untouchable" under penalty of the law of lese majesty, likewise of ancient Roman origin but also akin to the Christian
offense of blasphemy. According to the *Siete Partidas*, "It is necessary to refrain from touching [the king] in order to kill him, strike
him, or seize his person. For in seeking his death one would go
against the act of God . . . and the kingdom itself."[53]

Like kingship, resistance displayed a fundamental duality of
secular and sacred aspects, corresponding to the distinction made by
Fritz Kern between the Germanic and ecclesiastical rights to resist.[54]
In the first case the assumption was that, according to the *Sachsen-
spiegel*, "a man must resist his king and his judge if he does wrong";
in the second the injunction was to obey God rather than man. Modern ideas of resistance represented a convergence of these traditions.
In the extreme, resisting unjust and/or ungodly rule might entail
tyrannicide. The assassination of Caesar by Brutus was the most
celebrated precedent, but Christian tradition also recognized the
possibility of such recourse, as illustrated famously in John of Salisbury's distinction between true rulership and tyranny. "The Prince,
the likeness of the Deity, is to be loved, worshipped and cherished,"
wrote John in his *Policraticus*; "the tyrant, the likeness of wickedness, is generally even to be killed."[55]

In the early fifteenth century Jean de Terre-Vermeille drew a
similar contrast between kingship and tyranny, which for him (writing in the context of the civil wars of 1410–20) was represented by
the seditious behavior of John the Fearless, duke of Burgundy and

"destroyer of the kingdom" (*destructor regni*). Jean's three *Tractatus* were a "hymn to unity" and a celebration of the "mystical body of the kingdom" (*corpus mysticum regni*), employing a kind of "mystico-organic" analogy which, drawn from ecclesiastical convention, became common to royalist ideology throughout the early modern period.[56] Of this mystical body politic the king was by definition the head (*caput*) and fidelity its principle of life; and resistance or rebellion by any of the members was the worst sort of treason or lese majesty, the very institutionalization of "tyranny." The position of the rebels, of course, drawing on the very same political language, was just the reverse of this. Again, the kingdom and also political language were the objects of rivalry.

In Spain the sacral character of monarchy was much less evident, and so was insistence on ancient pedigree, to the extent that Spain had no Charlemagne or Arthur in its past, and at least one medieval king of Castile placed the crown on his own head. But Spain did have a long tradition of oppositional thought and practice. The legendary "liberties" of the Aragonese nobles, for example, were recalled (and embroidered upon) by François Hotman to give further substance to his arguments for resistance.[57] In the Spanish kingdoms, too, political protest became especially prominent under the rule of the Habsburgs, beginning with Ferdinand and Isabella's grandson Charles, who, though he might claim to be a descendant of the mighty Charlemagne, was only a foreign nuisance to many of his subjects. Ideas of protest and resistance spread to all classes, especially in the uprising of the communes (*Communidades*) in 1518 and the Christian brotherhood of Valencia (*Germanía*) in 1519. The *comuneros* may have brought anarchy to an area already "seething with discontent," but they did so, as Merriman remarked, in "the sweet name of liberty."[58]

There was thus a rich heritage of medieval resistance ideas and precedents deriving from the "liberties" asserted by communes as well as by the church and by feudal aristocracy against the pretensions of monarchy. Viewed in terms of the feudal compact, kingship was a precarial, and often precarious, institution that required fidelity from both parties. If vassals failed in their duty, they became felons; if kings fail in their duty, wrote Jean Meschinot in the 1460s, "let them fall."[59] This was the position taken by the League of the Public Weal, a cabal of French nobles who wanted to control King

Louis XI on the grounds—or as Philippe de Commines put it, "under the guise"—of maintaining this "Public Weal." The noble right to resist "tyranny" by force, asserted by Thomas Basin, was invoked a century later by the Huguenot propagandist François Hotman, who repeated these claims and added that these high nobles (the dukes of Bourbon, Berry, and others) had also "declared immunity from dues and taxes" as part of their campaign for the welfare of the state. Feudal ideas were reinforced by conceptions of contract associated with the coronation oath.[60] On this basis Jean Gerson, in his sermon *Vivat Rex* (1405), defended the right of resistance to tyranny and, under certain conditions, tyrannicide: "No sacrifice is more pleasing to God than the death of a tyrant."[61] Gerson also invoked the famous formula of Roman law justifying resistance to force by force (*vi vim repellere licet*).

The question of resistance was inseparable, then, from theories of kingly authority, and here appears another form of the dualism, in this case the rival ideas of divine right and popular sovereignty. "God chooses and the people establish a king," wrote a sixteenth-century royalist (*Eligit Deus, et constituit Regem populus*).[62] Although such a formula may be hard to reconcile with modern notions of authority, it is in fact essential for a society which assumed fundamental correspondences between earthly life and transcendent values, with a watchful God providing, confirming, preserving, and maybe overturning human institutions. The significant point here is that resistance, too, can be regarded as a human institution with its own kinds of legitimacy, and indeed was so regarded by jurists, so that its employment might be understood as not only a right but also a duty. As a result the "people" could be envisioned as acting on behalf of God in deposing a tyrant—which indeed happened more than once in scriptural record and in ancient, medieval, and modern historical memory.

Yet, while ideas of resistance flourished variously in contexts of conflicts between church and state, feudal rebellion, and uprisings of other social groups, these ideas were not given general and systematic expression before the sixteenth century. The great age of political resistance in Europe appeared in the wake of the Protestant Reformation, when religious enthusiasm fueled older, especially feudal and civic, sources of discontent and became a social and political force. First in time were the constitutional position taken by the

Lutheran princes—the original "Protestants"—against Charles V; the formation by them of the Schmalkaldic League in 1530, which coincided with the formulation of the Confession of Augsburg; and the civil wars in the Holy Roman Empire that lasted intermittently until 1648. Next there was the protest of the English exiles against the government of Queen Mary Tudor during the 1550s. Then, a decade later, came the wars of religion in France between the Calvinists—"Huguenots" as they began to be called in the 1560s—and the Catholic party, and the parallel revolt of the Dutch provinces, their Eighty Years' War (as they termed it), against the rule of the Spanish Crown. It was in the course of these interrelated conflicts, beginning with the Lutheran question and ending in the Thirty Years' War, that the modern theory of resistance was formed.[63]

In the sixteenth century political resistance became most conspicuous in those territories of the German empire where the princes who objected to Emperor Charles V's violation of their ecclesiastical rights joined forces with the Lutheran movement which the emperor was also opposing. The upshot of this fusion of a political party defending its constitutional "liberties" and a confessional movement representing an evangelical "liberty" was the first modern form of resistance theory. It was on the basis of secular legal arguments rather than Bible-based protest that Luther himself qualified his fundamentalist conviction that it was an offense to God to resist any legitimate authority and came to the conclusion that "if one may resist the pope, one may also resist all the emperors and dukes who contrive to defend the pope."[64] The arguments thus applied to the princes, and reinforced by the old maxim of civil law that force might be legitimately resisted by force were extended to cities such as Strasbourg and especially Magdeburg, which brought their own ancient civic liberties under the umbrella of this idea of resistance.

But if the grounds of opposition were the old liberties accumulated in the course of medieval communal struggles, it was evangelical dissent that precipitated active resistance. As the pastors of Magdeburg put it in 1550, "We will undertake to show that a Christian government may and should defend its subjects against a higher authority which should try to compel the people to deny God's word and to practice idolatry."[65] Scriptures offered many examples of "just wars" against religious "tyranny," and a ruler taking his orders from "the devil," and natural law furnished further legitimacy to such ideas of active resistance. This *Confession of Magdeburg* gained further notoriety when in 1574 Calvin's successor in the Genevan church, Theodore Beza, published his *Right of Magistrates over their Subjects* and subtitled it "a treatise essential at this time [just after the massacres of St. Bartholomew] to advise magistrates as well as subjects about their duty, published by those of Magdeburg in 1550 and now reviewed and augmented with many arguments and examples."[66]

In general evangelical resistance followed the lead set, however inadvertently, by Luther; and it was Calvin in particular who assembled the basic arguments, even if he did not proceed to draw their most extreme conclusions. Passive resistance was the most that private individuals could venture, but "magistrates of the people" (like their ancient counterparts) could take more active measures against tyranny. For Calvin, moreover—and this was a loophole through which a torrent of ideological extremism would eventually follow—there was always one exception to the rule of obedience to even divinely instituted authority; namely, that obedience to God superseded all other secular duties: "We must obey God rather than men" (Acts 5:29).[67] Calvin did not go so far as to argue that this justified resistance, but he did encourage his followers to leave the "Babylon" that Catholic states had become and join him in exile; and in France doing so meant violating the royal edict of 1556 forbidding such emigration—or else submitting to the martyrdom to which passive resistance and the need to avoid religious hypocrisy led.

In England the high point of resistance ideas came during the period of the Marian exiles (1553–58), who came into direct contact with continental Protestantism and its radical political implications. Yet the exiles' own predicament and hatred of the persecutions of "Bloody Mary" was at least as significant in provoking notions of resistance, expressed most famously in John Knox's *First Blast of the Trumpet*, John Ponet's *Short Treatise of Politike Power*, and Christopher Goodman's *How Superior Powers Ougt to be Obeyed*.[68] Once again resistance ideas were the product of dual inspiration— the opposition first to popish tyranny, which oppressed Christian liberty, and second to the secular government which supported the papal Antichrist. Addressing "the Lordes and commons of Englande," Ponet defended the "liberty of the people" in both senses and held out the possibility of tyrannicide. Goodman repeated Calvin's argument "that rather is God to be obeyed then men" but went further by suggesting that the initiative to disobedience rested not only with "inferior magistrates" but with all men, "of what state and condicion so ever they be."

Marian protest was cut short by the death of Mary and the accession of Elizabeth in 1558; but in France ideas of resistance were just entering their take-off period, as the "Calvinist cause" was visibly infiltrating the ranks of the higher nobility, constituting just those "inferior magistrates" who, sharing in sovereign power, might take the lead in resisting tyranny. In these years of emergent religious conflict—and of the "politicization" of Protestantism—in France, Calvin was often asked by his followers what recourse they had to the tyranny and persecution they were suffering at the hands of their "popish" rulers, meaning especially Mary Tudor in England; Charles V and Philip II in the Netherlands; and Henry II and his sons, under the influence of Catherine de Médicis, in France.[69] Calvin's own answer remained the same as that given famously in his *Institution of Christian Religion* twenty years before; but his younger followers, especially Beza and Hotman, went further. At least in private, they began to seek legitimate constitutional grounds for active resistance, to establish the political program of the Huguenot party, and, in effect and in the event, to formulate the propaganda that would evolve, twenty years later, into the classic works of modern resistance theory by those critics of absolutism whom William Barclay later called "monarchomachs."

≺ V ≻

From Resistance to Rebellion

Political resistance is the obverse of kingship, and yet it also claimed a sort of social legitimacy, stemming as it did from the right to petition and protest which all classes theoretically enjoyed, especially but not exclusively through parliaments, diets, or assemblies of estates. Official remonstrances and *gravamina* addressed to the king directly or indirectly questioned the legality, morality, or propriety of his actions, and often they are hardly to be distinguished from rebel petitions joined to violent protest.[70] And of course this extended to the lowest levels of society: the German peasants in 1525, the Norfolk uprising of 1549 against enclosures, and the French *croquants* in the early seventeenth century are only a few of the popular uprisings which claimed justification in law, immemorial custom, or some other higher principle.

When religious sentiment was added to social discontent, the grounds were prepared for a higher level of ideological dissent and political impact; and this condition was conspicuously the case with the German peasant wars, which provide the most sensational episodes of grass-roots resistance. In these complex uprisings the Lutheran themes of "Christian liberty," "priesthood of all believers," and the primacy of Scriptures were sounded, but in the most hyperbolic and ambiguous ways.[71] Preachers like Thomas Müntzer and Andreas Karlstadt emphasized the need of the people for shepherds but, at least indirectly, encouraged community action against the tyranny not only of popery but also of the nobility. "Freedoms," in the sense of privileges, were opposed by peasant leaders like Michael Gaismair,[72] but so was the tyranny of human "law," including scholastic theology and Roman law. In any case there was, among both religious and secular leaders, agreement on the independence of true Christian faith from human authority, on the significance of the "common man," and, finally—against the moderate counsel of Luther—on the need for immediate and not gradual action.

The most radical expression of resistance ideas in this context was an appeal "To the Assembly of the Peasantry May 1525."[73] The anonymous author, recalling the assassination of Julius Caesar and the rebellious foundations of the Swiss Confederation, defended active resistance against "false and unlimited power" and against the un-Christian institution of hereditary rule. Not only does a community indeed have "the power to depose its pernicious lords," declared this author, but "God wants it!"—and indeed, "Christ himself must be a rebel."[74] Therefore, the people should arm itself in the name of the Lord—for defensive purposes, of course—and preserve its unity in the just war that is likely to follow. The collapse of this sort of resistance and the tragic aftermath of the peasant uprisings obscured the ideals of the sermons and pamphlet literature of the mid-1520s, which would not become a significant part of the European canon of revolutionary activity until recovered and celebrated by Engels in the nineteenth century.[75]

Ideas of active resistance in a more secular mode were formulated most clearly by French and Dutch Calvinists during the wars of religion in the third quarter of the sixteenth century. In France the issue of resistance appeared first in the constitutional crisis produced by the death of Henry II in 1559 and the subsequent establishment of domination over the government and the young King Francis II, who was still a minor, by the Guise family, headed by Duke Henry and his brother the cardinal of Lorraine, and with the apparent complicity of the queen mother Catherine de Médicis. The grounds for complaint included not only the unfortunate political influence of these "foreigners"—referring to Catherine's Florentine background and the *fuorusciti* that remained in attendance on her, and the fact that the Guise family originated in Lorraine—but also to the continuing stream of legislation calling for the "extermination" of what the government called "the so-called reformed religion." Opposition took the form first of personal attacks on these usurpers, then of justification for resisting their "tyranny."

"We are often asked," wrote Beza (referring to himself and Calvin), "whether it is permitted to rise up against those who are enemies not only of religion but also of the real."[76] This was in September 1559, just two months after the death of Henry II and exactly at the time when active resistance was being organized against these enemies. Leaders of this "conspiracy" of Amboise, as critics later called it, applied both to Calvin and to princes of the blood (Antoine de Navarre and the prince of Condé) for approval and legitimacy. They failed in this effort, however; and this abortive episode—in effect the opening salvo in the civil wars—produced nothing except a few Protestant martyrs and a flurry of pamphlets which inaugurated constitutional and eventually revolutionary programs of the Calvinist (now commonly called Huguenot) party, including a violent protest entitled *The Estates of France Oppressed by the Tyranny of the Guise*. François Hotman took the cardinal of Lorraine as his principal target in his notorious *Tiger of France* of 1560, in which he suggested, not too subtly, that the cardinal, because of his religious intolerance as well as his constitutional usurpations, was at least as deserving of assassination as Caesar had been.[77]

All of these Huguenot pamphlets also called for a meeting of the Estates General in this time of political emergency, and this became a permanent demand on the part of the "Cause," as French Hugue-

nots called their politico-religious program. Efforts were made over
the next two years to reconcile the contending parties by means
both of a meeting of the Estates General (the first in over three-
quarters of a century) and a religious colloquy held at Poissy between Calvinists and Gallicans (with a dramatic confrontation between Beza and the cardinal), but nothing availed to prevent the
shooting war which almost everyone thought was inevitable, especially after the "massacre" of Huguenots at Vassy by the troops of
the duke of Guise.

The lines were finally drawn when the prince of Condé gathered
with other Huguenot leaders in Orléans in April 1562 and when his
legal champions, including Hotman and Beza, began to assemble
the public defense of and justification for their political resistance.
Letters seeking support, moral and financial, were sent out to the
German princes, to Elizabeth, and to the Genevan council. In the
"Treaty of Association" signed by himself and his followers Condé
protested that he was moved by no selfish passion and was entirely
loyal to the true government of France, that he wanted to achieve
the full "liberty" of the young king and his "legitimate counsellors,"
that he hoped to "relieve the poor people of the heavy burden of
taxation and debt" caused by the Guises, and that he would lay
down his arms if his opponents would do likewise.[78] Thus a religious
movement, based on the principle of "liberty of conscience," joined
with a neo-feudal faction to form a political party supported by an
army and international connections; and so the question of "resistance" was moved from the realm of theory to that of practice and
indeed, for the next generation, into national life in France.

Over the next few years the Huguenot cause became internation-
alized, as Condé and his successor Coligny established ties with
William of Orange, the leader of the Dutch revolt against Spanish
rule. Although the provinces of the Netherlands were involved in a
struggle of liberation rather than a civil war, they defended their
position on much the same grounds as those of their fellow Huguenots in France. In December 1565, three years after Condé's "association," a group of Dutch nobles formed their own "holy and lawful
confederation and alliance" against the introduction of the Spanish
Inquisition. In 1568 William took a public stand against the tyranny
of the Spaniards, "whose steady purpose it is only to bring [the Neth-
erlands] in intolerable slavery . . . despite the contracts, leagues, and

privileges which they violate every day"—and who in addition promulgated "edicts to extirpate the pure word of God."[79] As William wrote four years later (April 1572), "[A]fter expelling the tyrannical oppressors, together we shall see the Netherlands in their ancient freedom, governed again without any violence, with proper obedience to the king and security for your consciences, and according to the advice of the Estates general."[80] Thus the Dutch leadership also joined religious protest with constitutional ideals in their defense of resistance.

Ideas of resistance were escalated by one of the most sensational confluences of events of the century, which centered on the massacres of St. Bartholomew in August 1572. Besides striking a blow at Huguenot leadership by murdering Coligny, sending many of his followers to their deaths or into exile, and spoiling the plan of William of Orange—now called "redeemer of the freedom of the Netherlands"—to invade the Netherlands, these massacres pushed Huguenot ideas of resistance beyond a merely passive to an active level. Beza thus moved beyond the teachings of his spiritual father and predecessor to conclude, in his *Right of Magistrates* of 1573, "that we must honor as martyrs not only those who have conquered without resistance, and by patience only, against tyrants who have persecuted the truth, but also those who, authorized by law and by competent authorities, devoted their strength to the defense of true religion."[81]

The massacres of St. Bartholomew marked another turning point in resistance theory, for it led Protestants for the first time to direct their objections directly to the king himself and not to his foreign usurpers or "evil counsellors." Charles IX had taken full responsibility for the actions taken against "those of the religion," and so had made his royal person the target of criticism. The events of 24 August 1572 provoked not only resistance but also a resurgence of royalist pride, illustrated most outrageously by a medal cast in honor of the deed, depicting King Charles IX on his throne and holding a flaming sword and scepter, and featuring the words *"invictus in rebelles"*; on the reverse were a crown and fleur-de-lis between two columns, under which was inscribed *"24 Augusti 1572."*[82]

Beza's old colleague Hotman—himself a near victim of the massacres—reported hearing that His Majesty the King had been insulted by Huguenot protests. "But how can there be any 'majesty' in

such a monster," Hotman asked in a private letter to a Swiss Protestant, "and how can one accept as a king a man who has spilled the
blood of 30,000 persons in eight days?"[83] To question "majesty,"
that is, the sovereign power itself, was the most treasonable and
revolutionary position one could take even in wartime—literally
"lese majesty" (as, from the 1540s in France, was the crime of
heresy). This step was taken by William of Orange, too, a few years
later, when Philip II put a price on his head. In his *Apology* of 1580
William, admitting to the charge that he wanted "liberty of conscience," argued that the king himself had broken his royal word and
violated the customs and liberties of the Netherlands. A few months
later the Estates General of the United Netherlands formally abjured
Spanish sovereignty. "The prince is created for his subjects," this
document reads; and if the king does not live up to his obligations,
"according to right and reason his subjects . . . must no longer recog-
nise him as a prince . . . but should renounce him" and go on to elect
another.[84] This was a doctrine not only of rebellion but also, at least
by implication, of popular sovereignty, which would in effect be recognized in the treaties of Westphalia of 1648.

The last stage in the development of ideas of resistance in the
sixteenth century was the more theoretical and philosophical elabo-
ration of authors in the later sixteenth century, first Protestant and
then Catholic, in a massive outpouring of political polemic. Ideas of
constitutionalism and resistance received fullest expression in the
three classic treatises of the monarchomachs which were published
in the wake of the massacres. Beza's *Right of Magistrates*, Hotman's
Francogallia, and the *Vindiciae contra tyrannos* (later *Defense of
Liberty against Tyrants*), attributed to Hubert Languet and/or Philippe de Mornay, sum up the experience, grievances, reflections, and
conclusions of the post-Lutheran generation in western Europe.

The reasoning of the monarchomachs is complex and finds its
warrant in an eclectic mixture of authorities, including the Bible,
ancient philosophy, Roman law, medieval and modern history, legal
maxims, and natural law. Yet the major points can be summarized
quite simply along two lines of argumentation, religious and political. First, God must be obeyed before man; if a ruler forces his subjects to act against God's will, he loses his legitimacy and becomes
a tyrant; and it becomes not only the right but also the duty of
people to resist. Second, rulers are created for their peoples, not

peoples for rulers; and if a prince fails in his paternal obligations, again he becomes a tyrant and subject to overthrow, tyrannicide, or even replacement by another elected ruler. What makes such resistance legitimate is that such popular initiatives must be endorsed by political qualified leaders, such as the "lesser magistrates," or the ancient and sacred assembly of the Estates General—that is, the "Great Council" in its largest extension. (It is worth noting that this notion, which implied "mixed sovereignty," was itself regarded unofficially as a form of lese majesty at this time.)

Beza's book took the scholastic form of question-and-answer concerning the problem of obedience and the conditions under which it may be renounced. For Beza sovereignty was shared by the king with his officers (the "lesser magistrates") and with the estates, which were the repository of liberty and legislative authority and which traditionally possessed the power to elect and dethrone kings. In support of these views Beza offered examples from ancient and medieval history, including the famous Aragonese oath, which took the form of a contract: "We who are worth as much as you and can do more than you elect you king under such and such conditions."[85] Beza also invoked the *lex regia* of ancient Rome, according to which the prince received his sovereignty (*maiestas*) from the Roman people; and the conciliar thesis, rejected by the church, which placed the ecumenical council above the pope. If magistrates fail in their duty, Beza argued, "then each private citizen should exert all his strength to defend the legitimate institutions of his country."

It was the purpose of Hotman, Beza's old comrade in arms, to place these questions in a long historical perspective; and this he did, with a vast array of learning, including references to Fortescue and Seyssel, by tracing the liberties of the French people preserved in their ancient constitution. From the start the French had been threatened with Roman "tyranny"—the tyranny first of imperial and then of papal Rome—and the Italianate rule of Catherine de Médicis was simply the last manifestation of this vicious foreign influence. Hotman celebrated the "fundamental laws" circumscribing royal power and listed the "marks of tyranny" (evil counterparts to the marks of sovereignty celebrated by the king's legists), including forced obedience, the presence of "foreign body guards," and arbitrary rule without the consent of the assembly of the "great council," that is, the three estates. Like Beza, Hotman drew on ancient and medieval history for reinforcing parallels, including the very same text of the Aragonese oath.[86] In the first edition of the *Francogallia* Hotman invoked the principle of elective kingship, though he deleted this later when Henry of Navarre became heir presumptive to the throne. Hotman's main point, however, was the authority of the "public" and "sacrosanct" council, which included all those "marks of sovereignty," especially the law-making power that jurists had traditionally bestowed on kingship.[87]

If in some ways the *Vindiciae contra Tyrannos* seems more radical than the treatises of Beza and Hotman, this is because it reflects more directly the experience of the Dutch, who were fighting a war of liberation against foreign invaders. The *Vindiciae*, too, follows a question-and-answer method concerning the rights of resistance but is much more insistent on the contractual nature of rulership. "In all legitimate governments a compact is always to be found." The coronation of a king is accompanied by two covenants, according to the *Vindiciae*, "the first between God, the king and the people that the people will be God's people; the second between the king and the people that if he is a proper ruler, he will be obeyed accordingly."[88] But "if not"—the key phrase of the Aragonese oath, to which allusion is again made—then resistance is not only a right, it is a duty. Kings are established by the people and therefore may be deposed by the people, who are "greater than the king." What distinguishes the *Vindiciae* is the further argument that neighboring princes may be called in to help the victims of ungodly tyranny—as indeed happened in the case of the Dutch.

In general the drift of resistance theory in the wake of the Reformation was from the passive stance of martyrs to the active views of those who decided to take up arms in defense of their "cause" and in defiance of instituted authority. The extreme expression of this was the act of tyrannicide—and in this connection it should be remembered that the sixteenth century was an age not only of martyrs but also of political assassination. The French tended to blame this new practice on "Machiavellian" foreigners (in contrast to the civilized custom of duelling), but in fact it was a product of civil war not at all strange to French political tradition and revived in an atmosphere of religious fanaticism. On the Protestant side Coligny and William of Orange; on the Catholic side the two dukes of

Guise, father and son, Henry III, and finally, the former Protestant Henry IV—these are only a few of the more publicized "political murders" (Franklin Ford lists thirty-five "major political murders" in this period[89]) which, together with their theoretical justifications by Catholics and Protestants, testify to the impact, non-partisan and in extremis, of resistance theory in the period of religious conflict.

This legacy carried over directly into the seventeenth century, most notably into the adaptations made by the English in their own revolutionary experience, which likewise displayed religious as well as secular concerns, when the spirit as well as the letter of French and Dutch resistance literature had a second career. "For a century and more," as John Salmon has concluded, "the ideas born in the French Wars of Religion fertilized the ground of English politics."[90] In this afterlife the major difference was the increasingly abstract and philosophical style of argumentation, with legal, historical, and scriptural allegations being replaced by rational and moral considerations. Otherwise, the classic statement of Locke on behalf of resistance may be understood, from one point of view, as a recapitulation of the arguments of the monarchomachs—as well as an anticipation of the revolutionary thought of the following century.

≺ VI ≻

Liberty in Extremis

In various ways the cult of kingship was threatened by a counter ideology that called all aspects of sovereignty into doubt; and the result was a radical polarization of political thought, marked by the opposition between modern ideas of "divine-right" kingship and radical theories of violent resistance, which a century of massive printed propaganda had disseminated throughout European society.[91] In France the extremes were represented by the revolutionary views of the monarchomachs and the reinvigorated modern theories of absolute monarchy, expressed most famously in Jean Bodin's *Six Books of the Republic* of 1576, a work written at least partly in response to the subversive ideas of the Huguenot propagandists. Bodin asserted the indivisibility and inalienability of sovereignty, the purely auxiliary character of the royal council, and the perniciousness of a "mixed constitution." Although he in fact acknowledged traditional limitations on royal authority, his work continued to be read by later generations as a more or less unqualified statement of "absolute" royal authority. The reign of Henry IV—which saw the restoration of the Gallican liberties and an extraordinary outpouring of royal legislation—signalled efforts to reassert this royal authority against threats from both Protestant and Catholic extremes, which continued to haunt the monarchy even after the assassination of Henry in 1614.

In England this ideological polarity was recapitulated in the conflict between the Stuart monarchy and the constitutional opposition based on neo-feudal traditions of common law and parliamentary government. The Scottish founder of this dynasty, James I, had been brought up in traditions of civil law; and in his *Trew Law of Free Monarchies* he drew upon all the presumptions of political Romanism as well as the sacral, organistic, and patriarchal motifs of medieval and imperial monarchy, while his opponents responded with equally traditional arguments for limited kingship and fundamental rights.[92] In the course of the constitutional debates leading up to England's own civil war, the arguments of French ideologists of earlier generations were recapitulated and often drawn upon; and as in the Reformation and subsequent wars the conflict often took the form of a fundamental struggle for language—not only for the possession of the magical term "liberty" but also for the control of the terminology and legitimizing force of the concept. Both sides wanted "true law" and "true liberty" (as well as "true religion") on their side.

What of the rest of Europe? The German Empire continued to be divided, and Calvinism, introduced first into the Palatinate, was a particularly disruptive influence and indeed a major factor in the resumption of civil war in 1618. Like France and England, the Spanish monarchy made strenuous efforts at political and social recovery but soon faced rebellions within its own realm as well as the continuing conflict with the Netherlands. The turmoils came together in that maelstrom that was the Thirty Years' War, along with the marginal outbursts that Merriman grouped loosely under the rubric of "six contemporaneous revolutions."[93] "Liberty" was more than ever on the lips and in the publications of politically active men, but it was also, more than ever, a victim of the polarities which appeared in the wake of the Protestant Reformation and wars of religion.

In the disasters which Europe had experienced over the previous century (and would continue to face over the next generation and more) there were many factors—political, social, and economic—that need to be taken into account, but none more than religion. This was surely the view taken by contemporaries, and as illustration I cite a fascinating little pamphlet of 1622 entitled "Dialogue between Calvin and Luther, back from the New World, concerning the Affairs of Europe." The dialogue was cast as a dream in which the writer heard Luther and Calvin, speaking as colleagues and friends, discussing the condition of their religion just over a century after its beginning.[94]

"I have just learned from a German courier that our poor church has been ravished," Luther began, "and that we are forbidden to enjoy our liberty and to live according to the good laws and precepts which our free will [sic] gives us."[95]

"You may complain about your situation, my colleague and friend," Calvin responded, "but it is impossible for me to explain how much my poor children have been groaning under the oppressions which every day are inflicted on them by the king of France . . . It is easier to count the stars in the sky, the sands of the oceans, or the ships in the harbor of Calais than to number even part of the misfortunes and disasters which have been visited on our poor French churches in the past two and a half years"—referring to the campaigns of Louis XIII and the duc de Luynes in 1620–21 against the Huguenots.

Luther responded by pointing out the massive destruction which was ruining all Germany. Whichever of their churches was hardest hit, Calvin continued, the disaster—the appointment of hostile prelates and magistrates as well as the attacks on La Rochelle and other Huguenot refuges—kept his "poor children" from "living in our ancient liberty," and also from giving help to their resisting brethren in the Palatinate and other parts of the Empire.

Finally, the shades of the two Protestant founding fathers could not agree on who had been the more victimized by political leaders; and they departed for the resting place from which they had emerged to lament their mutual fates, the failure of their dreams of "reviving the ancient splendor of the primitive church," and the tragedy which they had helped to bring about.

In the end, then—taking the "crisis of early modern Europe"

as the end—the counterpoint of kingship and resistance was unresolved. Kingship remained a reality, and indeed an increasingly oppressive reality, while resistance continued to challenge such authority in the name of liberty. On the level of political ideals, however, one remarkable development was becoming apparent in the course of the seventeenth century, namely, the emergence of a rationally formulated theory of legitimate resistance—the anticipation, as it were, of the idea of revolution, which later generations would infer from the experiences and intellectual creations of the wars of religion.

To return to the Hegelian formula invoked at the outset of this chapter: champions of kingship knew that one, at least, was free; beneficiaries of successful resistance that some could be free; theorists of radical ideals that all should be free. Such has been the pattern—if not of political experience at least of political speculation and aspiration. Yet meanwhile, in the realm of reality, the conflict of wills and the search for contradictory notions of liberty continued to form the substance of political history, the unresolved theme of political thought, and the very essence of the human social predicament.

Parliaments in the Sixteenth Century
and Beyond

H. G. KOENIGSBERGER

IN 1500 MOST EUROPEAN STATES lived under a regime of *dominium politicum et regale*, a limited or mixed monarchy in which the ruler shared power with a Parliament or an assembly of estates. This was a development of the later Middle Ages and it has been discussed in chapter 5. *Dominium politicum et regale* contrasted with two other forms of regime, republics and *dominium regale*, or, as historians were later to call it, absolute monarchy. In Italy the three regimes co-existed. Outside Italy, the Swiss cantons were republics and so were many of the larger German cities, even though they acknowledged the suzerainty of the Holy Roman Emperor.[1] *Dominium regale* was rare north of the Alps, although its one generally recognized example, indeed its prototype, was the greatest power in Europe, France.

There was therefore no inherent reason why political liberty should not have developed relatively smoothly in most European countries. Even in France the die had not yet been definitely cast against political liberty, although by 1500, as many contemporary observers realized, it was already loaded against liberty. Yet by the year 1700 the map of political regimes looked very different. *Dominium regale* had triumphed not only in France but also in Spain, Portugal, Denmark, Russia, and in most of the Italian and German principalities, including the Habsburg dominions of the Austrian duchies and the kingdom of Bohemia. For the individual this meant not so much a loss of personal liberty; for in the private spheres of life, such as commercial transactions, inheritance, or disputes over property, the rule of law continued to operate. The nobility had some special legal privileges; but that was so, in varying degrees, under all regimes except republics. But under *dominium regale* there was a real loss of political freedom: the monarchy could make laws and tax its subjects without consent, and it could freely make wars or conclude peace according to the fashionable maxims of reason of state, that is, dynastic power politics.

By contrast, in 1700 *dominium politicum et regale* had survived only in some of the smaller German principalities, such as Württemberg and Mecklenburg, and in some of the outlying dominions of composite monarchies: Sicily and Belgium under the Spanish monarchy, Hungary under the Austrian Habsburgs, and the British colonies in North America. But three major states had acquired a regime for which there was no contemporary name and which is best described as a parliamentary regime. Here ultimate power lay with Parliament or the estates, regardless of whether the regime was formally a monarchy—Great Britain and Poland-Lithuania (and regardless of how much practical political power or influence the monarchy exercised at any given moment), or formally a republic—the United Provinces of the Netherlands. Sweden, the one great monarchy not in these lists, had in the seventeenth century swung between *dominium politicum et regale* and *dominium regale* and it continued to oscillate in the eighteenth century between *dominium regale* (the actual condition around 1700) and a parliamentary regime.

These three forms of regime were not hard and rigid. There were considerable variations in the distribution and exercise of political power within them, and of the nature and degree of liberty enjoyed by individuals and different classes. But the essence of these regimes was clear enough, and most people knew quite well under which type of regime they lived.

< I >

The Decline of Dominium Politicum et Regale

There is no simple answer which will account for the change which took place between 1500 and 1700. Parliaments had their origins in the rulers' need for the counsel and support of the most powerful persons, groups, and corporations in their countries (see chapter 5), and the form these parliaments took tended to reflect the social structure of their countries. Yet a purely social structural model cannot, by itself, explain the changes of these two hundred years. England, politically centralized and with a big capital city, but otherwise mainly aristocratic and rural, was structurally much more similar to France than to the highly urbanized and federated Netherlands; yet its political history was more similar to that of the Netherlands than to that of France. We find the same lack of symmetry in eastern and northern Europe. The social structures of Denmark and Poland and, in spite of the absence there of serfdom, also of Sweden had much in common: economies based mainly on agriculture, dominated to a greater or lesser degree by a nobility with large landed estates, but with relatively few and small towns, and an export trade in agricultural or forest products or minerals, largely in the hands of foreign merchants. Yet again their political histories were very different.

What all countries, in both western and eastern Europe, had in common, however, was that their constitutional crises, the rumbles of earthquakes along the geological fault lines of their political structures, were triggered by actions of their monarchies. Psychologically this was always likely. Kings were brought up to see themselves as singled out by birth to rule: exhorted by their clergy to fulfill their divine mission—they all prefixed their titles with the phrase *dei gratia*, by the grace of God—and assured by their Roman law jurists of the absolute power of the Roman emperors and hence of contemporary princes. Many European kings declared, or had their lawyers declare, that their realm was an empire. This meant that, like the Roman emperors, they acknowledged no earthly superior.

With the rapid spread of Jean Bodin's theory of sovereignty, from the last quarter of the sixteenth century onwards, one could dispense with the imperial argument. The Bodinian theory of sovereignty as being unlimited in extent and time could be used also by the German princes who recognized the suzerainty of the emperor. All rulers swore coronation oaths to maintain the laws of their countries; but this left plenty of room for the interpretation of such laws, and Catholic princes could, on occasion, get the popes, from their "fulnes of power" (*plena potestas*), to issue dispensations from particularly irksome points of their coronation oaths.

Beyond personal attitudes and ambitions there were impersonal pressures on princes and their ministers to try to increase their powers because government became a more complex business and warfare became ever more expensive and tended to absorb an increasing proportion of the country's resources. Much could be done within the limits of *dominium politicum et regale*. Bullstrode Whitelock, the ambassador of the English Commonwealth to Sweden in 1654, told the Swedish chancellor, Axel Oxenstierna, in a discussion they had about the constitutions of their respective countries:

We hold the government of England, as to the fundamentalls of it, to be the same now, as when we had a king; the same lawes, the same supreame power, and the same magistrates. Forrein negotiations, matters of peace and warre, raysing of monyes, and making of lawes, were the proper business of parlements in the time of our kings, so admitted by the best and most successfull of them; and though some of them, growing in power, would encroach more than others, yett all acknowledged the power of parlements in those matters, and so it is still.[2]

There was no doubt some special pleading here; for England had only just emerged from civil wars and political upheavals in which precisely these questions of liberty and power had been at issue. But Whitelock was making a point beyond trying to reassure the Swedes that Cromwell's England was a stable and safe diplomatic and trading partner. It was that the regime of *dominium politicum et regale* could both accommodate a strong monarchy and safeguard the subjects' liberty, and that England, in spite of the upheavals of the previous twelve years, during which it had abolished the monarchy, the House of Lords, and its established church, was still enjoying this regime.

Much would evidently depend on the political skill of the ruler. If the circumstances and the timing were just right, it was even possible to change *dominium politicum et regale* into *dominium regale* at one blow. This was what Duke Emmanuel Philibert of Savoy-Piedmont managed to do. For twenty-three years, from 1536 to 1559, his duchy had been divided and occupied by French and Spanish-Imperial armies who ruled their respective parts by decree. As part of the Peace of Cateau-Cambrésis between France and Spain, in 1559, Emmanuel Philibert was able to return to his dominions at the head of a victorious army. He had been Philip II's governor-general of the Netherlands and his experience with its difficult States General had not inclined him to look favorably on representative institutions. But, astute politician that he was, he summoned the

Parliament of Piedmont. Reflecting the country's relief at being rid of the occupying armies and having its own duke back, this Parliament did what all previous parliaments of the country had refused to do: it voted a huge salt tax. With the money thus raised the duke could pay his army; he then refused to confirm his country's privileges and he never summoned Parliament again. Nor did his successors. It was one of the very few cases in which a ruler used a standing army to establish princely absolutism and he was only able to do this because Parliament had been peacefully persuaded to pay for this army in the first place.

Whether the rest of Europe appreciated the mechanics of Emmanuel Philibert's *coup d'état* or not, from then on disputes over the control of armies became one of the flashpoints in relations between monarchies and parliaments. This was so both in the Netherlands, a few years later, and in England in the middle of the seventeenth century; and yet in neither case did the monarchy manage to win. Emmanuel Philibert had the advantage of trying it in a small country, demoralized by long years of foreign military occupation. He managed to repeat his trick in French-speaking Savoy; but he was careful to observe the golden rule of composite monarchies of not interfering in his outlying provinces, and he left the Parliament of the Val d'Aosta severely alone. In his two principal duchies of Piedmont and Savoy he bound the nobility to himself by allowing them a free hand in exploiting the peasants on their estates. The price paid for the *coup* by the ordinary citizens was high. Where the average annual revenue of the dukes of Piedmont-Savoy before the French invasion of 1536 had been between 70,000 and 90,000 ducats, Emmanuel Philibert's was about half a million, often higher and only rarely lower.[3] As Sir John Fortescue had put it, a century earlier: "Lo, this is the fruit of *ius regale*."[4]

But the counterforces to a sudden *coup d'état* by monarchies were still strong. Before the second half of the seventeenth century no monarchy managed to build up a reliable and reasonably efficient bureaucracy to govern a large country or a composite state. It remained necessary to rely on those who had local authority, and they were precisely those who valued their privileges and liberties. Monarchical power was still highly vulnerable when a strong ruler was succeeded by a woman or a child. In such cases, even when it was not a disputed succession which made the position worse, the regents would have to rely heavily on the support of independently powerful individuals and corporations. In the sixteenth century the prevalence of composite monarchies made the problems presented by regencies even more frequent because an adult male ruler might still have to govern a dependency by a regency.

Spain had the curious distinction of experiencing these problems both as a regency, when its king was absent, and as the metropolitan country whose king ruled his dependencies by regencies—and, because of the failure of the Habsburg family to produce enough males, by regencies headed by women.

Ferdinand of Aragon and his wife, Isabella of Castile, had won the disputed succession to the throne of Castile with the help of most of the towns. The towns had formed a league, a brotherhood (*hermandad*) in good medieval fashion, which performed many important state functions. After their victory, Ferdinand and Isabella shifted their favor to the nobility, who were more immediately useful to them than the towns in their campaigns against the Moors of southern Spain and north Africa and against the French in Italy. They allowed the nobles to encroach on the property of the cities and when they summoned the Cortes, which they did rarely, they insisted that the towns' deputies should have full powers; for this meant that they could the more easily be bribed or intimidated to agree to the Crown's demands. In the Cortes of 1480, for instance, the Crown spent four million *maravedís* on payments to deputies, a sum which it then recouped from the taxes the Cortes voted. When Isabella died, in 1504, Ferdinand had become so unpopular that Castile threw itself into the arms of Philip of Burgundy, the son of the emperor Maximilian I and the husband of Isabella's daughter, Juana the Mad. After Philip's early death, in 1506, Ferdinand managed to act, rather uneasily, as regent in Castile for Philip and Juana's infant son, Charles.

When Ferdinand died, in 1516, another regency was headed by the primate of Castile, Cardinal Jiménes de Cisneros. Very rapidly, the position of the Crown deterioriated further. Magnates and towns maneuvered against each other but combined to thwart the orders of the government. The classic problems of a composite monarchy now produced a major crisis. In 1517 the young Charles, speaking as yet no Spanish, arrived with his Burgundian court and his Burgundian ministers and only a very few Spaniards who were all, understandably, regarded as carpetbaggers. In a country seething with its own discontents, his relations with his first Cortes were correct but hardly cordial. In 1519 Charles was elected Holy Roman Emperor and needed money to finance his journey to Germany. To make sure of success Charles's ministers presented the town councils with a model formula of the powers they were to grant their deputies to a newly-summoned Cortes. They were "to keep, maintain, fulfill and pay, and to hold firm, acceptable, stable and valid, for now and for ever afterwards, as if we ourselves (i.e. the town councils) had done and granted it, supposing we ourselves had been present," everything the deputies might decide.[5] The deputies themselves were bribed with part of the proceeds of the tax they voted—very much as happened in French provincial assemblies where the Crown bribed the nobles. Even with these tactics, Charles obtained only a bare majority of the votes in the Cortes.

Quite unlike Emmanuel Philibert of Savoy, Charles V's government attempted its half-hearted coup not principally in order to change the balance of power between monarchy and Cortes but mainly to obtain money to extend the ruler's composite monarchy. The policy backfired immediately. The cities, led by Toledo and Valladolid, repudiated the taxes granted by the Cortes. In Segovia a mob lynched one of the deputies. The cities resurrected their fifteenth-century league, but now with a much more powerful executive (junta). They claimed that they did not seek their private interests, as the nobles did, but those of the whole kingdom, that indeed they were the kingdom. This claim was, at least implicitly, a denial of the very existence of the other two estates, the clergy and the nobility. Naturally, they also claimed, as other European assemblies had done in moments of crisis, that they had the right to assemble on their own initiative and to discuss all matters relating to the benefit of the Crown and the kingdom. In the civil war that followed, the comunero movement, the movement led by the towns, rapidly polarized opinion, as power in the cities shifted more and more to popular and radical elements. The nobles, at first not unsympathetic, became scared of social revolution and rallied to the Crown. On 23 April 1521 their army routed the comunero forces at the battle of Villalar.[6]

While the nobles had won the military victory, it was the Crown which reaped the political benefits. Its alliance with the nobility was to last, cemented by their mutual interest in the growing empire of Charles V and the patronage which this empire enabled the Crown to dispense. Owing to his imperial obligations, Charles V could spend only relatively short periods of time in Spain. The country had therefore to be governed by a succession of regencies. In these circumstances it was quite impossible to establish an effective *dominium regale* regime. The Cortes continued to be summoned and, while they never again challenged the Crown's ultimate authority, they continued to quarrel with the government about voting taxes only after their grievances had been dealt with and they frequently managed to circumvent the Crown's demand that the deputies be given full powers.

Much of this was a matter of expediency; for the deputies could not as easily travel back and forth over the long distances of the Castilian meseta as the deputies of Flanders or Holland who were constantly referring back to their nearby constituents, traveling comfortably in boats and barges on the ubiquitous Netherlands rivers and canals. In the Castilian Cortes the deputies could at times act as a kind of third force, mediating between the contradictory financial interests of the Crown and the cities—not so very different from the role of English members of Parliament. The Spanish monarchy, for its part, found it convenient to convert the *alcabalá*, the medieval sales tax, into the *encabezamiento*, global sums agreed by the Cortes and left to the individual towns to raise as they wished. In this way the cities maintained a great measure of control over parliamentary taxation and, at times, could prevent an increase in taxation and at least once, at the end of Philip II's reign, the renewal of a particularly heavy and odious tax at least for the rest of that king's reign.[7]

In the seventeenth century the length of the sessions of the Cortes increased, and the proportion of parliamentary taxation in royal revenues also increased, from about 25 per cent in 1573 to perhaps 60 per cent in the 1650s. Not surprisingly, the difficulties of getting agreement to these increased taxes increased in similar proportion. The monarchy tried to get its way by having titled noblemen and royal officials elected as deputies by the twenty-six cities represented in the Cortes. Even so, it proved necessary to pay huge bribes, not only to the deputies but also to the town councils. From the 1630s increasingly influential and insistent voices were heard in the king's councils, arguing that it would be easier and cheaper to do without the Cortes and negotiate directly with the city councils.

It was not a new idea. Charles V's government in the Netherlands had tried it sporadically in the 1530s and 1540s. The cities of the Netherlands, too, were in the habit of receiving handouts; but these did not usually go to individual deputies or city councilors but took the form of reductions in the quotas of the taxes levied on individual cities. Individual bribes were paid the other way round, by the provincial estates to royal councilors.[8] In the end, and after some wavering, the Dutch towns always refused to allow the government to divide them and grant taxes outside their representative assemblies. This firmness was undoubtedly one of the reasons, though certainly not the only one, for the eventual triumph of the Dutch estates over the Spanish monarchy. The Spanish king Philip IV (1621–65) was himself no friend of representative assemblies. In the Spanish Netherlands (Belgium) he did not summon a States General again after 1632 and he declared that "States Generals are pernicious at all times and in all monarchies, without exception."[9] There were none in the Spanish colonies in America. The Cortes of the kingdom of Valencia ceased to be called after 1645, those of Aragon after 1646. The Spanish viceroy of Naples asserted in 1643 that its Parliament could only damage the public peace and the king's service. It was never summoned again.[10]

In Castile, the government of Philip IV, beset by seemingly endless foreign wars, shied away from definite actions which might antagonize the cities. After 1665, with a weak and unpopular regency government by the Austrian mother of the infant Charles II, it was decided that it would be safer not to summon the Cortes. There were fears that the Cortes would want to exercise control over the regency council, as had happened during the last Castilian minority, in 1391. It is not clear whether the government meant this to be a final decision. When the taxes granted by the last Cortes of Philip IV ran out, it proved relatively easy to have them renewed by individual city councils. Petitions affecting individual towns and localities could still be granted. The Cortes had never played as important a role as the English Parliament in legislation for the whole kingdom.

And so the Cortes of Castile disappeared without even a whimper. There was no reaction to what, at least at first, appeared to be a non-event. The estate of the nobility had voluntarily withdrawn from the Cortes after a tiff about their exemption from taxation, in 1538. The clergy were not represented in any case. The only too evident tradition of the deputies and the city councilors to line their own pockets from public taxes had made them thoroughly unpopular. People forgot that, in spite of their failings, the Cortes had tried to protect the interests of the general public. They had refused a tax on flour, had halved the tax on salt, and had imposed taxes on the nobles as well as on the commoners. But taxes were simply very high.

The myth of the power of the Cortes had frightened the regent's advisers. It was probably an exaggerated fear. Only when it became clear, later in the reign of Charles II, that there would be no more Cortes, did the myth of the Cortes as the all-wise institution, capable of setting to rights all the ills of the country, gain widespread support. By then it was too late. In the eighteenth century the new Bourbon dynasty would be able to establish a geniune *dominium regale* with an extensive bureaucracy, unhindered by any claims to authority by a representative assembly.[11] When the struggle for freedom resumed in Spain in the eighteenth century, it had to start again from first base.

The history of the Cortes (corts) of Catalonia was very different, for here political freedom was preserved in its traditional form. Catalonia had been the metropolitan center of the medieval Aragonese empire in the Mediterranean. The union of the Crowns of Aragon and Castile and the succession of the house of Habsburg had changed Catalonia into a relatively small, outlying dominion of a world empire whose center was Castile. For a century and a half the monarchy observed all the rules for such a situation. It left the landowning nobility with its powers of jurisdiction over its peasants, and the administration of the country in the hands of Catalan officials. The corts of the three estates was traditionally uncooperative; but it was, also traditionally, summoned only rarely. Its functions of defending the country's privileges and of administering the parliamentary taxes were left to a small committee, the *diputació*.

Since the fourteenth century similar committees had been organized in different parts of Europe. Originally, their function had usually been to supervise the conditions which parliaments had imposed on their governments in between the full sessions of these parliaments. They could become very powerful and effective, as happened in the ecclesiastical principality of Friuli before it was conquered by the Venetians, in 1420.[12] More commonly, however, governments learned to control the appointments to these committees and manipulate their members in a way they could hardly manipulate a full Parliament.

In 1640 the government in Madrid, despairing of getting financial help for the war with France from the corts, decided on a campaign in the eastern Pyrenees in order to pitch Catalonia into the war. The smoldering hatred of the Catalan peasants against their tyrannical lords was now turned against the Spanish soldiers which the Madrid government billetted on them. The internecine feuds of the Catalan ruling families were also turned against the government, which was accused of riding roughshod over local privileges. In Barcelona a city mob, swollen by hordes of armed peasants, murdered the viceroy. Unexpectedly, the *diputació* now came to life as the defender of all local privileges when the government made the mistake of arresting one of its members. Its president, the energetic canon Pau Claris, turned rebellion into revolution. He proclaimed a republic in Catalonia—the ultimate symbol of freedom in early modern Europe. But within a week the advance of the Castilian army made it clear that there was no republican future for Catalonia. Unlike Holland in the sixteenth century, it was too near the center of Spanish power. In January 1641 the Catalans transferred their allegiance to the archabsolutist, the king of France, "as in the time of Charlemagne."

The outcome of the revolution, led by the *diputació* and the ruling elite of Catalonia in reluctant and fearful alliance with a peasant *jacquerie*, now depended on foreign intervention. When French help was withdrawn, because France had plunged into a civil war of its own, the Spanish monarchy had little difficulty in reconquering Catalonia. Philip IV was wise enough to let the Catalans have back all their old liberties and restore the condition of *dominium politicum et regale*. The peasants gained little but had at least got rid of the hated soldiery. Catalonia remained loyal to the Spanish Crown for another fifty years and loyal to the house of Austria during the War of the Spanish Succession when it was, ironically, the rest of Spain which now chose allegiance to the French Bourbons.[13]

≺ II ≻

The Impact of Religion: Central Europe

Five days before the battle of Villalar effectively ended the comunero movement, Martin Luther pronounced his famous defiance before the king of Castile, the emperor Charles V, at the Diet of Worms (18 April 1521). Outside Spain and Italy a new dynamic force now appeared in the relations between monarchies and parliaments. Religion, with its all-encompassing hold on men's minds, was the force which, more than any other, could break the basic striving for harmony in an aristocratic-patrician society. Inescapably, religion came to be entangled with political aims and necessities. For the monarchies this was summed up in the French lawyers' slogan: "One king, one law, one faith" (*un roi, une loi, une foi*). For the estates their rights and privileges now came to include their right to choose the "true" religion.

There was already one major precedent, the Hussite revolution in Bohemia, 1419–37. The theologian Jan Hus was burned as a heretic by the general council of Constance, in 1415; but his teaching for the reformation of the Catholic Church caught the imagination of his Czech countrymen. Tinged by strong anticlerical feelings, the Hussite movement brought together a surprisingly wide alliance: the great nobles, with their eyes on the government of the kingdom and on the land of the monasteries; the lesser nobles and the free farmers trying to free themselves from the control of the magnates, both lay and ecclesiastical; the petty bourgeoisie and the journeymen and urban laborers, hating the rich German merchants who ruled their towns; and the poor peasants, rebelling against crushing rents and dreaming of Christian communes where goods were held in common. The estates took over the government of the country, pronounced on religious as well as secular matters, and successfully organized the defense of Bohemia against successive "crusades" led by their king, the emperor Sigismund. Their armies also went on the offensive throughout central Europe, spreading universal fear and destruction but little political freedom.[14]

In the end, this unlikely alliance fell apart. The nobility, conservative in their interpretation of Hussite doctrine and anxious to consolidate their material gains, defeated the social and religious radicals and made a deal with Sigismund (1436). After his death in the following year, the estates continued to claim the right to elect the king.[15] It took two more confrontations, in 1546–47 and in 1618–20, before the Crown managed finally to defeat the estates, confirm the hereditary nature of the Bohemian monarchy (in the house of Habsburg), and establish an effective *dominium regale*. In both cases religion was a strong motive force for the estates in the defense of their privileges. In both cases the internal confrontation was closely involved with, and its outcome largely determined by, outside events and forces: in 1546–47 by the Schmalkaldic War and the military defeat of the Lutherans by Charles V; in 1618–20 by the religious and power-political tensions at the beginning of the Thirty Years' War and the military defeat of the Bohemian estates by the army of the king's ally, the duke of Bavaria.[16]

In Germany, the Reformation had, at least at first, few constitutional consequences. The imperial diets (*Reichstage*) continued as little more than the stage on which the emperor and the Catholic princes, on the one side, and the Protestant princes and imperial cities, on the other, argued their respective positions, passed unobserved and unobservable resolutions and compromises, and haggled over the financing of the defense of the Empire against the ever more menacing Turkish advance. For Charles V, his relations and wars with the Turks and with France had right of way, so to speak, before the religious and constitutional questions. Not until 1546–47 was Charles in a position to make a determined effort to cut the Gordian knot of the deadlocked political process and religious antagonisms of the Holy Roman Empire by waging a military campaign against the Schmalkaldic League of Lutheran princes and cities.

His victory, although it appeared to give him an unprecedently powerful position, failed to change the basic relationship between emperor and estates. The Catholic German princes were as little inclined as the Protestants to acquiesce in a fundamental restructuring of the Holy Roman Empire in favor of a strong monarchy. In 1555 Charles V's brother, Ferdinand I, agreed at the Diet of Augsburg on the principle of *cuius regio eius religio*, which allowed the princes, but not their subjects, to choose between Lutheranism and Catholicism for their own principalities. It was a compromise which gave Germany sixty years of peace but which left unresolved the

constitutional problems of the Empire and the sharpening religious confrontations of the age of the Counter Reformation.

Those German princes who introduced the Reformation in their principalities could usually rely on the support of their estates, especially of the nobility, with whom they shared the property of the secularized monasteries and convents, or to whom they sold this property on favorable terms, just as Henry VIII did with the property of the English monasteries. In these principalities there was therefore no serious problem between the princes and their *Landtage*. The usual disputes over princely demands for taxes did not escalate into serious crises, not least because the first half of the sixteenth century was a period of rising prices and economic expansion, which made increasing taxes acceptable to the propertied classes. The brunt of such taxes was, as usual, borne by "the common man," the peasants and urban workers. Step by step the princes were able to build up their political and administrative control over their principalities, even if they often still found it convenient and cheaper to leave the administration of parliamentary taxes to the estates. In 1654 the *Reichstag* enacted a law which gave the princes the right to tax all their subjects for purposes of defense without having to obtain the consent of their estates. Thus the assembly of the estates of the Holy Roman Empire, with its long tradition of trying to limit the powers of the emperor, enacted what a modern historian has appropriately called a Magna Carta of absolutism.[17]

The Catholic princes had greater problems. Quite often members of their high nobility, the lower nobility and gentry, and some urban patriciates had become Lutheran or were at least sympathetic to the Reformation, whether from personal conviction or from fear of "the common man" who tended to read the new religious teaching in economic and social terms. What more natural than that these Protestant elites should rely on their representative assemblies to defend their "liberty of conscience"? It was a term in many mouths, in the sixteenth century, though it meant different things to different people and rarely a really free choice.[18]

After the Council of Trent had given clear definitions of Catholic doctrine and had made sitting on a doctrinal fence much more

---

Opposite: Anonymous, *The Reichstag in Regensburg,* 1653. Engraving. Photograph courtesy of the late Professor Dr. Volker Press.

difficult than it had been in the first half of the century, the Catholic
princes, frequently advised by Jesuit and Capuchin confessors, went
on the offensive. Duke Albert V of Bavaria (1550–79) pioneered the
model of a two-pronged attack. By clever maneuvers, with initial
concessions to the moderate Protestants and only gradually harden-
ing policies, he managed to obtain increasing money grants from
his estates, until the *Landtag* of Munich, in 1577, begged him to
spare the country by not summoning any more assemblies. It was a
virtual capitulation to *dominium regale*. Albert's second prong of
attack was the systematic replacement of Protestant officials by
Catholics and the channeling of ducal patronage to his own, Catholic, supporters. Thus was the Protestant nobility won back to the
old church while the common people were re-educated by a Catholic clergy, now carefully protected from all Protestant competition.[19]

The Bavarian example was followed by other Catholic princes,
especially the Austrian Habsburgs. But the strategy could fail where
Protestant resistance was more determined than in Bavaria and
where, in a composite monarchy, neither the religious nor the constitutional issues could be resolved in a single, self-contained principality and where, moreover, outside forces were likely to intervene. In 1604 the Hungarians of Habsburg Hungary—the western
and northern third of the kingdom; the center and south was occupied by the Ottoman Turks and the northeast, Transylvania, had
become an independent Protestant principality—rebelled against
the Counter-Reformation policies of their king (Emperor Rudolf II).
The leader of the Hungarian estates, Stephen Bocskai, was elected
"Prince of Hungary" and waged open war against Rudolf. The estates of Upper and Lower Austria, of Bohemia and Moravia, all of
them dominated by Protestant nobilities, allied themselves with the
Hungarians and managed to obtain wide-ranging constitutional and
religious concessions from the archduke Matthias, the ruler of the
Austrian duchies.

An already tangled political situation was further complicated by
Matthias's ambition to overthrow the emperor. Some twenty years
earlier, Matthias had already played an equivocal role as governor-
general of the Netherlands, acting in theory for his cousin, Philip II
of Spain, but in fact by the grace of the rebellious States General
of the Netherlands. Rudolf tried to preserve at least the loyalty of

Bohemia—for most of his long reign he had resided in Prague—and he agreed to a kind of charter, the Letter of Majesty, for the estates of Bohemia which granted religious freedom to the Protestants (6 June 1609). But in 1611 Matthias forced Rudolf to abdicate and was himself elected emperor.

The basic conflicts between monarchy and estates and between Catholics and Protestants had not, however, been resolved. They broke out again in 1618. A year later the estates of Bohemia deposed their new king, the emperor Ferdinand II. They conferred the Crown of Bohemia on the Calvinist elector Frederick V of the Palatinate, the son-in-law of James I of England, and they summoned a States General from the estates of the Crown of Bohemia, of several of the Austrian duchies, and of Habsburg Hungary.

The Habsburgs had at times summoned assemblies of several of their provinces, usually in order to coordinate defense against the Turks. But they had always been ambivalent about such a policy, for fear that the estates of the different provinces might support each other in opposition to their ruler. The provincial estates had their own ambivalent feelings about *Generallandtage*, states generals. The privileges which rulers had sworn to observe were always the local privileges of the particular province and they usually included the privilege of assembling the estates only within the province. One did not lightly set aside such privileges and the strong feelings of local community and xenophobia which underpinned them. The Bohemian initiative of 1619 was therefore an indication of the depth of the crisis of *dominium politicum et regale* in central-eastern Europe. The Bohemian (Czech) and the Austrian aristocratic leaders were certainly aware of the issues of principle involved, and we know that some of them had read the tracts of the French monarchomachs. But, unlike some of the French and Dutch aristocratic Calvinists, they were unwilling to vary their aristocratic preconceptions sufficiently to mobilize the burghers of the towns and the peasants of their estates for their movement. The restriction of the movement to the nobility was undoubtedly a great weakness. The outcome, however, and it was entirely in favor of the monarchy, was decided by the relative effectiveness of outside military intervention for the two sides. And it was this intervention which engulfed Europe in the Thirty Years' War.[20]

The effects of the Thirty Years' War on the relations between the German princes and their parliaments were again ambiguous. The princes needed money for their soldiers and had to ask their estates for taxes. At times, they had to make concessions. But Germany was filled with armies, paid for by and owing allegiance to these very princes. There was therefore little chance of organizing effective resistance to princely power. By the middle of the seventeenth century *dominium regale*, by now fortified by the Bodinian theory of sovereignty and the introduction of a policy of "social disciplining," was almost everywhere in the ascendant.[21] Where assemblies of estates continued to function they were effectively harnessed to the process of "state building," which meant the progressive development of princely absolutism. In northern Germany, where towns were small, the princes won over the parliamentary nobility by allowing them a free hand on their estates and villages, just as the monarchy had done in Piedmont; only that in northeastern Germany the process went further and included the introduction or consolidation of the "second serfdom" for the majority of peasants. (The first serfdom had been the less onerous, medieval, one.) It was an appalling decline of liberty, even as against the later Middle Ages.

Yet even the very reduced powers of the assemblies of absolutist German principalities still had their uses for the princes' subjects; for they functioned as a brake on the often unlimited extravagance of many of these princes. With the political intelligence of a Louis XVI they tended to combine the diligence of a Louis XV and the ambitions of a Louis XIV. With palace-building programs to rival Versailles, they wanted to combine standing armies to rival those of Prussia. Not surprisingly, their creditors preferred the security offered by the estates for their steadily mounting loans. When some of the German princes, as for instance the rulers of Württemberg and Saxony, changed their own religion from Lutheran to Calvinist or Catholic, they found their Lutheran assemblies stubbornly refusing to follow suit. Confrontations could and did still happen.[22] But the *dominium regale* rulers of the later seventeenth century found they could no longer do what their predecessors in a *dominium politicum et regale* regime in the sixteenth century had found relatively easy: change the religious affiliation of their subjects. It took hard work on the part of the prince and the luck of several uninterrupted male successions, such as the Hohenzollern of Brandenburg-Prussia

enjoyed, to establish and confirm a genuine autocracy.[23] In the eighteenth century, the age of the enlightened despot, most German
princes were neither enlightened nor despotic.

≺ III ≻

The Impact of Religion: Western Europe

In western Europe the impact of the Reformation and the Counter
Reformation produced even more dramatic results than in central
Europe. In France the Valois kings had built up a very powerful and
apparently stable position for the monarchy in a paradigmatic regime of *dominium regale*. But in 1559 the regency in the unexpected
minority of Francis II found itself burdened by a huge debt contracted in the previous half-century of wars with the Habsburgs, and
with many of the monarchy's domain and regalia revenues given
away or mortgaged. There was an immediate political crisis as the
queen mother, Catherine de Médicis, and various factions of the high
nobility struggled to control the regency government. At the same
time, the Calvinist communities in France, the Huguenots, organized themselves as an effective military structure allied to one of
the noble factions, for the purpose either of gaining control of the
state or of at least achieving a degree of religious toleration for their
own doctrine. Much more effectively than Lutheranism, this doctrine, Calvinism, was able to bring into alliance social classes ranging from princes of the blood royal to shopkeepers and artisans in
the cities.[24]

The regency government, trying to maintain peace and to obtain
some financial support, summoned two successive meetings of the
Estates General, at Orléans and at Pontoise, in 1560 and 1561. These
were the first meetings of the Estates General since 1484 and, for
the first time, a political party tried to dominate them: the Huguenots tried to control the bailiwick and seneschalcy assemblies to
have them elect Huguenot deputies to the Estates General. But
while most delegates were agreed on the need for a reformation of
the Church, the majority did not want this to be done by the Huguenots and they differed on whether the Calvinist preachers should
be tolerated or suppressed by force. The one point on which all
delegates were agreed was not to grant new taxes, even by way of

recommendation to their own provincial assemblies. The regency had therefore got nothing financially from the Estates General, and on religious and political matters the tensions had, if anything, increased.[25] In 1562 open civil war began.

As civil war followed civil war, the stakes rose. Broken treaties, betrayals, and massacres eroded that minimum of trust necessary for the functioning of *dominium politicum et regale*. The monarchy, maneuvering between the extremes, hired troops in Germany. France's neighbors—Spain and Savoy on the Catholic side and England, the Palatinate, and the Dutch Sea Beggars on the Protestant—all feared the effects of the victory of the other denomination on their own precarious religious situations. But, inevitably, their interference was tinged with their own power-political ambitions, and they neither fully trusted nor were fully trusted by their French co-religionists on whose side they interfered.

Many Frenchmen thought the Estates General was the one institution which could solve the country's problems, and some of the most interesting tracts on the role of representative assemblies in the state and their relation to liberty were written in France during this period. But discussion of political theory was not enough. When Henry III, newly succeeded to the throne, summoned the Estates General again, in 1575, it only reflected the confusion in the country. The cities and the provinces were fearful of committing themselves to any clear line of policy and preferred to negotiate separately with the Crown.[26] The following year, the Huguenots boycotted an Estates General altogether and began to organize their own representative assemblies.

The civil wars, now inextricably interwoven with those in the Netherlands and with the war between England and Spain, increased in ferocity. In 1588 Henry III once more summoned the Estates General; but in the meantime he had unilaterally doubled the *taille* and trebled the *gabelle* on salt. This time it was the Catholic League, a nation-wide organization of hard-line Catholics, who dominated the Estates General. For the first time, the assembly pursued a clear, if one-sided, political and religious line: its decisions were to have the force of law and it demanded that the king pursue the war against the Huguenots with much greater vigor than he had been willing to do. Henry III replied by murdering the leaders of the League, the duke and the cardinal of Guise.

The League reacted by turning on the king himself, and after his assassination, in 1589, they fought his heir, Henry of Navarre (Henry IV), the leader of the Huguenots. The League organized revolutionary populist regimes in the cities which they controlled, setting up a network of autonomous League cities in France. Its propagandists borrowed much of the Huguenots' antiroyalist ideology and pushed it further into populism, but with its religious dynamic turned upside down, from Calvinism to Catholicism. The movement's leaders, from the princely house of Guise, were convinced royalists, with no interest in limiting royal authority in favor of representative assemblies. But, like the Protestant Bourbons, they found themselves carried along by the revolutionary movements they led and were quite willing to use assemblies for their own purposes. The resulting tensions could not be fully resolved. The League split into an aristocratic and a popular wing, and the country was divided between those who wanted to maintain the legitimate succession of Henry IV, provided he reconverted to the Catholic church, and those who wanted the Estates General to confer the crown on an unambiguously Catholic king.

The League summoned an Estates General to Paris in 1593 with great hopes of healing the disorder of the country. But between the irreconcilable parties and the self-serving maneuvers of Spain, the papacy, and other Catholic powers, the meetings soon ground to a halt. The great decisions were taken outside: by Henry IV abjuring Protestantism (1593), by his military victories over the League and the Spaniards, by the decision of more and more of the French elite to support its legitimate, native, and now again Catholic king in order to preserve the country from dismemberment. The Estates General and its cause of limiting the authority of the monarchy went down with the defeat of the League.[27] Henry IV, a man who abhorred religious fanaticism but whose temperament was as autocratic as that of Philip II, had no intention of resurrecting the Estates General. The assemblies of the Huguenots, to which he had never been very sympathetic when he was their leader, he now tolerated only as part of the territorially limited "state within the state," which the Huguenots had forced him to grant them, much as if they were assemblies in the outlying dominions of a composite state.

France remained a *dominium regale*, or rather, in its more modern form, an absolute monarchy, for almost two more centuries. The

myth of the Estates General all but disappeared; but not altogether: it was the straw at which a desperate monarchy clutched in 1789. But it became immediately apparent that it was no more than a resurrected mummy in historical costume. It had to be completely restructured and imbued with a new, democratic spirit before it could serve the purposes of late-eighteenth and nineteenth-century society.

The Netherlands had emerged from the civil wars of Maximilian's regency with a typical *dominium politicum et regale* regime in a composite state, made up of more than a dozen virtually autonomous provinces. When their ruler became king of Spain and, later, Holy Roman Emperor, the Netherlands also became part of a huge composite monarchy. They formed a vital part of this monarchy but were no longer its center. For nearly fifty years the Netherlands had regency governments, headed by two women, Charles V's aunt, Margaret of Austria and, from 1531, his sister Mary, widowed queen of Hungary. Their councils, appointed not by themselves but by the emperor, were a mixture of lawyer-administrators and Netherlands high nobility. Up to a point this arrangement satisfied the Netherlands elite. But it was the emperor and his immediate advisers, more and more Spaniards and hispanicized Italians, who made all ultimate policy decisions and controlled most of the monarchy's patronage in the Netherlands. Policy decisions, especially those about war and peace, depended on Charles V's assessment of the needs of his whole empire. They were not necessarily those of the Netherlands. The monarchy therefore had to operate on two levels. It had to persuade the provincial assemblies of the need to cooperate in, and provide money for, its purely Netherlands policies, such as the wars with the French-supported duchy of Guelders; and it had to persuade the deputies of the same provincial assemblies, coming together as a States General, to support an imperial policy which was for them always remote and often incomprehensible.

The system worked well as long as there was trust on all sides and an expanding economy made the imposition of imperial taxes bearable. But it was also a cumbersome system and exasperatingly slow just when rapid decisions were most needed. The delegates to the States General had to refer every proposal back to their pro-

Opposite: Lauros Giraudon, *The French Estates General of 1614.* Engraving. By permission of Bibliothèque Nationale, Paris.

vincial estates and these, in turn, had to refer back to their city councils. If there were disagreements, this process might have to be repeated several times or the governor of the particular province, usually a great lord with a seat in the regent's council, had to negotiate separately with recalcitrant city councils. In the personal absence of the ruler there was no way this system could be fundamentally altered without stirring up dangerous opposition. Thus Charles V failed to act on the urgent suggestion of Margaret of Austria that the States General should not be allowed to present requests before agreeing to the taxes proposed by the government. In the 1530s attempts to persuade the provinces into a closer union for the financing of defense broke down over their unwillingness to give up any important part of their autonomy. At most, the government could use Machiavellian tricks against difficult towns. In 1525 Charles advised Margaret to treat the obstinate delegates of Ghent "with great sweetness." When in this way Ghent had been brought to agree with the rest of Flanders to a tax, she should inform herself secretly about the ringleaders of the opposition and then arrest and punish them, "which would be an example to the others and in this way one could manage the people and bring them to reason."[28] It was hardly advice for a strong government, nor does it suggest a monarchy systematically on the offensive against the estates. When in 1537 Ghent once again refused to take part in an "*aide*" and would not be moved by "sweetness," the regency government was unable to do anything about it. The emperor had to come himself, three years later, with an army and bring Ghent to heel.

But, on the whole, cooperation continued until Charles V's abdication, in 1555. The government came to rely increasingly on money raised by the provincial estates from the sale of annuities (*rentes*). To make the obligation credible to buyers the government had to allow the estates to build up their own quite elaborate tax-gathering machinery. The experience of managing their own taxes taught the cities to cooperate through their provincial assemblies in provincial administration and it also taught them the value of sending their deputies to the States General in Brussels to defend their privileges, to cooperate with other provinces, and to win over members of the regent's council to their side. This last could best be done by outright bribes. The defense of liberty had to take account of the real world of politics.[29]

In the Netherlands, therefore, the States General and the provincial estates were a regular part of the political process and of political consciousness in a way they never were in France.[30] But it was not a stable situation. The two lady regents—arguably the most intelligent of all the sixteenth-century Habsburgs—were always aware of the fragility of the regime and they often warned the emperor of the danger of an imminent breakdown. In the 1550s the tensions increased rapidly. The economic expansion of the previous half-century came to an end, but the cost of the French wars continued to rise steeply. In 1557 both the Netherlands and the Spanish governments were forced to declare a moratorium and a rescheduling of their spiralling debts. Bad harvests caused near-famine prices and in the cities there was massive unemployment. In a States General of 1557–59 Philip II's governor-general, Emmanuel Philibert of Savoy, managed to negotiate a generous tax agreement. For the first time the delegates had officially met together for joint discussions—unofficially this had frequently happened before—and they obtained from the government the right to set up their own machinery to adminster the tax. In other words, they transferred the provincial pattern to the States General and the Netherlands as a whole. It was not a deliberate move to limit the king's authority; they simply wanted to make sure that the government spent the money for the purposes for which it had been granted, a point on which they had had bad experience. In the event, the machinery they set up did not work very well.

Some members of the government, however, took a more sinister view of the agreement. The king therefore determined that the States General should not be summoned any more, or at least not in joint sessions. It was a deliberate constitutional offensive and it came from the royalist side. In practice it was counter-productive since it greatly enhanced the myth of the States General as the all-wise representative of the true interests of the country in good *dominium politicum et regale* style. Philip II wanted to keep the *tercio*, a regiment of Spanish veterans in the country, as a safeguard against a renewed French attack. There is no evidence that the king wanted to use these troops to overthrow the country's liberties. But in the heated atmosphere of the time, that was precisely what people feared. The king gave way and withdrew the *tercio*, hoping that now at least the estates of Brabant would grant more money for defense. They did not, and the reasons lay mainly in a third and the most intractable cause of friction: the proposed ecclesiastical reorganization of the Netherlands which the king had agreed with the pope but without consulting the estates.

Fourteen new bishoprics were to be erected, mainly in order to boost the fight against the Protestant heretics. The plan proved enormously unpopular. The abbots of the great monasteries of Brabant resented their loss of income, for they were supposed to finance the new bishoprics. The nobility resented the loss of patronage and careers for younger sons for the new bishoprics were to be reserved for fully qualified ecclesiastics. The cities resented their loss of jurisdiction to the inquisition courts and feared that these would drive away the foreign merchants on whom their prosperity depended. And because all these groups were traditionally represented in the provincial estates and in the States General, the king's ecclesiastical plans were bound to affect the relations between the monarchy and these institutions.

The final breach of trust came when the king sent the duke of Alba with a large foreign army to punish the image-breaking riots and the somewhat haphazard armed revolts which had occurred in 1566 and which had been put down, with the help of the high nobility, by the regent, Margaret of Parma, in 1567. Even then, it is possible that the situation might have been saved if Philip II had been able to follow Alba to the Netherlands, as he had originally planned to do. But the Don Carlos affair—Philip's imprisonment of his insane only son—and, a little later, the revolt of the Moriscos of Granada (nominally Christianized Moors) prevented him from leaving Spain.

Alba set aside all Netherlands public law. A new court, the Council of Troubles, condemned over 12,000 persons to death or loss of property. In 1572 the provinces of Holland and Zealand succeeded in throwing the Spaniards out, mainly because Alba was preoccupied with Protestant invasions from France. The estates of Holland and Zealand set up an alternative government which functioned through committees of the assemblies of the estates. They appointed William of Orange, the richest of the Netherlands magnates and former governor of Holland who had gone into exile on Alba's arrival, as head of this government and he freely acknowledged that his authority derived from the estates.

This was no longer *dominium politicum et regale;* Orange headed a parliamentary government. It had started as a purely practical arrangement to deal with exceptional circumstances. In theory, at least, it was not yet seen as rebellion against the king's sovereignty, let alone an alternative regime to a monarchy. But this was exactly what it was. When the two sides came to negotiate, in 1575, both claimed, quite sincerely, that they wanted to return to the good old days of Charles V. But the king proposed a settlement at the extreme royalist end of the range of *dominium politicum et regale.* He would grant an amnesty and allow the Protestants to emigrate; but he would summon the States General only after peace had been restored, and he would accept its advice only on such matters as it had traditionally been asked to give. This excluded religion and sovereignty. The estates of Holland and Zealand could no longer accept such conditions, whatever had been the situation under Charles V. Philip II and Alba had destroyed the minimum of trust necessary for the functioning of any *dominium politicum et regale* regime.

No doubt, the estates of Holland and Zealand, having tasted sovereign power, were also unwilling to give it up. During the negotiations they argued that the States General had the right to deal with all matters whatsoever and that it could abrogate or amend all royal ordinances. They were later to make similar points in their negotiations with the duke of Anjou, the brother of Henry III of France, whom Orange had invited to become the new ruler of the Netherlands. As many had foreseen, the marriage of the French absolutist tradition with the new doctrines of the Netherlands estates did not work out; nor did that with the earl of Leicester, in 1587. In similar disputes about sovereignty, the Dutch spokesman Franchois Vranck declared that it resided in the *vroedschappen,* the town councils, constituted from the most notable persons of the whole community, and it was these who sent the deputies, with their very restricted powers, to the estates of Holland and the States General.

In 1576 the unpaid Spanish army in the Netherlands had mutinied and the king's authority had collapsed. The estates of Brabant and Holland invited the States General to meet, as the estates of Holland had done in 1463; and a purged council of state, cooperating closely with the States General, concluded peace with Holland and Zealand in the Pacification of Ghent, 8 November 1576.

These were all revolutionary acts to which the king had not

Frans Hogenberg, *Archduke Matthias of Austria, with William of Orange at his side, taking the oath as governor-general of the Netherlands before the States General in Brussels*, 20 January 1578. Engraving. Photo courtesy of Hambledon Press.

given his authority. His new regent for the Netherlands, his half-brother Don John of Austria, found he could not get on with the States General and work within a regime of *dominium politicum et regale*, now certainly tilted strongly towards the estates. Holland and Zealand did not accept him at all. In 1577 Don John restarted military action. The States General responded by appointing the archduke Matthias as governor-general, just as the estates of Holland had appointed Orange as their governor. The States General appointed Matthias's council of state, on whose advice he was required to act. Decisions on war and peace, on taxation, on all important legislation and appointments would need their consent, and they also claimed complete control over when and for how long they should be assembled.

Here was a fully organized parliamentary regime, as different from *dominium politicum et regale* as that regime was from *dominium regale*. Just as in Holland, the guiding spirit behind it was

William of Orange. William was probably quite clear about what he was doing, even if he could not see all its implications. Just as before in Holland, it was practical considerations which had driven him to this parliamentary solution. Its success would now depend on two conditions: firstly, the relative strength of the forces which king and States General, respectively, would be able to mobilize in the Netherlands; secondly, the effective help which the two sides would receive, directly or indirectly, from the neighboring powers.

In the event, revolutionary Calvinist movements in Flanders drove many previously anti-Spanish clergy, noblemen, and urban patricians back into the arms of the king. In 1579 they reached an accommodation (Union of Arras) which left the estates with considerable rights in the Walloon provinces. It was a return to *dominium politicum et regale*, although the pressures of the continuing war and the personal dispositions of Philip II and his successors came to tilt the balance of authority more and more towards the monarchy.

The States General could not hold Flanders and most of Brabant against the powerful royalist-Spanish-Catholic counteroffensive. But it did hold seven northern provinces, with Holland and Zealand as their core, to form the new state of the United Provinces of the Netherlands. Even this was only possible because, during the critical years of fighting, Spain was distracted by its war with England and with Henry IV of France; but it was possible also because, paradoxically, the loss of Flanders and Brabant, with their large, revolution-prone cities, had left the United Provinces with a much greater degree of social stability than the southern provinces. This social stability was due not least to the economic and financial preponderance of the province of Holland in the union, a preponderance which, ironically, was also due to the absence now of competition from Flanders and Brabant.[31]

Not all political and religious problems had been solved. The Calvinists, who had been in the forefront of the fight against Spain, gradually managed to win over the majority of the population to their beliefs; but they also managed to quarrel among themselves, and, inevitably in the early seventeenth century, these quarrels became mixed with political quarrels. The issues between the estates and the executive, in the form of the surrogate monarchy of the house of Orange, reappeared and, fanned by religious passions, still led to murderous crises.[32] The aristocratic court society of Europe despised the "bourgeois" republic with its clumsy confederal constitution and its new-fangled parliamentary regime whose functioning few outside the United Provinces understood. "It is a country where the gold-demon, crowned with tobacco, is seated on a throne of cheese," said a French wit. Yet by superior diplomacy and military and naval organization, the country played an effective great-power role throughout the seventeenth century. And it was a country whose political regime gave its citizens and the many distinguished foreigners who found a refuge there greater political and religious freedom than any other country in Europe for almost two hundred years.

England, like the Netherlands, emerged from its fifteenth-century civil wars with a typical *dominium politicum et regale* regime. Unlike the Netherlands, however, the England of 1500 was a unitary state, or at least much more so than any of the other great European monarchies. At the same time, the English ruling elite was more homogenous than that of most continental monarchies. Here were no great cities with proud histories of virtual autonomy from the central government or with strongly organized and politicized guilds with equally proud histories of revolutionary action. The great peasant revolt of 1381, while it was as strongly urban as rural, never became part of a parliamentary tradition, as similar revolts did in Flanders. The English boroughs, with only a few exceptions, were smaller than the towns which usually constituted the third estate in western European assemblies, and there were far more of them. Certainly by the fifteenth century, and probably much earlier, many of the members of Parliament representing the boroughs were country gentlemen,[33] and many of these were related to or were clients of the landed magnates who sat in the House of Lords, even when, after the Wars of the Roses, they were no longer military retainers.

As long as the monarchy did not offend this broad-based social elite, represented in Parliament, there was no reason why the traditional *dominium politicum et regale* regime should not continue to function, even when there were kings with such highly autocratic temperament as the first two Tudors, Henry VII and Henry VIII. It was this pattern which explains the relative ease with which the Reformation was introduced in England.

Just as in some of the German principalities, the initiative for the break with Rome came from the monarchy and, as in Sweden, even more than in Germany, the reasons for this break were in the first place political rather than religious. In Sweden, Gustavus Vasa had to conquer his kingdom from its legitimate king, Christian II of Denmark. Not least because his principal internal opponent was the archbishop of Uppsala, Vasa's anti-Danish campaign also became an anti-Roman campaign. Vasa had his own position and his title of king approved by the Swedish Parliament, the first full *riksdag*, at Västerås, in 1523. He won over the waverers by three ploys: he proclaimed his continued religious orthodoxy but favored the preaching of the "true gospel"; since the Swedish monarchy was elective, he threatened to resign and leave the country to chaos or to the well-known vengefulness of King Christian; and he got the *riksdag* to enact the return of all property donated by the nobility to the Church since the mid-fifteenth century. Monasteries and convents were to be placed under the administration of "good knights" who after allowing for a minimum for running costs, would share the income of these institutions with the Crown.[34]

Henry VIII, just as Gustavus Vasa, wanted to preserve his country from chaos, which, he feared, would follow if he had no legitimate male heir. Hence, when the pope would not, or could not, grant him a divorce from Catherine of Aragon (all of whose children except one girl had died in infancy) he also had to break with Rome. As a hereditary monarch he could not threaten to resign, a tactic which in any case would probably have been quite outside his comprehension. But, like Gustavus, he could, at least initially, proclaim his continued religious orthodoxy and fill the bishoprics with his own men. Once the break with Rome was final, the introduction of the Reformation was, if not inevitable, at least very likely in both England and Sweden; for the monarchy had created a religious vacuum which would attract the most active non-Catholic preachers. In this age these were the Calvinists and the Lutherans, respectively.

Again like Gustavus, Henry needed Parliament to enact the necessary legislation; and in the four sessions of the "Reformation Parliament" which did this, from 1532 to 1534, he experienced much less opposition than Gustavus had done with his *riksdags*. The pope lost all authority over the English church, in patronage of clerical appointments, in legislation, in finance, and in the determination of doctrine, while the English clergy were no longer permitted to appeal to Rome. All of this was underpinned by new treason laws. Henry VIII became "supreme head" of the Church of England. He had thus made his kingdom an empire, in the sense of freeing it from all outside authority. He had also effectively broken a fifteen-hundred-year tradition of Catholic Christian Europe of the separation of the ultimate authorities of church and state. Henry confirmed his revolution, just as Gustavas Vasa and the Lutheran princes in Germany had done before him, by dissolving the monasteries and convents and by selling off their property cheaply. Thus he associated large numbers of property owners with the new order in the country's religion.[35]

It is no wonder that royalist ministers and lawyers interpreted this sequence of events as signifying that Parliament was little more than another arm of government, useful for passing royal legislation and voting taxes but with few other necessary functions—in other words that England was now a *dominium regale* with a tame parliamentary appendage. These misconceptions did not have any immediate dramatic results; but the monarchy would pay dearly for them in the following century.

Religious passions now entered politics, in England as on the Continent, and raised the stakes of the political game; for religious differences now came to define men's political positions. Henry's family and foreign politics became linked with his own theological quests and gropings and with the increasingly bitter religious divisions of the country; and there was no hiding the fact that these politics were murderous. As yet, Parliament was not involved in these struggles and was willing to follow the monarch's lead; nor did Parliament and the country's ruling elite object to a sharp turn towards Calvinist Protestantism during the regency governments of Edward VI (1547–53). But where Henry VIII had personally initiated religious changes as "supreme head" of the Church and had used Parliament only to assure general approval and the legality of his acts, the regency parliaments became directly responsible with the Crown for all religious changes. This was something quite new. In *dominium politicum et regale* royal authority, though limited by Parliament, was never considered to be derived from Parliament and, consequently, neither was the king's "supremacy." Now, Parliament was not merely associated with royal actions but it had taken part in the exercise of the royal prerogative.[36] Henry VIII's caesaro-papism had become caesaro-parliamentary-papism. There remained the question of how far this position was appreciated and what its implications might be.

When Mary I (1553–58) wanted to return the country to obedience to Rome, it was immediately clear that this could only be done through acts of Parliament. For the last time, Parliament tamely followed the monarch's lead. Whatever the theologians were saying, for the majority of people, and not only in England, the lines of demarcation between the denominations were not yet completely rigid and did not become so until the decisions of the Council of Trent and the great Catholic counteroffensive that followed it. Even so, Mary failed to get Parliament to agree to a reversal of the property settlements of her father's Reformation. With the murderous nature of religious politics now becoming very visible in the pyres lit for the burning of heretics, with the queen's deeply unpopular marriage to Philip II of Spain, and with a disastrous war as Spain's ally against France—with all this, the historian may well wonder whether England was not heading for religious civil wars, like Scotland, France and the Netherlands: civil wars in which Parliament was likely to play a prominent role, as the States General was to do in the Netherlands.

At Mary's perhaps fortunate early death, in November 1558, England faced a typical succession crisis. Elizabeth, the daughter of Henry VIII and Anne Boleyn, was regarded by Catholics as illegitimate. The legitimate heir, in this view, was Mary Queen of Scots, at that time married to the heir to the French throne (Francis II, 1559–60). It was normal in European practice for parliaments to play important roles in such cases, although in England the precedents of 1399, 1460, 1483, and 1485 all pointed to usurpations of the Crown by force of arms—precedents which gave England a rather bad reputation in continental eyes. It was precisely to break this baneful tradition that Henry VIII had, in 1534, fixed the succession by parliamentary statute. Elizabeth, the entirely English candidate on the spot, had therefore no difficulty in obtaining Parliament's support, although Mary remained a real threat until her execution in 1587, and even beyond, when Philip II took up her claims for the Armada campaign.

The religious question was more difficult. In fact, however, Elizabeth had no choice but to return to Protestantism, both because of who she was and because the country clearly wanted it. There were, of course, those who opposed this reversion: the bishops appointed by Mary and a number of peers. Elizabeth arrested some of them and prevented others from attending Parliament. After that, it was relatively plain sailing to pass the Acts of Supremacy and Uniformity, carefully drafted to appeal to a wide range of Protestant opinion. The queen styled herself "governor," rather than "supreme head," of the Church of England.[37]

It had been a highly skillful piece of parliamentary management and such skill remained a hallmark of Elizabeth's reign. It was, however, a relatively easy pitch. The renewed vigor of the Counter-Reformation church was identified in England with royal absolutism, with massacres in France and the atrocities committed by the Spanish armies in the Netherlands, with plots against the life of the queen and, finally, with threats of invasion from Philip II's Armada. No wonder that Parliament and public opinion generally were passionately supportive of the queen. In its seven rather short sessions during Elizabeth's reign (1558–1603) Parliament passed no fewer than 433 acts—not as remarkable as the 222 passed by Henry VIII's Reformation Parliament in only seven years, but still witnessing to the effective functioning of *dominium politicum et regale* in England.[38] Often, but certainly not always, the initiative for debates in the House of Commons came from the queen's council or from a party in the council.[39] Such was usually the case in debates urging the queen to marry and provide the country with an heir. But in the long run this was a dangerous game for ministers to play. It confirmed them in their view that Parliament was simply an instrument of government, while at the same time confirming the country's view that its most important affairs should be debated in Parliament. Ministers mistook willing cooperation for outright domination and ignored the reality of the distribution of authority in a regime of *dominium politicum et regale*. This was the problem which would still have to be resolved in the seventeenth century.

Opposite: Presentation of the Speaker in the English Parliament, November 1584. From Robert Glover, *Nobilitas Politica vel Civilis*, 1608. By permission of the British Library.

SVMMI ET SVPREMI SENACVLI PARLAMENTARIS IN ANGLIA TYPVS

Proccrum   *Clattorius*   *Patfarum*   *primogeniti*

Cancellarij sedes ⁊⁊

Prolocutor

Milites Provinciarum & Burgenses (quos vocant) utrinq. qui Cameram Parlamenti inferiorem constituunt Prolocutorem conducentes.

≺ IV ≻

Resolution

In Sweden, *dominium politicum et regale*, so spectacularly confirmed at the *riksdag* of Västerås in 1523, worked reasonably well during the following seventy years. Just as other European monarchies, the Swedish one did its best to downgrade its Parliament. But the deposition of the insane Eric XIV, in 1568–69, and the succession of his younger brother, Johan III, could only be accomplished with the help of meetings of the high nobility and the *riksdag*—rather like the deposition of the emperor Rudolf II by his younger brother and the estates of Bohemia, forty years later. When Johan III tried to modify the now firmly established Lutheranism of his country in order to effect a reconciliation with Rome, he had only very superficial success and, if anything, confirmed the Lutherans in their convictions.

The confrontation, when it came, took the classic form of a succession crisis accompanied by the struggle between two opposed religious beliefs and by foreign intervention. Johan's son had been elected king of Poland, in 1587, as Sigismund III, and had converted to Catholicism. After his father's death, in 1593, he came to Sweden for his coronation and promised the *riksdag* that only the Lutheran religion would be practiced in Sweden; but secretly, he repudiated this promise. The situation now became thoroughly confused. Johan III's younger brother, Duke Karl of Södermanland, maneuvered for control of the government of Sweden. The great nobles of the *riksråd*, the royal council, who also formed the first estate of the *riksdag*, played for a greater role of the estates in the government, with special powers reserved for themselves. We know that some of them were, like the Austrian nobility, well versed in French monarchomach literature.[40] The Lutheran preachers roused the common people against the Catholic king.

In 1597 and 1598 there was open civil war. Sigismund invaded Sweden with Polish troops but was defeated by Duke Karl. The *riksdag* confirmed Karl as regent and effective monarch and, in 1604, persuaded him to accept the title of king, as Karl IX. It also acted as court for the trial of those members of the *riksråd* who, in the end, had chosen to maintain their loyalty to King Sigismund. They were executed.[41]

Karl IX and his son, Gustavus Adolphus, were certainly as autocratic by temperament as any of their contemporary fellow monarchs on the Continent; but they were better tacticians. Since they
were involved in almost continuous wars, with Poland, Denmark,
and the emperor, they took care to conciliate Swedish opinion
through the *riksdag* and they reconciled themselves with the great
nobility by continuing the *riksråd* in its predominant position in
government and by offering the nobles dazzling military and political careers on the Continent, supplemented by vast stretches of
alienated Crown land in Sweden. In 1654 the Swedish chancellor
Axel Oxenstierna gave this version of Swedish *dominium politicum
et regale*:

by our lawes, the boundaries of the king's power and of the peoples' rights
are sufficiently known and established; as the king can make no law, nor
alter or repeale any, nor impose any taxe, nor compell men to go out of the
kingdome, without the assent of the riksdag: and in that councell, which is
supreame in this kingdome, every man's vote and assent is included, by the
deputies of the clergy, burroughs and boores, which are respectively elected,
and by the chiefs of the nobility; so that all sorts of people have their share,
either in person or by deputies, in the supreame councell of the kingdome
by whome only those great matters can be done.[42]

As it turned out, Oxenstierna was too complacent. Even as he
spoke, the self-serving magnates of the *riksråd* had become thoroughly unpopular, and their unpopularity plumbed new depths during the regency for the child Karl XI, when they presided over a quite
disastrous financial and foreign policy. In 1680 Karl, now grown up,
carried out a *coup d'état* against the *riksråd*, with the connivance of
the rest of the *riksdag*. Then he calmly dispensed with this institution.[43] The king of Denmark had carried out a very similar coup
between 1660 and 1665.

Both the Scandinavian kingdoms were now ruled by absolute
monarchs, the latter-day version of *dominium regale*. But in Sweden
the distribution of power had not really been settled. After the death
of Karl XII, his sister Ulrika Eleonora, without an indisputable right
to the succession, and with other candidates waiting in the wings,
had to summon the *riksdag* again. It provided Sweden with a kind of
written constitution. But the stakes had risen. A return to a *dominium politicum et regale* regime was no longer seen to be possible.
Like the United Provinces of the Netherlands, Sweden acquired a

parliamentary regime. It remained a monarchy, but its government
now depended on the will of the representative assembly. Gustavus
III tried once more to reestablish absolutism, in 1772, but this regime came to an end with his assassination in 1792.[44]

In England it took longer for confrontations to reach their climax; but, characteristically, the fissures in the Tudor system became visible almost immediately on the accession of a foreign king,
James I. James was certainly willing to work the system of *dominium politicum et regale* which he had inherited from Elizabeth I,
but on his terms. In his first Parliament, in 1604, he remarked that
all parliamentary privileges were derived from royal authority. This
was not a particularly new or startling proposition. In the Netherlands, Philip the Good, in the fifteenth century, and Charles V and
his ministers, in the sixteenth, had made similar claims. The Netherlands deputies regularly sidestepped discussion of such claims,
preferring to return to the substantive matters put before them; and
ministers, in their turn, were usually quite content to get away from
political theorizing. But the English Parliament, half of whose members had sat in Elizabeth's parliaments, was anxious to impress the
new king with its rights and made counter claims. With the intellectual leadership in both the king's government and in the House
of Commons taken over more and more by lawyers, the arguments
over the royal prerogative and the rights and privileges of Parliament
and of all Englishmen tended to become more open and more clearly
defined. At the same time, the spread of theories of social contract,
of Bodinian sovereignty, and of reason of state sharpened political perceptions, intellectualized the clash of interests, and hardened lines
of division.[45]

The resulting strains on the system became apparent in the increasingly acrimonious exchanges between the king and a section of
Parliament and in royal tantrums, as when James tore out a page of
the Commons journal (December 1621) when the house had defied
his prohibition to discuss the proposed marriage of the Prince of
Wales to a Spanish infanta. It was an action reminiscent of that of
Margaret of Austria who, in 1528, took the seal from the chancellor
of Brabant and herself sealed an act of the estates which the chancellor had declared to be illegal in that it contravened the *joyeuse
entrée*.[46] The strained relations between James I and his parliaments
led to a sharp decline in parliamentary legislation. James's first Par-

liament, with sessions from 1604 to 1610, passed 228 acts, which was similar to the score of Henry VIII's Reformation Parliament. But in the final session of 1610 no acts were passed at all, nor were any in the "Addled Parliament" of 1614. James then did not summon another Parliament until 1621 and in its second session it again did not pass any acts, nor did the parliaments of 1626 and 1629.[47]

In the early years of Charles I England was at war again, with both France and Spain. These wars were mismanaged; yet both France and Spain were also engaged in other wars, and the danger to England was not as immediately obvious as it had been at the time of the Spanish Armada. In the middle of the La Rochelle campaign, in 1628, while Charles was trying to raise extra taxes and find billets for his soldiers, he justified imprisonment without the normal process of law of men suspected of subversive activities. If cause had to be shown for such imprisonment, he wrote to the House of Lords, "the service of the king would thereby be destroyed and defeated, and the judges had no rule of law to judge in cases of that transcendent nature," for otherwise "the very foundation and frame of our monarchy" would be endangered. "Without overthrow of our sovereignty we cannot suffer this power to be impeached."[48] The name of Bodin was not mentioned; but consciously or not, his was evidently the definition the king had in mind. He had moreover given a classic formulation of reason of state doctrine. The Commons certainly saw it as such. *Mutatis mutandis* it is also the same argument which modern governments use to justify the absolute secrecy and legal impenetrability of the work of their secret services. The opposition to this doctrine was also very similar, then and now. On 28 April 1628 Sir Benjamin Rudyard said in the House of Commons: "For 'reason of state' as it is used has not only eaten up law but almost all religion of Christendom."[49]

In speech after speech, during that spring of 1628, members of the Commons proclaimed their trust in the king, their desire to uphold his prerogative, their anxiety to provide financial means for the defense of the kingdom. But the stark truth was that they did not, could not, fully trust a king who imposed taxes without consent and imprisoned men at will and without due process of law. "I fear more the violation of public rights at home than a foreign army," proclaimed Sir Robert Phelps, on 22 March. He concluded his speech with a famous peroration:

Oh improvident ancestors! oh unwise forefathers! to be so curious in providing for the quiet possession of our lands and the liberties of Parliament, and to neglect our persons and bodies and to let them lie in prison . . . remediless. Why do we trouble ourselves with the dispute of laws, franchises, propriety of good . . . what may a man call his if not his liberty? [50]

But when the king accepted the Petition of Right (7 June 1628) as a declaration, and not as a law, prohibiting the billeting of troops, the imposition of taxes without consent, and imprisonment without cause shown, he still tacitly reserved his own right to do all these things in case of necessity.

With the acceptance of the Petition of Right *dominium politicum et regale* had been preserved, at least outwardly. No one as yet foresaw that there would be civil war, fourteen years later. To the historian, however, with his inescapable hindsight, it is clear that the dilemma of liberty and sovereignty had to be resolved. Charles I's decision, in 1629, to govern henceforth without Parliament had the same effect as Philip II's decision, in 1559, to govern the Netherlands without the States General: it vastly added to the strength of the myth of Parliament/States General as the one body which could remedy the country's ills, especially its religious ills. For there was now in England a strong feeling within the parliamentary classes that the king's and Archbishop Laud's Arminianism was little better than the hated and feared continental Roman Catholicism. The Puritans, the extreme Calvinists, were a minority, just as they had been in the Netherlands during the first years of the revolt against Spain. But there were many more, again as in the Netherlands, who strongly disliked the religious coercion now practiced by the Anglican church. And in both cases it was the king whom people held to be ultimately responsible, as indeed by his own doctrine he was. The fencing-off of the national church from interference by the papacy, accomplished to a considerable degree in Spain and completely in England, had seemed to be an added source of strength for their respective monarchies. In the age of heightened religious passions it turned out to be a point of vulnerability.

This was a particularly serious matter in a composite monarchy; for this was the condition of Charles I's monarchy, as it had been that of Philip II. And Charles, just as Philip II with the Netherlands and Philip IV with Catalonia, did not observe the ground rules of this situation: not to stir up trouble in a dominion in which he was not resident. Charles I interfered with the autonomous church and the autonomous government of Scotland and provoked an armed rebellion and the invasion of England by a Scottish army (1638–40). To finance a royal army it became necessary to summon Parliament again. But the distrust engendered by the frictions of the 1620s and the long intermission in the summoning of Parliament now resulted in open confrontation, and this at the very moment when the English Parliament had the potential support of an armed ally in the Scottish army. When Parliament forced Charles I to sign his minister Strafford's act of attainder, that is, his death warrant, the effect was similar to that of Mary of Burgundy being forced to sign the death warrant of her chancellor Hugonet, in 1477; the breach between the prince and the radical wing of the representative assembly became psychologically unbridgeable.

Even so, it is at least conceivable that civil war in England might have been avoided. That it was not was due largely to the complication introduced by the problems of Charles I's third kingdom, Ireland. To the Irish Catholics (the indigenous Irish population and the "old English" families who had settled in Ireland before the Reformation) the alliance between the Presbyterian Scottish "Covenanters" and the radical, Puritan wing of the English Parliament appeared as a deadly threat. There was a rebellion in Ireland and in England king and Parliament agreed that it had to be put down; but neither would trust the other any more with the control of the army. As tension escalated, it was the king who took the initiative in resorting to armed action—just as Philip II had done in the Netherlands and Philip IV in Catalonia.[51]

In the civil war the majority of the peers and a considerable minority of the commons joined the king, many not so much as true "cavaliers," than as supporters of the traditional English *dominium politicum et regale*. During the war Parliament proved that it had independent authority which translated into support in the country—precisely the point which Tudor and Stuart royalists had refused to admit. With its military victory, however, it also proved the parliamentary royalists correct: the basis for *dominium politicum et regale* was destroyed—again precisely the experience of the revolt of the Netherlands. Cromwell, the military leader of the parliamentary side, tried to reestablish this regime, and failed.

The Restoration succeeded; but the regime remained fragile because its balance was becoming increasingly unsustainable in an age of rapidly increasing state power. It was also still vulnerable to attack by an autocratic monarch, the Catholic James II. Once more *dominium regale* and Catholicism were linked in the public mind as enemies of freedom. The English ruling classes staged the Glorious Revolution of 1688–89 precisely to prevent this, to them, unholy alliance and confirm a Protestant *dominium politicum et regale*. Characteristically, the success of the revolution and even its initiation depended on massive foreign intervention, the huge armada, and strong forces which William of Orange (William III) brought with him from the Netherlands. It was also characteristic of the nature of composite monarchies that this revolution was not equally acceptable to all its component parts; for Ireland, with French help, fought for James II.

William III had never doubted that in the Netherlands he derived his authority from the estates. In Britain, although he and his wife, the Protestant daughter of James II, had excellent hereditary claims, it was also clear to him that his authority depended on Parliament, the more so as he needed its cooperation in the long war with France which followed the English revolution. The monarchy, having failed to beat Parliament, had joined it. In consequence it could, much more often than not, get its way on specific issues while, at the same time, the liberties previously won by Parliament remained firmly established.

To most Englishmen this political experience masked the fundamental change of regime. In Ireland, however, this was much more clearly visible. Its Parliament was now definitely subordinated to the English Parliament—British, after the union with Scotland and the Scottish Parliament, in 1707—and subject to the sovereign religious and economic legislation of Westminster. To make quite certain of this point the Westminster Parliament passed a declaratory act, in 1720, asserting its authority over the Irish Parliament.

In the American colonies the implications of the change of regime became apparent only in the 1760s. Then it was gradually realized that the *dominium politicum et regale* regime of the colonies could not coexist with the Bodinian sovereignty claimed by the parliamentary regime in Westminster. Resolution came through armed conflict in which, as usual, outside powers became involved. The conflict had, of course, many and complex causes; but not the least among them was the confrontation between two regimes, a confrontation which, in this form, was unprecedented and for which, in consequence, no one, not even Edmund Burke, had as yet thought out a peaceful solution.[52]

The founders of the United States of America solved this problem for themselves, but necessarily independently from Britain, by a definite rejection of parliamentary government and Bodinian parliamentary sovereignty in favor of a federal union and the division of powers between the executive, the legislature (with a vastly extended popular constituency), and the judiciary. It was a modernized and, as it has turned out, a very effective version of *dominium politicum et regale*.

Epilogue

R. W. DAVIS

I N THE LAST CHAPTER, H. G. Koenigsberger describes how factors
such as war, the nature of composite states, and religion determined the fate of parliamentary institutions in early modern Europe. In 1700 only Poland, soon to be joined by Sweden, shared such
institutions with the British Isles and the Netherlands—and neither
did so for long. Even in the Netherlands the parliamentary system
was in danger by mid-century. In England, it never would be again
after 1688–89; but it had been, in one way or another, for most of
the century before then. During the civil wars of mid-century, the
problems of what was, in effect, a composite state, with at least three
religions, lay at the very basis of the conflict. And it was only by the
good luck of the continental European states being preoccupied with
their own affairs that foreign intervention was never a real threat.

In 1688 things played out very differently. Religion united the
English nation against its Catholic king. Foreign intervention came
headed by a Protestant heir, William of Orange, anxious to line England up against the French threat on the Continent. Parliament was
willing to accept William jointly with his cousin and wife, Mary,
first in the line of succession if a Catholic half-brother were ignored,
which most members of Parliament were willing to do. Religious
divisions among English Protestants were eased by the so-called Toleration Act of 1689. The problem of the composite state was then
attacked, in the first instance literally, by crushing Irish resistance
in 1690, in the second by the Act of Union with Scotland in 1707.
Given the role Parliament had played in the Revolution Settlement,
it is extremely unlikely that after that it would ever have been in
much danger of disappearing. As it was, the wars with France and
the immense sums of money they demanded, which only Parliament could provide, made its position impregnable.

Yet even if the survival of Parliament was entirely a matter of good luck, which some might doubt, no one could doubt that its survival, for whatever reason, was important—to Britain itself, to its colonies, and to others who came under the influence of both to one degree or another. A similar point can be made about the significance of the States General in the century and more of the Netherlands' greatness. Without these two great representative institutions, the history of Western freedom would be very different.

Indeed Douglass North argues in this volume that the explanation of what he calls the paradox of the West lies in the contrasting political systems of East and West. Though the empires of the East had highly developed civilizations and cultures, their centralized political systems discouraged economic experimentation and thus the creation of a range of options that might have been employed to meet new economic challenges. In the West, in contrast, the lack of a large-scale political, and therefore economic, system at the beginning of the Middle Ages not only allowed experimentation, but actually encouraged it because of competition among the fragmented political bodies that made up western Europe. By creating a wide range of options, the system promoted economic growth. At the same time, it encouraged an independence of mind and spirit that would complement the later emergence of other kinds of freedom, associated, for example, with the growth of self-government in towns, the emergence of representative institutions, and the Protestant Reformation. In a less sweeping sense, the powerful economic component in the making of modern freedom assured that among its earliest elements would be a strong association between liberty and the security of property.

Both the general and more limited attitudes North writes about are apparent, in other volumes in the series, in the actions of substantial Dutch burghers in their States General and of English members of Parliament, who often championed similar commercial interests. A particularly good example is David Harris Sacks's discussion of the debates over monopolies in his chapter in *Parliament and Liberty from the Reign of Elizabeth to the English Civil War*, in which freedom of enterprise is specifically connected with the freedom of Englishmen. The relationship of liberty and property is also considered in broader context by Clive Holmes in the same volume; and in two essays on liberty, law, and property by Howard Nenner and

Henry Horwitz, respectively, in *Liberty Secured?: Britain Before and After 1688*. The Dutch are treated by Augustus J. Veenendaal in his chapter on fiscal crises and constitutional freedom in the Netherlands from 1450 to 1795, in *Fiscal Crises, Liberty, and Representative Government: 1450–1789*; and by Herbert H. Rowen in a discussion of the Dutch Republic and the idea of freedom, in *Republicanism and Commercial Society: from the English Civil War to the American Revolution*.

The connotations of democracy and freedom of speech, which Martin Ostwald finds in *eleutheria* by the fifth century B.C., would disappear as influential concepts as ancient Greece itself disappeared, not to revive again until they were reintroduced in early modern Europe through the efforts of the Humanist scholars of the Renaissance. After that, though they took a long time to be realized in practice, they became an important part of political debate. *Republicanism and Commercial Society* discusses, among other things, the classical influence on modern ideas of liberty.

Brian Tierney has pointed up the major influences of the medieval church on modern freedom. He stresses the lack in the West of the theocratic absolutism that prevailed elsewhere. Because neither church nor state ever managed to prevail over the other, it was impossible for any ruler to consolidate a position of absolute power, and divided power allowed freedom to grow in the interstices. As for the Church, its struggle with secular princes led it to advance theories of resistance to such authorities. It also promoted constitutional limitations on government, most evidently in religious affairs, which assisted in the growth of theories of religious liberty after the Reformation.

By the examples provided by cathedral chapters and Church councils, the Church also encouraged the election of secular officials and the growth of representative institutions. Here, of course, the Church reflected its own appropriation of the forms of the political system under which it had emerged from humble beginnings to greatness and power, the Roman Empire. And by its perpetuation not only of Roman political forms, but also of Roman law, with its provision for the election of emperors and its theory that their power derived from the people, the Church provided an intellectual justification for its own actions and of those who emulated them. The Church, then, served as the major conduit of Roman civilization to the modern world. By 1600, with the Reformation well under way and the unity of Christendom shattered, the Church's role, as discussed by Tierney, was over. By then, however, there was hardly an aspect of life it had not touched.

The Italian towns treated by John Hine Mundy had long since had their day. The towns of Flanders were still very rich, though their political independence was necessarily lessened by their gradual incorporation into larger states. But in the Middle Ages, as several authors stress, towns were important forces for change. In Italy, the towns, independent of both Church and outside secular control, provided examples of small self-governing states, with elected officials and often a democratic franchise. The northern cities, though not as free of outside influence, exhibited similar characteristics of government. In both the north and the south, towns helped to establish the principle of the sanctity of private property, naturally valued in merchant communities, as well as exhibiting a concern for the security of persons dictated by their popular electorates. As William Bouwsma argues, the influence of the Italian towns on the rest of western Europe, and thus on modern freedom, was greatest in their decline. Adversity generated political speculation among their citizens, on their own as well as the more distant past. The most prominent example is the writings of Niccolò Machiavelli. Several chapters in *Republicanism and Commercial Society* discuss the influence of Italian thought on modern freedom.

H. G. Koenigsberger's chapters on parliamentary institutions in the medieval and early modern periods are especially helpful in the background they provide for three volumes. The first of these, *Parliament and Liberty*, focuses its attention on the English Parliament and its promotion of liberty in the first half of the seventeenth century. The second volume, *Liberty Secured?*, ranges further in time, studying the causes and results of the Revolution of 1688 from 1660 to the end of the eighteenth century. It does not focus so exclusively on Parliament as does its predecessor, but the role of the legislature naturally figures prominently. The third volume, *Fiscal Crises, Liberty, and Representative Government: 1450–1789*, looks at the connection between governments' desperate need for money and the development of parliamentary institutions in Britain, the Netherlands, Spain, and France.

J. H. Baker's chapter is also vital to the understanding of the two English/British volumes. In examining the disappearance of villein status, complete by the end of the sixteenth century, he prepares the way for appreciating the impact of much of the legislation of the seventeenth century. For now all Englishmen were "freeborn" or "freemen" and therefore presumably entitled to all liberties old or newly discovered (that is, by legislation) and not specifically restricted. Such legislation increased significantly in the course of the seventeenth century. A prime example is the efforts to establish the right of habeas corpus, efforts which Baker traces up to 1600, and which finally succeeded with the act of the same name in 1679. Not only did the seventeenth century see the growth of liberty through the passage of such measures as the Habeas Corpus Act; that liberty was coming to be seen as the common heritage of all Englishmen, and women. David Harris Sacks's chapter in *Parliament and Liberty* discusses general attitudes toward liberty, as well as specific applications. Charles Gray's chapter in the same volume discusses law and legal institutions in the seventeenth century, including the "discovery" theory of legislation. The chapters by Howard Nenner and Henry Horwitz in *Liberty Secured?* also expand on Baker's points.

William Bouwsma sees the Renaissance as growing out of the chaos of fourteenth-century Italy. With old theories and methods discredited, Italians began to seek for new verities. One place where they sought answers was in their own world, the world of the Italian city-state. Out of this search came such ideas as the sovereignty of states and republican liberty, or citizen rule. They also went further back into the past, to the history of the Roman republic, studying its ideals of citizenship to define their own. From these studies came the identification of such virtues of civic humanism as loyalty, patriotism, and disinterested service to the state. On the basis of their examinations of the past, as well as their own experience, Machiavelli and others developed their theories of politics. The influences on modern freedom of ancient and late medieval and of Renaissance Italian thought are, again, among those discussed in *Republicanism and Commercial Society*.

For Bouwsma, the Reformation grows out of an approach similar to that which produced the Renaissance, but applied to a different subject. Christian scholars in northern Europe simply brought humanist attitudes and techniques to bear on religious questions. They approached ancient religious texts without any subsequent gloss, anxious to understand them as their authors had written them. The understanding was greatly aided by a better grasp of the classical languages, now expanded to include Hebrew. As scholars of a secular past achieved a new understanding by approaching their studies with new insights, new knowledge, and new rigor, so did religious scholars. In the latter case some of the most basic teachings of the Church became the subject of violent and growing controversy, which reached well beyond religion.

Luther's priesthood of all believers struck a blow at traditional notions of a social hierarchy and exalted the individual. So did his idea of Christian liberty in which people were free to do good for God's sake, not for the selfish and demeaning end of achieving their own salvation, a doctrine the Church had recently grossly abused. Calvin's doctrine of the sovereignty of God, whose will not even princes must be allowed to defy, gave a powerful impetus to resistance theories.

Donald Kelley also discusses resistance theories, particularly as they developed on both sides of the revolt in the Netherlands and in the French Wars of Religion. These theories now became part of the intellectual armory of Catholic as well as Protestant.

The French Idea of Freedom: The Old Regime and the Declaration of Rights of 1789, and an American volume, *Devising Liberty: Preserving and Creating Freedom in the New American Republic*, bring the series to the eve of the nineteenth century. With the American and French Revolutions, we reach a point where the influences discussed in this volume seemed fast to be losing their immediacy and perceived relevance in explaining events. True, this was largely because such influences had by then been thoroughly absorbed into European culture, of which America was, of course, a part. But new phenomena to which neither that nor any other past provided any apparent guide had already begun to appear. There was nothing in the background of an educated eighteenth-century Englishman or woman, on either side of the Atlantic, that prepared them for the evangelical enthusiasm of what on this side was called the Great Awakening. Neither would they have found ancient examples useful in understanding slavery in the American South. In economics they were not likely to look back further than their own century, and in politics not much beyond the previous one. It was to this more immediate past beginning around 1600 that people now began to look for knowledge and inspiration. It is this past, and more particularly its salient features for the making of modern freedom, that is examined in the six volumes immediately following this one.

Parliament and Liberty from the Reign of Elizabeth to the English Civil War, ed. J. H. Hexter (Stanford, 1992)

Liberty Secured?: Britain Before and After 1688, ed. J. R. Jones (Stanford, 1992)

Fiscal Crises, Liberty, and Representative Government: 1450–1789, ed. Philip Hoffman and Kathryn Norberg (Stanford, 1994)

Republicanism and Commercial Society: from the English Civil War to the American Revolution, ed. David Wootton (Stanford, 1994)

The French Idea of Freedom: The Old Regime and the Declaration of Rights of 1789, ed. Dale Van Kley (Stanford, 1994)

Devising Liberty: Preserving and Creating Freedom in the New American Republic, ed. David Thomas Konig (forthcoming, Stanford, 1995)

REFERENCE MATTER

Abbreviations

AHR	*American Historical Review.*
BIMA	*Bibliotheca iuridica medii aevi*, 3 vols. Bologna, 1888–1901.
BL	British Library, London.
Bod.L	Bodleian Library, Oxford.
Bracton	[cited in full first time]
Britton	[cited in full first time]
Co. Inst.	E. Coke, *Institutes of the Laws of England*, 4 vols. (1628–48).
CP 40	PRO, plea rolls of the Court of Common Pleas.
Cro. Eliz.	*The First Part of the Reports of Sir George Croke* (1661).
CRR	*Curia Regis Rolls* (1922–).
CUL	Cambridge University Library.
Degani	E. Degani, *Hipponactis Fragmenta et Testimonia.* Stuttgart, 1983.
Discourses	*Machiavelli: The Discourses*, trans. Leslie J. Walker. London, 1970.
Dist.	*Distinctio* in Gratian's *Decretum.*
DK[6]	H. Diels and W. Kranz, *Die Fragmente der Vorsokratischer*, 6th ed. Berlin, 1951.
Dyer	J. Dyer, *Ascuns Novel Cases* (1688 ed.). Some references are also made to Dyer's reports, published in the Seldon Soc. series, vols. 109–10 (1994).
EHR	*English Historical Review.*
Fleta	[cited in full first time]
Florentine Histories	Machiavelli, *Florentine Histories*, trans. Laura F. Banfield and Harvey C. Mansfield, Jr. Princeton, NJ, 1988.
Glanvill	[cited in full first time]
Hypomnemata	*Untersuchungen zue Antike und zu ihrem Nachleben.* Göttingen.

HLS	Harvard Law School (Treasure Room).
JEH	*Journal of Economic History.*
Kadmos	*Zeitschrift für vor- und frühgriechische Epigraphik.*
KB 27	PRO, plea rolls of the Court of King's Bench.
KB 29	PRO, controlment rolls of the clerk of the Crown in the Court of King's Bench.
LC	Library of Congress (MSS Division), Washington.
L.-P.	E. Lobel and D. Page, *Poetarum Lesbiorum Fragmenta.* Oxford, 1955.
Maehler	H. Maehler, ed., *Pindarus, Pars II.* Leipzig, 1989.
MGH	*Monumenta Germaniae historica*
Novae Narrationes	[cited in full first time]
PRO	Public Record Office, London.
Selden Soc.	Selden Society publications, over 110 vols. (1888–).
The Prince	Machiavelli, *The Prince*, in Peter Bondanella and Mark Musa, eds. *The Portable Machiavelli.* New York, 1979.
TUJ	*Tractatus universi juris.*
Vestigia	*Beiträge zur alten Geschichte.* Munich.
West	M. L. West, *Iambi et Elegi Graeci* 2. Oxford, 1972.
Y.B.	Year Books. Those in the "vulgate" edition of 1679–80 are cited by term, regnal year, folio, and placitum. Those in the Rolls Series and Selden Soc. series are so cited. Cases of Edw. 2 not in the Selden Soc. series are cited from the 1678 ed. by J. Maynard.

Notes

CHAPTER I

Brad Hansen, my research assistant, was a continual and much appreciated help in writing this chapter. Priscilla Scott provided encouragement and advice at just the right time. Avner Greif, Philip Hoffman, Joel Mokyr, and John Nye all read earlier drafts and gave me valuable suggestions.

1. Douglass C. North, *Structure and Change in Economic History* (New York, 1981), chap. 8.

2. Charles Previté-Orton, *The Shorter Cambridge Medieval History* 1 (Cambridge, 1960): 442–45.

3. Joel Mokyr, *The Lever of Riches* (New York, 1990), chap. 3.

4. R. DeRoover, "The Organization of Trade," in M. M. Postan, E. E. Rich, and E. Miller, eds., *The Cambridge Economic History of Europe* 3 (Cambridge, 1965): 46–70.

5. Richard Bean, "War and the Birth of the Nation State," *JEH* 33 (1973): 203–21.

6. Douglass C. North, "Institutions, Transactions Costs and the Rise of Merchant Empires," in J. Tracy, ed., *The Political Economy of Merchant Empires* (Cambridge, 1991), 22–40.

7. Paul Milgrom, Douglass C. North, and Barry Weingast, "The Role of Institutions in the Revival of Trade: The Law Merchant, Private Judges, and the Champagne Fairs," *Economics and Politics* 2 (1990): 1–24.

8. Max Weber, *The Protestant Ethic and the Spirit of Capitalism* (New York, 1958).

9. R. H. Tawney, *Religion and the Rise of Capitalism* (New York, 1926).

10. James Coleman, *Foundations of Social Theory* (Cambridge, MA, 1990), 6.

11. Alan Macfarlane, *The Origins of English Individualism* (Oxford, 1978).

12. Avner Greif, "Reputation and Coalition in Medieval Trade: Evidence on the Maghribi Traders," *JEH* 49 (1989): 857–82; id., "Cultural Beliefs and the Organization of Society: Historical and Theoretical Reflections on Collectivist and Individualist Societies," *Journal of Political Economy*, forthcoming.

13. Timur Kuran, "The Economic System in Contemporary Islamic Thought," *International Journal of Middle East Studies* 18 (1986): 135–64.

14. Ernst Benz, *Evolution and Christian Hope: Man's Concept of the Future from the Early Fathers to Teilhard de Chardin* (Garden City, NY, 1966).

15. Lynn White, *Medieval Religion and Technology* (Berkeley, 1978).

16. Joseph Needham, *Science and Civilization in China* (Cambridge, 1954–88).

17. R. M. Hartwell, "Markets, Technology and the Structure of Enterprise in the Development of the Eleventh Century Chinese Iron and Steel Industry," *JEH* 26 (1966): 29–58.

18. Eric Jones, *The European Miracle* (Cambridge, 1981).

19. Eric Jones, *Growth Recurring* (New York, 1988).

20. Karl Wittfogel, *Oriental Despotism* (New Haven, CT, 1957).

21. Andrew Watson, "The Arab Agricultural Revolution and its Diffusion, 700-1100," *JEH* 34 (1974): 8–35.

22. Claude Cahen, "Economy, Society and Institutions," in P. M. Holt, A. K. S. Lambton, and Bernard Lewis, eds., *The Cambridge History of Islam* 2 (Cambridge, 1970): 511–38.

23. Maxine Rodinson, *Islam and Capitalism* (New York, 1974), chap. 4.

24. William McNeill, *The Rise of the West* (Chicago, 1963), 556.

25. Henri Pirenne, *Early Democracies in the Low Countries* (New York, 1963).

26. Ibid., 168.

27. Frederic W. Maitland, *The Constitutional History of England* (Cambridge, 1963), 175.

28. Eileen Power, *The Wool Trade in English Medieval History* (New York, 1965).

29. William Stubbs, *The Constitutional History of England* (Oxford, 1896), 3:599.

30. G. R. Elton, *The Tudor Revolution in Government* (Cambridge, 1953), 4.

31. David Harris Sacks, "Parliament, Liberty, and the Commonwealth," in J. H. Hexter, ed., *Parliament and Liberty from the Reign of Elizabeth to the English Civil War* (Stanford, 1992), 86.

32. J. H. Hexter, "Introduction," in Hexter, *Parliament and Liberty*, 2,1.

CHAPTER 2

I here wish to acknowledge a debt of gratitude to my colleagues Professors A. J. Graham and James B. Pritchard for advice and assistance that has saved this chapter from many pitfalls. Responsibility for shortcomings remains my own.

1. M. I. Finley, "The Freedom of the Citizen in the Greek World," in *Economy and Society in Ancient Greece*, ed. B. D. Shaw and R. P. Saller (New York, 1982), 77–94, esp. 77, citing E. Leach, "Law as a Condition of Freedom," in *The Concept of Freedom in Anthropology*, ed. D. Bidney (Paris and The Hague, 1968), 74.

2. O. Patterson, *Freedom*, vol. 1: *Freedom in the Making of Western Culture* (New York, 1991), xiv–xvi, quote from xv.

3. M. I. Finley, "The Servile Statuses in Ancient Greece," in *Economy and Society in Ancient Greece*, ed. Shaw and Saller, 133–49.

4. See M. Ventris and J. Chadwick, *Documents in Mycenaean Greek*, 2d ed. (Cambridge, 1973), 123–24, 156, 164, 166–67, 353, 409–10, 417, and 418; see also 236.

5. Ibid., 298–300, 469.

6. K. Raaflaub, "Zum Freiheitsbegriff der Griechen," in E. C. Welskopf, ed., *Soziale Typenbegriffe im alten Griechenland und ihr Fortleben in den Sprachen der Welt* 4 (Berlin, 1981): 180–405, esp. 186–87.

7. See Y. Garlan, *Slavery in Ancient Greece*, trans. J. Lloyd (Ithaca, NY, 1988), 29–37.

8. Homer, *Iliad* 6.455, 16.831, and 20.193, where they are described as "booty" (*lēiadas*).

9. Homer, *Odyssey* 14.340 and 17.323.

10. See K. Raaflaub, *Die Entdeckung der Freiheit. Zur historischen Semantik und Gesellschaftsgeschichte eines politischen Grundbegriffs der Griechen* (= *Vestigia* 37) (Munich, 1985), 36–46. The Homeric texts are not sufficient to support Patterson's elaborate theory, in *Freedom* 1:50–54, which makes female slaves the main orginators of the idea of freedom, nor does *Iliad* 6.528 support Raaflaub's contention, in *Entdeckung der Freiheit*, 189 with n. 67, "dass eleutheros nur . . . im Hinblick auf Frauen erscheint."

11. Heraclitus, F 53 (DK⁶) as interpreted by Charles H. Kahn, *The Art and Thought of Heraclitus* (Cambridge, 1979), 207–10.

12. Alcaeus, fr. 72 (L.-P) (= D14) 11–13: σὺ δὴ τεαύτας ἐκγεγόνων ἔχηις / τὰν δόξαν οἴαν ἄνδρες ἐλεύθεροι / ἔσλων ἔοντες ἐκ τοκήων, as interpreted by D. Page, *Sappho and Alcaeus* (Oxford, 1955), 171–74. Two other occurrences of "free" in Alcaeus (120 and 306 [10] {L.-P.}) are in too fragmentary a state to be interpreted.

13. Semonides, fr. 7.57–58 (West).

14. The opposite, "a slave's fare," is found in a social and an economic sense in fragments of his contemporary Hipponax of Ephesus: δούλιον χόρτον and δούλιον ἄρτον (frr. 36.6 and 194.8 [Degani]).

15. Solon, fr. 36.6–15 (West).

16. An ingenious recent reconstruction is that of A. Andrewes in *Cambridge Ancient History* 3.3, 2d ed. (Cambridge, 1982): 368–84. See also P. B. Manville, *The Origins of Citizenship in Ancient Athens* (Princeton, 1990), 105–23.

17. Solon, fr. 4.7–19 (West).

18. See Raaflaub, "Freiheitsbegriff," 193 with n. 116.

19. On this point, see the excellent discussion of the Solonian reforms by Manville, *Origins of Citizenship*, chap. 6.

20. See D. Page, ed., *Poetae Melici Graeci* (Oxford, 1962), frr. 893.4 and 896.4 with M. Ostwald, *Nomos and the Beginnings of the Athenian Democracy* (Oxford, 1969), 96–136.

21. Herodotus 5.55.1, 62.1, 63.1, 64.2, 65.5, 78.

22. So, for example, Raaflaub, *Entdeckung der Freiheit*, 139–40, cf. 110.

23. See, e.g., the Lipit-Ishtar law code in J. B. Pritchard, ed., *Ancient Near Eastern Texts Relating to the Old Testament*, 3d ed. (Princeton, NJ, 1969), 160, no. 25: "If a man married a wife (and) she bore him children and those children are living, and a slave also bore children for her master (but) the father granted freedom to the slave and her children, the children of the slave shall not divide the estate with the children of their (former) master." We have here not only an example of slave concubines, but also of manumission and social rank in relation to inheritance.

24. See Pritchard, *Near Eastern Texts*, 163–80.

25. See R. Meiggs and D. M. Lewis, *A Selection of Greek Historical Inscriptions to the End of the Fifth Century B.C.*, 2d ed. (Oxford, 1988), no. 12. For a general survey of Egypt and the Near East, see A. B. Knapp, *The History and Culture of Ancient Western Asia and Egypt* (Chicago, 1988); for Anatolia, see H. Lewy, "Anatolia in the Old Assyrian Period," in *Cambridge Ancient History* 1.2, 3d ed. (Cambridge, 1971): 707–28, esp. 715–23. This applies also to those Mesopotamian localities which, though monarchically ruled, are believed by some scholars to display democratic features; see esp. the two articles by Thorkild Jacobsen, "Primitive Democracy in Ancient Mesopotamia" and "Early Political Development in Mesopotamia," both republished in *Toward the Image of Tammuz and Other Essays on Mesopotamian History and Culture*, ed. W. L. Moran (Cambridge, MA, 1970), 157–70 and 132–56. In general, see R. M. Glassman, *Democracy and Despotism in Primitive Societies*, 2 vols. (Millwood, NY, 1986).

26. See R. de Vaux, *Ancient Israel: Its Life and Institutions*, trans. J. McHugh (London, 1961), 68–79, 80–90. For other aspects, see L. I. Rabinowitz, "Freedom," in *Encyclopaedia Judaica* 7 (Jerusalem, 1971): 117–20.

27. On this point, see D. Daube, *The Exodus Pattern in the Bible* (London, 1963), esp. chap. 5: "A Change of Masters." See also M. Walzer, *Exodus and Revolution* (New York, 1985).

28. See Ventris and Chadwick, *Documents in Mycenaean Greek*, 298–300, 469.

29. Herodotus 2.135.2; 3.125.3; 4.95.1–2; 5.92η.3; and 6.58.1.

30. For valuable observations on this term, see L. Edmunds and R. Martin, "*Thucydides* 2.65.8: ἐλευθέρως," *Harvard Studies in Classical Philology* 81 (1977): 187–93.

31. Solon, fr. 9.3–4 (West) with Raaflaub, "Freiheitsbegriff," 193.

32. A curious passage is 7.58.2, where Gelon accuses the Greeks of not having assisted him in freeing "the trading posts from which great profits and advantages accrued" to the Greeks. Since the trading posts in question are likely to have been Carthaginian, their "freeing" seems to conceal imperialistic designs.

33. See Kurt von Fritz, "Die griechische ΕΛΕΥΘΕΡΙΑ bei Herodot," *Wiener Studien* 78 (1965): 5–31.

34. On this kind of imitation, see Patricia A. Rosenmeyer, *The Poetics of Imitation* (Cambridge, 1992).

35. Page, *Poetae Melici Graeci*, fr. 419, attributed to Anacreon in *Anthologia Palatina* 13.4.

36. See Rosenmeyer, *Poetics*.

37. The best treatment of this problem is still that by U. von Wilamowitz-Moellendorff, *Sappho und Simonides* (Berlin, 1913), 105–6; he dates this poem to the time before Anacreon moved to the court of Polycrates in Samos, sc. before 522 B.C.

38. For samples, see Meiggs and Lewis, *Greek Historical Inscriptions*, nos. 24–28 with discussion on 54–57. A large number are traditionally attributed to Simonides (c. 556–468 B.C.), collected in E. Diehl, ed., *Anthologia Lyrica Graeca* 2 (Leipzig, 1925): 85–118, and discussed by A. J. Podlecki, "Simonides: 480," *Historia* 17 (1968): 257–75. For a general discussion, see Raaflaub, *Entdeckung der Freiheit*, 72–82.

39. Meiggs and Lewis, *Greek Historical Inscriptions*, no. 26 (I), line 4, with discussion; W. C. West III, "Saviors of Greece," *Greek, Roman and Byzantine Studies* 11 (1970): 271–82.

40. Plutarch, *De gloria Atheniensium* 7 (= *Moralia* 350A) = Pindar, fr. 77 (Maehler).

41. Pindar, *Isthmian* 8.15, with E. Thummer, ed. and comm., *Pindar: Die Isthmischen Gedichte* 2 (Heidelberg, 1969): 131.

42. Cf. also external and internal freedom in Pindar, *Pythian* 1.71–75 (470 B.C.), where the battle off Cumae in 474 B.C. is said to have "pulled Greece out of grievous slavery"; and 60–65, where "freedom" is said to be built into the god-laid foundations of Aitna, according to Dorian norms.

43. Most accessible in Meiggs and Lewis, *Greek Historical Inscriptions*, no. 23 with discussion and bibliography.

44. N. G. L. Hammond, "The Narrative of Herodotus VII and the Decree of Themistocles at Troezen," *Journal of Hellenic Studies* 102 (1982): 75–93, ingeniously dates the original of the decree a year before the battles of Artemisium and Salamis.

45. *eleutheros* and *eleutheria* in the two fourth-century versions of the Oath of Plataea (the Acharnae inscription, lines 23–24, and Lycurgus, *In Leocratem* 81), respectively, speak of a personal freedom. See P. Siewert, *Der Eid von Plataiai* (= *Vestigia* 16), 9–19, 24, 53–56.

46. Diodorus 11.72.2.

47. Thucydides 2.71.2; Plutarch, *Aristeides* 19.7 and *de malignitate Herodoti* 42 (= *Moralia* 873b).

48. The cult is in Athens best attested through archaeological remains dating to c. 430 B.C.; see R. E. Wycherley, *The Stones of Athens* (Princeton, NJ, 1978), 42–43 with n. 40. For the literary evidence, see R. E. Wycherley, *The Athenian Agora* 3. *Literary and Epigraphical Testimonia* (Princeton, NJ, 1957), 25–30.

49. Sources and general discussion in Raaflaub, *Entdeckung der Freiheit*, 125–35.

50. M. Pohlenz, *Herodot* (repr. Stuttgart, 1961), 116 n.3, shows interesting linguistic parallels between Herodotus and Aeschylus's *Persae*.

51. See also Aeschylus, *Choephori* 1060 and *Eumenides* 175 and 340; Euripides, *Heracleidae* 790, 868, *Hecuba* 864, 869, *Heracles* 1010, *Electra* 911, *Phoenissae* 999, *Rhesus* 664. Related to this use is the claim of the Furies at *Eumenides* 603 that Clytaemnestra is "free from" (= innocent of) the charge of murder. Cf. also Sophocles, *Antigone* 399 and 445; Euripides, *Hippolytus* 1449–50, *Orestes* 1088; and [Hippocrates], *De Arte* 7. 25, *Letters* 11.37; cf. also *De septimestri partu* 4.24 on the delivery of a child.

52. Cf. also Sophocles, *Electra* 1509; and Euripides, *Electra* 868.

53. The code is most accessible in R. F. Willets, ed., *The Law Code of Gortyn* (= *Kadmos* Suppl. 1) (Berlin, 1967); for the date, see ibid., 8.

54. The Gortyn Code also recognized a type of free man called *apetairos* (= a person excluded from membership in *hetaireiai*): see ibid., 12–13; and a kind of household serf, called *oikeus*, mentioned in connection with property rights (cols. 3–4).

55. Sophocles, *Trachiniae* 63, *Ajax* 63, 1258–60, *Oedipus Tyrannus* 706, *Electra* 1256; Euripides, *Hippolytus* 421–22, *Andromache* 153, *Bacchae* 775, *Iphigeneia at Aulis* 930, 994, *Rhesus* 420. In this connection the increasing use of the adverb *eleutherōs* in the sense of "uninhibited" is worth noting (Sophocles, *Electra* 1300; Euripides, *Cyclops* 287, *Alcestis* 1008), as are the overtones of generosity and liberality in both *eleutherōs*, (Euripides, *Heracleidae* 559, *Orestes* 1170) and *eleutheros* (Euripides, *Alcestis* 569, 678).

56. E.g., Sophocles, *Trachiniae* 249, 267, 301, *Ajax* 1020, 1260. Cf. also Hippocrates, *De morbis popularibus* 6.7.1.35, *Oath* 21.

57. E.g., Sophocles, *Philoctetes* 996; Euripides, *Heracleidae* 789, 890, *Andromache* 12, 195, 433, *Hecuba* 234, 291–92, 367, 420, 550, 754, 864, *Iphigeneia among the Taurians* 1349, *Helen* 275.

58. E.g., Sophocles, *Trachiniae* 487; Euripides, *Ion* 855, *Helen* 730.

59. Aristotle, *Politics* 1.5, 1254a17–1255a3.

60. Euripides, *Heracleidae* 62, 113, 198, 244, 287.

61. See also the freedom of Troy at *Rhesus* 469 and 991.

62. Thucydides 1.122.3, 124.3; 2.63.2; 3.37.2; 6.85.1. For freedom from Persian rule, see 1.69.1; 2.71.2; 3.10.3, 54.4,; 6.76.4, 83.2.

63. Id. 6.59.4; 8.68.4.

64. Speeches: id. 1.69.1, 124.1, 3; 3.10.3–5, 13.3, 7, 39.7, 62.5, 63.3; 4.85.5–6, 86.1, 4, 87.2, 5–6; 5.9.9; 6.87.2. Indirect speech: 7.56.2; 8.48.5. Narrative: 4.52.3, 120.3, 121.1; 8.52.1.

65. Pindar, *Pythian* 8.98–100 with R. W. Burton, *Pindar's Pythian Odes* (Oxford, 1962), 174–93, and Raaflaub, "Freiheitsbegriff," 215. For Cos see [Hippocrates], *Epistle* 26.17 and 22, where Cos is enslaved by Athens and the Thessalians are appealed to to liberate her. However, the authenticity of the *Epistle* is very dubious. The only historical occasion suitable for this appeal is a period between 446/5 and 443/2 B.C.; see S. M. Sherwin-White, *Ancient Cos* (= *Hypomnemata* 51) (Göttingen, 1978) 375–77, who does not cite the Hippocratic letter.

66. Thucydides 2.8.4, 72.1; 3.32.2, 59.4; 4.85.1, 86.1; 8.46.3. Echoed in the fourth century in Isocrates 4.122.

67. Thucydides 1.84.1; 5.9.1. Interestingly enough, the Athenians claim internal freedom only for their "land" (2.36.1) and for their liberation from Peisistratid tyranny (n. 63 above).

68. So most explicitly at 3.45.6; 6.20.2; 8.43.3, but see also 2.62.3, 63.1; 3.12.1; 4.63.2, 64.5, 92.4, 7, 95.3, 114.3; 5.9.9, 99, 100, 112.2; 6.40.2, 69.3, 87.2, 89.6; 7.68.3, 69.2, 82.1; 8.45.4, 64.3–4, 71.1.

69. See M. Ostwald, *Autonomia: Its Genesis and Early History* (Chico, CA, 1982), especially 11–14.

70. E. J. Bickerman, "Autonomia: Sur un passage de Thucydide (1, 144, 2), "*Revue Internationale des Droits de l'Antiquité*, 3d ser., 5 (1958): 313–44.

71. Thucydides 2.72.1; 3.10.5, 46.5–6; 4.86.1; 6.77.1, 84.3

72. See M. N. Tod, *A Selection of Greek Historical Inscriptions* 2 (Oxford, 1948), no. 123, lines 10 and 20; even earlier is the Athenian treaty with Chios of 384 B.C., no. 118, line 2. Cf. also Athens and Chalkis (no. 124, lines 21–22 of 377 B.C.), Athens and Thrace (no. 151, line 16 of 357 B.C.), and the treaty between Alexander and Priene of 334 B.C. (no. 185, line 4). See also Isocrates 4 (*Panegyricus*) 117; 14 (*Plataïcus*) 24; 6 (*Archidamus*) 64; 8 (*On the Peace*) 58; *Epistle* 8.7; Demosthenes 1 (*Olynthiac I*) 23; 7 (*On Halonessus*) 30, 32; 17 (*On the Treaty with Alexander*) 8; 18 (*On the Crown*) 305.

73. Thucydides 2.78.4, 103.1; 3.73.1; 4.26.5, 80.3–4, 118.7; 5.34.1, 83.2; 8.15.2, 28.4, 41.2, 62.2, 73.5, 84.2.

74. For a simple social distinction, see, e.g., Aristophanes, *Plutus* 148; Andocides 4 (*Against Alcibiades*) 14, 23; Antiphon 6 (*On the Choreutes*) 19, 22; Lysias 5 (*For Callias*) 4, 5; 7 (*On the Olive-Stump*) 16; 23 (*Against Pancleon*) 9, 11–12; Isocrates 17 (*Trapeziticus*) 14, 17, 49; Aeschines 1 (*Against Timarchus*) 62, 65–66; 3 (*Against Ctesiphon*) 122, 169, 171. Legal distinctions in, e.g., Lysias 4 (*On a Wound by Premeditation*) 12, 14; Lycurgus 1 (*Against Leocrates*) 41, 65.

75. Andocides 4 (*Against Alcibiades*) 18.

76. Antiphon 6 (*On the Choreutes*) 23, 25.

77. Id. 5 (*On the Murder of Herodes*) 48–50.

78. Isaeus 8 (*On the Estate of Ciron*) 12; cf. also Antiphon 2 (*Tetralogy 1*) 3.4, 4.7; and 5 (*On the Murder of Herodes*) 31, 34.

79. Aeschines 1 (*Against Timarchus*) 7, 9, 12, 14, 15–17; cf. also Lysias 1 (*On the Murder of Eratosthenes*) 32.

80. E.g., Lysias 2 (*Funeral Oration*) 14, 62, 64; 3 (*Against Simon*) 23; 13 (*Against Agoratus*) 66; Isocrates 20 (*Aegineticus*) 6; Aeschines 1 (*Against Timarchus*) 43, 107, 123, 138, 159; 2 (*On the False Embassy*) 4–5, 127, 148.

81. E.g., Aristophanes, *Clouds* 1414; *Lysistrata* 379, 614; and especially *Ecclesiazousae* 721–24, 941.

82. Aeschines 1 (*Against Timarchus*) 42; 2 (*On the False Embassy*) 173; Lycurgus 1 (*Against Leocrates*) 49; Plato, *Republic* 4, 431c.

83. E.g., Xenophon, *Memorabilia* 1.2.29; *Symposium* 8.23.

84. Thucydides 2.37.2, 65.8; 6.85.2; 7.63.4; Aristophanes, *Clouds* 518; *Ecclesiazousae* 1145; Lysias 8 (*Calumny*) 16; Isocrates 4 (*Panegyricus*) 49; Aeschines 1 (*Against Timarchus*) 120, 156; 2 (*On the False Embassy*) 23, 70; 3 (*Against Ctesiphon*) 154. Note that sometimes *eleutheros* has the same connotations, e.g., Aeschines 1 (*Against Timarchus*) 42; Plato, *Laws* 7, 795e; cf. n. 55 above.

85. Antiphon F44A, col. 4.3–8; Plato, *Gorgias* 491e5–492c8, esp. c5.

86. See Xenophon, *Memorabilia* 1.2.5–6; 4.5.2; *Oeconomicus* 1.23; Aristotle, *Politics* 6.2, 1317b10–13.

87. E.g., Aristophanes, *Thesmophoriazousae* 102; Lysias 2 (*Funeral Oration*) 18; Isocrates 10 (*Helen*) 35.

88. Most clearly expressed in Plato, *Laws* 7.790a-b and 807d, cf. also *Protagoras* 312b.

89. Aristotle, *Politics* 1.5, 1254a17-b26; 1254b27–34.

90. Ibid. 6, 1255a4-b4; 3, 1253b21–22. Cf. n. 59 above.

91. For an excellent survey of the development of the notion of "liberal arts," see "Excursus: The *Liberales Disciplinae*," in J. J. O'Donnell, *Augustine: Confessions* 2 (Oxford, 1992): 269–78.

92. Aristotle, *Politics* 3.5, 1277b33–1278a13. It must be emphasized that Aristotle nowhere advocates that industrial workers be barred from citizenship in actual states; he merely expresses his view that membership in the community requires active participation: "If we regard an industrial worker as a citizen, we must regard the definition of the excellence of a citizen as we have been discussing it as not applying to all, nor only to a free person, but only as applying to all those who have been relieved from the necessity to work" (3.5, 1278a9–11).

93. Note the emphasis on leisure in 8.3, 1337b28–30.

94. Ibid. 8.2, 1337b4–21.

95. Ibid. 8.3, 1338b2–4.

96. Euripides, *Supplices* 353, 404–8.

97. Isocrates 12 (*Panathenaicus*) 68; 20 (*Against Lochites*) 1, 10; Aristotle, *Rhetoric* 1.8, 1366a4; *Politics* 3.8, 1279b39–1280a5; 4.4, 1290b1–3, 17–20, 1291b34–35; 5, 1292b38–39, 8, 1294a11, 15, 1299b26–27; 5.9, 1310a28–33; 6.2, 1317a40-b17, 1318a3–10.

98. Examples of a general nature are found largely at the end of the fifth and in the first half of the fourth century, e.g., Andocides 3 (*On Peace with Sparta*) 14; 4 (*Against Alcibiades*) 1; Lysias 2 (*Funeral Oration*) 24, 26, 33, 41, 44, 46, 48; 25 (*Subverting the Democracy*) 32; 33 (*Olympic Oration*) 6–7; 34 (*Subversion of the Ancestral Constitution*) 11; Isocrates 4 (*Panegyricus*) 52, 95, 104, 106, 123, 140, 185; 5 (*To Philip*) 104; 6 (*Archidamus*) 7, 43, 51, 83; 14 (*Plataïcus*) 5–6, 17, 18, 43, 61.

99. Referring to the Persian Wars of the early fifth century at: Andocides 1 (*On the Mysteries*) 142; 3 (*On Peace with Sparta*) 17–18; Lysias 2 (*Funeral Oration*) 35, 42, 47, 55, 60; Isocrates 5 (*To Philip*) 129; 8 (*On the Peace*) 42; 15 (*Antidosis*) 307; so also the spurious [Aeschines], *Epistle* 3.2.

Referring to the fourth century: Andocides 3 (*On Peace with Sparta*) 17–18; Isocrates 4 (*Panegyricus*) 185; 8 (*On the Peace*) 141; cf. also the Greek cities of Asia Minor at 5 (*To Philip*) 123 and *Epistle* 6.11.

100. Lysias 12 (*Against Eratosthenes*) 73; 13 (*Against Agoratus*) 17; 18 (*On the Property of the Brother of Nicias*) 27; 26 (*On the Scrutiny of Euandros*) 2; 31 (*Against Philon*) 26, 31–32; also 28 (*Against Ergocles*) 13–14, cf. Isocrates 7 (*Areopagiticus*) 65.

101. The relevant passages in Demosthenes are too numerous to cite. But see Lycurgus 1 (*Against Leocrates*) 42, 45, 47, 48, 50, 73, 147. Cf. Aeschines 2 (*On the False Embassy*) 60.

102. [Aeschines], *Epistle* 11.6 and 9 (spurious). See also the Oath of Plataea cited in Lycurgus 1 (*Against Leocrates*) 144 with n. 45 above.

CHAPTER 3

1. F. W. Maitland, *Roman Canon Law in the Church of England* (London, 1898), 100.

2. Matt. 16:15–17; Acts 15:28, "It has seemed good to the Holy Spirit and to us."

3. Brian Tierney, ed., *The Crisis of Church and State, 1050–1300* (Englewood Cliffs, NJ, 1964), 13.

4. E. Emerton, ed., *The Correspondence of Pope Gregory VII* (New York, 1932), 179.

5. Tierney, *Crisis*, 49.

6. Tierney, *Crisis*, 189.

7. John of Paris, *On Royal and Papal Power*, trans. J. A. Watt (Toronto, 1971), 94.

8. Tierney, *Crisis*, 79.

9. John of Paris, *On Royal and Papal Power*, 157–59.

10. Antony Black, *Guilds and Civil Society* (Ithaca, NY, 1984), 63.

11. *Digest* 1.3.31; *Code* 1.14.4.

12. John of Salisbury, *Policraticus*, trans. Cary J. Nederman (Cambridge, 1990), 46–49, 206–13.

13. *Decretales, D. Gregorii Papae IX . . . cum glossis diversorum* (Lyons, 1624), gloss *ad* 1.7.3. The various canonistic texts mentioned below are printed and discussed further in my *Foundations of the Conciliar Theory* (Cambridge, 1955) and "Pope and Council: Some New Decretist Texts," *Medieval Studies* 19 (1957): 197–218.

14. *Decretum Gratiani . . . una cum glossis* (Venice, 1600), *Dist.* 40 c.6.

15. Tierney, "Pope and Council," 206; id., *Foundations*, 41.

16. Johannes Teutonicus, *glossa ordinaria ad* C.24 q.1 c.9. In his gloss *ad Dist.* 19 c.7, Johannes wrote, "Where matters of faith are concerned . . . a council is greater than a pope."

17. Cardinal Zabarella made this point explicitly. He wrote that plenitude of power resided "fundamentally in the corporate body, and in the pope as the principal minister through whom this power is expressed." Tierney,

Foundations, 225. For the citation of Roman law mentioned above see ibid., 46.

18. Tierney, "Pope and Council," 201.

19. Tierney, *Foundations,* 58–63.

20. These various viewpoints are found, for instance, in the *Summa Et est sciendum,* the *Summa Duacensis,* and the *Apparatus* of Alanus on the *Decretum.* See Tierney, "Pope and Council," 214–18.

21. Thomas Aquinas, *Commentum in Libros IV Sententiarum* 2.44.2 ad 1 in *Opera Omnia,* 34 vols., ed. L. Vivès (Paris, 1874–89), 8:590.

22. Thomas Aquinas, *On Kingship to the King of Cyprus,* ed. G. B. Phelan and I. T. Eschmann (Toronto, 1949), 1.1.10, 7.

23. *Institutes* 1.2.6; *Code* 1.17.1.7; *Digest* 1.4.1.

24. Azo, *Lectura ad Cod.* 8.53.2, quoted in E. Cortese, *La norma giuridica,* 2 vols. (Rome, 1962–64), 2:176.

25. The conciliar movement grew up during the Great Schism of 1378–1417. Its leaders asserted that a general council was the supreme organ of church government and sought to establish a kind of parliamentary regime for the church. For the specific argument mentioned above see my *Religion, Law, and the Growth of Constitutional Thought, 1150–1650* (Cambridge, 1982), 58–60.

26. *The Works of . . . Mr. Richard Hooker,* ed. John Keble, 7th ed. rev. by R. W. Church and F. Paget, 3 vols. (London, 1888), 8.2.7, 3:346.

27. *Dist.* 4 *dictum post* c.3. For canonistic commentary on this text see Luigi de Luca, "L'Accetazione popolare della lege canonica nel pensiero di Graziano e dei sui interpreti," *Studia Gratiana* 3 (1955): 194–276.

28. De Luca, "L'Accetazione," 211.

29. Thomas Aquinas, *Summa Theologiae* 1.2ae.97.3, *Opera* 2:595. Aquinas also noted that not all communities were free in this fashion. Some were subordinated to the authority of the ruler.

30. These various opinions are presented in De Luca, "L'Accetazione," 201, 212, 213, 219.

31. On this question see most recently K. Pennington, *The Prince and the Law: Sovereignty and Rights in the Western Legal Tradition* (Berkeley, 1992).

32. John of Paris, *On Royal and Papal Power,* 96–105.

33. *Les Quodlibets onze-quatorze de Godefroid de Fontaines,* ed. J. Hoffmans, vol. 5 of *Les philosophes Belges* (Louvain, 1932), 76 (Quodl. 11 q.17).

34. Durand of St. Porçain, *De iurisdictione ecclesiastica* (Paris, 1506), fol. lrb.

35. John of Paris, *On Royal and Papal Power,* 124.

36. Marsilius of Padua, *Defensor Pacis* 1.9.5, in A. Gewirth, *Marsilius of Padua. The Defender of the Peace,* 2 vols. (New York, 1951–56), 2:32.

37. Ibid. 1.15.2, in 2:61.

38. Ibid. 1.9.2, in 2:29.

39. Ibid. 1.12.6, in 2:47–48. There has been much discussion on Marsilius's use of the term "weightier part" (*valentior pars*). It seems most likely,

as Gewirth argues, that he did not envisage a small ruling elite but rather a majority that included the more substantial citizens.

40. Ibid. 2.15.4, in 2:235.

41. Ibid. 2.16.16, in 2:252.

42. Ibid. 2.4.12, 2.6.12, in 2:122–24, 2:148–49.

43. Hervaeus Natalis, *Tractatus de iurisdictione*, ed. L. Hödl, in *De iurisdictione. Ein unveröffentlichter Traktat des Hervaeus Natalis O.P. (+ 1323) über die Kirchengewalt* (Munich, 1959), 14–15. See John Locke, *Two Treatises of Government*, ed. Peter Laslett, 2d ed. (Cambridge, 1967), 1.2, 286, "That the Power of a *Magistrate* over a Subject, may be distinguished from that of a *Father* over his Children, a *Master* over his Servant, a *Husband* over his wife, and a *Lord* over his slave."

44. Ibid., 16.

45. Ibid., 17.

46. M. V. Clarke, *Medieval Representation and Consent* (London, 1958), 296.

47. V. H. Galbraith, *The Constitution of the Dominican Order, 1216–1360* (Manchester, 1925).

48. O. Hintze, "Weltgeschichtliche Bedingungen der Repräsentativverfassung," *Historische Zeitschrift* 143 (1930): 1–47; G. de Lagarde, "L'Idée de représentation dans les oeuvres de Guillaume d'Occam," *Bulletin of the International Committee of Historical Sciences* 9 (1937): 425–51; E. Barker, *The Dominican Order and Convocation* (Oxford, 1913); Carl Schmitt, *Politische Theologie*, 2d ed. (Munich, 1934), 49.

49. On *plena potestas* and *quod omnes tangit* see especially Gaines Post, *Studies in Medieval Legal Thought* (Princeton, NJ, 1964), 91–220; J. G. Edwards, "The *Plena potestas* of English Parliamentary Representatives" in *Oxford Essays in Medieval History Presented to H. E. Salter* (Oxford, 1934), 141–54; Yves Congar, "Quod omnes tangit, ab omnibus tractari et approbari debet," *Revue historique de droit français et étranger* 36 (1958): 210–59.

50. *Code* 5.59.5.2.

51. *Dist.* 63 *dictum post* c.25.

52. *Decretales* 1.23.7.

53. Tierney, *Foundations*, 49.

54. These examples are from Congar, "Quod omnes tangit," 217, 233, 234.

55. William Stubbs, *Select Charters*, 9th ed. (Oxford, 1913), 480.

56. Aquinas, *On Kingship* 1.2.19; 1.4.30; 1.6.42; 12, 19, 24.

57. Aquinas, *Summa Theologiae* 1.2ae.105.1, *Opera* 2:675.

58. Ibid., "It was a democratical government in that rulers were chosen from all the people, for it is said, 'Provide wise men from all the people' (Exodus 18.21), and also in that the people chose them, whence it is said 'Let me have from among you wise men' (Deuteronomy 1:13)."

59. E. Gilson, *The Christian Philosophy of St. Thomas Aquinas* (London, 1957), 330.

60. Raimondo M. Spiazzi, ed., *In octo libros Politicorum expositio* (Turin, 1966), 3.6, 140.

61. John of Paris, *On Royal and Papal Power*, 206.

62. Susan Babbitt, "Oresme's *Livre de Politiques* and the France of Charles V," *Transactions of the American Philosophical Society* 75 (1985): 1-158.

63. Jean Gerson, *De potestate ecclesiastica* in *Oeuvres complètes*, 10 vols., ed. P. Glorieux (Paris, 1960-73), 6:248.

64. James Blythe, *Ideal Government and the Mixed Constitution in the Middle Ages* (Princeton, NJ, 1992), 307.

65. See my "Origins of Natural Rights Language: Texts and Contexts, 1150-1250," *History of Political Thought* 10 (1989): 615-45.

66. Michel Villey, *La formation de la pensée juridique moderne*, 4th ed. (Paris, 1975), 252, 261.

67. Gloss *ad Dist.* 56 c.7.

68. H. Singer, ed., *Rufinus von Bologna. Summa Decretorum* (Paderborn, 1902), 6.

69. For these canonistic texts see my "Origins of Natural Rights Language," 629-35.

70. Some examples are given in Charles J. Reid, "The Canonistic Contribution to the Western Rights Tradition: An Historical Inquiry," *Boston College Law Review* 33 (1991): 37-92.

71. On this development see Pennington, *Prince and Law*.

72. *An princeps* in *Guillelmi de Ockham opera politica*, 3 vols., ed. H. S. Offler (Manchester, 1956-74), 1:251.

73. Ibid., 230-32, 248-51. Ockham returned to this argument over and over again in his political works. For a list of references see A. S. McGrade, *The Political Thought of William of Ockham* (Cambridge, 1974), 141 n.179.

74. Gerson, *De vita spirituale animae, Oeuvres* 3:141, 143.

75. Ibid., 142.

76. Ibid., 129.

77. Ibid., 130, 135, 145.

78. There was an equivocation here in the use of the term *ius naturale*. Often natural law was taken to mean a body of enduring moral precepts that all were bound to obey (like Gratian's Golden Rule). But sometimes the term referred to a primeval condition of things that existed before the institution of human law and that had been subsequently modified by human law.

79. Ockham, *Octo quaestiones* 1.5, *Opera* 1:28.

80. C.12 q.2 c.68.

81. David B. Davis, *The Problem of Slavery in Western Culture* (Ithaca, NY, 1966), 90. Davis provides a good overview of medieval attitudes to slavery. For a collection of relevant texts see J. F. Maxwell, *Slavery and the Catholic Church* (London, 1975).

82. Aquinas, *Summa Theologiae* 1.2ae.19.5, *Opera* 2:189.

83. Gloss *ad Decretales* 5.39.44.

84. William Prynne, *The Soveraigne Power of Parliaments and Kingdoms* (London, 1643), 5–7, 31, 68, 73, 153; John Maxwell, *Sacro-sancta regum majestas* (Oxford, 1644), 16; Henry Parker, *Jus populi* (London, 1644), 26; George Lawson, *Politia sacra et civilis*, 2d ed. (London, 1689), 119. For a discussion of this material see Francis Oakley, "On the Road from Constance to 1688," *Journal of British Studies* 1 (1962): 1–31; id., "Figgis, Constance, and the Divines of Paris," *AHR* 75 (1969): 368–86.

CHAPTER 4

1. The commonplace on monarchy is in Ptolemy of Lucca's *De regimine principum* 4.2, in R. M. Spiazzi, ed., *Divi Thomae Aquinatis Opuscula philosophica* (Turin, 1954), no. 1033, 327. For the village, see n.46 below.

2. G. Tilander, ed., *Los fueros de Aragòn* (Lund, 1937), 280.

3. Ptolemy, *De regimine* 4.8, in Spiazzi, ed., no. 1056, 336.

4. Giles of Rome, *De regimine principum* 3.2.2 (Rome, 1607), 455.

5. Ptolemy, *De regimine* 4.8, in Spiazzi, ed., no. 1056, 336.

6. Salimbene, *Cronica*, *MGH Scriptores* 32 (Leipzig and Hanover, 1905/13): 643–44.

7. Giles of Rome, *De regimine* 3.2.2, 45.

8. Bartolo of Sassoferrato, *Tractatus de Guelphis et Gebellinis* 2, in D. Quaglioni, ed., *Politica e diritto nel trecento Italiano* (Florence, 1983), 136.

9. In E. Salzer, *Über die Anfänge der Signorie in Oberitalien* (Berlin, 1900), 302.

10. Bartolo of Sassoferrato, *De regimine civitatis* 2, in Quaglione, ed., *Politica*, 164–65.

11. *Das Sächsische Weichbildrecht: Jus municipale saxonicum*, A. von Daniels, ed. (Berlin, 1858), 1:66.

12. *Digest* 1.5.4.

13. Cicero, *Paradoxa* 34.

14. *Institutes* 1.2.2. For some clerical ideas on slavery, see Brian Tierney's chapter above.

15. Accursius, *Glossa in digestum vetus* on *Digest* 1.5.4 (Venice, 1488), 10va.

16. In E. Cortese, *La norma giuridica* (Florence, 1962–64), 1:82 n.109.

17. Azo, *Summa aurea* no. 6 (Lyon, 1557), 1050–51.

18. In P. Villari, *The Two First Centuries of Florentine History* (New York, 1901), 304.

19. Odofredo, *Lectura super digesto veteri* on *Digest* 1.5.4 no. 1 (Lyon, 1550), 1:18vb.

20. Dante, *De monarchia* 1.12, in G. Vinay, ed. (Florence, 1950), 72.

21. Ibid. 1.12, in Vinay, ed., 75.

22. R. L. Benson, "*Libertas* in Italy," in *La notion de liberté au moyenâge: Islam, Byzance, Occident*, G. Makdisi et al., eds. (Paris, 1985), 191, cited these passages from *Epist.* 6:2 and 3.

23. Alexander of Roes, *Noticia seculi* 12 and 13, *MGH Staatschriften des späteren Mittelalters* 1.i (Stuttgart, 1958): 159–60.

24. Philippe de Commines, *Mémoires* 5.18, J. Calmette, ed. (Paris, 1924–25), 2:211.

25. Landulf in G. Dilcher, *Die Entstehung der lombardischen Stadtkommune* (Aalen, 1967), 110.

26. Luke 6:35.

27. Gratian's *Decretum De penitencia* Distinctio 5.6.

28. Acts 4:32–35.

29. G. Lefèvre, ed., *Le traité 'De usura' de Robert de Courçon* (Lille, 1902), 33.

30. In J. Kirshner and K. lo Prete, "Olivi's Treatises on Contracts of Sale, Usury and Restitution," *Quaderni fiorentini per la storia del pensiero giuridico moderno* 13 (1984): 268.

31. *Naviganti* in *Decretalium Gregorii IX. Compilatio* 5.19.19.

32. John of Joinville, *Mémoires*, F. Michel, ed. (Paris, 1882), 9.

33. In H. J. Gilomen, "Wucher und Wirtschaft im Mittelalter," *Historische Zeitschrift* 250 (1990): 265.

34. *Digest* 50.17.32.

35. Gregory I, *Registrum epistolarum*, 5.59 in *MGH Epistolae* 1 (Munich, 1978): 371.

36. Ptolemy, *De regimine* 3.9, in Spiazzi, ed., no. 974, 308.

37. In V. Colorni, *Gli Ebrei nel sistema del diritto comune* (Milan, 1956), 15.

38. *Code* 3.19.3.

39. *Cronache e statuti della città di Viterbo*, ed. I. Ciampi (Florence, 1872), 518: "*in personis et rebus.*"

40. Alberic of Rosate, *De statutis* 2.2 no. 17, *TUJ* 2 (Venice, 1504): 28vb.

41. Albert of Gandino, *Quaestiones statutorum* 75, *BIMA* 3:193.

42. *De legibus et consuetudinibus Angliae, introductio*, S. E. Thorne, ed. (Cambridge, MA, 1968), 2:32.

43. A. Giry, ed., *Documents sur les relations de la royauté avec les villes en France* (Paris, 1885), *Sermo II ad burgenses*, 58–59.

44. *Digest* 3.4.1 and *Institutes* 1.2.1 in *Questiones statutorum* 44, *BIMA* 3:176–77.

45. Baldo, *Consilia* no. 372 no. 2 (Venice 1608–9), 5:91ra-b.

46. Ptolemy, *De regimine* 4.2, in Spiazzi, ed., no. 1035, 328.

47. Alberic of Rosate, *De statutis* 2.177 no. 5, *TUJ* 2:48vb-49ra.

48. Vegetius, *Epitoma rei militaris* 4 proem.

49. Giles of Rome, *De regimine* 2.3.7, 365.

50. Boncompagno, *Rhetorica novissima* 3.9, *BIMA* 2:285.

51. *Institutes* 1.1.1 and *Digest* 1.1.10.

52. *Code* 3.5.1.

53. Cino of Pistoia, *In digesti veteris libros commentaria* on *Code* 3.5 no. 2 (Frankfurt, 1578), 137va.

54. Baldo, *Tractatus de statutis* on *Arbitrium* no. 13, *TUJ* 2:89vb.

55. Alberic of Rosate, *Quaestiones statutorum* quaes. 4.32 nos. 4 and 5, *BIMA* 3:71rb.

56. *Code* 2.6–7 and 2.10 *lex unica*.

57. Azo, *Ad singulas leges XII librorum codicis commentaria* on *Code* 2.6.6 (Paris, 1577), 93.

58. Azo, *Brocardica aurea* Rubric 77 nos. 41 & 42 (Venice, 1566), 138.

59. Alberic of Rosate, *De statutis* 4.1.8, *TUJ* 2:66ra.

60. *Boncompagnus Boncompagni* 6, L. Rockinger, ed., *Briefsteller und Formelbücher* (Munich, 1863–64), 1:166.

61. Baldo, *Consilium* no. 335 (Venice, 1608–9), 3:91vb, and *Tractatus de statutis* on *Magnas*, *TUJ* 2:128va.

62. In G. Dahm, *Untersuchungen zur Verfassungs- und Strafrechtsgeschichte der italienischen Stadt* (Hamburg, 1941), 37–38.

63. John Bassiani, *Lectura on Institutes* 1.2.11 in E. Cortese, *La norma giuridica* (Milan, 1962–64), 2:413–14.

64. Alberic of Rosate, *De statutis* 1.3. 6–8, *TUJ* 2:2va.

65. Ptolemy, *De regimine* 3.20, Spiazzi, ed., a composite quotation from nos. 1019 and 1031, 322 and 326.

66. Brunetto Latini, *Li livres dou tresor* 3.73, F. J. Carmody, ed. (Berkeley, 1948), 392.

67. In G. Rossi, *Consilium sapientis judiciale* (Milan, 1958), 34n.

68. Alberic of Rosate, *De statutis* 1.4 nos. 1, 5, and 6, *TUJ* 2:2va.

69. Bonvesino della Riva, *De magnalibus urbis Mediolani* 5.19, in F. Novati, ed., *Bullettino dell'istituto storico italiano* 20 (1898): 147.

70. Odofredo called him "Postilla" in his *Lectura super digesto veteri* on *Digest* 3.1.10 (Lyon, 1550), 1:99va.

71. Boncompagno, *Cedrus* 6, Rockinger, ed., *Briefsteller und Formelbücher* 1:123.

72. Alberic of Rosate, *De statutis* 1.9, *TUJ* 2:5rb.

73. *Code* 5.59.5.2.

74. Alberic of Rosate, *De statutis* 1.4, *TUJ* 2:2va.

75. Odofredo, *Lectura super digesto veteri* on *Digest* 1.1.7 no. 2 (Lyon, 1550), 1:8ra.

76. Odofredo, *Lecturae in primam Codicis partem* on *Code* 1.14.8 no. 2 (Lyon, 1552), 39rb.

77. Alberic of Rosate, *De statutis* 1.135 no. 8, *TUJ* 2:19va.

78. *Oculus pastoralis*, D. Franceschi, ed., *Memorie dell'Accademia delle scienze di Torino*, ser. 4.11 (1966), 32–33 and 70, using Matthew 11:25 and *Code* 5.59. 5.2. The *Code's* well-known *Quod omnes tangit* means majority here, but see Ghent's "members" two paragraphs above.

79. Salimbene, *Cronica, MGH Scriptores* 32:156, using Ecclesiastes 1:15 and Wisdom of Solomon 6:26.

80. Marsiglio of Padua, *Defensor pacis* 1.13.8, ed. R. Scholz (Hanover, 1932–33), 1:76–77.

81. Ptolemy, *De regimine* 4.15, Spiazzi, ed., no. 1077, 344.

82. Ibid. 2.8.A, in Spiazzi, ed., no. 873, 285.

83. John of Viterbo, *De regimine civitatum* 11, *BIMA* 3:221a-b.

84. Salimbene, *Cronica, MGH Scriptores* 32:372–75 and Ecclesiastes 9:15.

85. In M. Sbriccoli, *L'interpretazione dello statuto* (Milan, 1969), 409.

86. Alberic of Rosate, *De statutis* 1.120 nos. 1, 7, and 10, *TUJ* 2:17va-b.

87. *Institutes* 1.2.2 and Acts 4:32–35.

88. In E. Cortese, *La norma giuridica* 1:101 n. 4, who says that this treatment of a theme found in Isidor of Seville (d. 636) was borrowed from Rufinus, an earlier canonist (1157–59): *Summa decretorum* 1.1, in H. Singer, ed. (Paderborn, 1902), 6–7.

89. Odofredo, *Lectura super digesto veteri Digest* 1.4.1 no. 6 (Lyon, 1550), 1:18ra.

90. Alberic of Rosate, *De statutis* 3.11 nos. 1–2, *TUJ* 2:60va. Brian Tierney finds the cited commonplace in the Ordinary Gloss (Paris, 1601) to *Decretum* Distinctio. 47.8.

91. Commines, *Mémoires* 7.18, Calmette, ed., 3:113–15.

CHAPTER 5

1. Philippe de Commines, *Mémoires* bk. 5 chap. 18.

2. Cf. M. Riedel, "Auf der Suche nach dem Bürgerbund," *Orientierungen für die Politik*, ed. P. M. Schmidhuber (Munich, 1984), 83–99.

3. H. G. Koenigsberger, "The Unity of the Church and the Reformation," in id., *Politicians and Virtuosi* (London and Ronceverte, 1986), 169–78; id., *Medieval Europe 400-1500* (London, 1987), chap. 2.

4. See B. Tierney, "Medieval Canon Law and Western Constitutionalism," *Catholic Historical Review* 52 (1966): 1–17.

5. G. C. Mor, "Modificazioni strutturali dell'assemblea nazionale longobardo nel secolo VIII," in *Album Helen Maud Cam* 2 (Louvain, 1961): 1–12.

6. T. N. Bisson, "The Military Origins of Medieval Representation," *AHR* 71 (1966): 1199–1218.

7. A. Marongiu, *Il Parlamento in Italia nel Medio Evo e nell' Età Moderna* (Milan, 1962), chaps. 1 and 2. Shortened English translation of this comprehensive study by S. J. Woolf, *Medieval Parliaments: A Comparative Study* (London, 1968).

8. Jean Sieur de Joinville, *The Life of Saint Louis*, trans. M. R. B. Shaw (Harmondsworth, Middlesex, 1963), 177.

9. Chronicle of Florence of Worcester, quoted by J. C. Holt, "The Prehistory of Parliament," in R. G. Davies and J. H. Denton, eds., *The English Parliament in the Middle Ages* (Manchester, 1981), 3. I am following Sir James Holt's arguments about the importance of information. Ibid., 4–5.

10. G. Post, "Roman Law and Early Representation in Spain and Italy, 1150–1250," *Speculum* 18 (1943): 228ff.

11. *Storia d'Italia*, ed. G. Einaudi, 1 (Torino, 1972): 416; D. Waley, *The Italian City-Republics* (New York, Toronto, 1969), 111–15.

12. D. Waley, *Siena and the Sienese in the Thirteenth Century* (Cambridge, 1991), 74–76.

13. Marongiu, *Il Parlamento*, 183–84, 192; H. G. Koenigsberger, "The Italian Parliaments from their Origins to the End of the 18th Century," *Politicians and Virtuosi*, 37–38.

14. J. Dhondt, "Les origines des états de Flandre," *Anciens Pays et Assemblées d'États* 1 (Louvain, 1950): 13–19; id., "Les assemblées d'états en Belgique avant 1795," *Anciens Pays et Assemblées d'États* 35 (Brussels, 1966): 238–41.

15. Dhondt, "Les origines," 20–21.

16. Holt, "Prehistory," 5–8.

17. The standard work on Magna Carta is J. C. Holt, *Magna Carta* (2d ed. Cambridge, 1992).

18. Cf. M. T. Clanchy, *England and its Rulers 1066–1272* (London, 1983), 241–60.

19. Ibid., 269–70.

20. Quoted in G. L. Harriss, "The Formation of Parliament, 1272–1377," in Davies and Denton, *The English Parliament*, 30.

21. A. Wolf, "Les deux Lorraines et l'origine des princes électeurs du Saint-Empire," *Francia* 11 (1983): 241–56; K. Bosl, "Repräsentierte and Repräsentierende," in K. Bosl and K. Möckl, eds., *Der moderne Parlamentarismus und seine Grundlagen in der ständischen Repräsentation* (Berlin, 1977), 102–7.

22. J. H. Denton, "The Clergy and Parliament in the Thirteenth and Fourteenth Centuries," in Davies and Denton, *The English Parliament*, 108. Convocation has survived into our own time, with three houses: bishops, clergy, and laity. In 1992 it decided the question of the ordination of women. Since the monarch is head of the Church of England, the positive decision on this point will require legislation by "the Queen in Parliament."

23. P. Blickle, *Landschaften im Alten Reich: Die staatlichen Funktionen des gemeinen Mannes in Oberdeutschland* (Munich, 1973), passim.

24. E. A. R. Brown, "Philip the Fair, *Plena Potestas*, and *Aide pur Fille Marier* of 1308," in *Representative Institutions in Theory and Practice. Studies Presented to the International Commission for the History of Representative and Parliamentary Institutions* 39 (1970): 1–17.

25. Ibid., 21–22.

26. R. Villers, "Réflexions sur les premiers états généraux de France au début du XIVe siècle," *Parliaments, Estates and Representation* 4.2 (1984): 93–97.

27. A. Marongiu, "Pre-parlement, Parlements, Etats, Assemblées d'États," *Revue historique de droit français et étranger* 57 (1979): 631–44.

28. G. L. Harriss, "War and the Emergence of the English Parliament, 1297–1360," *Journal of Modern History* 2 (1976): 45–47; id., "The Formation of Parliament," 40–52.

29. Harriss, "War and the Emergence of the English Parliament," 41.

30. J. B. Henneman, *Royal Taxation in Fourteenth Century France*

(Princeton, NJ, 1971); id., "The French Estates General and Reference Back to Local Constituents, 1343–1355," in *Representative Institutions in Theory and Practice*, 34–45.

31. E. B. Fryde, "English and French Fiscal Systems and the Officialdoms that They Created, c. 1270 and c. 1420," in id., *Studies in Medieval Trade and Finance* (London and Ronceverte, 1983), *passim*.

32. O. Hintze, "Typologie der ständischen Verfassungen des Abendlandes" (1930) and "Weltgeschichtliche Bedingungen der Repräsentivverfassung" (1931), in *Gesammelte Abhandlungen*, ed. G. Oestreich, 1 (Göttingen, 1962). English translation of the 1931 article, "The Preconditions of Representative Government in the Context of World History," in *The Historical Essays of Otto Hintze*, ed. and trans. F. Gilbert (New York and Oxford, 1975), 302–53. Cf. Koenigsberger, *Politicians and Virtuosi*, 6–8; id., *Medieval Europe*, chaps. 4 and 5.

33. The calculation is based on S. Peller, "Births and Deaths among Europe's Ruling Families since 1500," in *Population in History*, ed. E. V. Glass and D. E. C. Eversley (London, 1965), 87–100.

34. R. Van Bragt, "De Blijde Inkomst van de Hertogen van Brabant Johanna en Wenceslas (3 januari 1356)," *Anciens Pays et Assemblées d'États* 13 (1956); E. Lousse, "La Joyeuse Entrée de Brabant," *Schweizer Beiträge zur Allgemeinen Geschichte* 10 (1952): 139–62.

35. W. Näf, "Herrschaftsverträge und Lehre vom Herrschaftsvertrag," in *Die geschichtlichen Grundlagen der modernen Volksvertretung*, ed. H. Rausch, 1 (Darmstadt, 1980): 214–21. The document itself was in Flemish (Dutch) and was called *de blijde inkomst*.

36. R. Van Uytven and W. Blockmans, "Constitutions and their Application in the Netherlands during the Middle Ages," *Revue Belge de Philologie et d'Histoire* 47 (1969): 399–412; W. Blockmans, "Alternatives to Monarchical Centralisation: The Great Tradition of Revolt in Flanders and Brabant," in *Republiken und Republikanismus im Europa der Frühen Neuzeit*, ed. H. G. Koenigsberger and E. Müller-Luckner (Munich, 1988), 148–51.

37. W. Eberhard, *Monarchie und Widerstand: Zur ständischen Oppositionsbildung im Herrschaftssystem Ferdinands I in Böhmen* (Munich, 1985), 11–52.

38. F. L. Carsten, *Princes and Parliaments in Germany: From the Fifteenth to the Eighteenth Century* (Oxford, 1959), passim; K. Bosl, *Die Geschichte der Repräsentation in Bayern* (Munich, 1974), 45–120.

39. The documentation for these assemblies, mostly in German and Latin, is among the fullest we have for any medieval parliament: F. Thunert, ed., *Acten der Ständetage Preussens Königlichen Anteils (1466–79)* 1 (Danzig, 1896) and *Acta Stanów Prus Królewskich* 2–8 (1479–1526), eds. K. Górski, M. Biskup, and I. Janosz-Biskupowa (Toruń, 1955–93).

40. H. Schück, "Sweden's Early Parliamentary Institutions from the Thirteenth Century to 1611," in *The Riksdag; A History of the Swedish Parliament*, ed. M. F. Metcalf (Stockholm, 1987), 5–43.

41. G. Post, "Plena Potestas and Consent in Medieval Assemblies," *Tra-*

ditio 1 (1943): 355–408; J. G. Edwards, "The 'Plena Potestas' of English Parliamentary Representatives," in *Oxford Essays in Medieval History Presented to H. E. Salter* (Oxford, 1934), especially 151.

42. J. R. Maddicott, "Parliament and the Constituencies, 1272–1377," in Davies and Denton, *The English Parliament*, 83.

43. E. B. Fryde et al., *Handbook of British Chronology*, 3d ed. (London, 1986), 572.

44. A. L. Brown, "Parliament c. 1377–1422," in Davies and Denton, *The English Parliament*, 110.

45. H. G. Koenigsberger, *Estates and Revolutions* (Ithaca, NY, 1971), 52 n.127.

46. J. Russell Major, *Representative Government in Early Modern France* (New Haven, CT, 1980), 27.

47. Ibid., 32.

48. H. Helbig, "Königtum und Ständeversammlungen in Deutschland am Ende des Mittelalters," in Rausch, *Die geschichtlichen Grundlagen der modernen Volksvertretung* 2:99–116.

49. Koenigsberger, *Estates and Revolutions*, 80–93; id., *Politicians and Virtuosi*, 39–44.

50. Koenigsberger, *Estates and Revolution*, 22.

51. H. G. Koenigsberger, "The Beginnings of the States General of the Netherlands," *Parliaments, Estates and Representation* 8.2 (Dec. 1988): 101–14; id., *Monarchy and States General in the Netherlands in the Fifteenth and Sixteenth Centuries* (Cambridge, forthcoming), chap. 2; Henry VIII's speech and a critical discussion in G. R. Elton, ed., *The Tudor Constitution* (Cambridge, 1960), 230, 257 n.1, 270.

52. W. P. Blockmans, ed., *Le privilège général et les privilèges régionaux de Marie de Bourgogne pour les Pays-Bas* (Kortrijk—Heule, 1985), *passim*, but see especially the chapters by Blockmans and M.-A. Arnould; H. G. Koenigsberger, "Fürst und Generalstaaten: Maximilian I in den Niederlanden (1477–1493), *Historische Zeitschrift* 242.3 (1986): 557–79.

53. Olivier de la Marche, *Mémoires*, ed. H. Beaune and J. Arbaumont, 1 (Paris, 1883): 163.

54. Sir John Fortescue, "De Natura Legis Naturae," *The Works of Sir John Fortescue*, ed. Lord Clermont (London, 1869), 1:16.

55. Sir John Fortescue, *The Governance of England*, ed. C. Plummer (Oxford, 1885), 114–15.

56. The adjective *political*, deriving from Aristotle's *Politics*, was used all over Europe at the time, to indicate a limited or mixed regime. I find these two terms rather vague; and the German term *Ständestaat* is a modern construct and does not fit England very well.

CHAPTER 6

1. The primary meaning of *franchise* was freedom in a general sense: see the examples in *Anglo-Norman Dictionary*, ed. W. Rothwell and others, 6

fascicles (London, 1977–92), 316; J. H. Baker, *Manual of Law French*, 2d ed. (London, 1990), 120. But the specific legal sense soon overtook it.

2. The best text of the charter (with English translation) is in J. Holt, *Magna Carta*, 2d ed. (Cambridge, 1992), 448–73. Clause 39 was incorporated in c. 29 of the Magna Carta of 1225, which was treated as the first parliamentary statute, and is usually so cited.

3. 2 Edw.3, c. 8; 5 Edw.3, c. 9; 14 Edw.3, stat. 1, c. 14; 25 Edw.3, stat. 5, c. 4; 28 Edw.3, c. 3; 42 Edw.3, c. 3 ("no man shall be put to answer without presentment . . . or due process of law and original writ, according to the old law of the land"). Most of these statutes were directed principally against the extraordinary jurisdiction of the king's council.

4. *Bracton on the Laws and Customs of England*, ed. S. E. Thorne, 4 vols. (Cambridge, MA, 1968–77), 2:33, 110, 306 (fols. 5b, 34, 107). This book was compiled between the 1220s and 1240s; it is associated with the judge Henry de Bracton (d. 1268), but probably not written by him.

5. W. S. Holdsworth, *History of English Law*, 16 vols. (London, 1922–66), 3:464–66 considers that this was a "very new principle" when it was first clearly laid down in 1483 (Y.B. Trin. 1 Edw.5, pl. 13). It is found in 1457 in the form that the king cannot be a disseisor: Y.B. Trin. 35 Hen.6, fol. 61, pl. 1, per Moyle J.; cf. Danvers J., contra, at fol. 62.

6. *Bracton* 2:412 (fol. 146).

7. Note also, just after the end of our period, the development of *mandamus* and *certiorari* to challenge government decisions: E. G. Henderson, *Foundations of English Administrative Law* (Cambridge, MA, 1963).

8. For a fuller account of what follows, with suggestions for further reading, see J. H. Baker, *An Introduction to English Legal History*, 3d ed. (London, 1990), pt. 1.

9. In the case of highways, the fourteenth-century judges went so far as to say that one could not lawfully acquire a right to take toll-thorough save in special cases where the claimant had duties of repair, because it would oppress the people: *R. v. Chanceux* (1329), *Eyre of Northamptonshire*, ed. D. W. Sutherland, 1 (Selden Soc. vol. 97 [1983]): 61–67; *R. v. Walmersford* (1329), ibid., 122–23; *R. v. Abbot of Peterborough* (1329), ibid., 135; *Anon.* (1346), Fitz. Abr., *Toll*, pl. 3; *Case of the Bailiffs of Richmond* (1348), Y.B. 22 Edw.3, *Liber Assisarum*, pl. 58. Here we see something like a notion of freedom of passage.

10. See P. Brand, *Origins of the English Legal Profession* (Oxford, 1992).

11. For the origins of the collegiate system, see J. H. Baker, *The Third University of England: the Inns of Court and the Common-Law Tradition* (Selden Soc. lecture, London, 1990).

12. The principal Tudor statute touching on villeins was actually in favor of lords: 19 Hen.7, c. 15 (against feoffments of land to the use of villeins).

13. The statute of 1547 was never enforced, and was repealed in 1549: see C. S. L. Davies, "Slavery and Protector Somerset: the Vagrancy Act of 1547," *Economic History Review*, 2d ser., 19 (1966): 533–49. It is thought to have resulted from the influence of intellectuals influenced by Roman law.

14. Villein tenure has a different history, and by the early thirteenth century free men could hold lands in villeinage without any effect on their status: below.

15. What follows is based on Baker, *Introduction to English Legal History*, 3d ed., 532–37, and the reading there.

16. For contemporary legal confusion, see the anonymous annotator of *Britton*, ed. F. M. Nichols, 2 vols. (London, 1865), 1:195 n.(q), who taught that serfdom was something less servile than villeinage; and *The Mirror of Justices*, ed. W. J. Whittaker (Selden Soc. vol.7 [1893]), 77, 79, 165.

17. See F. Pollock and F. W. Maitland, *The History of English Law before the Reign of Edward I*, 2 vols. (Cambridge, 1895), 1:412–13, 430–31; R. H. Hilton, "Freedom and Villeinage in England," *Past and Present* 31 (1965): 3–19; C. Dyer, *Lords and Peasants in a Changing Society* (Cambridge, 1980), 103–5; J. Hatcher, "English Serfdom and Villeinage," *Past and Present* 90 (1981): 1–39.

18. *Glanvill*, ed. G. D. G. Hall (London, 1965), 57–58. This treatise was written at the end of the 1180s.

19. *Bracton* 2:300 (fol. 105b); 3:91, 109 (fols. 193, 200b). For the history of this maxim, borrowed from Civil and Canon law, see P. R. Hyams, *King, Lords and Peasants in Medieval England* (Oxford, 1980), chap. 12. It was frequently stated in the fourteenth century: e.g., Y.B. 19 Edw.2 (1678 ed.), fol. 652; Y.B. 20 Edw.3 (Rolls Ser.), pt. 2, 468 ("judgment was given in favour of liberty that the defendant was a free man . . . and the reason is the favour shown to liberty"); Y.B. Hil. 43 Edw.3, fol. 4, pl. 8 ("there is a great argument in favour of liberty"); Rot. Parl. 2:193a ("so is the law more favourable to the freedom of man's body than to put him in servitude [*servage*]"). (Quotations translated from French.)

20. Hyams, *King, Lords and Peasants*, 206.

21. See the later medieval authorities collected by Coke in Co. Inst. 2:45.

22. *Bracton* 3:91, 102 (fols. 193, 197b).

23. *Britton* 1:199 ("pur favour de fraunchise").

24. *Bracton* 2:34, 397, 438 (fols. 86, 141, 155b). Trespass would lie against third parties: ibid., 438. If the lord acted through a subordinate, the latter could be sued in trespass, but could plead a justification. However, it was held in 1359 that there had to be specific authority: a servant could not justify imprisoning a villein in the stocks by command of the lord except for cause (such as disobedience or rebellion): Pas. 33 Edw.3, Fitz. Abr., *Trespas*, pl. 253. Cf. Y.B. Trin. 5 Edw.2 (Selden Soc. vol. 33), 230, pl. 32; Mich. 6 Edw.2, 151, pl. 40; Selden Soc. 100:xxxix–xl.

25. *Bracton* 3:107 cites *Montacute v. Bestenovere* (1219), *Bracton's Note Book*, ed. F. W. Maitland (London, 1887), 2:62–63, no. 70, CRR 8:114; *Bestenovere v. Montacute* (1220), *Bracton's Note Book* 2:79–80, no. 88. See also *Britton* 1:196; *Fleta*, ed. H. G. Richardson and G. O. Sayles, 3 vols. (Selden Soc. vols. 72, 89, and 99 [1955–84]), 3:24. In reality, the distinction remained a fine one even in the fourteenth century, and we still hear of tenure "in bondage" at that period. From the later fourteenth century, vil-

lein tenure was increasingly known as "copyhold," a term which carried no hint of servile status.

26. *Bracton* 2:30–31 (fol. 5); 3:92, 94 (fols. 193, 194b). See, in accord with this, *Britton* 1:197; *Fleta* 1:13–14.

27. E.g., *Mareschal v. Prior of Ely* (1320), Y. B. Trin. 13 Edw.2 (1678 ed.), fol. 408; *FitzThomas v. Lechebere* (1326), Y.B. Hil. 19 Edw.2 (1678 ed.), fols. 651, 652; *Anon.* (1364), Y.B. Mich. 38 Edw.3, fol. 34.

28. The rule that a lord should not deprive a villein of his means of support ("wainage") was stated in Magna Carta, c. 14; *Bracton* 2:34 (fol. 6). It seems implicit in the pleading in *Oldbury v. Abbot of Hales* (1292), Selden Soc. 30:24, at 26, that a lord could not put a villein in close custody in irons, or pour water over him. On unjust treatment, see *Select Cases of Trespass in the King's Courts*, ed. M. S. Arnold, 2 vols. (Selden Soc. vols. 100, 103 [1984–87]), 1:xxxix-xl. See also *Mareschal v. Prior of Ely* (as to battery).

29. For the precarious existence of the fourteenth-century villein, see E. B. Fryde and N. Fryde, "Lords, Serfs and Serfdom," in J. Thirsk, ed., *The Agrarian History of England and Wales* 3 (Cambridge, 1991): 760–68.

30. *Bracton* 2:300 (fol. 105b): "I know of no other reason except that this is a concession made in favour of liberty, which is priceless" (apparently an allusion to Justinian's *Digest*, 50.17.106). The rule is also stated in *Glanvill*, ed. Hall, 54; *Britton* 1:202 ("en favour de fraunchise"); *Fleta* 2:173–74 ("propter favorem libertatis").

31. *FitzThomas v. Lechebere* (1326), Y.B. Hil. 19 Edw.2 (1678 ed.), fol.652, per Aldborough sjt. (translated from the French).

32. *Thorne v. Peche* (1310), Y.B. Pas. 3 Edw.2 (Selden Soc. vol. 20), 94, pl.15. The effect was the same if the plaintiff abandoned his suit: *Novae Narrationes*, ed. S. F. C. Milsom (Selden Soc. vol. 80 [1963]), clxvii.

33. *Fleta* 1:172 ("in odium servitutis"). Cf. *Brevia Placitata*, ed. G. J. Turner (Selden Soc. vol. 66 [1947]), 91, 214; *Registrum Omnium Brevium* (1634), fol. 87.

34. For the workings of the action in its heyday, see *Novae Narrationes*, intro., cxliii–cxlvii; P. R. Hyams, "The Action of Naifty in the Early Common Law," *Law Quarterly Review* 90 (1974): 326–50; id., "The Proof of Villein Status in the Common Law," *EHR* 89 (1974): 721–49.

35. John Jenour's book of entries provides precedents of naifty actions in 1425 and 1446 in which the alleged villein was found free: LC, Phillipps MS. 26752, fol. 135rv.

36. *Bracton* 2:85 (fol. 24b); 3:90, 91, 94 (fols. 192b, 193, 194b); *Britton* 1:198, 200; *Fleta* 3:24, 77. For later authorities, see Holdsworth, *History of English Law* 3:492 n.7; *The Reports of Sir John Spelman*, ed. J. H. Baker, 2 vols. (Selden Soc. vols. 93, 94 [1977–78]), 2:188–89; S. E. Thorne and J. H. Baker, eds., *Readings and Moots at the Inns of Court in the Fifteenth Century* 2 (Selden Soc. vol. 105 [1990]): 152. The principal instances were a grant to the villein, a covenant with him, or an action against him.

37. *Glanvill*, ed. Hall, 58; *Bracton* 3:85, 103, 104 (fols. 190b, 198); *Britton* 1:200, 209; *Fleta* 1:173. Glanvill said the villein must become a mem-

ber of the gild. Cf. *Paris v. Page* (1308), Y.B. Pas. 3 Edw.2 (Selden Soc. vol. 17), 11, pl. 1 (where an alderman of London raised the city privilege unsuccessfully because he had left the city).

38. *Bracton* 2:31 (fol. 5); 3:85, 103, 104 (fols. 190b, 198); *Britton* 1:200, 207; *Fleta* 1:172. For later authorities, see *Spelman's Reports* 2 (Selden Soc. vol. 94): intro., 189; but cf. *Glanvill*, ed. Hall, 58; *The Notebook of Sir John Port*, ed. J. H. Baker (Selden Soc. vol. 102 [1986]), 103; *Readings and Moots in the Inns of Court*, lxiv, 134; *St German's Doctor and Student*, ed. T. F. T. Plucknett and J. L. Barton (Selden Soc. vol. 91 [1974]), 272–73. These cases were problematic, because (i) there was the possibility of deraignment or degradation, and (ii) it was arguable that the villein status continued, even though the lord's rights over the body were diminished.

39. The two cases of enfranchisement by marriage were: (i) where a female villein married a free man, and (ii) where a male villein married his seigneress (a case first noted in *Britton* 1:198).

40. There is an anonymous fifteenth-century precedent, probably from Edward IV's time, in John Jenour's books of entries, LC, Phillipps MS. 26752, fol. 54rv (writ of entry in the *quibus*, in which the plaintiff not only is found free but recovers land against the putative lord as well). For other fifteenth-century precedents, see Robert Maycote's book of entries, LC, Phillipps MS. 9071, fols. 116–17; Anon. entries, BL, Add. MS. 37488, fols. 284v-285 (entry in *quibus*); BL, Harleian MS. 5157, fols. 226–27 (two cases of trespass, temp. Edw. 4); Robert Maycote's entries, LC, Phillipps MS 9071, fol. 116 (ca. 1500); W. Rastell, *A Collection of Entries* (London, 1566), fols. 681v-682r.

41. See Richard Broke's reading in Gray's Inn (ca. 1505), Selden Soc. 93:225. This was a general principle, not confined to villein cases: *Doctor and Student*, ed. Plucknett and Barton, 187–88. Only the ecclesiastical courts could certify bastardy in respect of a living person. But the alleged villein could obtain jury trial by alleging the bastardy in an ancestor: Mich. 14, Edw.4, BL, Harleian MS. 5157, fol. 353v, margin (dictum of Bryan and Littleton).

42. See, e.g., *Symonds v. Nichols* (1557), Dyer's unpublished reports (Selden Soc. 109:19, forthcoming), where it is explicitly stated that a villein was allowed by the tenant for life of a manor to bring a writ of entry with the intention of effecting a manumission; the defendant himself pleaded bastardy (as a bar to the writ of entry), and it was certified; the question (not answered) was whether the certificate barred the lord in reversion.

43. For such proceedings, see *Spelman's Reports* 2 (Selden Soc. vol. 94): intro., 191; D. MacCulloch, "Bondmen under the Tudors," in *Law and Government under the Tudors*, ed. C. Cross et al. (Cambridge, 1988), 91–108, at 101–7.

44. For a documented instance of collusion in 1523, when a villein paid his lord £20 before a Common Pleas action, see MacCulloch, "Bondmen under the Tudors," 104. Legal opinion differed as to whether a manumission by a tenant in tail or for life was absolute: see Holdsworth, *History of English Law* 3:504 n.3. Cf. n.38, above.

45. See R. H. Hilton, *The Decline of Serfdom in Medieval England* (London, 1969). However, it was by no means extinct: for an estimate of the extent of villeinage in the sixteenth century, see MacCulloch, "Bondmen under the Tudors," 92–94.

46. John Hody, Chief Justice of the King's Bench 1440–41, was the son of a villein: H. Maxwell Lyte, "The Hody Family," *Notes and Queries for Somerset and Dorset* 18 (Sherborne, 1925): 127–28. For an alderman of London seized as a villein in 1308, see Selden Soc. 17:11.

47. See *Bracton* 3:102 (fol. 197b). After 1540, the lapse of forty years would bar a claim as a result of the Limitation Act (32 Hen.8, c. 2): *Butler v. Crouch* (1567), Dyer 266b.

48. *De Laudibus Legum Angliae*, ed. S. B. Chrimes (Cambridge, 1942), 104 (translated above from the Latin). He argued that the common law was more favorable than the Civil law, in that the children of a free man are always free, and that a person once manumitted is always free.

49. *The boke of surveyeng* (London, ca. 1526), fol. 24v. Cf. *Doctor and Student*, ed. Plucknett and Barton, 213–14, where the Doctor asks whether the law of villeinage could stand with conscience, and the Student replies that it has been accepted for so long that it was too late to doubt it.

50. HLS, MS. 47, fol.59 (translated from French). Another reader from this period even argued that "free man" in Magna Carta included any villein other than the king's: BL, Harleian MS. 4990, fol. 161.

51. This had a long history in villein claims: see Selden Soc. 62:311–12; *Adam's Case* (1304), Y.B. 32 & 33 Edw.1 (Rolls Ser.), 55; Y.B. 33–35 Edw.1 (Rolls Ser.), 297; *Paris v. Pope* (1308), Y.B. Pas. 1 & 2 Edw.2 (Selden Soc. vol. 17), 11, pl. 1; *Herneswell v. Prior of Ely* (1318), Selden Soc. 61:292; *Okeover v. Okeover* (1318), Selden Soc. 100:36 (£70 recovered); *Marlingford v. Bery* (1329), Selden Soc. 100:32 (200 marks recovered); Y.B. Trin. 39 Edw.3, fol. 16; Mich. 40 Edw.3, fol. 36, pl. 6.

52. For examples from the early Tudor period, see *Spelman's Reports* 2 (Selden Soc. vol. 94): intro., 190.

53. An example from John Lucas's book of entries is *Shank v. Abbess of B[arking]* (1466), in which the plaintiff recovered £40 damages: LC, Phillipps MS. 11910, fol. 51v-53r, citing [KB 27/821], Trin. 6 Edw.4, m. 99. (In this context, replevin—*replegiare*—meant to restore liberty on receipt of surety to await the outcome of a trial.) Cf. Anon. entries, BL, Harleian MS. 5157, fol. 266.

54. *Thomson v. Lee* (1498), PRO, plea rolls of the King's Bench, KB 27/949, m. 33; *Port's Notebook*, 6; *Spelman's Reports* 2 (Selden Soc. vol. 94), intro., 190 n.9. Followed in the Common Pleas in *Lordwyn v. Thymbylby* (1510), Jenour's book of entries, LC, Phillipps MS. 26752, fols. 291v–292r, citing [CP 40/991], Pas. 1 & 2 Hen.8, m. 406 (in false imprisonment; writ of *non molestando* for alleged villein, on surety of two esquires). Cf., to the contrary, Y.B. Mich. 40 Edw.3, fol. 36, pl. 6 (in false imprisonment).

55. *Doctor and Student*, ed. Plucknett and Barton, 330; examples in *Spelman's Reports* 2 (Selden Soc. vol. 94): intro., 191.

56. *Salle v. Paston* (1498), KB 27/949, m. 95; Y.B. Mich. 14 Hen.7, fol. 5, pl. 12. This opened up the possibility of collusive actions. A probable example is *Annot v. Gryffyn* (1520), PRO, plea rolls of the Common Pleas, CP 40/1030, m. 647, where trespass was brought against a number of villagers (including a wheelwright and a yeoman), who pleaded the title of the lord, and the jury found the plaintiff free.

57. In 1499 £120 was recovered against a peer: *Revet v. Earl of Suffolk* (1499), KB 27/951, m. 66. In 1501 £200 was recovered: *Sheperd v. Worthe* (1501), KB 27/960, m. 52. And £340 was recovered for lying in wait in 1509: *Smyth v. Prior of St Neot's* (1509), CP 40/989, m. 419.

58. I. S. Leadam, "The Last Days of Bondage in England," *Law Quarterly Review* 9 (1893): 348–65; A. Savine, "Bondmen under the Tudors," *Trans. Royal Hist. Soc.*, 2d ser., 17 (1902): 235–89.

59. Dr. Daniel Dunn, fellow of All Soul's College, dean of Arches, manumitted in 1576: MacCulloch, "Bondmen under the Tudors," 92.

60. *Journals of the House of Lords* 1:94a, 99a.

61. I.e. who were not attached to a manor.

62. The last villein claim in the courts seems to have been *Pigg v. Caley* (1618), Noy 27.

63. This is challenged by MacCulloch, "Bondmen under the Tudors," 93.

64. Sir Thomas Smith, *De Republica Anglorum* (1583), 107–15, reprinted in ed. by M. Dewar (Cambridge, 1982), 135–42. Smith added that apprenticeship was an acceptable and necessary kind of bondage; as also was the compellability of servants to serve under the legislation of Edward III.

65. William Harrison, *A Description of England* [c. 1577], prefaced to *Holinshed's Chronicles* 1 (London, 1809): 275; reprinted with modern orthography in *The Description of England by William Harrison*, ed. G. Edelen (Ithaca, NY, 1968), 118.

66. There are references to the sale of prisoners in the sixteenth century: see, e.g., Mich. 36 Hen.8, Bro. Abr., *Propertie*, pl. 38; *Acts of the Privy Council*.

67. Sir Thomas Egerton's extracts from the lost Star Chamber register, Huntington Lib., MS. EL 2652, fol. 14r. Another example of a sentence to the galleys by the Star Chamber, for forgery, occurs in 1593: *Acts of the Privy Council 1592–93*, J. R. Dasent ed. (London, 1901), 486. The practice also began in the same century of sending convicted felons to the galleys instead of the gallows: E. K. Adair, "English Galleys in the Sixteenth Century," *EHR* 35 (1920): 497–512, at 510–11. Harrison, who proudly asserted the absence of bondage in England, was all in favor of introducing slavery as a punishment for theft: *The Description of England*, ed. Edelen, 190.

68. See Francis Hargrave's argument in *Ex parte Somerset* (1772), *A Complete Collection of State Trials*, ed. T. B. Howell, 20 (London, 1816): 1, at cols. 35–49.

69. Arnold, *Select Cases of Trespass*, intro., 1:xxxiii–xxxiv.

70. The Common Pleas held in *Anon.* (1577), BL, Hargrave MS. 4, fol. 15,

that "imprisonment is a restraint of liberty, which is not by words without an actual deed" (translated from French).

71. It was held in *Whele's Case* (1483), Y.B. Hil. 22 Edw.4, fol. 45, pl. 9, that a servant who has the key to a prison, if he knows someone is inside, is chargeable with the imprisonment, and that imprisonment even for one hour is actionable. See also Co. Inst. 2:52–55, 186–87, 482.

72. Only the LC MS (next note) departs from this tradition in asserting that "merchants and other men should be adjudged according to this statute by their peers." There was some warrant for this wider interpretation in Y.B. 30 & 31 Edw.1, 531 (jury of knights ordered). But that case was not printed until 1863 and probably had no influence. Cf. *R. v. Thomas* (1554), Dyer 99b (which said the usage had always been contrary and that an esquire could be tried by merchants).

73. Readings on c. 29 have not survived in large numbers. The following have been used: CUL, MS. Ii.5.43, fol. 40v; Bod.L., MS. Rawlinson C. 294, fols. 14v-15r; Derbyshire Record Office, MS. D3287, unfol.; LC, MS. 139, 34–35; HLS, MS. 13, 441–43. Still in the same tradition is Richard Blackwall's reading in Clement's Inn (Lent 1544), CUL, Add. MS. 8871, fols. 16v-17r. There are no known lectures on the Edw.3 statutes of due process.

74. CUL, MS. Ii.5.43, fol. 40v; Derbyshire Record Office, MS. D3287, unfol. (Both texts refer to a controversy on the question.) The issue of writs against infringers of Magna Carta was warranted by the Statute of Marlborough 1267, c. 5, though this provision bore little or no fruit in medieval times.

75. See *Spelman's Reports* 2 (Selden Soc. vol. 94): intro., 72–73. The earliest precedent so far discovered is from 1501. Actions were expressly founded either on Magna Carta or on one of the subsequent statutes of due process.

76. E.g. *Speccote v. Fry, Vyseke v. Fry* (1511), KB 27/1000, mm. 37, 38 (arising from a suit before Richard Empson, king's councilor).

77. Coke cites, "As taking one example for many, and that in a powerfull, and a late time, Pasch. 2 H.8. *coram rege* rot. 538, against the prior of S. Oswin in Northumberland.": Co. Inst. 2:55. The reference is mistaken, since this was in the Common Pleas. There are two actions against the prior of Tynemouth (St. Oswin's), founded on Magna Carta, in CP 40/991, m. 529 (by Younghusband) and m. 538 (by Brandelyng). They were brought for suing before the Council by writ of privy seal for taking a boat, and compelling the plaintiffs to appear before Atwater, dean of the chapel royal, and Wolsey, king's almoner; the cases end with an imparlance.

78. For the early history of bail, see E. de Haas, *Antiquities of Bail* (New York, 1940). The law was clarified by the Statute of Westminster I (1275), c. 15; 23 Hen.6, c. 9. In Tudor times, the power to bail in criminal cases passed from the sheriff to the justices of the peace. See Holdsworth, *History of English Law* 4:525–28. ("Irreplevisable" meant not susceptible of replevin: as to which, see above, n.53.)

79. The inns of court readings in HLS, MS. 13, 442, and LC, MS. 139, 35, say false imprisonment is appropriate. BL, Harleian MS. 1336, fols. 7v-9r (reading on Statute of Westminster 1, c. 15) says it must be an action on the case, because the original arrest was lawful.

80. *Oldbury v. Abbot of Hales* (1292), Selden Soc. 30:24, at 26 (pouring water on villein in irons); *Warwick v. Lorimer* (Eyre of London, 1321), Selden Soc. 86:108 (against jailer of Newgate, for putting plaintiff in lowest part of jail to extort money; verdict for defendant); ibid. 176 (similar action against sheriff); *Anon.* (1333), cited in E. Coke, *Twelfth Part of the Reports* (London, 1658), 127.

81. Cf. *Bracton* 3:410–12 (fols. 145b-46).

82. Appeals: C. Flower, *Introduction to the Curia Regis Rolls, 1199–1230* (Selden Soc. vol. 62 [1943]), 309–12. Writs: Milsom, intro. to *Novae Narrationes*, ccxi. The appeal was subject to the obvious disadvantage that the defendant might wage battle: *Britton* 1:123 ("for avoiding the perilous risk of battle, it is better to proceed by our writs of trespass"). It did not survive.

83. Milsom, intro. to *Novae Narrationes*, ccxi; id., *Studies in the History of the Common Law* (London, 1985), 15–16. Arnold, *Select Cases of Trespass* 1:35–61, has many examples. There is an example of an action against a constable in 1222, in CRR 10:324.

84. *Handlo v. Earl of Arundel* (1319), Selden Soc. 81:130 (no judgment).

85. *Warner v. Hudson* (1495), CP 40/934, m. 327 (heresy); Y.B. Hil. 10 Hen.7, fol. 17, pl. 17; cited in Dyer's manuscript reports; Co. Inst. 2:55; 3:42.

86. Y.B. Mich. 21 Edw.4, fol. 67, pl. 48.

87. Y.B. Hil. 22 Edw.4, fol. 43, pl. 4: Cf. 27 Edw.3, Lib. Ass. fol. 27, where the countess of Warwick claimed a franchise to imprison in her castle for three days and three nights before delivering to king's jail; the case was left undetermined.

88. *Gylys v. Walterkyn* (1486), Y.B. Hil. 1 Hen.7, fol. 6, pl. 3; CP 40/893, m. 244.

89. *Bradshawe v. Brooke* (1579), BL, Add. MS. 35941, fol. 56v.

90. *Simmons v. Sweete* (1587), Cro. Eliz.78 (false imprisonment against the mayor of Barnstaple). Cf. the habeas corpus cases of *Ex parte Marshall* (1572), below, n.122; *Ex parte Dean* (1599), Cro. Eliz.689.

91. *Clarke v. Gape* (1596), 5 Co. Rep. 64. Lord Chancellor Ellesmere (in 1616) criticized Coke for reporting this: "Observations upon Cookes Reportes," printed in L. A. Knafla, *Law and Politics in Jacobean England* (Cambridge, 1977), 297–318, at 309. Cf. *Kenrick v. Mayor of Northampton* (1573), Dalis. Rep. 103.

92. However, the writ *de homine replegiando* could not be used in respect of a taking by order of the king or his justices; this exception was mentioned in the writ itself, and seems to be based on the Statute of Westminster 1, c. 15.

93. There are virtually no records before Tudor times.

94. Huntington Lib., MS. EL 2652, unfol.

95. *Spelman's Reports* 1 (Selden Soc. vol. 93): 184; 2:351; Baker, *Introduction to English Legal History*, 3d ed., 293.

96. BL, Harleian MS. 2143, fol. 33 (citing lost Register, Pas. 19 Eliz., fol. 286). Cf. Huntington Lib., MS. EL 2768, fol. 45 (two justices of the peace fined "for wrongefull emprisonment of the quenes subjectes," c. 1580). The year-book authorities on constables support the decision: Y.B. Mich. 22 Edw.4, fol. 35, pl. 16. (As to stocks, see also Y.B. Mich. 49 Hen.6, fol. 18, pl. 21.) It was conceded, however, that a constable could imprison in his own house in case of necessity, where it was dangerous to move the prisoner: Y.B. Hil. 35 Hen.6, fol. 44, pl. 6 (arrest during Cade's rebellion); Pas. 8 Edw.4, fol. 8, pl. 20.

97. It is a command to the recipient to "have the body" of a named person before a named court on a specific day.

98. For its history in general, see M. Cohen, "Habeas Corpus cum Causa—the Emergence of the Modern Writ," *Canadian Bar Review* 16 (1940): 10–42, 172–97; R. S. Walker, *The Constitutional and Legal History of Habeas Corpus* (Stillwater, OK, 1960); W. F. Duker, *A Constitutional History of Habeas Corpus* (Westport, CT, 1980).

99. For an early example, see Selden Soc. 1:67 (1214).

100. Chancery: Y.B. 14 Edw.3 (Rolls Ser.), 204 (1341). Common Pleas: Y.B. 24 Edw.3, fol. 25; 48 Edw.3, fol. 22; Stat. 2 Hen.5, stat. 1, c. 2.

101. King's Bench, Trin. 29 Edw.1, m. 57; Mich. 33 & 34 Edw.1, m. 101; *Placitorum Abbreviatio* (London, 1811), 243, 257; *Hale's Prerogatives of the King*, ed. D. E. C. Yale (Selden Soc. vol. 92 [1976]), 207–8. Hale noted, "Whether it were a habeas corpus or a *homine replegiando* appears not."

102. Selden Soc. 82:72.

103. *Kayser's Case* (1465), KB 27/818, m. 143d; cited in Dyer's unpublished reports (Selden Soc. vol. 109:108) and in Co. Inst. 2:55; 3:42. The Elizabethan cases cited in 2:55, from Dyer's unpublished reports, were also cases of privilege.

104. The wording of this writ required the body of N. to be produced, "together with the day and the cause of his detention, to undergo and receive (*ad subjiciendum et recipiendum*) whatever our court should order": see the form in Baker, *Introduction to English Legal History*, 3d ed., 626–27.

105. For this reaction, see *Spelman's Reports* 2 (Selden Soc. vol. 94): intro., 70–74.

106. PRO, controlment rolls of the King's Bench, KB 29/150, m. 34 (Mich. 1518); Selden Soc. 109:77.

107. KB 29/150, m. 18 (Trin. 1518): "committed by command of the lord king alone, and this is the cause and no other"; recommitted to the Tower. For the feud see J. A. Guy, *The Cardinal's Court* (Hassocks, 1977), 76–78. Sheffield died in the Tower the same year.

108. Co. Inst. 2:55 refers to an indictment for imprisonment contrary to Magna Carta; but the reference given there is wrong.

109. KB 29/179, m. 13 (Pas. 1546).

110. KB 29/179, m. 4d (convicted as accessories to William Hynde of Southwark); *Letters and Papers of Henry VIII* 21:pt. 1, 571, no. 1166(18) (pardon for Heyth, 7 June 1546).

111. *Ex parte John Hynde* (1576–77), in *The Fourth Part of the Reports... Collected by... William Leonard* (London, 1675), 21; BL, Hargrave MS. 373, fol. 226r, and other MS reports; Selden Soc. 109:lxxx; *Spelman's Reports* 2 (Selden Soc. vol. 94): intro., 74.

112. E.g., *R. v. Smyth* (1534), *Spelman's Reports* 1:52, 169 (clerk attaint removed from ecclesiastical prison to establish effect of pardon).

113. What follows is derived from the intro. to *Cases from the Lost Notebooks of Sir James Dyer* (Selden Soc. vol. 109), lxxvi–lxxxiii. The principal new sources are MS law reports, and the controlment rolls of the King's Bench (KB 29), which were used by Selden and others in the 1620s but have still not been exhaustively studied. The printed sources are noticed in Holdsworth, *History of English Law* 5:495–97; 6:33–34; 9:112–14.

114. He found a precedent in John Jenour's book of entries, now in LC, Phillipps MS. 26752. The precedent is on fol. 23v, and probably dates from Edward IV's time.

115. Saunders' reports, BL, Hargrave MS. 9, fol. 22v.

116. Printed in State Tr. 3: col. 109–26.

117. They include the cases of Aprice (1518) and Hogges (1546), noted above.

118. *Ex parte John Lamburne* (1565), KB 29/199, m. 31; cited by Sir Edward Coke, *Twelfth Part of the Reports*, 54. The outcome is not there recorded.

119. *Ex parte Edward Mytton* (1565), Selden Soc. 109:lxxix, 107. Mytton was subsequently indicted at common law, but died in 1568 before trial. For later struggles between the common-law courts and the ecclesiastical commissioners, see R. G. Usher, *The Rise and Fall of the High Commission* (Oxford, 1913). One of the principal issues was that of compulsory self-incrimination by the oath *ex officio*.

120. *Ex parte John Hynde* (1576–77), above, n. 111. Note also the judges' resolution of 1591 in Holdsworth, *History of English Law* 5:495–97.

121. *Ex parte Edmunde Newport* (1557), KB 29/191, m. 45d (committed to Tower "by command of the queen's councillors"; bailed); *Ex parte Thomas Lawrence* (1567), KB 29/202, m. 35d (committed to sheriffs of London "by order of the queen's council"; bailed); *Ex parte Robert Constable* (1567), KB 29/202, m. 68 (committed to the Tower "by command of the queen's Privy Council"; bailed).

122. *Ex parte Marshall* (1572), BL, Hargrave MS. 8, fol. 163rv (mayor of Exeter not allowed to imprison a non-freeman for failing to find surety for good behavior). The matter was pressed by the court to arbitration, "pur

avoider le graund disobedience del cittizens al magistrate que poet ensuer si judgment serra done." Cf. the similar cases of *Ex parte Starkey* (1589), 4 Leo.61; *Ex parte Dean* (1599), Cro. Eliz.689.

123. *Searche's Case* (1587), printed in *Reports and Cases of Law . . . Collected by . . . William Leonard* (London, 1658), 70.

124. Henderson, *Foundations of English Administrative Law,* 95, traces this practice to 1589.

125. See Elizabethan precedents collected by Sir Edward Coke, *Twelfth Part of the Reports,* 54.

126. *Ex parte Humfreys* (1572), BL, Add. MS. 35941, fol. 30r; Dal. 81, pl. 22. Cf. *Stepneth v. Lloyd* (1598), Selden Soc. 12:xxxix; Cro. Eliz.647; Co. Inst. 4:97; A. K. R. Kiralfy, *Source Book of English Law* (London, 1957), 301.

127. *Rector of Edington's Case* (1441), Y.B. Pas. 19 Hen.6, fol. 63, pl. 1 (translated from French).

CHAPTER 7

1. Cf. Orlando Patterson, *Freedom in the Making of Western Culture* (New York, 1991), x.

2. Walter Ullmann, *Principles of Government and Politics in the Middle Ages* (London, 1961); *The Individual and Society in the Middle Ages* (Baltimore, 1966). For a critique of Ullmann for his identification with medieval culture generally of what I call "traditional culture," see Francis Oakley, "Celestial Hierarchies Revisited: Walter Ullmann's Vision of Medieval Politics," *Past and Present* 60 (August, 1973): 3–48.

3. Quoted by Charles Stinger, *Humanism and the Church Fathers: Ambrogio Traversari (1386–1439) and Christian Antiquity in the Italian Renaissance* (Albany, 1977), 295. On this point Traversari was not a typical Renaissance humanist.

4. For the general point see Gordon Leff, *The Dissolution of the Medieval Outlook: An Essay on the Intellectual and Spiritual Change in the Fourteenth Century* (New York, 1976). On nominalism and the relation between "modernity" and the loss of confidence in reason, see also Hans Blumenberg, *The Legitimacy of the Modern Age,* Robert M. Wallace, trans. (Cambridge, MA, 1983), 137–38, 152–54, 532–33.

5. For this movement, with suggestions for additional reading, see William J. Bouwsma, *The Culture of Renaissance Humanism* (Washington, 1973); and Albert J. Rabil, ed., *Renaissance Humanism: Foundations, Forms, and Legacy,* 3 vols. (Philadelphia, 1988).

6. The classic work on the origins of Renaissance humanism is Paul Oskar Kristeller, *Renaissance Thought: The Classic, Scholastic, and Humanistic Strains* (New York, 1955).

7. Quoted by Quentin Skinner, *The Foundations of Modern Political Thought* (Cambridge, 1978), 1:3. This work is now fundamental for the subject of the present chapter.

8. Quoted by John H. Mundy, *Europe in the High Middle Ages, 1150–1309* (London, 1973), 449.

9. *Villani's Chronicle*, Rose E. Selfe, trans. (London, 1906), 312–13.

10. A. J. Carlyle, *Political Liberty: A History of the Conception in the Middle Ages and Modern Times* (London, 1963), 12–13.

11. Hans Baron, "The Evolution of Petrarch's Thought," *Bibliothèque d'Humanisme et Renaissance* 24 (1962): 28. David Thompson, ed., *Petrarch: An Anthology* (New York, 1971), 65–81, translates Petrarch's exhortation to Cola.

12. On the general point, see Peter Riesenberg, *Citizenship in the Western Tradition, Plato to Rousseau* (Chapel Hill, 1992), 87–199.

13. I quote in the translation of Laura F. Banfield and Harvey C. Mansfield, Jr. (Princeton, NJ, 1988), 95; Machiavelli was, of course, employing the categories of Aristotle's *Politics*.

14. This development is traced by Eugenio Garin, "I cancellieri umanisti della Repubblica Fiorentina da Coluccio Salutati a Bartolomeo Scala," *Rivista Storica Italiana* 71 (1959): 185–208.

15. The best study of Salutati is Ronald G. Witt, *Hercules at the Crossroads: The Life, Works, and Thought of Coluccio Salutati* (Durham, NC, 1983). For Salutati's humanism, see also Charles Trinkaus, *"In our Image and Likeness": Humanity and Divinity in Italian Humanist Thought* (Chicago, 1970), 1:51–102.

16. For Bruni see above all Hans Baron, *The Crisis of the Early Italian Renaissance: Civic Humanism and Republican Liberty in an Age of Classicism and Tyranny* (Princeton, NJ, 1955); I cite from the one-volume edition of 1966. On Bruni's history, see Donald J. Wilcox, *The Development of Florentine Humanist Historiography in the Fifteenth Century* (Cambridge, MA, 1969), 32–129. Bruni's major writings are available in the English translations of Gordon Griffiths, James Hankins, and David Thompson, *The Humanism of Leonardo Bruni: Selected Texts* (Binghamton, NY, 1987).

17. As translated from Bruni, *Historiae Florentini Populi*, by Renée Neu Watkins, in *Humanism and Liberty: Writings on Freedom from Fifteenth-Century Florence* (Columbia, SC, 1978), 46, 62.

18. Quoted by Baron, *Crisis*, 419; Baron discusses this oration at length, 412–21.

19. See n. 14 above.

20. Gene A. Brucker, *Renaissance Florence* (New York, 1962), 234–37, the best general discussion of the "Baron thesis" and its critics. Peter Burke, *Culture and Society in Renaissance Italy* (London, 1972), 268–70, generally agrees with Brucker.

21. Skinner, *Foundations* 1:27–35.

22. J. G. A. Pocock, *The Machiavellian Moment: Florentine Political Thought and the Atlantic Republican Tradition* (Princeton, NJ, 1975), 74–75, 157, 320, 329. Pocock also emphasizes the Aristotelian element in civic humanism.

23. Quoted from Bruni, *History of the Florentine People* by Wilcox, *Florentine Humanist Historiography*, 72–73.

24. Francesco Patrizi, quoted by Skinner, *Foundations* 1:175.

25. As recently as November of 1992, the "Baron thesis" stimulated a lively discussion at the Villa I Tatti, the Harvard Center for Italian Renaissance Studies in Florence. Baron's views were exposed to a vigorous attack by James Hankins, to which William J. Connell made an equally vigorous response.

26. For Savonarola as republican, see Donald Weinstein, *Savonarola and Florence: Prophecy and Patriotism in the Renaissance* (Princeton, NJ, 1970).

27. Sebastian de Grazia, *Machiavelli in Hell* (Princeton, NJ, 1989), 31, 289. In spite of its lurid title, this is probably now the best study of Machiavelli's writings and thought.

28. Cf. de Grazia, *Machiavelli*, 76–79.

29. Machiavelli, *Discourses* 1.38. I cite in the translation of Leslie J. Walker, *Machiavelli: The Discourses* (London, 1970).

30. Machiavelli, *Florentine Histories*, 186.

31. Machiavelli, *The Art of War*, in *Machiavelli, the Chief Works and Others*, trans. Allan Gilbert (Durham, NC, 1965), 2:622.

32. In the last chapter of *The Prince*, entitled "Exhortation to Liberate Italy from the Barbarians." I use the edition of Peter Bondanella and Mark Musa in *The Portable Machiavelli* (New York, 1979).

33. Carlo Morandi, "Il concetto della politica di equilibrio nell'Europa moderna," *Archivio di Storico Italiano* 98 (1940): 3–19.

34. Felix Gilbert, *Machiavelli and Guicciardini: Politics and History in Sixteenth-Century Florence* (Princeton, NJ, 1965), 113–14.

35. Machiavelli, *Discourses* 2.2.

36. De Grazia emphasizes this point, *Machiavelli*, 176–93.

37. Machiavelli, *Discourses* 1.16

38. Machiavelli, *Florentine Histories*, 122.

39. Cf. de Grazia, *Machiavelli*, 180.

40. Machiavelli, *Discourses* 2.2, 3.12, 1.19, 1.59, 1.58.

41. Ibid. 1.11.

42. Ibid. 1.59.

43. Cf. ibid. 1.2.

44. Cf. Skinner, *Foundations* 2:114–34, 174–78.

45. Machiavelli, *Discourses* 1.10; id., *Florentine Histories*, 95.

46. For Venetian republicanism see, in general, William J. Bouwsma, *Venice and the Defense of Republican Liberty: Renaissance Values in the Age of the Counter-Reformation* (Berkeley, 1968). On its reverberations in the rest of Europe see also Bouwsma, "Venice and the Political Education of Europe," in J. R. Hale, ed., *Renaissance Venice* (London, 1973), 445–66.

47. Giorgio Spini, "Riforma italiana e mediazioni ginevrine nella Nuova Inghilterra puritana," in id., *Ginevra e l'Italia* (Florence, 1959), 454–55.

48. Pocock, *Machiavellian Moment*, traces its importance for England and America.

49. Baldassare Castiglione, *The Book of the Courtier*, trans. Charles Singleton (New York, 1959), 303–6.

50. Giovanni Botero, *Relationi universali* (Venice, 1640), 764; this work was first published in 1591.

51. Among recent studies that deal generally with the importance of cities for the Reformation are Bernd Moeller, *Imperial Cities and the Reformation*, trans. H. C. Erik Midelfort and Mark U. Edwards, Jr. (Philadelphia, 1972); Steven E. Ozment, *The Reformation in the Cities: The Appeal of Protestantism to Sixteenth-Century Germany and Switzerland* (New Haven, CT, 1975); Thomas A. Brady, Jr., *Turning Swiss: Cities and Empire, 1450, 1550* (Cambridge, 1985); Peter Blickle, *Communal Reformation: The Quest for Salvation in Sixteenth-Century Germany*, trans. Thomas Dunlap (New York, 1992). There are also many studies of the Reformation in particular cities.

52. Machiavelli, *Discourses* 1.55; id., *The Prince*, chap. 10.

53. Moeller, *Imperial Cities and the Reformation*, 53.

54. On the contrast between the northern and the more secular Italian conception of community, see Thomas A. Brady, Jr., *Ruling Class, Regime and Reformation at Strasbourg* (Leiden, 1978), 17.

55. Robert C. Walton, *Zwingli's Theocracy* (Toronto, 1967), 4–16, is illuminating on this.

56. Quoted by Brady, *Turning Swiss*, 27.

57. J. Toussaert, *Le sentiment religieux en Flandre à la fin du Moyen Âge* (Paris, 1963), 67.

58. Martin Luther, "Preface to the Epistle of St. Paul to the Romans," in John Dillenberger, ed., *Martin Luther: Selections from His Writings* (New York, 1961), 30.

59. Quoted by Gerhard Ebeling, *Luther: An Introduction to His Thought*, trans. R. A. Wilson (Philadelphia, 1970), 169.

60. Philip Melanchthon, *Loci communes theologici*, trans. Lowell J. Satre, in *Melanchthon and Bucer*, ed. Wilhelm Pauck [Library of Christian Classics, 19] (London, 1969), 123.

61. On this possibility, see M. A. Screech, *Rabelais* (Ithaca, NY, 1979), 88–94.

62. In François Rabelais, *Gargantua and Pantagruel*, bk. 1, chaps. 52–58. I quote in the translation of Donald Frame, *The Complete Works of Francois Rabelais* (Berkeley, 1991).

63. Martin Luther, *Secular Authority: To What Extent It Should be Obeyed*, in Dillenberger, *Selections*, 392.

64. Quoted by Ebeling, *Luther*, 170.

65. Cf. George Forell, *Faith Active in Love: An Investigation of the Principles Underlying Luther's Social Ethics* (New York, 1954), 84–85, 123.

66. Melanchthon, *Loci communes*, 126.

67. Heiko Oberman, "Headwaters of the Reformation: Initia Lutheri—Initia Reformationis," in Heiko Oberman, ed., *Luther and the Dawn of the Modern Era: Papers for the Fourth International Congress for Luther Research* (Leiden, 1974), 46–47.

68. Martin Luther, *The Freedom of a Christian*, in Dillenberger, *Selections*, 73.

69. Peter Blickle, *The Revolution of 1525: The German Peasants' War from a New Perspective*, Thomas A. Brady, Jr., and H. C. Erik Midelfort, trans. (Baltimore, 1981).

70. Brady, *Turning Swiss*, 187.

71. Ibid., 30–42.

72. Quoted by Moeller, *Imperial Cities*, 78.

73. Walton, *Zwingli's Theocracy*; Moeller, *Imperial Cities*, 75–78.

74. Brady, *Strasbourg*, 245, n. 36, is illuminating on the tension in Bucer's thought between republicanism and respect for political authority.

75. Moeller, *Imperial Cities*, 81; see also Miriam Usher Chrisman, *Strasbourg and the Reform: A Study in the Process of Change* (New Haven, CT, 1967), and Lorna Jane Abray, *The People's Reformation: Magistrates, Clergy, and Commons in Strasbourg, 1500–1598* (Ithaca, NY, 1985).

76. I quote in the English translation of Lowell J. Satre, in *Melanchthon and Bucer*.

77. On Calvin generally, see William J. Bouwsma, *John Calvin: A Sixteenth-Century Portrait* (New York, 1988); for his attitudes toward liberty, chaps. 12–13.

78. Cf. Michael Walzer, *The Revolution of the Saints: A Study in the Origins of Radical Politics* (Cambridge, MA, 1965), 1–113.

79. John Calvin, *Institutes of the Christian Religion*, IV, xx, 8. I quote in the translation of Ford Lewis Battles (London, 1960).

80. Comm. Is. 3:4, quoted in Bouwsma, *Calvin*, 195.

81. For much of this Calvin was indebted to Bucer; cf. Hans Baron, "Calvinist Republicanism and its Historical Roots," *Church History* 8 (1939): 30–41.

82. Calvin's social and political views were stated most coherently in the final chapter of the *Institutes*. See also Harro Höpfl, *The Christian Polity of John Calvin* (Cambridge, 1982).

83. Cf. Bouwsma, *Calvin*, 136–38; see also Jane Dempsey Douglass, *Women, Freedom, and Calvin* (Philadelphia, 1985).

84. See, in general, J. Wayne Baker, *Heinrich Bullinger and the Covenant: The Other Reformed Tradition* (Athens, OH, 1980); and Charles S. McCoy and J. Wayne Baker, *Fountainhead of Federalism: Heinrich Bullinger and the Covenantal Tradition* (Louisville, KY, 1991), which includes English translations of Bullinger's major writings on the covenant idea.

85. I follow for this contrast the classic discussion of Ernst Troeltsch, *The Social Teaching of the Christian Churches*, Olive Wyon, trans. (New York, 1960). See also George Huntston William, *The Radical Reformation*

(London, 1957), and Michael Mullett, *Radical Religious Movements in Early Modern Europe* (London, 1980).

86. This position is most fully developed in Erasmus, *De libero arbitrio* [*On the Freedom of the Will*], trans. E. Gordon Rupp, in *Luther and Erasmus* [Library of Christian Classics, 17] (London, 1969), 35–97.

87. I quote from the edition of George M. Logan and Robert M. Adams (Cambridge, 1989), 97.

88. I quote from *The Essential Thomas More*, James J. Greene and John P. Dolan, eds. (New York, 1967), 208.

89. Available in an English translation by Roland Bainton, *Concerning Heretics by Castellio* (New York, 1935). On the general subject, Joseph Lecler, *Histoire de la tolérance au siècle de la Réforme* (Paris, 1955).

90. Cf. Perez Zagorin, *Ways of Lying: Dissimulation, Persecution, and Conformity in Early Modern Europe* (Cambridge, MA, 1990).

91. For this development, see Hugh R. Trevor-Roper, "The General Crisis of the Seventeenth Century," *Past and Present* 16 (1959): 31–64.

CHAPTER 8

1. G. W. F. Hegel, *The Philosophy of History*, trans. J. Sibree (New York, 1944), 104.

2. *Digest* 1.4.1.

3. Bernard du Haillan, *De l'Estat et succez des affaires de France* (Paris, 1619 [1580]), f. 135v: "Ce nom specieux de liberté, qui est un breuvage qui empoisonne les entendemens des hommes"; and f. 142r: "la plus belle, le plus douce et la plus trompereuse chose du monde."

4. Thomas Cooper, *Thesaurus linguae Romanae et Brittanicae* (London, 1565).

5. See especially Gerd Tellenbach, *Church, State, and Christian Society at the Time of the Investiture Contest*, trans. R. Bennett (Oxford, 1940); and Victor Martin, *Les Origines du gallicanisme* (Paris, 1939).

6. "Les libertez de l'eglise gallican," in (among other places) Jean du Tillet, *Recueil des roys de France* (Paris, 1607), 283–95 (3d pagination); English trans. by Henry C. Vedder in Crozier Theological Seminary, Historical Leaflet no. 7 (1911).

7. Emile Benveniste, *Le Vocabulaire des institutions indo-européennes* (Paris, 1969), 2:9–17; Fritz Kern, *Kingship and Law in the Middle Ages*, trans. S. B. Chrimes (Oxford, 1956), 12; more generally Walter Ullmann, *Principles of Government and Politics in the Middle Ages* (London, 1961), and Bernard Guenée, *States and Rulers in Later Medieval Europe*, trans. J. Vale (Oxford, 1985).

8. See above all Ernst H. Kantorowicz, *The King's Two Bodies* (Princeton, NJ, 1957).

9. See Denys Hay, *Europe: The Emergence of an Idea* (Edinburgh, 1968), and Marie Tanner, *The Last Descendant of Aeneas: The Hapsburgs and the*

Mythic Image of the Emperor (New Haven, CT, 1993); also Robert Folz, *Le Souvenir et la légende de Charlemagne dans l'empire germanique medi-éval* (Paris, 1950); Robert W. Hanning, *The Vision of History in Early Britain* (New York, 1966); José Antonio Maravall, *El Concepto de España en la edad media* (Madrid, 1964); and Emil Hölzle, *Die Idee einer altgermanischen Freiheit vor Montesquieu* (Berlin, 1925). But see also Teofilo F. Ruiz, "Un-sacred Monarchy: the Kings of Castile in the Middle Ages," in Sean Wilentz, ed., *Rites of Power* (Philadelphia, 1985), 109–44.

10. Marc Bloch, *The Royal Touch: Sacred Monarchy and Scrofula in England and France*, trans. J. E. Anderson (London, 1973).

11. Yves Bercé, *Le Roi caché* (Paris, 1990).

12. See especially Ralph E. Giesey, *The Royal Funeral Ceremony in Renaissance France* (Geneva, 1960); Lawrence M. Bryant, *The King and the City in the Parisian Royal Entry Ceremony* (Geneva, 1986); Richard A. Jackson, *Vive le Roi: A History of the French Coronation from Charles V to Charles X* (Chapel Hill, NC, 1984); Percy Ernst Schramm, *A History of the English Coronation*, trans. L. Legg (Oxford, 1937); Jacques Krynen, *Idéal du prince et pouvoir royal à la fin du moyen age* (Paris, 1981); and Jean Céard, "Les Visages de la royauté en France, à la Renaissance," *Les Monarchies*, ed. E. Le Roi Ladurie (Paris, 1986), 73–89.

13. Sidney Anglo, *Spectacle, Pageantry, and Early Tudor Policy* (Oxford, 1969), 30.

14. Jackson, *Vive le Roi*, 178. And in general see Colette Beaune, *The Birth of Ideology: Myths and Symbols in Late-Medieval France*, trans. S. Huston (Berkeley, 1991).

15. "Models of Rulership in French Royal Ceremonial," in Wilentz, *Rites of Power*, 53.

16. Charles Dumoulin, *La premiere partie du Traicté de l'origine, pro-grez, et excellence du royaume et monarchie des françois, et couronne de France*, in id., *Opera omnia* (Paris, 1681), 2:1034.

17. Bernard du Haillan, *De la fortune et virtue de la France* (Paris, 1570); and cf. *Histoire generale des roys de France* (Paris, 1615).

18. Guillaume Budé, *Annotationes in . . . quatuor et viginti pandec-tarum libros* (Paris, 1535), 67–68, commenting on *Digest* 1.3.31 ("princeps legibus solutus est").

19. Sir Thomas Smith, *De Republica Anglorum*, ed. Mary Dewar (Cambridge, 1982), 56 (bk. 2, chap. 9).

20. J. H. Elliott, *Imperial Spain, 1469–1716* (New York, 1963), 144.

21. See above, n.2. But the *lex regia* could also be used on behalf of resistance theory: see below at n.76, and Joseph Canning, *The Political Thought of Baldus de Ubaldis* (Cambridge, 1987), 91.

22. See especially Percy Ernst Schramm, *Der König von Frankreich* (Weimar, 1939); Maravall, *El Concepto de España*, 432ff; and Sergio Mochi Onory, *Fonti canonistiche dell'idea moderna del stato* (Milan, 1951).

23. *Siete Partidas* 2.1.5, on which see Gaines Post, *Studies in Medieval Legal Thought* (Princeton, NJ, 1964), 483.

24. Charles Merbury, *A briefe discourse of Royall Monarchie* (London, 1581), 40; and cf. Claude d'Albon, *De la maiesté royall* (Lyon, 1575).

25. Erasmus, *The Education of a Christian Prince*, trans. Lester K. Born (New York, 1936), 174, 175.

26. See, e.g., John of Paris, *On Royal and Papal Power*, trans. Arthur P. Monahan (New York, 1974), 7; and J. Beneyto Perez, *Textos políticos de la baja edad media* (Madrid, 1945).

27. Otto Gierke, *Political Theories of the Middle Ages*, trans. F. W. Maitland (Cambridge, 1900), 9.

28. Claude de Seyssel, *The Monarchy of France*, trans. J. H. Hexter and ed. D. R. Kelley (New Haven, CT, 1981), 48.

29. Sarah Hanley, "Engendering the State: Family Formation and State Building in Early Modern France," *French Historical Studies* 16 (1989): 4–27, and "Toward a Reassessment of Political Culture through Gender Concerns in Early Modern France" (unpubl. MS); and see R. E. Giesey, *Juristic Basis of Dynastic Right to the French Throne* (Philadelphia, 1961), a new edition of which is forthcoming.

30. Sir John Fortescue, *The Governance of England*, ed. Christopher Plummer (Oxford, 1885), 111, and *De laudibus legum Anglie*, ed. and trans. S. B. Chrimes (Cambridge, 1949), 24–29; cf. John of Paris, in Fortescue, *Laudibus*, 88, and Aristotle, *Politics* 1252a15, distinguishing between a royal (*basilikon*) and a civil (*politicon*) ruler.

31. Merbury, *Briefe discourse*, 44.

32. Seyssel, *The Monarchy of France*, 49–57; and in general see Jean Barbey, *Le Roi et son gouvernement en France de Clovis à Louis XIV* (Paris, 1992).

33. R. E. Giesey, *If Not, Not: The Oath of the Aragonese and the Legendary Laws of Sobrarbe* (Princeton, NJ, 1968).

34. R. B. Merriman, *The Rise of the Spanish Empire* 3 (New York, 1918): 441.

35. See below, section 5.

36. See J. H. Elliott, "A Europe of Composite Monarchies," *Past and Present* 137 (1992): 48–71.

37. Garrett Mattingly, *Renaissance Diplomacy* (Boston, 1955), and J. H. Hexter, *The Vision of Politics on the Eve of the Reformation* (New York, 1973).

38. Kantorowicz, *The King's Two Bodies*, 189.

39. Ferdinand Lot and Robert Fawtier, *Histoire des institutions françaises au moyen age* 2 (Paris, 1958): 40–42.

40. Charles de Grassaille, *Regalium Franciae libri duo*, followed by Jean Ferrault, *Tractatus . . . iura seu privilegia* (Paris, 1545), and Barthélmy de Chasseneux, *Catalogue gloriae mundi* (Geneva), 417ff; and see Julian Franklin, *Jean Bodin and the Rise of Absolutist Theory* (Cambridge, 1973), 6–7.

41. George Whetstone, *The English Mirror* (London, 1586), 201.

42. Francis Yates, *Astraea: The Imperial Theme in the Sixteenth Century* (London, 1975).

43. Maravall, *El Concepto de España*, and *Carlos V y la pensamiento político del rinascimiento* (Madrid, 1960); and more recently, J. N. Hillgarth, *The Spanish Kingdoms* (Oxford, 1978), especially 2:197.

44. Cited by Fernand Braudel, *The Mediterranean and the Mediterranean World in the Age of Philip II*, trans. Siân Reynolds (New York, 1972), 2:674.

45. G. R. Elton's controversial *Tudor Revolution in Government* (Cambridge, 1953) opened up this question.

46. Seyssel, *Monarchy of France*, 37.

47. *The Tudor Constitution*, ed. G. R. Elton (Cambridge, 1982), 84.

48. A useful summary (with diagram) in J. H. M. Salmon, *Society in Crisis: France in the Sixteenth Century* (London, 1975), 66-70; see also the authoritative works by Roger Doucet and Gaston Zeller of the same title and date—*Les Institutions de la France au XVIe siècle* (Paris, 1948).

49. A nice summary (with diagram) in Elliott, *Spanish Empire*, 167-78.

50. Fritz Hartung, *Deutsche Verfassungsgeschichte* (Stuttgart, 1950), 13ff.

51. Elliott, *Spanish Empire*, 245.

52. *Digest* 48.4.1.1 ("Lex Iulia maiestatis").

53. Cited by J. H. Mariéjol, *The Spain of Ferdinand and Isabella*, trans. B. Keen (New Brunswick, NJ, 1961), 116-17. See also Jean Du Belloy, *De l'autorité du roi et crimes de lèse-majesté qui se commettent par ligues, désignations de successeur et libelles escrites contre la persaonne et dignité des prince* (s.l., 1587).

54. Kern, *Kingship and Law*, 81ff.

55. *The Statesman's Book of John of Salisbury*, trans. John Dickinson (New York, 1927), 335 (*Policraticus* 8:17).

56. Jean Barbey, *La Fonction royale: Essence et legitimité d'après les Tractatus de Jean de Vermeille* (Paris, 1983), 185.

57. Giesey, *If Not, Not*, 22off.

58. Merriman, *Rise of the Spanish Empire* 3:76; and see John Lynch, *Spain under the Habsburgs* (Oxford, 1965), 1:39ff.

59. P. S. Lewis, *Late Medieval France* (London, 1968), 91.

60. *Francogallia*, ed. R. E. Giesey and trans. J. H. M. Salmon (Cambridge, 1972), 442/43.

61. Lewis, *Late Medieval France*, 89.

62. Claude Gousté, *Traicté de la puissance et authorité des roys* (s.l., 1561).

63. More detailed discussion, with bibliography, in D. R. Kelley, *The Beginning of Ideology: Consciousness and Society in the French Reformation* (Cambridge, 1981); Martin Van Gelderen, *The Political Thought of the Dutch Revolt* (Cambridge, 1992); Perez Zagorin, *Rebels and Rulers* (Cambridge, 1982); *The Cambridge History of Political Thought 1450-1700*, ed. J. H. Burns (Cambridge, 1991), 193-253, the chapters by Robert M. Kingdon and J. H. M. Salmon on Calvinist and Catholic resistance theory.

64. Martin Luther, "Disputation Concerning the Right to Resist the Emperor" (8-9 May 1539), in *Christianity and Revolution*, ed. Lowell H. Zuck

(Philadelphia, 1975), 134; and in general see Quentin Skinner, *The Foundations of Modern Political Thought* 2 (Cambridge, 1978), 194.

65. Confession of Magdeburg, in Zuck, *Christianity*, 137.

66. *Du Droit des magistrats*, ed. Robert M. Kingdon (Geneva, 1971), trans. in part in Julian H. Franklin, *Constitutionalism and Resistance in the Sixteenth Century* (New York, 1969).

67. John Calvin, *Institutes of the Christian Religion*, bk. 4, chap. 20.

68. See D. R. Kelley, "Ideas of Resistance before Elizabeth," in *The Historical Renaissance*, ed. Heather Dubrow and Richard Strier (Chicago, 1988), 48–76.

69. Kelley, *The Beginning of Ideology*, 253ff.

70. See Yves-Marie Bercé, *Revolt and Revolution in Early Modern Europe*, trans. Joseph Bergin (New York, 1987); and Gerald Strauss, *Law, Resistance, and the State: The Opposition to Roman Law in Reformation Germany* (Princeton, NJ, 1986), 104.

71. Texts collected in Michael G. Baylor, ed., *The Radical Reformation* (Cambridge, 1991), with bibliography. See also Gerald Strauss, *Law, Resistance, and the State: The Opposition to Roman Law in Reformation Germany* (Princeton, NJ, 1986); Peter Blickle, *The Revolution of 1525* (Baltimore, 1981); R. Scribner and G. Benecke, eds., *The German Peasant War of 1525—New Viewpoints* (London, 1979); and G. H. Williams, *The Radical Reformation* (Kirksville, MO, 1992; 3d ed.).

72. Michael Gaismair, "Territorial Constitution for Tyrol," 1526 in Baylor, *The Radical Reformation*, 255.

73. Baylor, *The Radical Reformation*, 101–29.

74. Ibid., 118, 123.

75. F. Engels, *The Peasant War in Germany* [1850] (Moscow, 1956).

76. Letter to Bullinger (12 Sept. 1559), in Beza, *Correspondance* 3, ed. H. Aubert, H. Meylan, and A. Dufour (Geneva, 1963): 20.

77. See D. R. Kelley, *François Hotman: A Revolutionary's Ordeal* (Princeton, NJ, 1973), 105–25.

78. *Remonstrance de monseigneur le prince de Condé . . . sur le jugement de rebellion* (s.l., 1562); and see also Robert M. Kingdon, *Geneva and the Coming of the Wars of Religion 1555–1563* (Geneva, 1956), 107–8.

79. Herbert H. Rowen, ed., *The Low Countries in Early Modern Times* (New York, 1972), 38.

80. Ibid., 42.

81. Franklin, *Constitutionalism and Resistance*, 135.

82. *Figure des medailles de la conspiration des Rebelles . . . le 24 jour d'aoust 1572* (Paris, 1572), copy in Bibliothèque de l'Arsenal.

83. Letter to Gualter, 10 Jan. 1573, in Zurich, Zentralbibliothek, F. 39, f. 49r. In general see Robert M. Kingdon, *Myths about the St. Bartholomew's Day Massacres, 1572–1576* (Cambridge, MA, 1988).

84. Zuck, *Christianity*, 180, 183.

85. Beza, *Droit des magistrats*, 38 (Franklin, *Constitutionalism*, 119).

86. Hotman, *Francogallia*, 306–7 (Franklin, ibid. 70).

87. Ibid., 332–33 (Franklin, ibid. 73); and cf. Bodin, *Les Six livres de la Republique* (Paris, 1583), 211 ("Des vrayes marques de souveraineté").

88. *Vindiciae contra tyrannos*, Traduction française de 1581, ed. A. Jouanna et al. (Geneva, 1979), 25 (Franklin, ibid. 143).

89. Franklin Ford, *Political Murder: From Tyrannicide to Terrorism* (Cambridge, MA, 1985); and see Roland Mousnier, *The Assassination of Henry IV*, trans. Joan Spencer (New York, 1973).

90. *The French Religious Wars in English Political Thought* (Oxford, 1959), 163.

91. The classic works are John Neville Figgis, *The Divine Right of Kings* (Cambridge, 1896), and *Political Thought from Gerson to Grotius: 1414–1625* (Cambridge, 1907).

92. *The Political Works of James I*, ed. C. H. McIlwain (Cambridge, MA, 1918).

93. See Roger Merriman, *Six Contemporaneous Revolutions* (Oxford, 1938).

94. *Le Dialogue de Calvin et de Luther revenus du nouveau monde* (s.l., 1622), a pamphlet of 15 pp. (Protestant Library in Paris).

95. Note that this entirely violates Luther's teaching on the question of free will.

CHAPTER 9

1. For republics see *Republiken und Republikanismus in Europa der Frühen Neuzeit*, ed. H. G. Koenigsberger and B. Oestreich (Munich, 1988); H. G. Koenigsberger, "Republicanism, Monarchism and Liberty," in *Royal and Republican Sovereignty in Early Modern Europe*, ed. G. Gibbs, R. Oresko, and H. M. Scott (Cambridge, 1995); H. G. Koenigsberger, *Early Modern Europe 1500–1789* (London, 1987), chaps. 1 and 2.

2. B. Whitelock, *A Journal of the Swedish Embassy*, ed. C. Morton, 1 (London, 1772): 320.

3. H. G. Koenigsberger, *Estates and Revolutions* (Ithaca, NY, 1971), 73–79.

4. J. Fortescue, *The Governance of England*, ed. C. Plummer (Oxford, 1885), 115.

5. *Cortes de los Antiguos Reinos de Leon y Castilla* 4 (Madrid, 1882): 285ff.

6. A. Maravall, *Las Comunidades de Castilla* (Madrid, 1963); S. Haliczer, *The Comuneros of Castile* (Madison, 1981); Koenigsberger, *Estates and Revolutions*, 181–90.

7. J. I. Fortea Pérez, "The Cortes of Castile and Philip II's Fiscal Policy," *Parliaments, Estates and Representation* 11. pt. 2 (Dec. 1991): 117–38; C. Jago, "Philip II and the Cortes of Castile: The Case of the Cortes of 1576," *Past and Present* 109 (Nov. 1985): 24–43.

8. J. D. Tracy, *Holland under Habsburg Rule 1506–1566* (Berkeley, 1990), 53–54; Koenigsberger, *Estates and Revolutions*, 166–75.

9. J. Gilissen, *Le régime représentatif avant 1790 en Belgique* (Brussels, 1952), 117.

10. H. G. Koenigsberger, *Politicians and Virtuosi* (London, 1986), 46.

11. I. A. A. Thompson, "Crown and Cortes in Castile 1590–1655," *Parliaments, Estates and Representation* 2.1 (June 1982): 29–45; id., "The End of the Cortes of Castile," ibid. 4.2 (Dec. 1984): 125–33.

12. Koenigsberger, *Politicians and Virtuosi*, 46.

13. J. H. Elliott, *The Revolt of the Catalans: A Study in the Decline of Spain* (Cambridge, 1963); id., *Spain and its World* (New Haven, CT, 1989), 71–91.

14. Popular memory of the Hussite raids survived into the twentieth century. In the 1920s my godmother, who came from a small village in Silesia, used to speak of the Hussite terror as if she had lived through it herself.

15. H. Kaminsky, *A History of the Hussite Revolution* (Berkeley, 1967), especially 296–309; D. Hay, *Europe in the Fourteenth and Fifteenth Centuries* (London, 1966), chap. 9.

16. W. Eberhard, "The Political System and the Intellectual Traditions of the Bohemian Ständestaat from the Thirteenth to the Sixteenth Centuries," in *Crown, Church and Estates: Central European Politics in the Sixteenth and Seventeenth Centuries*, ed. R. J. W. Evans and T. V. Thomas (London, 1991), 23–47; K. J. Dillon, *King and Estates in the Bohemian Lands, 1526–1564* (Brussels, 1976), 110–40.

17. V. Press, "Vom 'Ständestaat' zum Absolutismus: 50 Thesen zur Entwicklung des Ständewesens in Deutschland," in *Ständetum und Staatsbildung in Brandenburg-Preussen*, ed. P. Baumgart (Berlin, New York, 1983), 324; Cf. Koenigsberger, *Early Modern Europe*, chaps. 2 and 3.

18. See chap. 8.

19. K. Bosl, *Die Geschichte Repräsentation in Bayern* (Munich, 1974), chap. 4, especially 141–57.

20. Apart from general histories of the Thirty Years' War see the following from Evans and Thomas, *Crown, Church and Estates*: G. Heiss, "Princes, Jesuits and the Origins of the Counter-reformation in the Habsburg Lands," 92–109; K. Benda, "Habsburg Absolutism and the Resistance of the Hungarian Estates in the Sixteenth and Seventeenth Centuries," 123–28; J. Pánek, "The Religious Question and the Political System of Bohemia before and after the Battle of the White Mountain," 129–48; W. Schulze, "Estates and the Problem of Resistance in Theory and Practice in the Sixteenth and Seventeenth Centuries," 158–75; G. Schramm, "Armed Conflict in East and Central Europe: Protestant Noble Opposition and Catholic Royalist Factions, 1604–20," 176–95; I. Auerbach, "The Bohemian Opposition, Poland-Lithuania and the Outbreak of the Thirty Years War," 196–225.

21. G. Oestreich, *Neostoicism and the early modern state*, ed. B. Oestreich and H. G. Koenigsberger, trans. D. McLintock (Cambridge, 1982).

22. H. Schilling, *Konfessionskonflikt und Staatsbildung: Eine Fallstudie . . . am Beispiel der Grafschaft Lippe* (Güersloh, 1981).

23. F. L. Carsten, *The Origins of Prussia* (Oxford, 1954), 165–277.

24. Koenigsberger, *Estates and Revolutions*, 226–33; D. R. Kelley, *The Beginnings of Ideology: Consciousness and Society in the French Reformation* (Cambridge, 1981), 253–97.

25. J. Russell Major, *The Estates General of 1560* (Princeton, NJ, 1951); id., *The Monarchy, the Estates and the Aristocracy in Renaissance France* (London, 1988), 460–76.

26. J. Russell Major, *Monarchy, Estates and Aristocracy*, 701–15.

27. J. H. Mariéjol, *La Réforme et la Ligue* (Paris, 1904), 365–82.

28. Koenigsberger, *Politicians and Virtuosi*, 64–65.

29. Tracy, *Holland under Habsburg Rule*; Koenigsberger, *Estates and Revolutions*, 166–75.

30. Koenigsberger, *Estates and Revolutions*, 125–43.

31. Ibid., 190–210; id., *Politicians and Virtuosi*, 97–119, 63–76; id., *Early Modern Europe*, chap. 3.

32. H. H. Rowen, *The Princes of Orange: The Stadtholders in the Dutch Republic* (Cambridge, 1988).

33. J. S. Roskell, *The Commons in the Parliament of 1422* (Manchester, 1954), chap. 7.

34. M. Roberts, *The Early Vasas: A History of Sweden, 1523–1611* (Cambridge, 1968), 75–82; H. Schück, "Sweden's Early Parliamentary Institutions from the Thirteenth Century to 1611," in *The Riksdag: A History of the Swedish Parliament*, ed. M. F. Metcalf (Stockholm, 1987), 39–42.

35. M. A. R. Graves, *The Tudor Parliament; Crown, Lords and Commons, 1485–1603* (London, 1985); G. R. Elton, "The Reformation in England," in *New Cambridge Modern History* 2, 2d ed. (Cambridge, 1990): 269–72.

36. Elton, "The Reformation in England," 283.

37. N. Jones, *Faith by Statute: Parliament and the Settlement of Religion* (London, 1982); G. R. Elton, *The Parliament of England 1559–1581* (Cambridge, 1986), 350–79.

38. S. E. Lehmberg, "The Role of Parliament in Early Modern England," in *The Swedish Riksdag in an International Perspective*, ed. W. Stjernquist (Stockholm, 1989), 77.

39. P. Collinson, "The Monarchical Republic of Queen Elizabeth I," *Bulletin of the John Rylands Library of Manchester* 69.2 (1987): 394–424; G. Q. Bowler, "An Axe or an Acte: The Parliament of 1572 and Resistance Theory in Early Elizabethan England," *Canadian Journal of History* 19 (1984): 349–59; H. G. Koenigsberger et al., *Europe in the Sixteenth Century*, 2d ed. (London, 1989), 289–99, 354–56.

40. K. Strömberg-Back, *Lagen, Rätten, Lären: Politisk och kyrklig idéblatt: Sverige under Johan III's tid* (Lund, 1963).

41. H. Schück, "Sweden's Early Parliamentary Institutions," in Metcalf, *The Riksdag*, 52–58; Roberts, *The Early Vasas*, 295–393.

42. Whitelock, *Journal*, 224–26.

43. G. Rystad, "The Estates of the Realm, the Monarchy and Empire,

1611–1718," in Metcalf, *The Riksdag,* 73–83; A. Upton, "Absolutism and the Rule of Law: The Case of Karl XI of Sweden," *Parliaments, Estates and Representation* 8.1 (June 1988): 31–46.

44. M. F. Metcalf, "Parliamentary Sovereignty and Royal Reaction, 1719–1809," in id., *The Riksdag,* 112–64.

45. Cf. *Parliament and Liberty: From the Reign of Elizabeth to the English Civil War,* ed. J. H. Hexter (Stanford, 1992).

46. Koenigsberger, *Politicians and Virtuosi,* 65.

47. S. E. Lehmberg, "The Role of Parliament," in Stjernquist, *The Swedish Riksdag,* 77.

48. *Commons Debates 1628,* ed. R. C. Johnson et al., 3 (New Haven, CT, and London, 1977): 372.

49. Ibid., 134.

50. Ibid. 2:61–63.

51. Cf. C. Russell, *The Fall of the British Monarchies, 1637–1642* (Oxford, 1991).

52. I have developed these arguments further in "Composite States, Representative Institutions and the American Revolution," *Historical Research* no. 148 (June 1989): 145–53.

Index

In this index an "f" after a number indicates a separate reference on the next page, and an "ff" indicates separate references on the next two pages. A continuous discussion over two or more pages is indicated by a span of page numbers, e.g., "57–59." *Passim* is used for a cluster of references in close but not consecutive sequence. Entries are alphabetized letter by letter, ignoring word breaks, hyphens, and accents.

Library of Congress Cataloging-in-Publication Data

The origins of freedom in the West / edited by R. W. Davis
    p.   cm. — (The Making of modern freedom)
    Includes index.
    ISBN 0-8047-2474-1
    1. Liberty—History. I. Davis, Richard W. II. Series.
    JC599.E9075   1995
    323'.09—dc20   94-20717
                                    CIP

∞ This book is printed on acid-free, recycled paper.